Sarasvatichandra Part I

Buddhidhan's Administration

Govardhanram Madhavram Tripathi was born on 20 October 1855 at Nadiad, in Gujarat. He published the first part of *Sarasvatichandra* in 1887, the second part in 1892, the third in 1898, and the fourth in 1901. He is also the author of *Snehmudra* (1889), *Navalram Nu Kavijivan* (1891), *The Classical Poets of Gujarat and Their Influence on Society and Morals* (1894), *Lilavati Jivankala* (1905) and *Dayaram No Aksherdeha* (1908). He presided over the first session of the Gujarati Sahitya Parishad in 1905. He died on 4 January 1907 in Bombay.

Tridip Suhrud works at the Sabarmati Ashram Preservation and Memorial Trust, Ahmedabad.

To the first part he gave all his art. The novel is imbued with aesthetic delight; the characterisation is matchless. The second part depicts Hindu society, his art went deeper in the third part, and he gave all that he wished to give to the world in the fourth part.

M. K. GANDHI

No other work has left such an indelible mark on the life of Gujarat as *Sarasvatichandra* has. In fact ... Govardhanram is the only one before the arrival of Gandhiji who had the greatest success in shaping the cultural life of Gujarat.

UMASHANKAR JOSHI

In the great celebration that is India, Gujarat has two gifts to offer: Mahatma Gandhi, and the jewel among books *Sarasvatichandra*.

MANUBHAI PANCHOLI 'DARSHAK'

Sarasvatichandra Part I

Buddhidhan's Administration

Govardhanram Madhavram Tripathi

Translated from the Gujarati

by Tridip Suhrud

Orient BlackSwan

SARASVATICHANDRA PART I

ORIENT BLACKSWAN PRIVATE LIMITED

Registered Office
3-6-752 Himayatnagar, Hyderabad 500 029 (Telangana), India
e-mail: centraloffice@orientblackswan.com

Other Offices
Bengaluru, Bhopal, Chennai, Guwahati,
Hyderabad, Jaipur, Kolkata, Lucknow,
Mumbai, New Delhi, Noida, Patna, Vijayawada

Originally published in Gujarati as
Buddhidhan Nu Karbhar (Bombay: N. M. Tripathi and Co., 1887).

First published by Orient Blackswan Private Limited 2015
Reprinted 2017

ISBN 978 81 250 5990 5

024513
23112016

Typeset by
Le Studio Graphique, Gurgaon 122 001
in Adobe Jenson Pro 11/13

Printed at
B.B. Press
Noida

Published by
Orient Blackswan Private Limited
3-6-752 Himayatnagar,
Hyderabad 500 029 (Telangana), India
e-mail: info@orientblackswan.com

For Megha

Let us walk with light and in friendship to old age.

Contents

Translator's Acknowledgements *ix*
Translator's Introduction *xi*
Preface I *liii*
Preface II *lv*
An Offering *lxi*

1. The Guest of Suvarnapur 1
2. Buddhidhan's Family 6
3. Buddhidhan 20
4. Buddhidhan (Continued) 30
5. Buddhidhan (Conclusion) 43
6. Intrigues in Rajeshwar 68
7. Pleasure Garden 75
8. At the Counsellor's House 85
9. The Consequences of Intoxication 93
10. Instruments of Intrigue and the Warcraft of Karbharis 109
11. In Readiness for Court 123
12. The King, Palace and Administration 136
13. On the Way 175

14.	Destiny Fulfilled	199
15.	Sarasvatichandra	212
16.	Buddhidhan and Saubhagya Devi	262
17.	Pramaddhan and Kumud Sundari	266
18.	The Karbhari and his Administration	275
19.	Night Life: The Rising Curtain and the Ordeal by Fire	300
20.	Leave Taking	333
21.	Walking Away	338

Translator's Acknowledgements

Taralika—friend and mother—more than anyone else, desired that I attempt this translation. She knew as mothers often do that this text that she knew intimately would teach me humility. Taralika chose to leave us and become one with the immortals. This translation owes much to Taralika and Suhrud. They introduced me to *Sarasvatichandra* when I was ten. They cultivated in me a fondness for Gujarati language and literature, which has informed much of what I have done, and continue to do, and has given me the fitness to attempt this translation.

During the last eight years that this translation has been in the making, I have incurred debts of friendship. The most pleasurable of these is to Harmony Siganporia. Over the last two years, she has tried to educate me in the architecture and cadence of poetry and helped me with the translation of the plethora of verses that form part of this four-part novel. Thank you, Harmony.

Achyut Yagnik and Ashis Nandy taught me to patiently deepen my engagement with the Gujarat of an earlier age, while retaining my anxieties and unease with the literary and political culture of Gujarati in my times.

Sudhir Chandra, whose work on Govardhanram Tripathi, among others, remains a pathfinder for all those who seek to understand the social and intellectual history of the nineteenth century, has nourished this translation and the translator. He was the first reader of this translation and his patient care and careful reading has made this a better work. Thank you, Sahib.

For someone like me whose knowledge of Sanskrit is non-existent, Arindam Chakrabarti has been an exerting and encouraging teacher. In Shimla and from Hawaii, he has answered my queries, pointed to texts and traditions of translations of these, tried to teach me Sanskrit grammar and, when all else failed, rendered Sanskrit verses in English for me with flair. The friendship with Vrinda and Arindam has been one of the many gifts of the Indian Institute of Advanced Study.

Hank Heifetz, in a remarkable act of generosity, translated for a complete stranger verses from Magha's *Shishupala Vadha*, which have been included in this and the forthcoming volumes of this translation. Thank you.

My very first conversation with Vidya Rao was about *Sarasvatichandra*. She is the primary reason for the long relationship that Orient BlackSwan and I have developed. Mimi Choudhury has been supportive as always. It has been an absolute delight and joy to work with Moyna Mazumdar; her understanding and fondness for works of translation have evidently informed the many improvements she suggested, making the text read better than it would have otherwise.

Over the years, *Sarasvatichandra* has travelled with me to Shimla. Peter Ronald deSouza gave me sanctuary when I most needed it. His friendship, the long walks in the misty mountains, and conversations which he set up at the IIAS have been a source of joy and solace. Thank you, Peter.

Binita Desai has given a gift of friendship like none else to me and mine. As always, thank you.

Katyayani will hopefully not read *Sarasvatichandra* in translation, especially now that she has threatened to be literate.

This is for Megha.

Tridip Suhrud

Translator's Introduction*

I

> I wish to produce, or see produced, not this or that event—but a people who shall be higher and stronger than they are, who shall be better able to look and manage for themselves than is the present *helpless* generation of my educated and uneducated countrymen. What kind of a nation that should be and how that spark should be kindled for the organic flame: these were, and are, the problems before my mind. I lay down this as, for the present, the only one fixed objective before me ...[1]

* Earlier versions of this text have been published by the translator as part of an essay titled 'Govardhanram Tripathi and "the Philosophy of Consumption": A Reading of *Sarasvatichandra*,' in *Early Novels in India*, edited by Meenakshi Mukherji (New Delhi: Sahitya Akademi, 2002); and as part of 'Consumption as Dharma' in *Writing Life: Three Gujarati Thinkers*, Tridip Suhrud (New Delhi: Orient BlackSwan, 2009).

[1] K. C. Pandya, R. P. Bakshi and S. J. Pandya (eds), *Govardhanram Madhavram Tripathi's Scrap Book* (Bombay: N. M. Tripathi and Co., 1959), 29–30; emphasis in the original. This first scrap book covers the years 1884–1894 of the author's life. The scrap book for the period 1894–1904, compiled and edited by the same editors, was also published in 1959. The scrap book for the period 1904–06, edited by K. C. Pandya was published earlier in 1957, both volumes by N. M. Tripathi and Co., in Bombay. These volumes are, herein, referred to as *Scrap Book* I, II and III respectively. Although the chronology of publication goes against this arrangement, this has been done for the convenience of citation as well as to maintain the chronology in which they were originally written. Govardhanram Tripathi began writing the scrap books in January

With these words, Govardhanram Madhavram Tripathi (1855–1907) articulated his *swadharma*. Govardhanram was born on 20 October 1855, in a Vadnagara Nagar brahmin vaishnav family at Nadiad.[2] The family had no remarkable tradition of learning. For at least three generations, this family had practised money lending. Govardhanram spent his formative years in Bombay and Nadiad. He acquired primary education in the Buddhivardhak Gujarati Shala in Bombay and Government English School at Nadiad. In 1871, he passed his matriculation examination as a student of Elphinstone School, and joined Elphinstone College for his graduation. Between 1871 and 1875, he studied history, economics, nyaya and nitishastra. He passed his B.A. examination at the second attempt at the age of twenty.

After passing his B.A., Govardhanram made three resolutions which he hoped would govern his entire life. He resolved to acquire a law degree, to start an independent legal practice, and to give up legal practice at the age of forty and, thereafter, dedicate his life to the service of the people through literature.

In 1876, he passed his first LL.B. examination. He was forced by circumstances to accept the post of a personal secretary to Samaldas Parmananddas, the *Dewan* of Bhavnagar state. This gave him the opportunity to observe and participate, in close proximity, the functioning of a native state. He had hoped that his stay at Bhavnagar would be short and only a minor aberration in his plan. He was repeatedly frustrated in his attempts to pass the remaining LL.B. examinations. He failed thrice and eventually passed it in 1883 on his fourth attempt. He immediately left Bhavnagar for Bombay, where

1885 after he had achieved some stability in his profession as a lawyer in Bombay, and stopped maintaining them in November 1906. During this period, he filled seven notebooks, all of which were written in English. He had no intention of publishing them. They were published as a part of the celebrations to mark his birth centenary.

[2] This biographical section is largely based on K. C. Pandya, *Sriyut Govardhanram* (Bombay: N. M. Tripathi and Co., 1910, 1965).

at the age of twenty-nine he started independent legal practice. His practice at the Bombay High Court flourished. At the height of his legal career, Govardhanram fulfilled his long cherished dream. At the age of forty-two, he retired from the practice to contemplate the state of his people and society in the quiet solitude of his ancestral house in Nadiad.

II

For Govardhanram Tripathi, the original cause of the universe lies in what he describes as the 'Great Will' or the 'Great Force'. Individual beings are a mere point, a manifestation of the Great Will. 'Our will is a manifestation, at a point, of his will. His will is universal, ours is a point of it.'[3] The vocation of human beings, according to him, is to understand the Great Will and function in harmony with it. 'We are unable to enter into the actual motives of the Great Will, but we can understand and join its music and poetry ... Our final cause—like all final causes—is to understand our proper function in this symphony and join it properly.'[4]

A perfect conscience, according to Govardhanram, recognises that 'I is a fiction,'[5] and it is at this moment of recognition of self-identity that the individual being is in perfect harmony and union with the Great Will. In this union and realisation of identity lies salvation. But how is this salvation to be attained? The central question for Govardhanram is: How can an individual reconcile his vocation of final union with the Great Force, and his obligation towards his family, the society and the country? For Govardhanram, this reconciliation can be achieved only through what he describes as a Philosophy

[3] Pandya, Bakshi and Pandya, *Scrap Book* I, 45.
[4] Ibid., 123.
[5] Ibid., 46.

of Consumption.[6] 'Total sacrifice of the individual for the good of the whole is consumption ... Complete dissolution and sacrifice of the self for others is consumption. It is through consumption that individual existence and life achieve completion.'[7] 'Consumption' for Govardhanram is an all-encompassing philosophy and praxis. It is by leading a life of consumption that an individual offers his body and soul to the *yajna* [ritual sacrifice] of the Great Force. 'We must consume, both body and soul, ... in the Great and Patent *Yajna* that is blazing around us, we throw as *Havis* (oblation) the patent *Yajna* of body and soul ...'[8]

The philosophy of consumption becomes the sole mediator between the individual and the Great Will and also the individual and society. Through the philosophy of consumption, Govardhanram attempts to offer a critique of the philosophy of Vedanta, which was one of the earliest and most powerful influences on him. Vedanta, Govardhanram believes, leads to asceticism as the mode of attaining salvation. 'Patent is a thing to be avoided, and latent to be sought ... as to the censures passed against the Patent, as to the exclusive acceptance of the Latent as Transcendental Idea.'[9]

In 1877, aged twenty-two, Govardhanram offered a critique of the practice of renunciation as a mode of attaining salvation in an essay entitled 'Practical Asceticism in My Sense of the Word'. Care for the 'self' is at the heart of the practice of renunciation, he observed. Salvation cannot be attained through a self-centred mode. 'The great Bacon has said,' he wrote, 'it is a poor centre of man's action, himself, and it is true. But I go some steps beyond him. I say it is a poisonous

[6] The term 'Philosophy of Consumption' is Govardhanram's coinage. In Gujarati he uses the term *uttsargsiddhi*, or the attainment of higher ideals through sacrifice.

[7] Ramprasad P. Bakshi, *Govardhanram Nu Manorajya*, 2nd ed. (Bombay: N. M. Tripathi and Co., 1992), 14–15.

[8] Pandya, Bakshi and Pandya, *Scrap Book* I, 148.

[9] Ibid., 100.

centre of man's action—himself.'[10] Asceticism for Govardhanram is an act of rebellion against the Great Will. It is as unjustified as suicide. A real ascetic hands over the care of the 'self' to the Great Will and 'consumes' it for society. 'Asceticism, in its usual sense, is a mistake and a substitution of miscarriage for consumption. Asceticism, in its real sense, is most beautiful consumption.'[11] Consumption of an individual is conditioned by the capacities of the person. 'Consumption ... is not a promiscuous or unlimited duty. It is actually limited, and potentially unlimited, that it may be enlarged according to capacity.'[12] Notions of morality, ethics and justice are also contingent upon the idea of consumption. Defining vice and virtue, Govardhanram wrote:

> Whatever makes a man feed on the flesh of the world is ordinarily vice. Whatever is his consumption in order to feed the world is a virtue. Whatever is inconsistent with such consumption and the means of attaining it is vice. Whatever is consistent with it is innocent. Whatever furthers it is virtue. Whenever feeding oneself is instrumental to such consumption, it is virtue.[13]

For Govardhanram, poetry and philosophy, ethics and religion must converge in any philosophical system. He is aware that in his philosophy of consumption, he has created an all-encompassing world-view, a mode of life, his swadharma. 'To my mind ... Poetry and Philosophy, Ethics and Religion must eventually converge, and in Ethics, I include the world in all its aspects. Need I say that my vision of Philosophy of Consumption, with all its imperfections, reaches this very point?'[14]

A person who recognises virtue and vice, adopts the former and shuns the latter has a sense of duty. Thus for Govardhanram

[10] Pandya, *Sriyut Govardhanram*, 63.

[11] Pandya, Bakshi and Pandya, *Scrap Book* I, 146.

[12] Ibid., 125.

[13] Ibid., 52.

[14] Pandya, Bakshi and Pandya, *Scrap Book* II, 87.

consumption is not only a virtue but it is *dharma*. This conception of dharma informed his vocation and defined his understanding of personal duty towards the country. While clarifying for himself 'Duties in regard to the country', Govardhanram set before himself the goal of moulding a generation of people who shall be 'higher and stronger' and 'better able to manage for themselves'.

In this articulation of swadharma, Govardhanram denies the relevance and the efficacy of *events*. Events are for him acts uninformed by deep industry and knowledge. It was also not his aspiration to produce an event, which for him was a mere reflection of deeper societal processes. 'To produce a particular event—be it a political constitutional agitation or a social reform effervescence—this is too little for my mind and aspiration.'[15] He also eschewed commenting upon events. 'So obsessive was this concern for clarity that, unlike most of his contemporary creative writers in different Indian languages, Govardhanram tended to avoid journalism.'[16]

Aware as he was of 'the evil consequences which we may inflict on our country by our well-meaning follies', he decided to 'attempt or wish to assist nothing' before proper study; because, 'without study there is no sight and without sight no efficacy of action.'[17] In order to attain the requisite clarity to play out his conflicting, contradictory emotions, desires and ideas, Govardhanram regularly maintained his personal diaries. Readers of his *Scrap Books* cannot but be affected by his constant struggle and deep agony to attain the state of *aptavachana*—in which a person has a certain vision of life and society, and wishes to conduct his life accordingly.

This sense of duty was also conditioned by awareness of his capabilities as 'there is no duty beyond capacities'. He was aware that

[15] Ibid., 34.

[16] Sudhir Chandra, 'A Nineteenth Century View of the Hindu Joint Family: Notes from Govardhanram Tripathi's *Scrap Book*', Occasional paper, 2, Centre for Social Studies, Surat.

[17] Pandya, Bakshi and Pandya, *Scrap Book* I, 29–30.

it was not given to him to be a 'public' person—which he would be forced to be if he wanted to produce an event—he wanted to cultivate the *sakshibhav* [bearing witness to] of a *sthitapragna* [one whose intellect is secure]. 'Glory, Public applause, Eminence, Moneys, Public Leadership, etc., are *Things I do not want at all*.'[18]

His desire to achieve the state of sthitapragna and his disinclination to produce an event should not lead us to conclude that Govardhanram is advocating either *nivritti* [detachment] or a form of asceticism. Asceticism for him is an act of rebellion against the Great Will. The state of sthitapragna does not entail a denial of duties. A sthitapragna is not one who is dislocated from the world; on the contrary, he is someone who experiences deeply the world around him, but who does not submit to the rule of the senses. Govardhanram would say that all acts of a sthitapragna are acts of consumption. He describes this state of being as a state of 'Practical Asceticism'.

He was aware that his goal of shaping a generation of people who shall be 'higher and stronger' and who shall be 'able to manage for themselves' and the act of 'kindling the spark of the organic flame'—which will bring about long lasting mediation in the forces shaping the destiny of his nation—was not a task given to mere mortals. At times he is plagued by deep doubts of self-worth: 'I am a pigmy and the pigmiest of pigmies ... I may never be able to attempt so much as a beginning in the right direction for the simple reason that abilities may be extinct ashes ....'[19] He was aware that the life of a country is much longer than that of an individual. Neither the magnitude of the task nor such daunting realisations could deviate him from his chosen path. 'I must fancy', he says, 'that I am an *Ajaramar*, when planning my duty to my country.'[20]

[18] Pandya, Bakshi and Pandya, *Scrap Book* II, 176; emphasis in the original.

[19] Pandya, Bakshi and Pandya, *Scrap Book* I, 151.

[20] Ibid., 27.

III

It was as a part of his duty towards the country that Govardhanram embarked upon a project which was to consume him for nearly fifteen years. At the age of thirty, in 1885, he started writing his novel *Sarasvatichandra*. When the fourth and final part was published in 1901, fourteen years had elapsed since the publication of the first part. He did not wish to write the novel at all. His initial plan was to write philosophical essays on the human condition; but he found the essay form limiting. This limitation arose from the form, its restricted reach, and the inability of the general reading classes to appreciate and comprehend discursive prose. Given the limiting circumstances, he came to the conclusion that illustrations of actual and ideal life were the most appropriate mode of communication.

> The conviction has also grown upon him [the author] that reality in flesh and blood under the guise of fiction can supply the ordinary reader with subtler moulds and finer casts for the formation of his inner self than abstract discussions, and that this is especially so with *a people who must be made, and not simply left, to read.*[21]

Govardhanram selected the novel form not for its aesthetic possibilities but for its potential as a medium of 'moulding inner selves' of people. 'Both women and the novel desire to be beautiful', he says, 'but fulfilment of this desire must be a means to achieve higher goals. Striving for mere aesthetic pleasure is not only undesirable, it is futile—indeed it could be harmful—to attain that step and not rise upwards.'[22] He is keenly aware of the functions and possibilities of the

[21] Govardhanram Madhavram Tripathi, 'English Preface' in *Sarasvatichandra*, Part I, 18th ed. (Bombay: N. M. Tripathi and Co., 1887, 1977), 8; emphases added. There are two prefaces to the volume, one in Gujarati and the other in English, with substantial variations between the two.

[22] Tripathi, 'Prastavana' [Gujarati Preface] in *Sarasvatichandra*, Part I, 9. See also p. lvi of this volume.

novel, which he calls a 'universal luxury', and says this form of literature is unrivalled in its popularity and reach amongst the educated middle classes.

He felt disappointed that the true potential of the novel form was not being utilised by authors, and that instead they used it as a medium to gratify the instincts of the reading classes. Functions of the novel, he says, are 'much higher and sacred'. An author who desires to use it as a means of education must be aware of his audience. Govardhanram takes a critical look at his readership and classifies them into three categories. In the first category are the scholars who read novels to acquire a deeper understanding of the human condition. The second class comprises discerning readers who read the novel to enrich their inner lives. And the third class is the general readership. This class reads novels either because it entertains them or gratifies some of their instincts. This is the class that for Govardhanram 'must be made, and not simply left, to read'. Most novels address themselves to this class and therein lies the reason for their popularity. According to him, the element of fiction or magic does not constitute the central concern of the novel—its function is to 'educate' and 'raise' the reading classes. The novel must show them the path of virtue. The characters and situations depicted in the novel thus assume centrality. Depiction of ideal types cannot inspire readers to aspire for a higher life. Nor can the depiction of evil alienate masses from it. Therefore, Govardhanram says that his novel will depict humane characters who constantly strive to raise their condition.

With the progress of his enterprise, we sense a certain satisfaction of accomplishment. 'The purpose of the writer is to enable the reader to rise to a stage higher than where he was ... *Sarasvatichandra,* thus undertaken at this point, *works* without doubt, and people *feel* the book. This is a mere literary work and will work on society.'[23] Eleven years after the publication of the first volume, Govardhanram notes with satisfaction that 'the progress of the reading classes is equal to the

[23] Pandya, Bakshi and Pandya, *Scrap Book* I, 31; emphases in the original.

aspirations of the writer to interest them in the principal problems of the day.'[24]

The sense of achievement also brought with it a sense of greater responsibility for Govardhanram, who was plagued by the fear of illness and untimely death. 'I think I owe it as a duty to the world that I should finish before dying.'[25] India, he felt, was undergoing a strange transition in all spheres of community and personal life, and that certain 'forces have cast a gloomy shadow over our eyes'. Henceforth, his objective was not only to 'raise' readers but also 'to help his countrymen in groping their way out of the darkness into some kind of light'.[26]

Govardhanram captures the predicament of his society: both the advocates of change and those who wish to give 'eternal rigidity to the present' are uncertain as to how this transition will be harmonised. Will the process, which is heterogenous in its inception, result in an inward homogeneity? In this time of transition, only one certainty exists: 'Indian society must yield to the irresistible process of reciprocal assimilation'.[27] Can this society find repose? For Govardhanram, the realm of creative imagination can provide repose in such turbulent times—for the 'only place where we can safely look for a peaceful picture in spite of transient facts is in art and poetry'.[28] Henceforth, he resolved that the purpose of the novel would be to work towards a vision of a harmonised future. The narrative which had hitherto been a blend of the actual and the ideal, enters a different phase as 'the latter acquires a distinct predominance over the former'.

While dealing with the causes of the transition experienced by Indian society, Govardhanram refutes the widespread belief that India

[24] Tripathi, 'English Preface' in *Sarasvatichandra*, Part III, (Bombay: N. M. Tripathi and Co., 1898), 3.

[25] Pandya, Bakshi and Pandya, *Scrap Book* II, 172.

[26] Tripathi, 'English Preface' in *Sarasvatichandra*, Part IV, (Bombay: N. M. Tripathi and Co., 1901), 6.

[27] Tripathi, *Sarasvatichandra*, Part III, 4.

[28] Ibid.

was witnessing a fusion of two different civilisations—the modern West and the East. Indian civilisation has passed through many phases in its evolution and what we are witnessing today, he says, is a fusion of three civilisations—the modern West, the modern East and the resurgent traditions of the ancient Indian civilisation. He is confident that this will one day result in 'reciprocal assimilation and harmony'. It is the possible visions of that day which are the source of anxiety for Indian people. His endeavour would henceforth be to provide one possible path to this assimilation and a vision of the future. In this 'drama of transition', the intellectuals, or those whom he calls the educated Indians, have a crucial function as they are 'directly involved by the actual contact and growing reactions of these civilisations.'[29] Their role is one of mediation between these civilisational forces and the masses so as to bring about the inevitable transition. 'It has fallen to the lot of the educated classes to serve as organic sheaths and conductors between multiform sets or organisms forming a repository of these energies.'[30] Although living through ambivalent times, Govardhanram is able to identify the problematic and its possible resolution with a rare sensibility and awareness.

Writing the novel for Govardhanram is a conscious act of tempering the souls of his countrymen. It is through this act that he wishes to fulfil his historical role of an 'organic sheath' between the great civilisational forces and the Indian masses.

IV

Sarasvatichandra is not 'one' unitary text. The novel was not only published in four parts but was also written in four parts over a period of fifteen years. Each part has a distinct thematic content, its own cast of characters and independent beginnings and ends. This is not to

[29] Tripathi, *Sarasvatichandra*, Part IV, 8.

[30] Ibid., 9.

deny either the aesthetic or thematic unity of the novel. But readings which privilege one story—the story of Kumud, Sarasvatichandra and Kusum—as the principal theme and consider all others as unnecessary diversions do not allow an appreciation of the complete text.

The increasing influence of the East India Company in the affairs of the 'native states' provides the backdrop for the first part, *Buddhidhan's Administration*. It deals with one individual's sustained efforts to assume complete control of the administration of a native state, Suvarnapur, and to rise above his circumstances. Govardhanram describes Buddhidhan's impoverished beginnings, his constant victimisation by Shathrai, the prime minister of the state, and Buddhidhan's opportunistic alliance and friendship with Bhupsinh—a cousin of the ruling king and a claimant to the throne. Together they seek support of the British Resident officer of a neighbouring area, and with his intervention, Bhupsinh is declared the legitimate ruler. With patience, wisdom and foresight, Buddhidhan is gradually able to secure the complete trust of the new ruler, and to rid the state's administration of the influence of Shathrai. He also regains the post of prime minister which his family had traditionally held.

Part II of the novel, *Gunasundari's Household* deals with the state of a Hindu joint family in the latter half of the nineteenth century. Gunasundari and Vidya Chatura were married as children. Vidya Chatura was educated in Bombay and appointed as a teacher in an English school at Ratnanagari, another native state. He also obtained the post of tutor to the young prince, Maniraj of Ratnanagari. Gunasundari had acquired functional literacy, but as her name suggests, she was endowed with virtues 'natural' to women. Vidya Chatura trained and educated his young wife, enabling them to indulge in the pleasures of the mind and thereby avoiding the fate of many couples married in childhood. But just as they begin to experience a 'conjugality' driven by circumstances, Vidya Chatura's relatives come to live with them as dependents. From being a young, joyous wife, Gunasundari has to perforce become a *grihini* and manage a household of thirteen to fourteen people, all with different needs and personalities.

In this second part, Govardhanram achieves the height of his descriptive powers as a novelist. His minute descriptions of the dynamics of a joint family, his observation of human nature and its strengths and fragilities, his unencumbered prose and his characterisation have made this part most endearing to generations of readers. Govardhanram describes with a touch of humour—otherwise, entirely lacking in his prose—the interpersonal conflicts in the joint family, and pregnant Gunasundari's constant struggle to keep the family united and each member contented. She and her father-in-law, Manchatura, together succeed in both reforming and rehabilitating all constituent units of the joint family, without breaking the 'jointness' of the joint family.

The narrative thus far is a blend of actual and ideal aspects of life. From the third part on, the ideal acquires a distinctive predominance over the actual—a contrast which is immediately recognisable with the first part. Part III, *Ratnanagari's Statecraft*, deals with the attempts of an enlightened ruler, along with his feudal chiefs and advisors, to create a responsible polity in times of general decay. Ratnanagari had survived the onslaught of British expansion because of the strength and vision of its rulers. It was governed by the concern for the welfare of all sections of society.

From state and society, Govardhanram moves on to dharma. The fourth part, *The Dreamland of Sarasvatichandra and the Culmination*, presents the ideal community of Sundargiri. This community of ascetics leads their life in perfect harmony with nature and her Creator, in accordance with the principles of dharma, under the benevolent gaze of Vishnudas. Their strivings are those of souls wishing to achieve complete non-duality with the Creator.

The love story—the story of Kumud, Sarasvatichandra and Kusum—links Govardhanram's reflections on state, society and dharma. Kumud, the naturally virtuous daughter of Gunasundari and Vidya Chatura, was engaged at an early age to Sarasvatichandra. Born into great wealth, Sarasvatichandra, as his name suggests, was a scholar and a luminary amongst the intellectuals of Bombay. Ascetic by nature and given to deep reflection on the state of his country, he was greatly enamoured by the natural charm and virtues of Kumud, and they fall in love with each other before marriage. But his insecure, jealous stepmother engineers a misunderstanding between the devoted son and the loving but short-sighted father, which results in Sarasvatichandra leaving home, renouncing not only his family and wealth but also Kumud. Kumud is disconsolate. He decides to live a life of an 'intellectual vagabond', travelling to remote parts of the country to experience the living reality of his countrymen.

As an unknown, rootless traveller with an assumed identity, in desperate search for purpose and peace, Sarasvatichandra reaches Suvarnapur. There he is invited to be the guest of Buddhidhan. Kumud's parents have by then married their uncomplaining daughter to Pramaddhan, the unworthy and debauch son of Buddhidhan. Sarasvatichandra, carrying the burden of his guilt, once again leaves Kumud to her fate, but not before Pramaddhan suspects the tenderness of their relationship. Before he can cause greater misery to Kumud, Sarasvatichandra disappears, and is given up as dead. Through a series of accidents he reaches Sundargiri, where he is celebrated as the heir to Sadhu Vishnudas. Kumud, believed to be drowned in a river, also reaches Sundargiri and lives in the care of *sadhvis* as an ascetic. Widowed Kumud—though she remains unaware of Pramaddhan's death for a long time—and Sarasvatichandra suffer greatly because of their mutual love. Vishnudas asks them to spend five nights together in a cave to contemplate their fate. Under divine intervention, they travel to the 'Land of the Enlightened' in their dreams where they experience a union of souls and emerge from the cave enlightened and pure. The novel ends with the inauguration of Sarasvatichandra's project for the regeneration of the country, and a new phase in the lives of Kumud, Kusum and Sarasvatichandra.

V

For those who came of age in late-nineteenth century India and felt concerned about the state of their society and nation, colonial rule was a fundamental reality. Awareness of subjection coupled with a profound uncertainty about the present and future shaped their response to the British presence in India. Given this ultimate objective—'one which never ought to be lost sight of'—of moulding his people into a great people who would be able to take care of themselves, Govardhanram grappled with the meaning of British rule. In an entry in *Scrap Book* I, dated 13 April 1891, he wrote:

> India is invaded and subdued already. There is no question of Offensive or Defensive here, and Elasticity would be a nice helpmate in Constitutional Warfare. The rulers are a clever set of people—an admixture of selfish aggressors and disinterested, benevolent helpmates. India is worked by 'push and pull' among these, and naturally the Home Interest generally carries the day. Yet even here we win morsel by morsel, though often it is snatched away—sometimes even from near the lips.[31]

The only unambiguous, unqualified statement here is the fact of India's subjection. Accepting the British presence as given, Govardhanram advises his people to cultivate 'elasticity'. 'Coming after offense and defense have been ruled out, "elasticity" becomes the very epitome of ambiguity. The term here seems to suggest pragmatism.'[32] Relations between the rulers and the ruled are mediated by the idea of warfare. But this is neither an offensive nor a confrontation. The concept of 'constitutional'—given by the colonial rulers—and the need to cultivate elasticity, introduces an element of caution, of pragmatic moderation. Moving on to a depiction of the rulers, Govardhanram again displays ambivalence and a mixed assessment of British presence. Yet he is

[31] Pandya, Bakshi and Pandya, *Scrap Book* I, 51.

[32] Sudhir Chandra, *The Oppressive Present: Literature and Social Consciousness in Colonial India* (New Delhi: Oxford University Press, 1992), 23.

aware that in the ultimate analysis, 'the home interest carries the day' and that whatever ground is gained by Indians through their elasticity is snatched away.

Govardhanram may have been ambivalent towards British rule, but he displays remarkable consistency in his analysis of the 'native states', and the capacity of his people to effectively counter the colonial aggressor—he has no faith in their ability to take premeditated action and believes they can only indulge in 'well-meaning follies'. He has some faith in the Congress, owing to its 'well-chosen leadership' of A. O. Hume and Sir William Wedderburn.

> But in other matters our leaders are unfit. In view of these things, I would like to leave many things to our rulers rather than to our native leaders, for the former are at least most sensible people. If natives act, I shall not hinder them. If Europeans act I shall have some confidence.[33]

The high standards he had set himself in private and public conduct may have made him sceptical of the abilities of his own people. This severe denouncement and total lack of confidence in the abilities of Indians informed his vocation of creating a generation which shall be 'better able to look and manage for themselves'. This negative assessment of his countrymen to manage the political and social implications of the colonial encounter pervades all his reflections—whether in the *Scrap Books* or the novel. On the question of British presence, he did not allow any wishful thinking to colour his assessment. In a lengthy entry titled 'India and the foreigner', he wrote:

> India is under foreign control and the foreigner is the kindliest of all foreigners available. To get rid of the foreigner by force or fraud is an idea associated with all incidents that remind us of the rule being foreign. The idea naturally haunts our uneducated instincts; to educated instincts the idea is both foolish and fallacious. It is foolish because it is not practicable, and because

[33] Pandya, Bakshi and Pandya, *Scrap Book* I, 58.

> any experiment founded upon it would send the country from the frying pan into the fire. It is a fallacious idea, because the distinction between a native and a foreigner is only transient, and the distinction is not a guarantee of a native being a better ruler than the foreigner in such a mass of heterogenous people as my country is.[34]

Govardhanram is not only emphasising his lack of faith in the strategies employed by Indians to get rid of the British but is also questioning the basic premise of 'foreign' and 'native' interests being mutually exclusive. Moreover, his absence of trust in the abilities of natives to manage a heterogenous people with differing aspirations and needs also colours his assessment of the problem. He goes on to articulate the real problem: '[the] problem is not the absolute eviction of the foreigner, but *his accommodation to the native element* ... where India and England *become one on Indian Soil* ...'[35] One can assume that while cautioning against attempts to evict the foreigner completely from Indian soil, he is referring not just to the physical presence, but to a civilisational encounter, and his stand is informed by the awareness that Indian culture and society will be transformed by this 'drama of transition.' The source of his anxiety lies in the uncertainty about the future and how these opposing tendencies will be harmonised and what kind of a resolution will emerge. To bring about a resolution where 'India and England become one on Indian Soil', he required to 'create a homogeneous nuclear class.'

This also was the central concern of *Sarasvatichandra*. At the same time, he was not unaware of the opposition between foreign and native interests. He elaborates in the same entry:

> In India the sovereign is enlightened and yet has an interest foreign to the country. Two things have to be done. This interest has to be made to cease to be foreign; and while it is foreign, we want the natives that shall guard against the civic temptations to

[34] Ibid., 149.

[35] Ibid., 150; emphases in the original.

> which the foreigner is exposed by his position, that shall enable the native interests to grow and develop during their minority without any hindrance from the adverse interests of the rulers, that shall in fact watch over the real interests and develop the future welfare of the country. And it is possible to do these both loyally and patriotically.[36]

In the four volumes of *Sarasvatichandra,* Govardhanram attempted to demonstrate this wisdom. The first part of the novel—which is the depiction of reality according to him—portrays the expanding British influence over the native states. It is one of the most severe indictments of native states in the literature of that period. Govardhanram depicts a polity based on personal interests, plagued by widespread erosion of morals and values. The efforts of Buddhidhan and Bhupsinh to overthrow Shathrai's corrupt administration were in the final analysis motivated by personal animosity and gain. 'Buddhidhan had meanwhile turned Bhupsinh and his administration into mere instruments for his festering rage.'[37] The only thing that differentiates Buddhidhan from Shathrai is the former's high sense of personal morality.

A more condemning attitude towards the native states is perhaps reflected in the *Scrap Books,* where Govardhanram feels no compulsion for moderation. While he was contemplating retirement from legal practice, he had many tempting offers from the native states in Gujarat to join the administration as dewan. Given his financial insecurities, a few years of dewanship would have put many fears at rest. This position would have also provided him an opportunity to work for the good of society. Giving his reasons for refusing these offers, he writes: 'Baroda, Junagadh, Kutch, Bhavnagar, and what not?—all native states in fact stand before my eyes, with their whole nudity of weaknesses, complications and difficulties—from subjects, officers, the princes themselves and even from Agencies ....' The mere thought of being in that environment filled him with a 'vision of pettiest

[36] Ibid.

[37] See p. 68 of this volume.

jealousies, meanest natures, foolishest ambitions, ridiculous follies and vanities, and adamantine obstructions.'[38] Perhaps this assessment of the native states has much to do with his unhappy stay at Bhavnagar in the service of the Dewan. He also felt that efforts made in the native states for the betterment of society were unlikely to bear fruit. This would amount to narrowing his vision. He adds in the same entry:

> Besides, the greatest result available in this field can only be local influence—while the kind of influence that is wanted is one that could permeate and stimulate the whole constitution of India. This larger effect must be begun and produced in British India where the plant, if sown, can have a freer, larger growth along what Telang called the line of least resistance.[39]

During this period, he returned to this theme with regularity. Perturbed by his thoughts of retirement from active legal practice his family and friends tried to persuade him to take up tempting offers. A few days after the entry quoted above, he elaborated upon the 'thorns of inferior society in Political life in Native States.'[40] His chief objection to working in a native state was that he would have to deal with people of inferior intellectual abilities. 'No Prince can be equal to your education, and no fellow servant disposed to have your conscience in the present state of things.' This situation he says is 'not much dissimilar to the marriage of a man of my education and age with an illiterate girl of twelve, whom you must try to please and educate with all the arts of one attempting to make love with such an odd match.'[41]

Govardhanram's other concern is about moral life in the native states. One may be forced to work with people who may not have any sense of duty, and even if they do, it is likely to be 'in a disfigured,

[38] Pandya, Bakshi and Pandya, *Scrap Book* II, 43.

[39] Ibid.

[40] Ibid., 51.

[41] Ibid.

mutilated, and even perverted form'. And therefore, 'I shall have to guard warily against the Fallacious Persuasions of the Serpentine Tempter, if ever he takes me near the Tree of Service'.[42] Govardhanram's assessment of the native states is without doubt largely negative and he does not see in them much potential for 'kindling the spark of organic flame'. Nevertheless, large parts of the country were under the administration of native states; he thus felt the imperative to turn his attention to them in the novel. The third part of *Sarasvatichandra*—subtitled *Ratnanagari's Statecraft*—deals with the creation of an 'ideal' native state. From Part III onwards, the narrative enters a different phase, and normative considerations are given primacy over the depiction of reality.

VI

We are concerned not only with the fate of his societal endeavours, but also with the fate of Govardhanram and two other individuals irrevocably bound to him. Their minds and souls were the first that he tried to cultivate in accordance with his ideals and philosophy. These two were Lalita, Govardhanram's second wife, and Lilavati, their daughter. It is important for us to consider the fates of these three individuals not only because they were played out almost simultaneously to his public endeavour, but also because for Govardhanram there was no marked disjunction between giving his country a vision of an ideal society and of educating and 'raising' his wife and daughter. These two projects were essentially the same—both were integral to his personal dharma towards the country. And as Govardhanram himself put it, 'my country is a term which must be confined in the beginning and made to expand in course of time only'.[43]

[42] Pandya, Bakshi and Pandya, *Scrap Book* I, 51.

[43] Ibid.

Govardhanram shows a keen awareness of the intertwined fates of those inhabiting the inner worlds he created through his fiction, and of his own self and his family. At many places in the *Scrap Books* he draws parallels between his life and the novel, compares his wife to his heroine and asks his daughter to follow in the footsteps of Gunasundari. His life and his fiction seemed to him to mirror each other. Jayanti, another daughter of his, was betrothed at a tender age, a decision which upset him. Two days after the engagement he wrote: 'Curious coincidence! Jayanti betrothed on 25th, and I get the first proof of the second part of my novel on the 26th. The betrothal pinches me, and I compare myself to Vidya Chatura, who accepting in haste a woman's arguments, betrothed Kumud to Pramad, and dropped all talk of Sarasvatichandra.'[44] In a moment of rare passion, Govardhanram says: '*I only want their souls*'.[45] Moreover, the only source of deriving some understanding about the possible fate of his societal endeavour is from the lives of Govardhanram, Lilavati and Lalita, who tried to live a life of consumptive virtue. It is in their biographies that Govardhanram's 'grand project' unfolds itself completely.

Govardhanram's marriage to Harilaxmi was fixed before their birth. A close 'conjugal' relationship developed between the two. But the relationship between adolescent Harilaxmi and Govardhanram's dominating mother Shivkashi was one of constant conflict. Torn between love for his young wife and his sense of duty towards his mother, Govardhanram seriously contemplated running away from his conflict-ridden house to start life anew.[46] His first marriage ended tragically—Harilaxmi died in 1874 while giving birth to their child, who also died soon after. Govardhanram was to express his deep anguish and a sense of permanent loss in two verses—*Hridayruditshatakam* and *Snehmudra*—that he wrote in memory of

[44] Ibid., 93.

[45] Ibid., 27; emphasis in the original.

[46] Pandya, *Sriyut Govardhanram*, 16–17.

Harilaxmi and in which he paid her glowing tributes.[47] Reflecting on his first marriage, he wrote in 1893: 'My first marriage was meant to be a cruel hoax which my wife lived and was eventually to leave me a widower'.[48] Though delighted 'at the prospect of a living relieved from future marriage',[49] Govardhanram was married again to Lalitagauri in 1876. Years later, he complained: 'I was then married, under conditions to which I would have never assented, if I had not been kept ignorant of them, to a girl reputedly ill-bred ...'[50] Secure in his faith in the philosophy of 'consumption', he tried to cultivate in his 'ill-bred' wife the high ideals of this philosophy. 'My duty does not end with satisfying her poor ideals, but I am bound to enlarge them. This is my marital duty ...'[51] Govardhanram lists his 'duties' towards his wife as under: 'a) to train her up b) to raise her life c) to make her free d) to provide for her e) to fulfill her aspirations with such luxuries etc., as a husband in love and duty ought to give her'.[52] His primary obligation towards his wife was to 'train' her. By training he did not imply 'educating' her in the conventional sense of imparting literacy, as he time and again laments that he was not able to educate her.[53] Training for Govardhanram primarily meant imparting to her those virtues and ideals which would enable her to lead her life according to the tenets of his philosophy of consumption.

For Lalita, the first thirteen years of her life with Govardhanram were years of training under his constant guidance and close supervision. Not given to impassioned display of his feelings, he is nevertheless ecstatic in his praise of Lalita's moral strength to

[47] *Hridayruditshatakam*, a long verse in Sanskrit, was written in 1875. *Snehmudra*, an adaption of the former, was published in 1889.

[48] Pandya, Bakshi and Pandya, *Scrap Book* I, 167.

[49] Ibid.

[50] Ibid., 167–68.

[51] Ibid., 64.

[52] Ibid., 61.

[53] Ibid., 62.

continuously lead a life of self-negation and self-inflicted deprivation. There are repeated references of Lalita's moral virtues and a life of self-sacrifice in his *Scrap Books* of this period. He writes:

> last thirteen years have been a life of training for her, and her life is high. Industrious to the fullest extent, virtuous and charitable, active and clever, enthusiastic and untiring in her domestic work and in the work of rendering me happy and all in the family, she has nobly – successfully – and touchingly borne, and willingly undertaken, the heaviest self-sacrifice for all this – the sacrifice of health, of liberty, of all luxuries, of all enjoyments – of her own wants and aspirations, and the most usual of worldly enjoyments, – of her tastes and temper – and of everything possible under the sun ...[54]

Govardhanram cannot hide his feelings of a personal success and achievement in training Lalita. 'I have trained wife from the beginning to do voluntary and loving service and sacrifice to my people. She has done it. She has worked like an ass for my people ...'[55] Lalita's sole aspiration of life becomes making Govardhanram and his family happy. For this she earns his unqualified praise. Her latest change of disposition compels Govardhanram 'to adore and make *arti* to her soul—to her goodness, to her virtue—to her understanding—and to her moral power.'[56] Lalita's sacrifice compels Govardhanram—who constantly lived with a feeling of his own moral and intellectual superiority—to put her on a pedestal even higher than himself. 'Her life is higher than mine.'[57] This was the greatest recognition that Govardhanram could have given to any one; he called her the 'Family's Angel.'[58] Lalita succeeds in acquiring respect even from the quarrelsome Shivkashi. Govardhanram compares Lalita to

[54] Ibid., 62–63.

[55] Ibid., 184–85.

[56] Ibid., 26.

[57] Ibid.

[58] Ibid.

Gunasundari—the ideal and perfect embodiment of consumption created in *Sarasvatichandra*.[59]

But his 'heaven' does not last long. The familiar discord re-enters their lives. Govardhanram records instances of conflict between Lalita and Shivkashi, and Lalita and his brother's wife. He records, with some satisfaction, his own efforts to be an 'impartial judge' in these conflicts and reflects on 'Family misunderstandings and the way to remove them'.[60] As the conflicts and discord become deeper, he is forced to re-evaluate Lalita's morals and virtues and is ruthless in his condemnation: 'My wife is inadequate to be my heroine, alas, she falls far too short of my Gunasundari'.[61] Lalita's failure to continuously lead a life of consumption forced Govardhanram to grapple with a more fundamental question of how to successfully 'raise' our women. He also reflects on his own failure to do so.

> Are our women to be raised? How? Take a particular woman, and see, how? ... I have tried ... with my mother, my wife ... The result of my labours has been that both mother and wife have turned into discontented imperfect machines—square pegs in round holes—my mother the peg and my wife the hole![62]

Even this clear admission of failure does not introduce any element of doubt regarding his mission of cultivating minds and tempering the souls of his countrymen. Instead, quite characteristically, he sees in this failure a new raison d' etre for his endeavours: '99 out of 100 individuals will give up without thinking of the society,' he says, but 'my crucifixion in my own family must direct me to rise from this grave and try to relieve my countrymen from the troubles from which

59 Ibid.

60 Ibid., 113–15.

61 Ibid., 200.

62 Ibid., 236–37.

I could not relieve myself. *The next generation must always benefit by the adversities of its predecessors*.'[63]

Govardhanram was unwavering in his resolve to cultivate the minds of others, but by 1892 Lalita was not prepared to lead a life of continuous self-negation. Lalita becomes a victim of many physical and mental ailments: 'Mrs. has been suffering from premonitory symptoms of consumption ... she is doomed.'[64] As her physical condition further deteriorated, her mental health also suffered. She became a patient of 'Monomania' and was admitted to a sanatorium at Sion.[65] Lalita's illness forced Govardhanram to examine the cause of her hysteria, which he does with clinical detachment, as is evident from his jottings in *Scrap Book* I:

> *Cure for wife's hysteria:*
>
> 1. Cause of hysteria: *Prolonged* and *compulsory* abstinence from natural tendencies and sentiments and sickness and agitations of soul and frequent irritations, etc., etc., caused by a sense of enduring injustice and ill-treatment, etc.
> 2. *Result*: Bodily hysteria, and abnormal and incessant irritability and pain of mind, and melancholia and hypochondria, etc.
> 3. *Remedy applied*: A general abstinence on my part from contradicting her and allowing free scope of her *will* and *frenzies* ... and showing sympathy for her real and imaginary miseries ...
> 4. *Shortcomings in the remedy*: I sometimes lose patience and temper, and sometimes fail to study her mind and mood.[66]

Despite care and medical treatment, Lalita's condition progressively worsened and she was faced with imminent death. 'Poor Lalita! Your life is hanging upon a most apparent uncertainty. Most people affected

63 Ibid.; emphasis added.

64 Ibid., 162.

65 Ibid., 166–68.

66 Ibid., 182; emphasis in the original.

as you are die after lingering pains.'[67] The possibility of Lalita's death compels Govardhanram to articulate his own guilt: 'Poor beloved Lalita, sweet sharer of my cares, brave bearer of the heavy burdens that I have placed on thy frail personality, in this way am I bound to witness thy pangs and smoldering ...'[68] The Great Will willed otherwise, and Lalita survived. But hereafter, Govardhanram gave up his efforts to cultivate Lalita. After her illness, Lalita acquired the self-confidence to rebel against the regimentation imposed by Govardhanram. He indicates that she would frequently taunt him:

> You taught me from childhood to love and serve your people; how do you ask at this stage and age, to be indifferent to their opinions and remarks, and their wounded feelings, simply on the ground that you agree with me in thinking they are mistaken? Why should they mistake? How can I change my nature now? My only way to bliss is to see them love me whatever the sacrifice.[69]

Govardhanram's philosophy had the resources to contain such rebellions. Centred as it was in the ideal of continuous self-negation, without an accompanying awareness of this sacrifice, his philosophy made Govardhanram respond to Lalita's questions in a characteristic manner: 'If she did not feel the sacrifice, she should be right.'[70]

Govardhanram may have been able to respond philosophically to Lalita's taunts but Lalita's life, her 'failure' to be the embodiment of 'consumption', her illness—hysteria which pushed her to the margins of insanity—posed fundamental questions to Govardhanram's philosophy of consumption and his declared mission to cultivate the minds and souls of his countrymen. Neither Govardhanram nor his philosophy had a creative response to this. His only response was silence. After his self-chosen retirement and final shift to Nadiad

[67] Ibid., 166.

[68] Ibid., 163–64.

[69] Ibid., 224.

[70] Ibid.

from Bombay to complete his novel and dedicate himself fully to contemplate the fate of his country and countrymen, there are no references either to Lalita's consumptive lungs, her mental illness, or her being the 'Family's Angel'. When Lalita entered Govardhanram's life, she was around twelve years old. She had received her primary *sanskara* [traditional mores and values]—for Govardhanram, 'ill-breeding'—from her natal home. And as Lalita herself so accurately posed the question: 'Is it possible to divert the branches of the tree at the fag end of their growth without breaking them?'[71]

VII

In 1881 Lalita gave birth to their first child—daughter Lilavati. In 1885, Govardhanram started writing *Sarasvatichandra,* at the same time as Lilavati's education began. He assumed complete control of her education and upbringing. In Govardhanram's project neither chance nor *lila* had any play. Each action was to be based on proper study and intense reflection. This 'obsessive concern for clarity' is also reflected in the detailed curriculum that he worked out for Lilavati's education. Govardhanram believed that the sanskara of any individual is the sum total of the accumulated sanskara of her/his *swagotra,* the sanskara imparted at the natal home and the individual's own philosophy of life. Govardhanram did not have any control over Lilavati's accumulated sanskara, but he was determined and duty-bound to impart all those values to her which formed the core of his own philosophy.

Govardhanram believed that keeping girls completely unlettered was both a sin and a curse. His wisdom told him that education without a clear aim could be dangerous, especially for girls. To arrive at a decision regarding Lilavati's education he formulated a guiding principle: 'The decision must be made after considering the in-law's

71 Ibid.

house, mental capacities of the girl and her future prospects'.[72] He defined, specifically for girls, the role of education: 'In the dark wintry night that this world is, there is no protection, support and light against the piercing blizzards comparable to good knowledge, to guide the helpless girls on the righteous path and give them warmth and solace'.[73]

Lilavati was admitted to a girl's school in Zaverbaug, Bombay, at the age of three. But Govardhanram soon realised the narrow vision of such institutions. After a few months he took his daughter out of the school, and 'keeping in mind her age, sex and body, appropriate facilities were created at home for her play and enjoyment'.[74] Lilavati was never to go to a school after this. This brief stay at a girls' school was to be her only excursion to the world outside—before marriage—without the ever present gaze of her father.

Govardhanram was seized by a sense of urgency about Lilavati's education, which he wanted completed before she was married and sent to live with her husband, as he firmly believed that there were too many obstacles in the path of education once a girl starts living with her husband.

Initially, Lilavati was given basic literacy in Gujarati. Govardhanram was conscious of the fact that his child was destined to live through the 'drama of transition' and hence, that she must be systematically exposed to both traditional Indian wisdom and knowledge systems as well as Western education. A private tutor was hired to teach Lilavati basic Sanskrit and English. She was taught Professor Bhandarkar's *Sanskritmargopadesika* and the English 'First Book'. Once she had acquired basic knowledge of Sanskrit, Govardhanram appointed Shastri Jivram Lallubhai (later Professor of Sanskrit, Elphinstone College, Bombay) to educate her in Sanskrit literature and the *shastras*.

[72] Govardhanram Madhavram Tripathi, *Lilavati Jivankala*, 4th ed. (Bombay: N. M. Tripathi and Co., 1905, 1961), 57–58.

[73] Ibid.

[74] Ibid., 61.

Before giving him the responsibility of his daughter's education, Govardhanram reminded Shastri of his obligations and the goals of knowledge.

> Shastriji, Lilavati is destined to live in a foreign environment. Neither I nor her mother will be able to guide her in good and bad times. Moreover, how are we—worldly beings—to provide her with wisdom? So, if you give her knowledge, give that type of Knowledge which will be a good friend of her intellect and constantly guide her, wherever she may be, on the right path.[75]

They decided to combine the knowledge of literature with that of the shastras because,'Literature is useful in invoking and tempering higher desires and *rasas* of life while, development of the frail intellect requires the support of the *shastras*'.[76] Lilavati was too young to be exposed to *shringara* [an aesthetic of beauty pertaining to love]; hence, together they selected those parts of the texts which did not have shringara as the dominant *rasa* [aesthetic; flavour]. Shastriji taught her Bhartrhari's *Niti Sataka,* Aryashrenishvara's *Chandakaushik* and the fourth part of the *Shakuntal.* While she studied the *Savitri Natak* on her own, at a later stage she was allowed to study other parts of *Shakuntal* herself. Of the shastras, Lilavati was taught *Laghutark Kaumudi, Ishavasya* and *Ken Upanishad, Bhagvad Gita* and *Panchikaran.* As Lilavati went deeper into the Sanskrit tradition, she became disinterested in English education. Govardhanram allowed her to discontinue her English studies. In order to make sure she did not remain completely ignorant of Western life, she was given Karsandas Mulji's *Travels in England* (in Gujarati). To familiarise her with societal issues, she was made to read a daily, *Gujarati,* and some other journals. Through such complete education, 'the emotional and intellectual core' of Lilavati's life was formed.[77]

75 Ibid., 4. For details of Lilavati's education, see 57–58.

76 Ibid., 65.

77 Ibid., 66.

Govardhanram was aware that the prevailing social consciousness was inhospitable for a girl who was learned but did not have any housekeeping skills. Therefore, along with the training of her mind she was initiated into the intricacies of household work.

> In this training her mother was made her teacher. It is always desirable that a mother should initiate a daughter in this work because this training demands love and delicate tutoring while, at the same time, the teacher should have the right to punish. There is no other person who inspires the same level of confidence in a child as compared to her mother.[78]

From a tender age Lilavati was given the responsibility of cooking for the entire joint family of twelve or thirteen members. Lalita and other women of the house were given strict instructions not to interfere in her work. Lilavati's mornings were spent doing the household work while the rest of the day was devoted to studies. Lilavati's education was comprehensive. No area was left untouched. So total was Govardhanram's involvement with Lilavati that he neglected his two other daughters, Jayanti and Jasu, and also his son Ramaniyaram's education and upbringing. In later years, he would often lament that in his own preoccupation with his literary and professional activities and total involvement with Lilavati, he had neglected his other children. Govardhanram notes that even Lilavati had noticed the wide gulf which separated her from her brother and sisters. She even questioned her father on this, and his meek defense left her unsatisfied.[79]

[78] Ibid., 62.

[79] Ibid., 50. One incident captures this divide. Once while he was going to Bombay from Nadiad, Jayanti requested her father to get for her a book on religious and ritual observances, *Somvar Ni Katha*. After she left the room, Govardhanram expressed his sorrow and his sense of failure to his friend and relative, Chandrashankar Pandya. 'I could not educate this poor girl and therefore she has to ask for books like *Somvar Ni Katha*, otherwise like Lilavati she would have demanded excellent books.' Pandya, *Sriyut Govardhanram*, 207–08.

Lilavati was engaged to marry at the age of three or four. While choosing a husband for her, Govardhanram went against the established norm of his caste of choosing a family from his own native town Nadiad. She was engaged to Himatbhai, third son of Manilal Gangashankar of Petlad. Govardhanram's family was against Lilavati's betrothal to an impoverished and indebted family. But Govardhanram was uncompromising and argued that even his own family was indebted at the time of his marriage to Lalita, but that her parents had posed complete faith in their ability to overcome the crisis. He argued that they had no right to reject Himatbhai's family on grounds of indebtedness.[80] Lilavati's marriage to Himatbhai took place in 1891 when she was twelve years old. Her marriage at this tender age irked Govardhanram, but he eventually decided to go ahead with it, reasoning that her happiness had to be sought within the existing social structure, and that marriage was necessary to achieve that.[81]

Lilavati's education continued even after she was sent to live with her in-laws. Both Govardhanram and Lalita wrote her frequent letters, in which they counselled her in *grihinidharma*. In one such letter, Lalita wrote:

> You should not differentiate between the natal home and the house of your in-laws ... As long as you differentiate between the two families you shall never be happy. Therefore, it is your duty to consider them as your own and worship them like Gods. You once asked me, who was virtuous? Virtuous is one who considers the in-laws' house as her natal home and who treats all members—whether young or old—with utmost respect.[82]

Father Govardhanram urged her to follow the ideal and noble path of Gunasundari. 'Gunasundari was surrounded by all types of people and she made all of them her own through her *niti* and cleverness.

[80] Tripathi, *Lilavati Jivankala*, 16–17.

[81] Pandya, Bakshi and Pandya, *Scrap Book* I, 89.

[82] Tripathi, *Lilavati Jivankala*, 6.

Keep her in mind and follow her example. Notwithstanding the character of others we should always be good and virtuous because ultimately *Dharma* always emerges victorious.'[83] Reminding her of the education and wisdom he had imparted to her, he says: 'Make your mind so strong with the help of your knowledge that the unhappiness of this world does not generate any remorse in you.'[84]

Lilavati made this philosophy of life integral to her existence. She followed each tenet as the truth itself. Govardhanram lists many examples—and not without great satisfaction and some degree of pride—to prove that Lilavati had been worthy of all the knowledge he had given her and that she had completely internalised this knowledge and the principles of 'consumption'. Some rumours regarding her ill health and unhappiness prompted Govardhanram to write a rather concerned letter to her. In reply, Lilavati reminded her father of his swadharma, suggesting that it was his dharma not to be concerned about the wellbeing of a married daughter living with her parents-in-law. She quoted a verse from Govardhanram's own poem *Snehmudra* to remind him that when a bird leaves its nest, it flies on its own. Similarly, a girl leaves her father after marriage and is on her own. She further reminded him of a verse in *Shakuntal* in which Rishi Kanva says that a girl is another's property and the father is relieved by returning her to her husband,[85] prompting Govardhanram to observe: 'My sweet child admonished me in my own words and pointed the way to my happiness.'[86] By reminding her father of his swadharma, Lilavati showed that she had indeed internalised her education. Govardhanram notes many instances to reinforce that Lilavati lived her life in accordance with the two basic tenets of the philosophy

83 Ibid., 10.

84 Ibid., 11.

85 Ibid., 4.

86 Pandya, Bakshi and Pandya, *Scrap Book* II, 230.

of consumption: *yajmandharma* and *manojnadharma.*[87] His success in creating an embodiment of the principles of consumptive virtue through Lilavati was complete.

A writer can bring his literary creations to an ideal end, but life is rarely so kind. Lilavati lived in Junagadh, which suffered a series of epidemics. Her parents repeatedly asked her to come back to Nadiad. But Lilavati refused to leave her in-laws' house until she had nursed every member of the family to health. When Lilavati finally reached Nadiad, it was too late. She had in fact 'consumed' herself through self-inflicted privation; she was diagnosed as suffering from the 'disease of consumption', tuberculosis. She refused to blame anyone or even her fate in the face of imminent death. Reassuring her mother that she had fulfilled her grihinidharma, Lilavati said:

> Mother, in those days of fever epidemic there were only two possible outcomes. If I had pampered and loved myself and not cared to nurse others, someone else would have lost life. But I did not do so, and I do not care what fate awaits me now. Either I could have saved my life or someone else's life, and it is desirable that I lose my life.[88]

Lilavati, the embodiment of consumption, sacrificed her life. Govardhanram wrote: 'Lilavati! By following the righteous path of *Dharma* as suggested by your parents, you sought, like Nachiketa, death. And death shall give you your fulfillment.'[89] Lilavati died at the age of twenty-one, on 8 January 1902. It is perhaps not a

[87] Govardhanram defined virtue as consumption of the self in order to feed the world, while vice entailed feeding upon the flesh of the world. The dharma of the virtuous is to be a *yajman,* while those who feed on others are *atithi.* He imagined his ideal virtuous individual to be a follower of *yajmandharma.* The other quality of the virtuous is to know even the unarticulated feelings and desires of others and conduct their lives accordingly; he calls this *manojnadharma.* He attributed these qualities to the sadhvis of Sundargiri in *Sarasvatichandra.*

[88] Tripathi, *Lilavati Jivankala,* 28.

[89] Ibid., 29.

coincidence that the two projects which had taken complete hold of Govardhanram's life and being ended almost simultaneously. He completed the fourth and final part of *Sarasvatichandra* and it was published in 1901.

Govardhanram did one final act of duty towards the sacred memory of Lilavati and his country. He wrote her biography, *Lilavati Jivankala*. Even this final act was done not to glorify her memory, but to place before society an ideal life. 'I am not writing this book to glorify you. But I feel that your life, your philosophy and your actions have a message for the society. You are the real author of this work.'[90]

One question must be asked: Who or what was responsible for Lilavati's tragic and untimely death? Father Govardhanram, who assumed complete control of her existence and tried to create a real embodiment of his philosophy at the cost of her life? Or was it his philosophy which demanded a negation of the 'self'? Or should we hold Lilavati's husband and his parents responsible? Or was it perhaps the Great Will? *Lilavati Jivankala* does not provide any answers. We must turn to Govardhanram's *Scrap Books* to understand his real emotions. Initially, Govardhanram is tempted to attribute her pain and suffering to the desire of the Great Will.

> My best, Sweetest, meekest, wisest and most patient child, who has done nothing in this life to deserve this situation, a situation which can only be accounted for by a speculative desire of Providence to kill her, or to test or toughen the 'Philosophy' of which alone her education and wealth consists.[91]

This attribution to the Great Will was only temporary. He feels that neither Lilavati's husband nor her parents-in-law deserved to have such a noble soul like Lilavati in their house. Emotions which are restrained in *Lilavati Jivankala* find free expression in *Scrap Book* II, where there are repeated references to the ill-treatment, agony and prolonged suffering that she was subjected to by her parents-in-law.

[90] Ibid., 3.

[91] Pandya, Bakshi and Pandya, *Scrap Book* II, 191.

> Her services were not only accepted without the slightest effort at limiting her struggle to serve them, but she was taunted for her groans and complaints, which she could not have made except in extremities. Her complaints were belittled, she was allowed to pass latest hours of a coldest winter on a damp ground floor, working to do them superfluous service without being relieved. And when she had fever and shiverings and was in need of warm blankets to cover her, nobody looked to these things. She lay so, listening to talks with hard words about her making too much of her body.[92]

Govardhanram does not see any escape from this situation. If she were to live, she will have to go back to her husband. Only death can save his daughter from this misery, he feels, and he secretly desires her death.

> Not being able to see how the girl can be happy living with such people as those at her husband's, I have never been able to persuade myself to offer a single prayer for her life, and all that I could do in my affection, which cannot bear the idea of her death, has been to request the Great Will to do what is best for her welfare, and for his inscrutable objects, or to make her live, *provided* she is destined to be happy by living.[93]

Blaming others may have given temporary solace to Govardhanram the father, but the thinker in him is not convinced. He knows that the final decision regarding Lilavati's marriage was his, and that he had gone against both the norms of his community and express wishes of his family while taking this decision. He gives a long, agonising justification for his action.[94] Such post-facto wisdom does not however lessen his burden. His search for the truth finally leads him to the realisation: 'I am responsible.'[95] The realisation invokes in him a strong feeling of having sinned: 'I have to thank myself for my having

[92] Ibid., 224.

[93] Ibid., 213; emphasis in the original.

[94] Ibid., 223.

[95] Ibid., 191.

committed this inexplicable sin against my poor child, by choosing for her an unsuitable family.'[96] With her death, this feeling of having sinned becomes magnified and possesses him.

> At 5.30 p.m. yesterday my poor Lilavati died after a stainless, spotless life of suffering. She was a martyr to the cause of our Hindu Social System, to her father's exercise of his power of disposing of her in early marriage ... and to the services she rendered to her mother-in-law and her father-in-law.[97]

Govardhanram's expiation and atonement can now lie only in 'realising my faults and weakness, and my sins against her life and merits.'[98] He also concludes that 'her soul and holiness were superior to *mine* and to that of every other person I see about me.'[99] Only one idea gives him solace: 'I can only feel proud to have had a child like this during my worldly sojourn, rewarded at the idea that I had the privilege of looking after the education and elevation of so aspiring a soul.'[100] His search for atonement leads him to examine the education and 'elevation' of her soul. 'In Lilavati's life, I and her mother always taught her the way to do her duty to her husband and his family, and to seek reward and consolation in the idea of Duty. She was quite equal to her task and her body paid for it.'[101] He continues,

> and with the philosophy and sweetness that her education and innate powers were able to develop in her, her life became one of martyrdom, among other things, to her own very high sense of duty, in which point she outdistanced not only me and mine but all the characters that I have been able to spin out in my books.[102]

[96] Ibid., 216.
[97] Ibid., 220.
[98] Ibid., 228.
[99] Ibid.; emphasis in the original.
[100] Ibid., 228.
[101] Ibid., 224.
[102] Govardhanram Tripathi to Janmanshankar Buch, in *Lilavati Jivankala*, 131.

In the opening lines of *Sanskarkala-Shodashi,* a long poem on Lilavati, Govardhanram laments: 'I had conceived a Gunasundari in my head. In real life I fathered you, a better version of Gunasundari. You did penance like Gunasundari but unlike her, did not enjoy the fruit thereof. I produced a thesis, you sacrificed your life to prove it right!'[103] Aware that it was his education and his philosophy which was the cause of Lilavati's pain, suffering and ultimately, death, Govardhanram is forced to re-evaluate his project of cultivating minds and elevating souls.

> My daughter Lilavati suffered because of high virtues and would have fared better if she had not got the virtues! Is it right then to teach these virtues to our daughters? So many people tell my wife that she has killed Lilavati by making her virtuous; the charge comes home more to me. Is a parent right in educating his children in this way at their cost?[104]

He questions the idea of virtue itself. But he is not ready to give up either his project or his faith in the essential goodness and desirability of virtue. For one last time, he reasserts the validity of his principles of consumption: 'This question must be answered in *affirmative* for people like *myself*; my children, like their father and mother, have been educated in virtue, *irrespective of its consequences*.'[105]

The power of his vision did not allow Govardhanram to abandon his project, but with Lilavati's death, his creative self died. He lived his final years lonely and miserable, seeking solace and strength from Lilavati's memory.

> No misery that will reach me now can be higher or more excruciating than that borne by my Lilavati, and I can do no

[103] Govardhanram Madhavram Tripathi, 'Sanskarkala-Shodashi' in *Lilavati Jivankala,* 4th ed. (Bombay: N. M. Tripathi and Co., 1905, 1961), 133–55. The translated verse is from Sonal Shukla, 'Govardhanram's Women', *Economic and Political Weekly*, WS 65, 31 October 1987.

[104] Pandya, Bakshi and Pandya, *Scrap Book* II, 290–91.

[105] Ibid.; emphases in the original.

> better reverence to her sacred memory than by walking in her gentle and yet, firm, steady, virtuous and heroic footsteps in facing any circumstances that may befall me. [May] Her sweet and lofty virtues be my divine beacon-light in my mundane struggles henceforth! May her example inspire my soul and draw me closer unto hers wherever and whatsoever she now may be![106]

He died on 4 January 1907 after a long illness.

VIII

While commenting on the high point that Gujarati poetry had achieved during the seventeenth century through Akho, Premanand and Samal, Govardhanram observed that the vocation of a writer is to expand the human nature by placing before the people 'purer and higher ideals of social life' in a 'beautiful and ennobling' manner. Akho, Premanand and Samal could achieve this only because they were 'above the society in which they live'.[107]

Govardhanram Tripathi's own mission as a writer, of influencing and improving contemporary society, was fulfilled, perhaps beyond his expectations, through *Sarasvatichandra*. 'The educated youth of Gujarat lived in the dreamland of Sarasvatichandra, Kumud and Kusum ... No other book of fiction has made so powerful an impact on its contemporaries as *Sarasvatichandra* ...'[108] For over a hundred years, *Sarasvatichandra* has remained the canonical text of Gujarati literature; perhaps no other work of fiction has been able to match its range of concerns or popularity. 'No other event, before the arrival of Gandhi, had so captured the imagination of the society and had

[106] Pandya, Bakshi and Pandya, *Scrap Book* II, 256.

[107] Govardhanram Madhavram Tripathi, *Classical Poets of Gujarat and Their Influence on Society and Morals*, 3rd ed. (Bombay: Forbes Gujarati Sabha, 1894, 1958), 33–34.

[108] Mansukhlal Jhaveri, *History of Gujarati Literature* (New Delhi: Sahitya Akademi, 1978), 98.

succeeded in moulding the minds of the people on the path of moral, civilised conduct as this epic novel.'[109]

Govardhanram's attempt was to create a new moral universe for the emerging middle class. As mediators of India's colonial encounter, this emerging class experienced deep uncertainties about the old order and felt ambivalent insecurities about new modes of thought, conduct, morality, faith, and culture, creating permanent disjunctions in their public and personal lives. Largely due to industrialisation, the distance between the public and domestic spheres increased, as people came in contact with new ideas and ideologies. This group was in search for new models of thought and conduct which would provide some sense of permanency in times of transition.

Govardhanram provided them with a new ideal through his 'graduate hero'. Sonal Shukla has beautifully captured the essence of this new ideal, which went on to become a dominant thematic category for Gujarat literature.

> He has done extremely well in his studies. He is sensitive and generous but also somewhat haughty and aloof. He has a mission, but no job. He usually belongs to a wealthy family, but does not mind living in poverty, although towards the end he is usually comfortably placed all over again. The novelist and his heroine admire this greatly. Sarasvatichandra is the first modern Gujarati hero of this type.[110]

This acute awareness of having to provide anchors introduced caution in Govardhanram's enterprise. He is willing to question the assumptions and normative principles underlying social and political institutions; he is also willing to reject their moral superiority in some cases. Nevertheless, he does not consider it desirable to posit options which might fundamentally alter the old order and introduce new anxieties. This caution is quite evident in his attitudes towards widow

[109] Vishnuprasad R. Trivedi, *Govardhanram: Chintak Ne Sarjak* (Bombay: N. M. Tripathi and Co., 1962), 95.

[110] Shukla, 'Govardhanram's Women', WS 63.

remarriage. This overwhelming desire to provide anchors to society led him to the creation of a new idealised woman—the 'Domestic Angel'.[111] Govardhanram's personal life and the novel reflect a remarkable engagement with women and femininity. For a major part of his life he tried to 'educate' and 'raise' the virtues of his wife, Lalita. So complete and intense was his identification with his daughter Lilavati that he neglected his only male child Ramaniyaram. The novel *Sarasvatichandra* is anchored in the characters of women that he created—Gunasundari, Kumud and Kusum. What could be the reason for his intense encounter with womanhood?

For Govardhanram, tradition was to be 'the bedrock of social reconstruction through much of this transitional phase, when two civilisations confronted each other'.[112] In times of transition, women and womanhood became ideal embodiments of traditional virtues. Govardhanram introduced to Gujarat the Victorian ideal of the 'naturally virtuous woman'. Govardhanram established the moral and cultural superiority of women over men. For many, awareness of the colonial encounter and its social and cultural implications provoked deep insecurities regarding their own traditions and belief systems. In Govardhanram's moral vision, it was through women that harmony and virtue, in both family and society, were sought to be achieved. Women became the sites where the conflict between tradition and modernity was being played out. Govardhanram's philosophy of consumption also placed additional burden on women. Consumption with its emphasis on continuous self-denial, without an accompanying awareness of sacrifice, and valorisation of pain and humiliation as an ideal to be sought to further one's consumption, crushed womanhood.

Govardhanram Tripathi sought to create such an ideal woman in his life, as in his fiction. When his 'domestic angel'—his wife Lalita—became hysterical under his regimentation and ultimately gathered the courage to question his ideals, he made another attempt

[111] Ibid., WS 65–67.

[112] Chandra, *The Oppressive Present*, 82.

through his daughter Lilavati. Govardhanram's vision demanded, and received, heavy sacrifices from women. Gunasundari paid through her consumption, Kumud by submitting her desires to a higher ideal of ascetic renunciation, Lalita, through her hysteria, and Lilavati paid with her life. Little did he realise that it is impossible to create one ideal woman through two lives and one fiction.

Tridip Suhrud

Preface I[†]

Novels have in these days become a universal luxury and in competing for public interest have succeeded to an extent almost unrivalled. The very natural result has been that the bulk of fiction in the West has ceased to aspire beyond an artistic display of such of the sentimental and emotional idiosyncrasies of mankind as happen to tickle the fancy of the ordinary reader. It is however certain—and the higher class of novelists never fail to recognise and claim—that the functions of the novel are more numerous, higher and more sacred than the mere pandering to the taste of the novel reading public.

The writer of these pages admits that the origin of his undertaking was in the first instance neither so ordinary nor so ambitious. Like all who live and look around, he had his memoranda of what may be called the substrata of this our world of human affairs. When he first desired to give an objective existence to all that so sketched out in his mind's book, he intended to give it the form of essays. Second thoughts discovered that the reading class in Gujarat were, for various reasons, difficult to reach through abstruse or discursive matter, and that illustrations of real or ideal life would be the best medium, best in the sense of being attractive and impressive, for communications like those which the writer has to make. Hence, the present contribution.

[†] As earlier stated, there are two prefaces, one in English and the other in Gujarati. This is the original English preface.

The conviction has also grown upon him that reality in flesh and blood under the guise of fiction can supply the ordinary reader with subtler moulds and finer casts for the formation of his inner self than abstract discussions, and that this is especially so with a people who must be made, and not simply left, to read.

It remains to note that by inducing reality under fiction it is not meant to convey any personal allusion whatever in any part or even a line of the book. The actualities of life or locality are referred to only and strictly so far as they belong to any of the varied conditions of life amongst our people. And even these are on occasions ideal. The ideal and actual are in some places inseparable.

Bombay
April 1887

G. M. T.

Preface II†

We live in times where the means of attaining eternal fame in this world are becoming frayed with each passing day. Human sensibility today is not what it was yesterday, and it will be different tomorrow from what it is today. It is difficult to imagine in the present what would be pleasing in the future. In this age of new discoveries every day, classical texts of today are rendered useless tomorrow. Similarly, that in these times of changing sensibilities, novels which by very character are ephemeral would acquire longevity and bind the author to the future through a chain of fame is a belief contrary to experience. Novels in the hands of readers have displaced plays that people watched. This example illustrates the argument. The lust for fame harboured in the writer's heart appears to be futile and lifeless, but its possibility enthuses him in the present. If the value of goods were to rest upon utility, it is a desired outcome. If this utility were to take its seat on the throne vacated by fame, it would possibly expand the scope of the fruits of literary endeavours and give to them a certain enduring significance. But the condition of the Western world and the shadows it casts on us is such that humans are enticed not by innate utility but outward beauty, thereby establishing what is secondary over the primary. But the fact is that beauty, however illusory, allows a thing to be assimilated easily; the beauty of illusion makes the aesthetic

† This is a translation of 'Prastavana', the Gujarati preface to the first 1887 edition.

sensibility refined, gives it higher aspiration and force; this makes the difference between human life, that acquires newer forms, and animal life sharper. But illusion merges in the essence—illusion seeks that essence—hence, the end of illusion is the beginning of the essential nature of a thing. As illusion disappears, essence must emerge; the egg-shell of illusion must give birth to new life that is essence. This one must not forget. Both women and the novel desire to be beautiful, but fulfilment of this desire must be a means to achieve higher goals. Striving for mere aesthetic pleasure is not only undesirable, it is futile—indeed it could be harmful—to attain that step and not rise upwards.

What then should be the essence of a novel? If one were to know in whose hands the novel would reach, from what perspective they would make use of it, the essence of a novel could be determined.

1. The seekers after truth read novels to study the psychology of the human mind.
2. Those with an assimilative intellect search in a novel aspects such as beauty and leave out the rest.

It is not that writers can relate to these two classes through the means of novels alone. This relationship can be forged through many forms, but one must not forget that these classes also take delight in novels, because among the reading classes they occupy the position of crown jewel. They are small in numbers, but their worship, their God-like control are accepted by all.

3. The number of readers in the third class is countless. They are drawn to reading novels for one or more of the following reasons:
   (a) The sense of anticipation that a story creates. This sensibility is present in all children; among women it is considered characteristic and some do not lose it even with advancing age.
   (b) Minds that have surrendered to stories of passion and women. Such minds become restive at the very sight of a novel and

excessive intercourse with such novels eventually makes their minds impotent.

(c) The addiction of reading tales is similar to the addiction of opium or alcohol, it does not go away even after an effort.

(d) The toil of reading classical and obtuse texts. Many among the literate are lazy and after they emerge from the state of being a student, there is no one who counters their unwillingness to labour over a text.

(e) Uncultured sensibility about the classics.

(f) Illiteracy and leisure.

A large segment of both literate and illiterate classes makes up this last class, and this is the reason for the triumph of novels these days. It should be the purpose of a story teller to ponder over such matters and create something that would eventually not harm, in fact benefit, readers of all classes. The manliness of a virile writer is proven not by submitting to the sensibilities of readers but by submission to a nobler aesthetic, and in an endeavour to produce this sensibility in his readers.

The ability to administer wisdom by mixing it in the sense of anticipation of an enticing story, the skill of alluring feeble minds that can be led onto the good path through pictures of ideal lives, the dexterity of administering the potion of virtue to an addict of stories, the ability to produce industriousness among the lazy literati, to fill the enchanting pictures with substance from the classics and infuse the ideal with good aspirations and produce among the illiterate a sensibility for good life and many similar aims of poetry are not unknown to writers of India, and they are considered the epitome of cultivation in Europe as well. Our scriptures say that such stories counsel like a friend, like a woman.

Pandering to the ordinary class of readers might appear to be easy, but satisfying the seekers after truth and the assimilating classes is complex as the ability to cultivate the mind requires greater means and capabilities than the ability to be pleasing to the mind. The scholarly group can sift truth from what appears to be fiction, and to fill their hands with good things requires knowledge akin to the riches of a prosperous man. Some minds that appear to be entwined in this worldly affair have the capacity to enter spaces which remain unseen by others and experience deep poetry. Such consciousness is eager to hear the song of the heart in the midst of commonplace prose. To satisfy them requires the blessings of a pure poetic conscience. Those scholars who study society examine with minute gaze the canopy of a novel in search of history that stands out in the gathering like a groom. They also discern with whom morality, like a bride, would unite. In short, the scholarly class looks for thousands and thousands of details in a novel which inhabit the universe of the human mind. The preceding one is only an example of this quest. If this class can be satisfied even on rare occasions, it would be a matter of great satisfaction.

Such is the pure essence of a novel. It is true that a story should have illusory capacity, but that is secondary. A form bereft of essence is lifeless and its consumption, harmful. The comparison of the extent to which this novel has been able to preserve essence and form should be left to the assessors. And yet, it would add to the story if certain special objectives of the writer are alluded to here.

This novel entwines like a garland of flowers more than one story. The secondary hero draws attention to himself before the hero of the novel makes unambiguous appearance. This breaks the norm prevalent in Europe that the story line must be harmonious and continuous, but it does uphold the divine law of history which introduces many stories in one narrative. It is not the principal objective of this novel to uphold artificial norms. The endeavour is to present a picture of the divine play.

Some books consider it their duty to draw attention only to the impure passions of man. It is true that in God's creation these impure passions have a place; but our life does not find fruition in these passions; scholars have other means available—in the classical texts—to find pictures of these passions and therefore, to the extent possible, the dreary drudgery of etching impure pictures has been kept at a distance in this novel.

If humans, who must rise above, are shown the topmost step of a ladder, it is likely that they would lose courage. But merely showing the base ground also does not accomplish movement upwards. For these reasons the characters of the novel are not supreme, or else readers would see them as merely fictitious and imaginary and not consider emulating their example. At the same time the characters are not so commonplace and everyday that they can neither enthuse anyone nor show the upward path. We have drawn pictures of humans who are subject to our ordinary passions and failings—frailties that need to be pardoned—and yet struggling against them, endeavouring to steady them and rise above their present condition. The attempt is not to find kindred feelings in weak human beings for others who are weak like them. But rather, the path adopted is to suggest possible ways of swimming against the current in the worldly sea. In order to do this it has become necessary to bring in, like black marks, descriptions of impure passions while drawing pictures of unsullied persons as the observation of these impurities allows for a truer measure of the glory of purity.

An attempt has been made to depict the conditions and the evolution of men and women living in light, as also in shadow and in dusk—like a state in-between knowledge, wealth, power, autonomy and purity. So that each reader is able to identify with some character and acquire an exemplar. Human beings are an amalgam of good and bad. There is nothing in the world that is unsullied goodness or pure evil. This complex composition has been shown here and through it, experiential wisdom has been shared.

The time that the story occupies is very close to our times and it is located within the people of Gujarat. This would enable us to hear more clearly the echoes of the past, view the present without obstruction and possibilities of the future to be intertwined, and those aspiring for the uplift of the country would find some suggestions.

Other objectives would become apparent to an assessor, and only then would they be considered fulfilled. So believing, they have not been narrated here.

Vasant G. M. T.
Vikramsamvat 1943
Bombay

An Offering

You planted the seed of the mind's succour
You manifested the very universe of love
Imbuing this child with aspirations
Even so, neither the sun nor the moon rose in the sky.
Fate, despite all actions, prevailed
And the chariot of the mind there remained contained
Prosperity played truant, gazing from afar
And yet the heart, it blossomed.
Days passed, and more inevitably shall
That which would blossom, has blossomed
Nurtured while delicate
Strong and beauteous it must become.
As she dances, flowers fall at the gardener's feet
Smell these fragrant flowers, O' gardener of my heart
Bless this child of yours
Let this heart in bloom play among the trees of heaven
This I pray, every day.

Man's hour on earth is weakness, error, strife.
... Even in his darkest hours
Still doth he war with Darkness and the Powers
Of Darkness, – for the light he cannot see
Still round him feels; – and, if he be not free,
Struggles against this strange captivity.

—*Faust*, Goethe

Bends and then fades silently
One frail and fair anemone.

...

Some star
... Climbs and wanders through steep night.

...

Ere it is borne away, away,
By the swift Heavens that cannot stay.

...

And the gloom divine is all around.

—*Prometheus Unbound*, P. B. Shelly

1 The Guest of Suvarnapur

A weary waste expanding to the skies:
Where'er I roam, whatever realms to see
...
Bless'd be that spot, where cheerful guests retire
To pause from toil, and trim their ev'ning fire;
Bless'd that abode, where want and pain repair;
And every stranger finds a ready chair.[1]

Suvarnapur is situated where the river Bhadra meets the Arabian Sea. It is spread out on the slope of a hill cradled by the sea with riverine hands like a child held at the waist. In the month of Magha, a vessel laid anchor in the harbour of this town. Small and large boats went up to the vessel to unload its cargo and passengers. Some merchants climbed onto one such boat. A young man got off with them and sat on the side of the boat, as if concealing himself. His eyes moved between the sea and Suvarnapur, almost in response to the boat swaying on the sea waves or like a child imitating the movements of the boat. The man appeared to be twenty-three or twenty-four years of age. His clothes were not bright; his face was withered. While he did not betray signs of dejection, his visage suggested that many a sigh filled his heart. His beauty was illuminating, his features delicate.

[1] Author's note: 'The Traveller, Or, A Prospect of Society', Oliver Goldsmith, 1764.

These set him apart from the rest of the merchants with their harsh country-folk features, immersed in joyous revelry.

The boat came ashore, and passengers disembarked with their bedding and baggage in a hurry. He too walked ashore, melancholic and somewhat indifferent. For a while he stood there, gazing into the distance, his hand on his chin. People were walking in the direction of the town. He slowly began to walk the other way. He walked apart and alone on a road surrounded by an expanse of trees and bushes, like a lone engine on a wide bridge. He carried a small bundle and walked with a steady step, looking in turns at the sky, the earth, the road before him, and behind. The young sun of the early morning suited him, dressed as he was in light clothing, and yet at times a strong gust of wind would force him to cross his arms over his chest. The effort of walking and the sun caused a film of perspiration to appear on his large forehead. His lotus-like face and cheeks turned red. At last, he reached a Shiva temple. Looking around, he entered its gates.

This was the temple of Rajeshwar Mahadev. It was built by the ancestors of Buddhidhan, the Counsellor of Suvarnapur. The temple was surrounded by a tiled square, and a roofed corridor bound it. A stone wall plastered with dung, built years ago, skirted this corridor. A small window-like opening led to a courtyard out back. In the courtyard there were fruit and flowering trees appropriate for the worship of Mahadev, as also a bel tree. This courtyard was encircled by a cactus fence with a few gaps in it. On either side of the corridor there were two large platforms. Towards the right was a small lake with an embankment, called Rajsarovar. On the other side, facing the temple, was a well. When crowds gathered at the temple on festival days, worshippers could stand on the well's high platform and have a darshan of Mahadev. The entry to the temple was slightly elevated but was purposefully placed lower than its threshold. The idea was that anyone entering the temple would—knowingly or unknowingly—have to bow before the deity on entering. The corridor was paved and wayfarers used it as a dharamshala. The paving had come loose at places but had been patched afresh. Travellers had inscribed their names with stone, brick, or coal on the walls of the corridor with a view to seek immortality, fame, or out of sheer playfulness. Some had even etched their names with nails. These 'writings' included crude poetry, correct and incorrect verses, idioms, foul abuses, blessings, advice, threats to the owner of the dharamshala, dates that signified arbitrary events; images of Gods and other beings drawn well and not so well could be seen at every step. The Shiva temple itself stood in the middle of the square. It was unremarkable: it had the requisite ten or twelve steps, a platform, and a Nandi.

Upon entering the temple, the newcomer looked around and gazed into the sanctum sanctorum. He climbed its steps, rang the bell that hung from the outer dome and perfunctorily bowed to the God. He sat on the threshold of the sanctum sanctorum and placed his bundle in front of him. The priest performing rituals inside signalled to him, so he got up and sat outside.

Murkhdutt, the priest, was a brahmin, about thirty to thirty-five years of age. He had an unkempt stubble and appeared careless and unconcerned. His association with the family of the Counsellor and the habit of imitating the servants of that family had given him some semblance of civilised conduct. His natural language was crass and of the mofussil, yet he could pepper it with smart turns of phrase on occasion. He was given to speaking for long, would try to please and plead, and would succeed in small deceits but get caught when he tried treachery in any important matter. He was given to scolding insignificant persons and strangers in the name of the powerful to satiate his ego. One moment he would quarrel with the Counsellor's staff, and the next, join them in some petty conspiracy. He made a show of being a poor priest in front of the Counsellor's family, sought pity and got his way. Despite this, the Counsellor considered him a naïve simpleton and provided for him.

When he saw the young stranger, Murkhdutt made a show of elaborate worship. He poured enough water to cause a flood, placed a heap of bel leaves and flowers on the Shivalinga, and belted out his impure chanting. The temple was at a distance from the town and therefore rarely visited. However, since the festival of Shivaratri was approaching, Murkhdutt was inebriated with the thought that the Prince and his retinue, the family of the Counsellor, and the townsfolk would soon visit the temple. The youth's arrival was an auspicious beginning, and it had an intoxicating bhang-like effect on Murkhdutt.

The young man watched the scene without so much as blinking an eyelid. He smiled at this show of ever-increasing worship. Murkhdutt felt that his display was having its desired effect. Pleased with himself, he concluded the ritual and loudly clearing his throat, unfurled a string of questions with much pomp: 'You appear to be a believer. What is your name? From where have you come? Are you thinking of doing some job or business here? How come here, at this time? You seem new to this town. I am the hereditary priest of this Mahadev. My name is Murkhdutt.' And then he got up and brought the flowers and bel leaves placed on the Linga to the youth.

The young man touched the consecrated offering to his eyes and said, 'My name is Navinchandra. I am a brahmin. I disembarked at the harbour and came straight to the temple. I wish to stay in this dharamshala for a few days, for which I need your assistance. I have no objection if you want to cook my meals with yours.'

Murkhdutt was surprised at the phrase 'no objection', at which point Navinchandra threw a rupee onto the floor. The clink of the coin on stone captivated the priest and silenced all further queries. He welcomed Lakshmi, the Goddess of Wealth, and rose as if in a trance or a joyous dream. He led the way, and as Navinchandra followed him, Murkhdutt let loose his tongue.

'Bhai Navin Chandar, your name is difficult on the tongue! I will call you Chandar Bhai, and you, like all the others, should call me Dutt. Come along, Chandar Bhai! I have a room in the corridor where I cook. If you have any valuables keep them in my trunk; you may keep the key if you wish. There is a courtyard at the back and a pond adjoining it. You may bathe in the pond, or pour water over yourself in the courtyard. I will call you when the food is ready; you wouldn't like to sit in the smoky kitchen and will prefer the courtyard to the corridor outside. Moreover, tomorrow is Shivaratri. The women of the Counsellor's family are expected to visit to oversee arrangements for the rituals, and if you are in the courtyard they will be shielded from your gaze. Come along. This is my room.'

2 Buddhidhan's Family[†]

Navinchandra went into the courtyard. Clouds of smoke billowed out of Murkhdutt's room. Soon, the creaking and squeaking of carriages and trotting hooves could be heard. Murkhdutt, his hands covered with dough, rushed to the front of his room, craned his neck to look out, tried to arrange his shikha with his wrists, and rubbing his eyes looked in the direction of the gate. Just then, four or five beautiful young women walked in, their anklets tinkling as they climbed up the temple steps with evident effort.

Two women led the group. At the front of the train was Buddhidhan's daughter Alak Kishori, about twenty to twenty-two years old. There was about her an air of unrestrained sensuality. Walking a step behind was a girl of fourteen or fifteen. Her charm was tender, her beauty like the breaking dawn—calm, despite the exhilarating passions suited to her age. Her gait was swan-like. She was Kumud Sundari, the new bride of Buddhidhan's son, Pramaddhan. Lightning dazzles and brightens a dark night, but when the rain-laden clouds disperse, it is gentle moonlight that illuminates the sky. Likewise, Alak Kishori's splendour was followed by the soothing beauty of Kumud Sundari. She was shy, restrained, with the hint of a smile on her lips; she illuminated the temple with her radiant beauty.

[†]Author's note: Chapters 2, 3, 4 and 5 deal with historical details and do not carry the story forward.

The differences in appearance, disposition, demeanour and thought between the two sisters-in-law were apparent. This was in large measure due to their respective families, their histories, and education. The seeds of this difference were sown from birth, but their lived contexts had contributed to the growth of these innate dispositions.

Alak Kishori was what women would describe as gorgeous. Her golden complexion glowed like the mid-day sun. She attracted and impressed all those who set eyes on her. Her body was proportionate and full: the eyes of the beholder were 'filled' by her figure. Her demeanour was restless, forceful and authoritative. Those who faced her experienced the anxiety of facing a large assembly. She spoke as one used to exercising authority; most people felt naturally inferior in her presence. Just as Buddhidhan ruled by the power of his office, Alak Kishori ruled with her captivating gaze. Most people with average intelligence believed that she owed her power to her physical beauty. They were not wrong. Bedazzled in her presence, their judgement was paralysed. However, those capable of more real and detailed analysis, or who thought about her in her absence, found themselves able to think of Alak Kishori's many shortcomings. But even such persons found themselves helpless before her captivating beauty. And if someone still felt an impulse to rebel, just the presence of this doe-eyed beauty melted their pride and they felt stupefied in the face of her vibrant sensuality. Her unrestrained, passionate youth attracted a large group of admirers, and she wielded over them a power akin to that of a goddess.

Alak Kishori's mother Saubhagya Devi was a woman of average beauty and qualities. Buddhidhan was fond of her because of her maturity. Alak Kishori was spoiled by her father's affection from an early age. Buddhidhan's preoccupation with public affairs left him little time to pay attention to household matters. Saubhagya Devi did not necessarily approve of everything her daughter did, but her own unwillingness and inability to bear the burden, her retiring disposition, and Alak Kishori's own forceful character led this unabashed young woman to wield authority over Buddhidhan's household, his family, clan, relations, and when possible, even in affairs of state.

Nothing happened in the household without Alak Kishori's approval. No one could point out her shortcomings. No one could impede her. Outsiders saw her as the very life-force of the Counsellor's family. They sought to influence the Counsellor through her and showered her with praise and flattery. Some even believed that the family would be plunged into darkness the day Alak Kishori left for the house of her in-laws. The Counsellor was aware of this and always on his guard, lest someone take advantage of the situation. He always had his way, but kept up the pretence of his daughter's authority. He did not have the power to change what the world believed, and he did not want to use his power in a way that would hurt his daughter's pride. He was also curious about the blind ways in which the world formed its opinions. Sometimes however, without his knowledge, Alak Kishori actually wielded power, thus reinforcing the common belief. The household of the Counsellor of Suvarnapur functioned in this manner.

Alak Kishori was still childish. She had never as much as seen poverty. She always got her way, did exactly what pleased her, issued orders, and ensured that they were obeyed. She knew only praise. The ascendancy of the Counsellor coincided with her birth. She had seen people superior to her in age, wisdom, experience and beauty remain subservient to her. No one told her what was right; no one dared tell her what was wrong. It was in no one's interest to point out to her desirable from undesirable, or cause tedium and boredom by recounting to her stories of the family's past. It was believed that to point out to her the future that awaited her would cause a strain upon her imagination and pain her. Hence, her gaze was fixed on events unfolding in the present and her vision limited by the immediacy of the obvious. Consequently, arrogance like a dangerous snake lurked in her delicate mind. It swayed upon her brows, danced in her eyes, hissed through her tongue and endowed her body with a poisonous vibrancy. She did not possess the nectar of knowledge that could have countered the poison since she had never experienced the goodness and bounty of association with the righteous. Her hauteur was contained only by the natural goodness of the Counsellor's family.

Her glory was like the sun at high noon. Her in-laws obeyed her wishes. Her haughtiness pricked her husband, but causing injury to her heart appeared to him ungrateful. People had hoped that her brother Pramaddhan would marry at the right age and become a householder, thereby deflating Alak Kishori's arrogance as the Counsellor's family would then be ruled by someone else. But those who had harboured such hopes were soon forced to reconsider.

Counsellor Buddhidhan's son Pramaddhan had received many marriage proposals. But the parents and the daughter differed in their estimation of the girls' beauty, virtues, and lineage, which is why his marriage could not be fixed. Finally it so happened that Kumud Sundari, daughter of the Minister of Ratnanagari, Vidya Chatura, became available for marriage.

Kumud Sundari was previously betrothed to Sarasvatichandra, the learned son of Laxminandan, a wealthy and reputed merchant of Bombay. As the day of marriage drew nearer, God knows why, Sarasvatichandra suddenly disappeared without a trace. Ultimately, Vidya Chatura received a letter from Sarasvatichandra, posted from Bombay. Therein he had written: 'There is a reason why I have left my home and identity behind. I do not desire marriage. Like a wave in the ocean of life, I shall roam the world alone and unrecognised. I will not be traceable. Do not worry about me. It would have been my good fortune to marry the virtuous Kumud Sundari, but I cannot convince myself that I could have given her any joy. Please get her married. May she experience everlasting conjugal happiness.' Upon receiving the letter, and ascertaining its veracity, Vidya Chatura had become dejected and anxious about Kumud Sundari's fate. She had crossed the marriageable age and he could not think of a match comparable to Sarasvatichandra for her. He had a younger daughter, Kusum Sundari. He had no son, but his two jewel-like daughters gave him immense joy. The thought of Sarasvatichandra and Kumud Sundari as a couple had filled his heart with supreme bliss. Hence, this misfortune grieved him even more than a son's death would have. Vidya Chatura could not fathom what had possessed his intelligent and wise son-in-law-to-be. Resigned, and with the thought that such was God's will, he let bygones be bygones and looked towards the future.

The news spread far and wide, was published in newspapers, discussed in the community and outside of it. Learning was blamed. Sarasvatichandra's juvenile conduct was on every tongue. Pramaddhan read and heard about it, and talked of it at meal time. Kumud Sundari's misfortune was discussed; everyone took pity on her. Somehow, talk veered towards her virtues and beauty. Suddenly, Alak Kishori said, 'Isn't that girl a suitable match for my brother?' Saubhagya Devi said she was suitable. Buddhidhan said Vidya Chatura was an old friend, that he was high born, and that his wife was intelligent, virtuous and literate. Saubhagya Devi said, 'I have seen the girl. We met during Rajchandra's marriage and sang songs together. She is beautiful and intelligent'. Alak said someone should be sent the next morning to seek Kumud's hand in marriage. Everyone agreed. The family priest, also present at the meal, declared,'The following morning is auspicious; the proposal will be accepted'. Pramaddhan followed the goings-on, spent the day in a spirit of festivity, and the night as in one long, sweet dream. The next morning, a messenger left for Ratnanagari with the proposal.

The Minister of Ratnanagari was still gripped by worries. It was his wife who ran the household. She found the groom and his family suitable. She had little idea about the groom, but she reasoned that since the family was good, the groom would be, too. She spoke to her husband. Agitated as he was, he agreed to the proposal without much thought. Buddhidhan's messenger ran back to Suvarnapur with the good news. When Vidya Chatura regained his composure, he reconsidered the decision; but having agreed to it, he could not now decline the proposal. If it is God's will, it must be for the good, he reasoned and stopped worrying. The marriage was solemnised, and Kumud Sundari had barely spent ten, fifteen days with her in-laws when the incident narrated at the beginning of our story took place.

The credit for finding such a fine match for Pramaddhan was accorded to Alak Kishori. The mother gave birth to him, and the sister found him a wife. Alak Kishori's prestige in the household rose even higher; the brother loved her even more. Kumud Sundari's placid disposition was amenable to this domestic arrangement.

Gunasundari, Kumud Sundari's mother, and Vidya Chatura were married as young children. She had not been to school. Her husband, who was learned, and who had the opportunity, conviction and enthusiasm, imparted to her a little learning before she gave birth to their first child.

Gunasundari was clever, quick-thinking, and emotional. But she was practically illiterate when she got married and could not fathom his deepest concerns. She would often ask, 'Beloved, what causes you such grief?' Vidya Chatura would let out a deep sigh, put his hand on her shoulder, and think to himself, Oh, sweet bird! Your voice is sweet, but only if a mynah could understand human grief could you understand my pain. What good is it to tell you? Weep at my tears like a child, my sweet bird, and make me weep even more. He would then immerse himself in his books or worldly affairs. His face shone with joy when he read good books, thought new thoughts, heard news about the country's welfare, or when God's lila filled his mind. At such times, his wife would gaze upon his moon-like face, and an innocent but uncomprehending joy would envelop her. But there were times when her heart ached because she could not partake of his joys and sorrows, and when sorrow pierced his heart, she felt helpless. Sometimes words that came naturally to her or actions that were insignificant caused her husband disproportionate pain, who made as if he had lost his all to a shipwreck. Other times, even the most gigantic efforts on her part seemed inconsequential to him. Her deepest joys seemed to him childish. This caused her great confusion and turmoil. There was no way out of this. Gunasundari would shed silent tears lying on her bed, or with her head on the dressing table, while looking out onto the river, the fields and the sky from her window, or when she lay her head on her husband's lap.

One day, the couple was up on the terrace. It was midnight and a huge moon was overhead. It was as if spring had embellished her friend the sky with jewel-like stars and white clouds. The unrestrained moonlight played with this beautiful woman. Vidya Chatura was reclining on a bolster, gazing at the moon, lost in thought. Gunasundari lay with her head in his lap, holding his hand in hers and ignoring the magnificent moon, she gazed at the resplendent visage of her husband. For a time, they lay together in silence. Then, of a sudden, from his poet's heart sprang a song:

Touching foreheads we remained
Conversing in soft whispers
As if for the first time
We spoke in endearments
Our hands held in close embrace
And in this chosen dream, was the night spent.[1]
Smiling childlike and innocent, morning breaks
And stands before our bed
Suddenly shy, sensuality
Hides in the blush of your cheek
The joy of togetherness sleeps in our eyes.

As his song rose and reverberated through the skies, the lovely Gunasundari was entranced, captivated by the sonorous sounds. Satiated and joyous, the words receded and merged into each other, finding repose in the last stanza. Gunasundari asked, 'Beloved! What was it you sang? What do these beautiful words mean? Explain it to

[1] Translator's note: This verse is an English rendering of a free Gujarati translation of the *Uttararamacharita* by Manibhai Nabhubhai Dwivedi (1858–1898), Gujarati poet, writer, philosopher and Sanskrit scholar. The literal translation of the original Sanskrit would be: '(Here) while we talked at random of this thing and that in most gentle tones, resting close together, cheek to cheek, and one arm of each engaged in close embrace, the night itself ended without our noticing how the watches flew.' From M. R. Kale, ed. and trans. *The Uttararamacharita of Bhavabhuti*, Act 1, Verse 27, 5th ed. (Delhi: Motilal Banarsidass, 1934, 2010), 8. [Hereafter, unless specified, all notes are by the translator.]

me.' The poet hesitated, 'Will you understand…? But of course, you will.' And Vidya Chatura explained the narrative and the song to her at length. As she listened, enrapt, her liquid eyes shone. She responded, 'Oh, it is beautiful indeed! I tremble with joy, my very hair stands on end. How can I understand your song for myself? You fulfil all my desires. I am dependent on you for life and shall forever remain so. But I cannot understand your thoughts or fathom your mind. I do not want to stare blankly at you at such moments and in times of joy and sorrow. Tell me, what am I to do?' Vidya Chatura smiled, 'Come, even that will happen. You will learn what I shall teach, will you?'

The very next day Gunasundari commenced her studies, and she persisted with them through the course of her first pregnancy. Thereafter, she became embroiled in household matters and motherhood, and had to give up her lessons. But she was no longer discontented. True, her learning was of no use in her husband's affairs. But she felt worthy of entering the sanctum of his heart, sharing his bed, his pleasures and his delights. While lessons with the husband had to cease, as she matured, Gunasundari learnt to disentangle herself from her household tasks and further her learning. Eventually, her efforts and enthusiasm bore fruit. In their moments of leisure and pleasure, the potent seed of Vidya Chatura's learning and his aesthetic sensibility impregnated Gunasundari's eager mind. This light grew daily, and young Kumud Sundari benefited from it.

A renowned scholar has likened men to tailors. Each wants others to be dressed in his own likeness, and if possible, in clothes of his own making. It is a general principle: the literate desire that all should be literate. While Kumud Sundari was still an infant, Gunasundari, in her love for the child and passion of first motherhood, decided to educate her. In our country, many obstacles are placed in the way of women's education. If they do go to school, what girls typically study is worthless. And after they marry and become householders, study becomes even more difficult. Although knowledge is worshipped, household duties, association with illiterate female friends and relatives, the need to satisfy the base animal instincts of the husband and oneself, caring for one's children, the many ailments that women have to bear, and the lack of belief, ability and opportunity in women's education do not allow Hindu women to acquire learning. Gunasundari, intelligent and persevering, overcame these obstacles and acquired some learning. She was determined that her daughter should study before such obstacles were placed in her path and before she became a householder.

Vidya Chatura was increasingly embroiled in public affairs, which cast a shadow over all his other activities. Even so, he supported, facilitated, improved, guided and furthered Gunasundari's commendable enthusiasm, insistence and effort in their daughter's education. In conversation, humour and by example, he helped bridge the gap and overcome the shortcomings of this effort. In just a few years, Kumud Sundari learnt much. She learned to think for herself, and her parents could rejoice that their efforts had borne fruit. She began to learn English and Sanskrit before marriage. The duties of a householder, aesthetic sensibility and refinement, worldly wisdom, and moral conduct which act as custodians of a householder's life, came to her effortlessly and stood guard as this princess entered the temple that was Buddhidhan's household. Her parents desired the learned Sarasvatichandra to be the consort for their princess. Though his refusal and disappearance pained and disappointed them greatly, Kumud Sundari bestowed heavenly bliss on her parents.

Kumud Sundari was quite different from Alak Kishori in appearance. Her complexion was fair, her structure delicate. She embodied the description: 'a delicate woman with a pearl nose-ring'. She did not attract by virtue of dazzling beauty. Her bearing was not haughty. Some thought she was a meek cow; some said she was worthless. Anyone could look upon her face. She wore the markers of a married woman but little else by way of ornamentation. Her clothes had simple, muted patterns and covered her entire body, except her childlike and delicate hands and equally dainty hennaed feet. Her movements were imperceptible, and she rarely emoted through bodily gestures. Like the outline of the moon shrouded by clouds in spring, a faint smile would play on her face. She spoke little, but when she did, her sweet voice had a silvery, bell-like ring to it. The virtuous could rest their gaze upon her and feel a natural, innocent and quiet attraction. Male aesthetes could discern about her visage a pure beauty. Intelligent women found her eyes alive and expressive. Middle-aged women found her mature. Charming young women were entertained by her conversation. Refined women liked to keep her company, observed her demeanour, her manner of speech, imitated her, and asked other women to do the same. Her delicate bearing, beauty, intelligence, modesty, charm and tenderness were observed, analysed and discussed in her absence. Children would stop playing and gather around her. Anyone who pointed out aspects of her beauty was praised; others joined in with their own views. Blessings were showered upon her as if unbidden. All those who looked at Kumud Sundari, heard her or conversed with her felt the same sensation of having bathed in gentle moonlight—they were immersed in nectar and showered with joy.

For Kumud Sundari, Buddhidhan's household was a world apart. She had settled in well with her in-laws. Alak Kishori ruled by habit; Kumud Sundari had learnt obedience. Women of the Counsellor's family did not have to do household work, which is why there was no conflict between them. Of money there was plenty; desires could be fulfilled without discrimination. Moreover, Alak Kishori was given credit for suggesting this match; therefore dressing up the bride, bringing her to the fore, adding to her glory, introducing her to the community, and acquainting and instructing her about the family customs were also her responsibility, and Alak Kishori performed them with enthusiasm. In all such matters, Saubhagya Devi's consent was perfunctorily obtained, Buddhidhan merely informed, and Pramaddhan's preferences sought. The family servants spoke about the new bride to her husband to seek his favour. Alak Kishori indulged in banter with her brother. The family's time was thus spent in this newfound and innocent joy.

When she first moved to her in-laws', Kumud Sundari still remembered Sarasvatichandra and shed silent tears. When alone, she sighed deeply, and when with others, she participated in their play and festivities with an empty heart. Her lacklustre smile hid a wounded and broken heart. However, this was seen as bashfulness and her tears seen as tears of joy. She wished and attempted to forge a bond with Pramaddhan, but her heart trailed behind. Even so, the force of time, the experiences of a new life, the surging joy of others around her, her young mind's capacity for adjustment to the new, the intelligence to obey the imperatives of God's will, the wisdom to cede to forces beyond her control, and the knowledge that so much as thinking of another man violated her virtue enabled the young but determined woman to rein in her mind and perform the duties expected of her. Gradually, the past began to recede; joy returned to her face. However, her happiness was like the waning moon at dawn, and no one but Gunasundari could have discerned this. If she were with her daughter, her loving heart would have shattered. Pramaddhan's joy was a superficial one. To him, as to other onlookers, it was apparent that Kumud Sundari had attained the zenith of bliss. What they did not see they were not capable of seeing.

There was no one in Buddhidhan's household to nurture Kumud Sundari and her refined ways. Pramaddhan had been an errant student. Student life had seemed constricting; he felt belittled at school. Studies were to him a source of boredom and drudgery, and learning, merely a poor man's means of earning a livelihood; and if it had any other use, he believed he could avail of it by retaining educated men as servants. The school teacher was a case in point: a respected man of learning, but his advice was never sought in the administration of the state. Pramaddhan believed that English education was glorified because it was a foreign language—the language of the rulers. Sanskrit was for him the language of the shastris, who, despite their learning, were poor and dependent. He considered mathematics, philosophy, Vedanta, and other such subjects fit only for the purposeless, the old, mendicants, people without means, and others who, though respectable, were in a real sense good for nothing. His father was the source of such notions, but Pramaddhan had nourished them owing to his own lazy disposition. He reasoned that as a dutiful son, it was not given to him to challenge his father's ideas. His associates flattered him and there was no one to tell him bitter truths. He had no disagreeable experiences. For these and other reasons, like many others, he too harboured a high opinion of his own intelligence.

Pramaddhan led a wanton and dissolute life. He took the family's wealth and prosperity for permanent and, eyes closed, floated along on the tide of time, believing, however, that he swam on the back of his own strength. Having done with his political intriguing, he read novels or whiled away his time in the company of friends who praised him, belittled others, and narrated their encounters with women. He behaved fancifully, imagined exciting situations, and wandered about freely anywhere any time. His speech was indiscreet. The Counsellor's son considered such a course of things to be his lot and a good use of his wealth. Apart from this, his character was good, his temperament joyous and content. He aspired to satisfy all of Kumud Sundari's desires and strived conscientiously to make her happy. He took pride in her beauty, praised her learning, and considered their union as precious as that of a jewel with gold.

The conduct of Pramaddhan, Alak Kishori and the entire household of the Counsellor of Suvarnapur were wholly foreign to what Kumud Sundari had been used to at Vidya Chatura's. Her natal home and her in-laws' household differed from each other in demeanour, in what constituted pleasure, thought and action. Believing that her new home would have books as well, she had brought none with her. In this new world, she had only one thing that linked her to her past and reminded her of it. Alongwith his letter to Vidya Chatura, Sarasvatichandra had also sent a letter for Kumud Sundari. The letter contained just one verse, written in golden ink. The handwriting was familiar to Kumud Sundari, as was the verse, which is how she knew who the author was.

Enchanting Night!
Do not allow separation from the waning moon to blind you
By day, holding the hands of the one you desire,
Become a joyous bride.

She had neither shown nor shared this verse with anyone. She guarded it in her blouse, close to her heart. In opportune moments of solitude she would take it out to read, although she knew it by heart. She would hum it to herself and weep. If she saw anyone approach her, she would quickly hide the letter, compose herself and be on guard. She often looked at the letter angrily, her eyebrows raised. At such times, her face reflected pity, pain and anger simultaneously. She would look up at the sky, sigh deeply, and wipe away her tears. In her new household, she could mask her feelings and no one could gauge her troubled emotions. In the eyes of the world, there was nothing amiss. To all outward appearances, the Suvarnapur Counsellor's family seemed festive and joyous. The nubile beauties of this family gracefully climbed up the stairs of the Rajeshwar Mahadev, their breathing heavy with effort. None but the priest Murkhdutt witnessed this scene. If a Yaksha were to behold them, he would be pardoned for believing that these were celestial beings rarely seen by mortal eyes, come down to earth to imbue it with life-giving nectar and worship the God of the Gods, Mahadev.

The priest hurriedly washed his hands, wiped them on a piece of cloth, adjusted his dhoti, and rushed out to receive the ladies. 'Welcome! Welcome!' he exclaimed and entered the sanctum of the temple. He took some bel leaves and other consecrated offerings and gave them to the women saying, 'Behn! Everything has been arranged just as you desired. All items required for the Shiv puja have been procured. I will follow your orders.' In the company of these beautiful women, Murkhdutt reminded one of Mahadev's ghostly attendants standing beside Parvati. Just as he was receiving instructions for the following day's festivities from them, a soldier rushed in, 'Behn, Behn! The Counsellor is on his way here, possibly accompanied by the King!'

'Is it possible for us to return unseen?'

'No, the flag-bearers and riders can be seen where the road forks.'

'What then?' asked Alak Kishori, flustered.

Those who have had to deal with certain situations know best how to respond to them. Murkhdutt rushed down the steps and said, 'Come, follow me to the courtyard. The King has only come for darshan and will not spend much time here. I will lock you in and open the door only after their party has left.' Murkhdutt had forgotten that Navinchandra was in the yard.

The women followed him. Alak Kishori turned to Kumud Sundari and said, 'We will be confined here for at least an hour or two. The King has not come merely for darshan. He will spend some time here. It was a mistake to come at this hour; it completely slipped out of my mind!'

Kumud Sundari looked up at her sister-in-law to indicate that she understood it was no one's fault that this had happened, delicately withdrew her gaze and kept on walking with her eyes lowered on the ground.

The women entered the yard. Murkhdutt quickly banged the door shut and locked it behind him.

3 Buddhidhan

Rajeshwar Mahadev was at a distance of four to five miles from Suvarnapur. Not many came that way. It was therefore a place for the secret rendezvous of rich wastrels and those bent on political intrigue. This contributed substantially to Murkhdutt's income—he had learnt the craft of pleasing all patrons by accommodating their needs and demands. Most times, patrons informed him of their meetings beforehand, thus avoiding the awkwardness of encountering others. However, the two persons meeting here at this point in our story were no ordinary men. One was the ruler of the city, and the other the patron of the temple. It was the duty of the priest to ensure that they were left undisturbed.

'Your kindness be upon us all, Your Grace!' announced the usher, as the ruler of Suvarnapur entered the temple accompanied by Buddhidhan. The princely retinue spread out a carpet woven with gold thread near the Nandi. Both men sat on it, and the servants left them to their conversation. Murkhdutt kowtowed thrice to them in greeting and then returned to his room to resume his cooking. Like the moon and a solitary star visible through a break in the clouds on an overcast monsoon night, the King and his Counsellor were left alone in the temple.[1]

[1] Author's note: This narrative is resumed in Chapter Six. The intervening part provides the story of Buddhidhan's life thus far.

Rana Bhupsinh was about thirty-seven or thirty-eight years old. The previous ruler had left no legitimate male heirs. His administrators and queens had failed to install an heir after his death. Their machinations to foist a ruler of their choice failed because of divisions in the ranks. Bhupsinh was a close cousin of the deceased king. Through the influence and cunning of his family, and support of the British Resident, he had ascended the throne. He had, by now, ruled over Suvarnapur for three, four years.

Rana Bhupsinh had had a normal upbringing, under ordinary circumstances. As a child, he had been shielded from the poisonous air of the palace. This was why he was still in possession of common sense. He had known poverty. Therefore, while not generous, his own memories of deprivation ensured that he was benevolent to the poor. He had dealt with administrators, officials and soldiers while trying to protect his father's *garas*, the family inheritance. He had had to plead and please, submit to insults, face wily officials, offer bribes, and suffer being pushed around. Therefore, he had an inkling of the difference between outward expressions and genuine feelings of love, trust and respect, even among those in the ruler's inner circle. He had heard of and experienced the wilful conduct of palace officials. He had resolved to put these learnings and experiences to good use after assuming the throne. He was personally acquainted with many in the state administration. He felt duty-bound to avenge the insults heaped upon him in the past and took pride in rewarding those who had stood by him. Bhupsinh had not the faintest idea of the real duties of a ruler: he firmly believed that by punishing insults and rewarding supporters, he would be performing his duty and securing glory. This belief stemmed from his past and was nurtured by his present. The rumblings beneath the surface were ever ready to erupt. When Bhupsinh assumed the throne, the chief administrator, the Karbhari of Suvarnapur palace had offered no resistance; he had changed his colours and displayed generosity. The wily administrator's scheming seemed to have borne fruit—Bhupsinh's temperament had seemingly undergone a change. The leisure and pleasures of the palace had doused his fire. His anger and thirst for revenge had subsided under the coat of gratification. And the old palace guard had heaved a collective sigh of relief.

In the torpor of power, in unthinking selfishness, in the inebriation of passion, in the grandeur of ostentation, in the web of everydayness, encircled, slumbering, comatose, bedazzled and enmeshed, as the change of ruler became a thing of the past, the old and new guards grew negligent. The only person who remained awake and vigilant was the Counsellor of Suvarnapur, Buddhidhan. He observed, listened, thought ahead and devised new manoeuvres. While the world around him slept, Buddhidhan kept awake like a doctor keeping vigil by the side of an ailing patient, or like an ever-watchful lion with his sight fixed on his prey, lest it escape. His aspiration was that the administration of Suvarnapur be regarded as the finest. He desired that his authority should take root, and thus render the state his plaything. This would ensure that the ruler and the populace of Suvarnapur became the bountiful kamdhenu for him and his family. Such thoughts constantly haunted Buddhidhan and kept him awake and restless. Perchance if another thought entered his mind and blurred his vision momentarily, he would soon return to his obsessive ambition. This unceasing worry corroded his joy, his being. It was not given to ordinary eyes to either witness or comprehend this churning.

Some four or five generations ago, Buddhidhan's ancestors had been the chief administrators, the karbharis of Suvarnapur. They had since lost this position; but the family continued to accept even lowly work in the state administration just in order to keep a foot-hold in the Suvarnapur palace. Wheels of fortune move rapidly, not only changing from one generation to the next but also within a single generation itself. This family, which had once taken pride in its wealth, had to see its riches dwindle to rags. Buddhidhan had inherited nothing but a strong sense of family pride from his father. This pride brought with it certain other qualities as well. His mother was intelligent and wise. She maintained the household even in poverty, but was equally capable of generosity in times of prosperity. It was said of her that had she been a man, she would have reclaimed the post of chief administrator for the family. Her son had inherited these qualities from her. As they observed his abilities flourish and grow day by day, his parents anticipated and hoped for a better, brighter future. Shivaji Maharaj was raised and encouraged by his mother Jijabai. Similarly, Buddhidhan's mother told her son rousing stories about his ancestors; how Ramrai had obtained the position of chief administrator; how young Laxmanchandra had gained the ruler's confidence and affection; how Krishnadas had amassed amazing riches and lifted the family's fortunes under the rule of Sundarsinh. The child Buddhidhan listened attentively to all these stories, hanging onto her every word. His illiterate mother's descriptions were not refined, but her narration had a natural flair, an innate charm, an attraction, and the power of suggestion. It had the delicacy of a woman's tongue and the cultured air attendant to it. The unadorned prose of this wise and beautiful woman unobtrusively etched itself into the mind of her young listener. The dreams and aspirations of the mother mingled and became part of the child's unconscious, and there they flowered effortlessly. His father boastfully recounted past glories of the family and blamed fate for allowing the new rank of uncultured youth, born in poverty, to rule and rise arrogantly in power. He laughed disdainfully at such officials and considered them of no significance. Buddhidhan's tender mind was filled with such ideas, and he resolved young that he would rectify Brahma the Creator's error and attain a position of power befitting his significant abilities.

The boy destined to be chief administrator went to school, but found education purposeless and spent many days in a quandary. Eventually, he realised that literacy was a craft, a means to a livelihood, and that those who possessed it could write dazzling prose and decipher obscure documents. The mother argued that education enhanced intelligence. The son never challenged this view, but was convinced that on this score his mother was in error. Believing this, he studied little at school, and instead spent time observing the school master at work, how he increased his number of pupils, how he flattered their parents, and how he dealt with dullards. He also observed how the students played pranks on the master behind his back. Buddhidhan found such observations both pleasurable and instructive. Initially, in his ranking of the most intelligent persons, the second slot, after his mother, had belonged to his school master. However, he was soon dropped from this exalted position. Gradually, the master became for him a specimen of stupidity and low intelligence. Buddhidhan satisfied the master with his learning and intelligence, and by also giving him money. As he entered the real world, Buddhidhan was armed with the conviction that all educated men must be like the school master. He changed his opinion only later in life, following a handful of instances, when faced with irrefutable proof to the contrary.

Success in the real world was harder than success in school. Over time, Buddhidhan experienced much that was new which would cause him to change his mind. As a child, he had dreamt of an easy and rapid rise to power. Bitter lived experiences doused this dream. Buddhidhan decided that he had no choice but to be satisfied if after years of toiling, he was mid-way but on course to his desired destination. The ultimate position he desired, for which he would have to overcome many obstacles by dint of hard work, face agonising disappointments and allow for the vagaries of fate, would only come to him gradually. Having taken this decision, he set himself adrift in the sea of the world without a raft.

Buddhidhan never thought highly of his father's intelligence, but benefited from his experience. While he often disregarded his mother's lessons and instructions, he was often forced to go back to her to seek counsel. Despite the fact that his mother's instruction was agreeable to him, day by day, his estimation of her intelligence lowered. He began to be moulded by worldly experiences, and with age his intellect matured. He increasingly found his mother's domestic wisdom wanting and fit only for women; his father he found weak in body and in mind. The young bird was learning to fly alone. The role of the parents became confined to expressions of endorsement or anxiety. As their ability to deal with his world decreased and their focus shifted to other concerns, their resolve weakened and their affection for their son deepened. This they expressed amply. The son recognised that it was his duty to ensure that their affection was not wasted like rain on barren land. He realised that it was his duty to respond to it in equal measure and give them joy. It did not come naturally to this worldly-wise man to make a display of his emotions, which usually remained unseen, unrecognised. But his reasoning enabled him to express a recognisable verisimilitude of filial love.

Buddhidhan was now required to decide the stream he would follow, to get to the port where he would cast anchor. His aged parents tried to mould his thinking to their aspirations. The father wanted to see his dream realised within his lifetime. He wanted to use his family connections and be instrumental in Buddhidhan making his acquaintance with the ruler of Suvarnapur. Poor as he was, he wanted this to be his inheritance to his son. The chief administrator was a distant relative of Buddhidhan's mother. Through the intercession of her cousin, she desired that her son be given a position higher than others of his age and stature. The old couple endlessly discussed the relative merits of their proposals. Buddhidhan understood the purpose of these discussions. But he wanted his own desires fulfilled, using the means suggested by his parents. They all agreed that wealth must be obtained, for it was a means to other ends. Their differences were over the source of this wealth. Political power or trade—which was it to be? Trade involved the risk of loss, needed initial capital, the goodwill of officials, and was a source of perpetual worry. For these reasons, Buddhidhan decided to seek wealth through the state. His concern was to find a way of achieving this. If he were to join the state service, his first job would be petty, bring in little money and no prestige. Political power would be a distant dream and he would be at the mercy of strange and stupid officials. Consign such a job to the flames. Throw dust over it! Business, however difficult, would not be so disagreeable. Buddhidhan was plagued by such doubts. He vacillated day and night, at home and in the world, solitary and deep in thought; he sought a solution to this dilemma. Often, even in the company of his parents, his heart empty, his gaze vacant, his ears would shut out all sound.

Sitting by himself, he would imagine thousands of situations, study how other people carried on their livelihoods, sincerely ask them how they had found this resource initially, and consider if these means were available to him. One path would appear unsuited to his temperament; another would not be free of risk; a third would not bring him riches; and a fourth was hazardous and full of obstacles. He measured each path and calculated on his fingertips, in the air, scribbled in the dust; but it would all come to naught. He would murmur to himself: What is to happen I do not know. I fear a failed future, I preempt, resolving it all in my mind.

But even this seemed to him foolish and at times he would laugh out aloud at himself. Finally, Buddhidhan decided to look for a job. He decided to wait patiently and secure suitable employment. His parents were unaware of what was raging in his mind. Sometimes they would ask, 'Bhai! What is it that you wish to do?' No response was ever satisfactory.

Through all of this, Buddhidhan appeared outwardly cheerful. He found ways to keep himself occupied, and his mother supported his endeavours. Though not deeply enamoured of learning, he went to the Kazi Sahib, an old acquaintance of the family, and learned Persian. This gave him gravitas and an air of wisdom. He heard instructive stories from the *shastris* and *puranis*. Moral sense tempered his conscience. He kept the company of ascetics and obtained peace and calm, while acquiring some understanding of the nature of divinity. This also helped him cultivate a philosophical attitude in his dealings with worldly matters. In his spare time he indulged in banter with old men who, in the strength and intoxication of youth, had done things great and base, had fallen and plotted, seen success and defeat, had been tempted and entangled, and had even managed to salvage themselves. Some were administrators, others traders. Some had wasted their youth in the company of prostitutes, while some in their stupidity had seen nothing of the world. Some had been lazy and allowed things to take their own course; others had been victims of intrigue. These wizened men narrated their stories variously, some without regret, some with a touch of pride, some with dejection. All these tales seeped into Buddhidhan's heart. At times, irrespective of whether the occasion demanded it or not, Buddhidhan would recite Persian verses, narrate instructive tales, or illustrate a point with a story told by one of his elderly companions. On these occasions, his mother would join in enthusiastically with stories of her own. These stories came alive for Buddhidhan and were etched permanently on his mind. Like Brahma who witnessed happenings in this illusory world without the necessity for action, Buddhidhan's father, the family patriarch, witnessed all this and experienced a quiet joy.

While cleaning his teeth, bathing, at lunch and dinner, while lying in bed, sitting around a winter fire, chatting on a moonlit night, in the cool nights of summer, while listening to the rain fall from laden clouds on dark monsoon nights, the 'chief administrator's family' of Suvarnapur, without a teacher or text, unconsciously learnt lessons from the world. The delicacy of a woman's charm, imagination, metaphor, affection, aesthetic sensibility and sensitivity now entered the conscience of this man who had hitherto harboured little regard for womanly intelligence. It had the same beautiful, nourishing and positive effect that the morning breeze wafting in from over a river has on the human body. The Persian couplets, moral lessons, verses, and idle chatter of old men became easily digestible for Buddhidhan owing to the nurturing touch of this woman—his mother.

Buddhidhan's father, like his ancestors, was entitled to a privy purse of two hundred rupees annually. The amount came in handy in hard times and gave them prestige among the people. Once a year, the new administrators were reminded of the 'chief administrator's family'. Buddhidhan's ancestors had amassed wealth and acquired land. From this holding, only enough survived to pay the land revenue. If Buddhidhan were to gain political power, he too would amass wealth anew. But for his family, such power was a thing of the past, not reclaimable even in their dreams. Money begets money, but his family had no wealth; which is why entry and success in palace politics through bribery was difficult to accomplish. They had to submit to the wealthy and influential, and could hope to secure justice only when the competition was level; even this hinged upon the industriousness, enthusiasm, and alertness of the concerned official. Nevertheless, affairs of the household rolled on. This was due to the able intelligence and parsimony of the woman who ran it. The family faced no apparent hardship. In any case, they were used to bearing difficulties. Leisure and pleasure were regarded as unpalatable. The joys, riches and pleasures of the family were confined to the chatter of the mother and son.

Buddhidhan was betrothed to a girl of a family living in similar circumstances. Her mother was dead; she was raised largely by Buddhidhan's mother, and under her upbringing she had acquired her true potential and capabilities. Her father-in-law had named her Saubhagya Devi. The young couple was the only wealth of this impoverished household—and their only hope.

Days passed. The haughty inebriated world did not cast so much as a glance in their direction. Buddhidhan's condition was like that of a potent seed growing underground, unknown even to the rays of the sun. He had passed through no fiery ordeal. His only real concern was to acquire power and to be considered important. This desire plagued and consumed him like a constant low fever. Not even his family knew what ailed him. Only he felt the torment in moments of solitude.

But this did not last long. Troubles burst upon this growing sapling. The father suddenly died of cholera. Buddhidhan was in no way prepared for this. The blow was sudden and swift. His resolve seemed to crack. Given his character, he was unlikely to find a virtuous companion among the pleasure-seeking youth. His poverty precluded any friendship with the rich, except one based on flattery; the poor were not similarly cultured. Even if he found a friend, the difference in intellect always remained apparent. Buddhidhan was friendless. In his moment of crisis there was no one to give him solace—save for his mother who was now a widow and herself submerged in grief. It became Buddhidhan's duty to give her succour. The avalanche of difficulties had not yet subsided.

> When parents are alive, their words should be implicitly obeyed. After death, on their death anniversary, the Shradh should be performed with generous offerings of food. At least once in a lifetime, Shradh (Pind Danam) should be performed in Gaya. These three actions alone make a son worthy of being called a true son.

This verse resonated within the brahmin youth. He found it pleasing. Reformers believed that a son following his own inclination also brings prestige to his father. Buddhidhan wanted to be a good son by fulfilling his father's aspirations. He drowned the sorrow of his father's death by dealing with the exigencies of daily life and thus proved himself a model son. He suffered agonies; he borrowed money; he worked hard. Hardships fell on him like axe blows on a sandalwood tree. His body withered, but his innate intelligence blossomed. Difficulties encircled him, but he pushed them aside and moved on ahead. He had no opportunity to turn back and ponder over the past. Alone and without support, Buddhidhan used all his strength to confront the hardships that threatened to crush and overwhelm him.

4 Buddhidhan (Continued)

The motherless Saubhagya Devi had lived with her in-laws since she was a child. She was no longer a child. Her body and mind changed, visibly and invisibly. With the death of her father-in-law, her widowed mother-in-law observed confinement. Saubhagya Devi had to shoulder the entire burden of the household. Her mother-in-law instructed and guided her from her room, and it was Saubhagya Devi's duty to obey her, even anticipate her wishes. She thus became a householder even before she was married. Hitherto, she had not spoken with Buddhidhan. But in these difficult times, gradually, unseen by others, and with trepidation, the two began to converse, initially standing well apart from each other. However, the young unmarried couple, in anticipation of pleasures to come, began to experience sensations hitherto unknown. Their hearts blossomed under force of youthful passion and even in the midst of very real difficulties, this tender attraction, unbeckoned by either, grew and dreamt innocent dreams. Neither was aware of this. In moments of playfulness, worldly responsibilities receded into the background; but their everyday lived reality compelled them to forget their tenderness. They had little scope to comprehend the two conditions. Sometimes their awakened desires sought to play themselves out and their growing familiarity allowed the playfulness of touch. Still children, they were in 'love'. If this sorrowful world was a sari dark as a moonless night, their love was resplendent like the Milky Way; in the belief that the whole world slept, it twinkled brightly. Sorrows and joys do not come in monotones. Flung against the rocks of difficulty, Buddhidhan's courageous mind grew tougher. At the same time, he was also tempered by delicate feelings. A love of pleasure and passion took root deep within his grave and sombre disposition. No one in the world was aware of this development.

One day, the mother-in-law and daughter-in-law sat reminiscing about the past. The mother-in-law was overcome with emotion. Not wanting the child to see her tears, she sent her out of the room, saying, 'Daughter-in-law, will you get me some water?' The girl promptly got up to fetch water. She went to the other part of the house and filled a tumbler from the pot. Buddhidhan was sitting on a swing, deep in thought. He stopped swinging when he saw her, the one who brought a sparkle to his eyes, the light of the house. He stared unblinking at Saubhagya Devi as she filled water. He looked at her face and eyes, which were uncovered, but his imagination led him to visualise her tender and sensuous body which was covered. He oscillated between that which was seen and that which was imagined. Saubhagya Devi grew aware of his intense gaze. Both stared at each other, and they forgot all else. She forgot that her mother-in-law had asked for water.

Meanwhile, the mother-in-law had shed her tears and regained her composure. She wondered where Saubhagya Devi was, and felt that her daughter-in-law had understood her pain and was probably crying all alone somewhere. She stepped out of the room, forgetting that she had to observe a widow's customary confinement. She mumbled to herself, You are the good fortune of this house, our hope, the goddess who will perpetuate our lineage. Can you ever be happy while I'm drowning in sorrow? Dear God! she sighed and stepped out. She retreated the moment she saw the tender young couple. She could not believe her eyes. Overcome with curiosity, and to be certain, she looked on, hidden from their view. This beautiful and joyous sight melted away her pain and sorrow. Just a moment ago her pain had been unbearable, but now she thanked God. Her moist eyes forgot that an elder was not supposed to witness such tender scenes. She stood there, transfixed.

Buddhidhan and Saubhagya Devi gazed at each other unblinking, as if in a trance. The spell was about to break. Any moment, Buddhidhan expected Saubhagya Devi to sprinkle water on him, and he was prepared for it. But the expected did not happen. Instead, he saw her eyes well up with tears. He got up. He took the tumbler from her and put it aside, then took her hand and asked, 'What is the matter?' In response, she broke down and began to sob quietly, her eyes downcast. He drew her close, embraced her and gently caressed her back.

Buddhidhan's mother suddenly realised that she had broken the customary limit. She retreated back to her room, deep in thought. She knew she had seen what was not for her to see.

Saubhagya Devi, too, realised what she had done. She freed herself from his embrace, and said, 'Nothing, nothing at all,' picked up the tumbler of water and hurried back to where her mother-in-law was waiting for her. Buddhidhan kept standing there, surprised, stupefied.

This was the first time they had crossed the limit. Both experienced new desires surface in their mind and body. Deep in thought, Buddhidhan slowly walked back to the swing. The mother surmised that the wise step would be to solemnise their marriage immediately and not wait for her husband's death anniversary to pass. She felt some remorse, but she forgave them as she recalled the days of her own youth. It is the natural instinct of Indian mothers to try and cover up the indiscretions of their children. The girl had reached puberty, but her father-in-law's death had delayed the marriage. The mother in her wisdom realised that God's will knew no such barriers, and hearts already united would not wait long for the marriage to be solemnised.

But there was another reason as well that delayed the marriage. Buddhidhan was required to incur the customary expenses on death rituals. To then spend money on a wedding was to invite trouble. But he could not bring himself to say this to his mother. The marriage was organised, and the bride and groom were declared a couple in the eyes of the world. The festivities were over. They were householders now.

Buddhidhan now had to face his debts and creditors. The household expenses could be met from the privy purse, but that was not enough to pay back the creditors. The family felt in want of various things for the new household. The produce from the land was not sufficient. Buddhidhan could not share his concerns with either his mother or his wife, for it would cause them much anxiety. He had to be the man of the house and keep up pretenses. Alarming the women would be like cutting off his feet himself. Buddhidhan's body withered, his face lost its lustre, his body appeared drained of blood, and although young, he soon started looking aged.

Even so, a solitary lamp spread light and hope. At the end of a tiring day, he would sit down and talk to his widowed mother. Saubhagya Devi would join them with her childlike innocence. Finally, alone with her, he would be able to listen to her sweet voice, her melodious song and experience a nectar-like passion. Tired and fatigued, with her he would experience a momentary bliss. This was the only source of joy in a life otherwise full of sorrow and strife. The height of a householder's joy is attained only while living in poverty.

This dream, too, proved short-lived. The joys of domesticity were not a remedy to his problems. Buddhidhan began to have bouts of fever. He did not submit to them, but the fevers soon developed into a chronic condition. His body was aflame and ultimately he was bedridden. In his state of acute anxiety, no medicine, no remedy could alleviate what ailed him. There were many vaidyas in town, but most of them were quacks. Each one suggested a different concoction.

Although poor, the 'chief administrator's family' still commanded some prestige in Suvarnapur. Many visitors crowded around Buddhidhan's sickbed, irritated him, found faults in the welcome accorded them owing to the absence of another man in the house, commented upon the family's circumstances and criticised the family members. They felt or feigned compassion, cast lecherous glances at the young woman who sat beside the ailing man, made many conjectures, stole what they could, made a lot of noise, and rose and left for their homes with or without taking the family's leave. Saubhagya Devi and her mother-in-law were grief-struck; these random comings and goings only alarmed and distressed them further. No remedy seemed to work and every visitor added to their confusion by suggesting new potions. Finally, the widow decided to come out of her confinement and sat by her ailing son when he had visitors. The young daughter-in-law, nervous and anxious, somehow managed the house. But the sole hope and support of the family, Buddhidhan showed no signs of recovery.

Suffering followed suffering. A year passed since Buddhidhan's father died. The administrator refused to continue the privy purse. Secretly, they were informed that the allowance could continue if the palms of the administrator and other petty officials were greased. This was impossible for the impoverished and hard-pressed family. The women felt helpless and distraught, but they did not inform Buddhidhan. His illness was a prolonged one. There was no money in the house, the income had stopped, and in the absence of a man to look after affairs, produce from the land declined further. There was no one who could go to the market. The vaidya lost interest in administering the medicines and his visits became infrequent. The visitors too became disinterested and stopped visiting. The house fell silent; there was nothing to draw attention away from the ailing man. The two women also began to look ill. Their suffering seemed endless. They had nowhere to turn but the sky above them and the water below.

Buddhidhan's distress increased as newer diseases assailed him. Bedridden, with sunken eyes and vacant gaze he stared at his old mother and childlike wife. His wife shed silent tears. Her eyes became swollen and bloodshot. The mother's anguish knew no bounds. She looked at her son and daughter-in-law, and smote her forehead in vain when she was alone. She nursed her son courageously, stayed close to her daughter-in-law and ensured she was not left alone with her consuming worry.

Finally, all visits ceased. Only the vaidya, moved by compassion, administered his preparations to the poor man. In addition, one elderly neighbour, whom Buddhidhan had spent hours listening to before his illness, continued to visit him, sit by his side and give him solace. It was this same man who now helped the widow by running errands to the market and the vaidya's house; it was also on his counsel that Buddhidhan had not been informed about the cessation of the privy purse. One day, feeling unwell, the old man could not visit Buddhidhan. The vaidya too had not been around. The widowed mother who was in confinement, found herself in a quandary. Sending her daughter-in-law out of the house seemed to her inappropriate. Therefore, early next morning, the doting mother decided to abandon societal norm and custom. She told the daughter-in-law not to feel embarrassed and to sit by her husband's side in her absence. Then like a thief stalking the shadows, she walked to the vaidya's house.

The daughter-in-law closed the door behind her and sat by her husband's bedside. Buddhidhan was asleep. His weak and withered body looked lifeless as he slept. A dhoti covered his torso; one emaciated hand rested inert by his side. The mother-in-law's absence allowed Saubhagya Devi to give vent to her grief. She looked at the shriveled body and withered face of her loving husband, and her heart cried out in anguish. Tears streaming down her eyes, she sang softly to herself.

Sad is the wife whose husband is away
For she is content only in his presence
My only beloved
Give up your foreign land and return
For my heart breaks when you are away ... when you are away

As she sang, her eyes on the deathly pallor of his face, her imagination ran wild. Inauspicious images flashed before her eyes as if in a macabre dance. The force of these visions was such that emotions buried deep within burst forth. She could no longer contain herself and let out a loud wail, 'Hai!' She smote her head against his feet and sobbed without restraint, not realising she might wake him. Her warm tears wet the bed. Buddhidhan woke up startled. For days now, he had not been able to as much as sit up in bed unsupported. Who knows from where he now found the strength. He pulled his wife close with his skeletal hands and weakly tried to press her to his emaciated chest. It was futile, since what little strength he had was already spent in this exertion. Buddhidhan was profoundly saddened at the sight of his agitated and frightened wife. He fathomed instantly the cause of her grief. He regained his calm; his eyes were moist with unshed tears. His voice trembled and broke as he said, 'Devi! Why are you doing this? Be patient. God is with those who have no one else.'

Saubhagya Devi continued to gaze intently at Buddhidhan as if crazed. The torment in her eyes seemed to admonish God as it were, convinced that His will did not favour her. She put her hands on her husband's shoulders and kept sobbing with downcast eyes as she haltingly spoke. 'What can I do? I cannot bear it any longer! Mataji did all she could. She sold her ornaments and paid off our marriage debts. She bears the household expenses with what little remains. I beg and plead with her, but she refuses to sell my ornaments. Now, disregarding her confinement, she has gone to the vaidya's house. Hai! O why did God create me? You had to incur debts to marry me. I am so utterly useless that I cannot even leave the house, and Mataji was forced to go despite her confinement. Who else could do what she has done! Her life is fulfilled. Alas, I am utterly useless, so are my ornaments. You could not make use of them. If the Privy Purse has been stopped, so be it—but what about my ornaments? If they are of no use to you, I do not need them either. What use are they to me!' And saying so, one by one she removed all her ornaments and flung them against the wall in helpless rage. 'I am born accursed because I have to see you in this state. I cannot bear it anymore!' she wailed.

Buddhidhan felt even more helpless and wretched. 'Why are you doing this, Devi? Why was I not told that the Privy Purse has been stopped? So be it. You are not useless. Why would you think so! You are my support, my beloved. Be patient, my Devi. Those who have no one else have God. These auspicious ornaments are symbolic of our union. Do not throw them away.'

'Who can be more auspicious for me than you? I have no fondness for ornaments. Where has the lustre of your face gone? God helps those He wants to, but what am I to do? Oh God! Do lie down, you will get weaker. Even at such times, I only add to your suffering!' She composed herself and helped him to lie back in bed. There was a knock at the door just then, and Saubhagya Devi hurriedly went to open it.

The mother entered the house. She looked dejected. Her face hid neither her rage, nor her red and moist eyes. She saw her distraught son and daughter-in-law, and the gold ornaments strewn about the room. For a moment, worry and suspicion assailed her. Her lips quivered and her heart pounded.

In a voice weak with exhaustion, Buddhidhan said, 'Ma, where have you been? Was it right not to inform me about the Privy Purse? Why do you appear so shaken?'

Realising then that he knew, the mother cast a reproachful look at her daughter-in-law.

Saubhagya Devi got up, embraced her and wept, 'Mataji, please forgive me! But at least put my ornaments to some use!' she pleaded.

Shutting the door behind them, both women sat near Buddhidhan's bed. 'Devi my daughter, you are still a child and immature. Why won't we use your ornaments? We will have to when the need arises. Let me take care of you while I'm there. May God preserve these ornaments upon your body forever. Do not weep, my daughter, put them on.' And wiping her tears, the mother let escape a deep sigh. 'Son, what shall I say? What all shall I recount?' The vaidya had gone out of town. His wife was a lowly character. The vaidya had not told her that he was treating Buddhidhan for free. There were many needy persons who could not pay, but the vaidya incurred his wife's wrath if he gave them free medication. The wife had abused and driven away Buddhidhan's mother without disclosing where her husband was. A compassionate neighbour had then informed her that the vaidya had to suddenly leave town on work. She had to return dejected. On her way back, she decided to pay a visit to the administrator, a distant relative, to discuss the matter of the privy purse. On reaching his house, she encountered his daughter at the threshold. The latter made a face and mocked her. But need can compel one to make a mother of a donkey; so disregarding the mockery, she entered the house. The administrator was in the courtyard, brushing his teeth, surrounded by servants. The moment he saw her, he knew why she had come. He also knew there was nothing to be gained from someone who lived a hand-to-mouth existence. Not wanting to waste his morning on something so futile, his face expressed displeasure. He sent a servant to say that 'the Kamdar is busy. Go back. Send your application to the palace.' She had hesitantly crossed the threshold; she now quickly turned back. She had only walked a few paces when she saw a woman come out of the administrator's house and catch up with her. Though a widow, the woman had adorned and embellished herself.

'You must have gone to the Kamdar's house to speak about the Privy Purse.'

'Yes.'

'Your work will be done if you follow my advice.'

'I have no money to pay a bribe; I am poor.'

'You have something more valuable than money.'

Startled, Buddhidhan's mother looked at the woman with suspicion and fear. 'What?' she asked.

'Send your daughter-in-law to me. I will ensure that your work is done. The Kamdar's son and I have good relations. I suggest this for your own good.' A poor man's wife is sister-in-law to all.

The old widow clenched her teeth and pursed her lips. Anger shone through her eyes. But she knew it was dangerous to get into a verbal duel with this shameless and unchaste woman. So concealing her righteous anger, she simply said, 'I do not want the Privy Purse,' and walked away, not wanting even the shadow of this woman to fall on her. In native states, the son is the chief of police, the brother is the judge, and the father the administrator. Who is one to complain to, or seek justice from? Helpless, the poor woman quietly walked back home.

She had decided to keep all this from her son, not wanting to cause him greater distress in his already weakened state. But Buddhidhan had divined from her face that something untoward had occurred. To satisfy his curiosity, she merely said, 'The fate of the poor is wretched. The vaidya is out of town.' The rest she did not mention. They spoke of unrelated things which did not make many demands on the ailing man's mind. Buddhidhan drifted back to sleep. Mother-in-law and daughter-in-law quietly got up and went to the adjoining room. The girl put her head on her mother-in-law's lap and cried herself to sleep. The elderly widow sat deep in thought. She patted the daughter-in-law with one hand and tried in vain to wipe away the tears that flowed incessantly down her cheeks. Just then, the elderly neighbour Dayashankar opened the door. The widow signaled to him to enter quietly. He came in, closed the door, and sat down quietly. In low tones, he explained the previous day's absence and asked after Buddhidhan.

The old widow was overcome with emotion and wept anew.

For when your own people appear
Sorrow breaks through as if a gate has opened.[1]

In company of a kindred soul, sorrow finds a voice. She narrated in detail to Dayashankar her experiences at the homes of the vaidya and the administrator. She also told him about what had transpired between her son and daughter-in-law. 'Hai! What will become of this orphaned flower? Dayashankar, I am old. But if this child were to be widowed like me, how will I have the courage to face her? What hardships will she have to bear? I will die soon; then who will look after my Devi?'

The compassionate Dayashankar tried to console her. 'Behn, have courage. Your fate will take a turn for the better. No doubt, Buddhidhan will certainly recover. He will come back with leonine strength. My conscience bears testimony to this, and you must believe

[1] Hank Heifetz, trans. *Kumarasambhavam,* Sarga 4, Verse 26, in *The Origin of the Young God,* (New Delhi: Penguin, 2014).

it to be true. I have read your daughter-in-law's birth chart, and it foretells that she is not destined to become a widow. This year is a bad one for Buddhidhan, but things will eventually turn for the better.'

It was not as if Dayashankar had deep faith in astrology, but his words gave hope to the suffering widow. She felt better for having unburdened herself. Her tears also ceased. Meanwhile, Saubhagya Devi awoke, and sat up with propriety. All of them went to Buddhidhan's bedside.

The rustle of Dayashankar's feet had awakened Buddhidhan. Illness had made his hearing sharper. And he had overheard their entire conversation. As he listened to them, emotions of pity, helplessness, rage, hope, enthusiasm ... all swept through his mind. By the time the three of them came in, Buddhidhan had regained his composure. Dayashankar sat by his bed, put a hand on Buddhidhan's forehead, and felt for his pulse. 'Are you feeling better? You look better to me, but your face betrays anxiety.'

'Yes Kaka, I am better today. I felt angry when I heard what mother said to you. You see for yourself how cunning the Kamdar is. That entire clan is shameless and wicked; they work only for the benefit of a few.' Buddhidhan appeared pensive as he said this, and seething in a quiet rage.

'Bhai, that is just the way it is. Keep that in mind when *you* become chief administrator,' Dayashankar said with a smile. 'Behn, don't think such a thing cannot happen. You know well that there was a time the present administrator had no food to eat. Who knows how the wheel will turn! You belong to the original chief administrator's family. Fifty years later, you may well regain that position. Is anything impossible before God?'

Buddhidhan looked at the old woman. The widow sighed deeply and said, 'We do not want to be administrators or any such thing, bhai. We are not going to get lakhs and become millionaires. My only consolation is these two. They are my heaven. Once my son recovers, finds an occupation, and they find happiness again, I will feel as fulfilled as if I had bathed in the Ganga. All this suffering and ignominy will then only be a memory. Then all I will seek and await is the call of God.' The son keenly felt the mother's pain.

Dayashankar consoled, 'Do not worry. All will be well. What do you say, bhai?'

'Kaka, I will feed you sweets when that happens. At this moment however, it seems like mockery. But I have taken note that this cunning administrator has heaped scorn upon my poor and virtuous mother, and that his son has insulted my family in hard times. Bear this in mind: Buddhidhan will have his revenge. In God's plan, every misfortune has a silver lining. It is good that the Privy Purse has been stopped. Now I am no longer under the Kamdar's thumb. I was unable to escape his power. That anxiety has now been taken from me—I am free. I am my own master. Thank God! The Kamdar has himself unwittingly removed these obstacles from my path. Now, I *will* get better. My desire to live has been rekindled. These two jewels are dearest to me—what would I not do for their sake! Yes, I am poor. I have neither money nor friends. Whether I become chief administrator or not is for fate to decide. But what is certain is that I will ruin this administrator. He shall be forced to acknowledge me, and to praise me. Yes, I *have* that power, and the world shall recognise it one day. Revenge: this fire will burn day and night in my heart, it will scorch the Kamdar and his family, and be quenched only thereafter. I too am a man born into a family of true administrators, not a family of savages like the present administrator. Ma, I was born of you! I do not wear bangles.' Buddhidhan trembled uncontrollably as he spoke, twisting and turning in his bed, gritting his teeth and biting his lips, at times thumping his emaciated chest with frail bony hands. The effort of this long passionate speech completely exhausted the sick man. His hands fell limp and hung lifeless by his side, his eyes flickered unsteadily and started to close. Drained by the excitement, the patient soon fell into a deep sleep. Gradually, his extreme agitation and tremors subsided, but his eyebrows were still raised and his forehead remained creased in a frown, betraying that even in sleep, Buddhidhan was gripped by a powerful dream.

The three of them stared at him as if stupefied. As he drifted swiftly into sleep, they got up, anxious and pensive. 'Let him sleep. Let him sleep,' advised kindly Dayashankar and returned home.

It was thought that Buddhidhan's words were borne out of delirium and rage. But when the vaidya resumed his visits the following day, his medicines miraculously seemed to take effect. Within a few days, Buddhidhan was well enough to move around the house. Quite soon, he was completely rid of his disease. The only traces left behind were the fires of revenge and anger still burning inside him. Like the comet that blazes a trail in the midnight sky, his unceasing rage manifested itself on his perpetually creased brow. It was a sign that the administrator's doom was certain.

5 Buddhidhan (Conclusion)

The false utterances of the influential and important are often taken as true, while the honest words of the less important are dismissed as false. Kindly Dayashankar had laughed at the anger of the weak, ailing, impoverished Buddhidhan. In time, Buddhidhan's family, too, forgot about it.

God has made the minds and hearts of people inscrutable. While those of little or no means have occasion to fathom the thoughts of the rich and powerful, the latter—intoxicated and blinded by power—fail to read the minds of the poor and the wretched. Those whose vision is thus blinded consider the deeds of the poor innately meaningless, thoughtless, foolish, insubstantial, and transient. Even if there be in the company of the blind a one-eyed man who considers a poor man's intelligence worthy of being tested, it is only to prove himself superior to the latter.

Prior to his illness, Buddhidhan used to visit the administrator, Shathrai, on occasion. Despite the insult to his mother, after his recovery, Buddhidhan resumed these visits. During gatherings, when the administrator sat surrounded by sycophants, chatting, boasting, disparaging others, seeking pleasure and pride in another's harm, indulging in depravities, plotting schemes, turning morality on its head, dreaming foolish and vile dreams fueled by a mistaken sense of superiority and abject flattery, Buddhidhan would sit at the back among the lowliest of workers and engage his eyes, ears and mind fully to observe this world. No one ever noticed him. Eyes fixed upon

Shathrai and his son Dushtarai, Buddhidhan would stoke the rage that burned within him. Sometimes Dushtarai would look at him from the corner of his eye, his gaze disdainful and arrogant, and gesture mockingly; this would remind Buddhidhan of his wretched and lowly status. The genuflection of his subordinates gave Dushtarai a supreme sense of power and authority.

In comparison, Dushtarai's father Shathrai was a better and more intelligent individual. Not that he was incapable of behaving like his son, but that he would do so only for a reason. In as much as was possible, nothing but pure self-interest moved him. Therefore, Buddhidhan had to rarely deal with Shathrai. However, on the occasions they did meet, Shathrai had realised that Buddhidhan was sharp and intelligent, albeit not as 'sharp' and 'intelligent' as himself. This assessment was in no way likely to either benefit or harm Buddhidhan, because Shathrai was unlikely to grant or deny him any favours because of his qualities. By the same token, Buddhidhan's status was such that he was incapable of causing any harm to the administrator. For Shathrai, he was neither a friend, nor a foe. Whatever enmity there was burned secretly within Buddhidhan's mind. This fire had been kindled, unbeknownst to them, by both the administrator and his son. Those without ordinary virtues are incapable of discernment; they see no reason for it either. But God punishes even those who falter unknowingly, and the consequences of indiscretion—realised or unrealised, seen or unseen—inevitably take root. When these consequences become manifest, ignorant men blame God. They forget their insolence, or are unable to see the link between their arrogance and the consequences thereof.

Blessed are those whose conscience is shielded by virtue and right judgment, for they are enlightened by their power of discernment even in times of darkness and sorrow. Examining Shathrai and Dushtarai minutely, reflecting upon their crimes and their future implications in moments of controlled rage, Buddhidhan would ponder, and arrive at conclusions and decisions known to him alone.

On one such occasion, seated right at the back of the gathering, Buddhidhan was deep in thought. Everyone had got up and left. But he continued to sit there and stare blankly ahead of him, as if seeing images flit past in a dream. Seated upon a window ledge, he was lost to the world. Just then, a sweeper entered the hall, swinging his broom. He thwacked the broom hard, releasing clouds of dust. Startled, Buddhidhan broke out of his reverie and realised he was alone. He got up, stretched his limbs and slowly walked to the door.

Just outside Shathrai's house, he met a Rajput Garasia. He wore a pagdi embroidered with gold and silver thread on his head, a tight-fitting intricately patterned angarkha, and tight pajamas buttoned at the ankles. He carried a silver hookah, a dagger, a sword, and a carved knife tied to his waist. The mojris on his feet had red embroidery. He was followed by another Garasia in simple attire, and a few others. They walked with slow deliberate steps. The Rajput Garasia leading them addressed Buddhidhan and said: 'Buddhidhan Bhai, how are things? Where are you headed? Is the Kamdar at home?'

'Welcome, welcome Bhupsinhji! The Kamdar has just left.'

'I see,' said Bhupsinh with a scowl. 'Then why did he ask us to be here! So be it. It is his day today. Buddhidhan, why have I not seen you around? You should visit us sometime. The Kamdar's house may be filled with gold, but none of it is going to be of any use to you. Instead of wearing your shoes out at his doorstep, if you were to come to us, we might be of some use to you. It is entirely up to you.'

'Why do you say this, Bhupsinhji? I have been intending to visit you for many days now.' From that day on, Buddhidhan strengthened his acquaintance with Bhupsinh.

Bhupsinh was the closest cousin of Rana Jadsinh, the ruler of Suvarnapur. Because he was still a minor, Bhupsinh's garas was under the Rana's administration. The Receiver appointed to administer the land under the garas, together with Shathrai, had siphoned off as much revenue from it as they could. They had also tutored the Rana to treat Bhupsinh as just another cousin. To this end, Bhupsinh was only paid paltry sums from the revenues earned from his garas. Being a minor, he feared for his life and stayed with his maternal relations, away from Suvarnapur. However, having recently attained adulthood,

Bhupsinh now wanted his family inheritance returned to him. He had come back to Suvarnapur to claim it, putting his life in jeopardy. No one heeded his demands and he was pushed around. He therefore harboured considerable enmity for both Rana Jadsinh and Shathrai. But his anger was impotent; Bhupsinh was incapable of actually doing anything. He kept the company of lowly, scheming bureaucrats and through them sought ways of reclaiming his inheritance. The only way suggested to him was to bribe the administrator. Shathrai and his hangers-on demanded at least fifty thousand rupees. The Rana wanted the same amount as a gift.

In times like these, the foe of a foe becomes a friend. Emboldened, Buddhidhan took up cudgels on behalf of Bhupsinh, who had the financial and moral support of his maternal family. Buddhidhan no longer had to worry about finding a source of income and livelihood. He decided to fight it to the finish with those who ruled the state. Owing to the people's fear of Shathrai, Bhupsinh was friendless. Buddhidhan's allegiance was therefore useful to him. Bhupsinh and his advisor would meet at night, contemplating their present and their future. They were not yet important enough to attract any attention.

But in due course, their association became public knowledge and alongside the one, the other too came to be regarded as an enemy by Shathrai. And so eventually, Buddhidhan too felt the need to be prepared for a counterattack. He sold his house and land in Suvarnapur and decided to move out with his family to an area under British control. He later came to know that Dushtarai had hatched an evil plan to abduct Saubhagya Devi the very day they left Suvarnapur. This reinforced Buddhidhan's conviction that his decision to move his family had been the right one.

Buddhidhan and Bhupsinh both made Lilapur, a seat of British administration, their new home. Both rented separate houses in Lilapur.

Some three miles from the village lived the Agent of the British Government, Colonel Buskin Sahib. Suvarnapur, Ratnanagari, a few other native states, and seven or eight taluks were under his jurisdiction. These native states were of different sizes and brought in revenues ranging from ten to fifty lakhs per annum. A military man, Buskin Sahib was a jolly fellow. He liked taking quick decisions and lost his temper if his orders were not carried out promptly, or if suggestions were made to the contrary. He always did things correctly and suspected others of wrongdoing. Even his strong sense of fairness did not prevent him from using all available means against such persons. He was capable of taking wise and insightful decisions, but preferred to work through his Shirastidar.[1] He would often seek the Shirastidar's opinion about the goodness or otherwise of plaintiffs, and was pleased when his own views were confirmed. He had come to regard the Shirastidar as an efficient and a good man.

This Shirastidar was a Dakshini[2] man called Sadashiv Pant whose command over the English language was good. He was clever and adept at conforming to the Sahib's wishes whilst maintaining the façade of autonomy. He had once obtained the Dewanship of Shantigarh through the largesse of Buskin Sahib. Since he owed his position to the Sahib's influence, he had come to regard that he had no duties towards the ruler of Shantigarh. When in need, he would flatter the courtiers, and discard them as soon as his ends were achieved. Therefore no faction regarded him as their own man. The newspapers praised Sadashiv Pant's neutrality and fairness, causing him to rise in the Sahib's esteem. This foreclosed any possibility of complaints against him, and the Shirastidar used this to satisfy his secret wants and desires, giving full play to his greed and brazenness. He appointed many outsiders in his administration on the grounds that the locals were incapable, unable to remain impartial, or unworthy of the responsibility entrusted. He could not but find anyone save fellow Dakshinis to fill these positions. Eventually, the ruler, the palace officials, Garasias, and the local people, everyone complained of his tyrannical ways. But the enemies of the state and the ruler went to

[1] Literally, one who knows the local customs and procedures.

[2] This term usually refers to persons from Maharashtra.

Buskin Sahib and attested to the Dewan's fairness; so he disregarded these complaints. Once however, perceiving himself to be slighted, the ruler personally went to the Sahib with a complaint. Other palace machinations also surfaced. Buskin Sahib surmised that the Dewan was unable to manage competing factions due to his honesty. Sadashiv Pant was therefore recalled to his earlier position. The Sahib increased his personal allowances and promised him a higher position when the time was right.

Buskin Sahib also exercised judicial authority over this area. Government pleaders were appointed for the same, and to liaise on account of native states. Buddhidhan approached the Sahib, and impressing him with his intellect, obtained a pleader's license. With this, he acquired an individual income and the prestige of associating with Government officials. Befriending Sadashiv Pant, Buddhidhan then introduced Bhupsinh to him. He convinced Sadashiv Pant that Bhupsinh was likely to inherit the Suvarnapur throne, and was in a position to spend some money to obtain his garas. He also kept creating opportunities to see Buskin Sahib in a professional capacity, and he so impressed him with his honesty, cleverness and discernment that, although reliant on Sadashiv Pant for counsel in most matters, when it came to issues represented by Buddhidhan, the Sahib need heed no one else. Careful not to displease the Shirastidar, Buddhidhan would first meet him, humour him, and only then approach the Sahib. In this, he saw nothing amiss.

However, as Sadashiv Pant cultivated relations with Bhupsinh, he began to see Buddhidhan as a thorn in his side. Buddhidhan had taught Bhupsinh to be generous, and his counsel was always sought in the exercising of this generosity. This practice ceased. Buddhidhan had calculated the worth of this relationship differently between the other two men. He felt that if Bhupsinh were to obtain his garas soon, he would squander it in pursuit of pleasure, which would douse his fiery aspirations. If this were to happen, Bhupsinh would not be in a position to cultivate relations with the British. Buddhidhan wanted to keep Bhupsinh in Lilapur primarily for this purpose, and to this end, though taking care to appear neutral, he would praise Bhupsinh in front of the Sahib. On the other hand, Buddhidhan fostered acquaintance with Sadashiv Pant in the hope that longstanding personal relations could be used to greater advantage in the future. Therefore, he also made no serious attempt towards claiming Bhupsinh's garas immediately; he wanted to use this time to expand Bhupsinh's understanding of the world. Sadashiv Pant foiled this plan. Bhupsinh and Buddhidhan drifted apart; but Buddhidhan pretended he was unaware of any such change in their relationship. He now plotted and schemed to counter the situation and right the wrong.

The norm 'good ends and good means' was unknown to Buddhidhan. But because his conscience was clear, he instinctively searched for means that were pure. And yet, he was satisfied only when the ends were also beneficial. He believed therefore that good ends could be achieved by using any means. He had not been taught that this was wrong, and there was no one around him to do so now. In this instance, when pure means did not provide themselves, he felt it necessary to deploy impure ones. For the present, he gave up attempts to inculcate right thought and conduct in Bhupsinh, instead allowing their conversation to be mired in subjects of leisure and pleasure. Sadashiv Pant was addicted to liquor, a womaniser and a nocturnal creature. To profit from these weaknesses while himself remaining untouched, Buddhidhan masterfully created opportunities for Bhupsinh to indulge in them, but in ways that Bhupsinh never realised that he had done so.

The young Rajput Garasia now began to idle away his days and nights at Sadashiv Pant's residence. When the Shirastidar was busy with office work during the day, and when he headed out by night, Bhupsinh took up with his wife, Ramabai. Buddhidhan could no longer meet Bhupsinh at the latter's residence. Even so, he would regularly visit his house and wait a while, keeping an eye on developments there. Bhupsinh's wife Rajba had very high regard for Buddhidhan. Neither harboured unchaste thoughts about each other. However, in Bhupsinh's absence, the two now had occasion to spend time alone with each other. Discontent and jealous of her husband's debauchery, Rajba felt she was no longer bound by the chastity contingent to her wifely duties. And she gradually grew to be infatuated with Buddhidhan. One day as they sat talking, she abruptly fell silent and looked intently at him as if struck by a sudden thought. Buddhidhan met her gaze, and he saw her passion. His piety was shaken. They both stood up. Involuntarily, as if compelled by some unseen force, they drew closer together, and their fingers intertwined. Their pulses raced, their bodies trembled, felt fevered. They lost the capacity to think and could only look at each other, stunned. Rajba's sari slipped off her shoulder. Just then there was a loud noise and the two were jolted back to their senses, their hands falling apart. Saying that he would return the next day, Buddhidhan walked out of the room, troubled and deep in thought. Rajba made as if to call him back, but the words failed her and she sat down petrified. Unable to think, in a state of extreme agitation, she sat there alone, crying. Then, like one reborn, with new resolve she sought to distract herself with household work.

Buddhidhan's conscience was aflame with repentance and remorse. He felt this incident was a bad omen. He resolved not to spend any more time alone with Rajba. But his imagination ran amuck and vivid images played and replayed in his mind's eye. The vision of Rajba—her sari askew, standing before him, holding his hand in hers, intense and eager—refused to disappear; her image chased away his piety. Thus bewildered, distraught and pale-faced, he reached home.

When Buddhidhan saw his mother's face, she somehow seemed different to him, although nothing had changed. Feeling impure and incriminated, he stood at a distance and could not bring himself to look at her pious and radiant visage. Entering the bedroom, Saubhagya Devi greeted him with a loving embrace. But he stood petrified, unable to respond, as if his very touch would defile her. He made as if he were trying to shun this touch even in his mind. Burning with remorse, he felt as if he had been unfaithful to his wife, his Devi. He looked at her pure, innocent face. The thought that he had cheated on her troubled him. And that she had no inkling that the husband who now stood before her had been so wicked. He looked at her face again and found her even more beautiful—Rajba paled in comparison with his wife. He found repulsive the very idea that he had been attracted to her even momentarily and could not fathom why reason had failed him or how he had thought of forsaking his swan-like beauty for that ugly crow. He finally resolved that his virtuous wife alone was worthy of his affections, and he grew eager to reciprocate her love. He also decided he would not visit Bhupsinh's home, but that if he had to do so, he would ensure that he spent no time alone with Rajba. Buddhidhan felt a deep gratitude that God had saved him from committing a great sin. Tension eased from his body as if he had received an oil massage followed by a bath, ministered by loving hands. He slept soundly, with his virtuous, beautiful and content wife by his side. Even in sleep, her image stayed with him. He dreamt that Saubhagya Devi was a deity in a temple: the temple of the heart, the Hriday Mandir. She was seated on a throne and emanated a light soft and soothing like the moon's rays. Grateful and fortunate, he fanned his Goddess lovingly, held her insignias, and when some fifty-odd women resembling Rajba arrived at the temple gates, he chased them away. The Goddess chided him fondly saying, 'Wait there, you crook!' and raised her hand to give him an affectionate pat. Just then, Saubhagya Devi's hand caressed his forehead: even in sleep, her lips quivered in a delicate smile.

The following day, Buddhidhan became engrossed in his routine work. But when evening fell and it was time to visit Bhupsinh's house, he remembered Rajba. Forgetting his resolve of the night before, he grew eager to see her. As he was dressing to leave the house, Saubhagya Devi came in to ask him something. Buddhidhan's conscience reasserted itself—her mere presence ensured that he remained chaste and faithful. No! I am not going to visit Rajba, he firmly told himself, and went about other business someplace else. From that moment on, this thought lost its grip over his mind.

But Rajba was a clever woman; she was obstinate and not one to give up easily. The Rajputani was also very courageous. Despite his promise, Buddhidhan had not come. He must be busy today; he will surely come tomorrow, she thought. Or the next day. Or the one after. Seven or eight days passed, but Buddhidhan did not come. Finally, one day as Bhupsinh was leaving the house to visit Ramabai as usual, consumed by jealousy, Rajba decided to follow him. She went back, and carefully disguised herself as a man, bearing a weapon at her waist. At around eight in the evening, she found herself in front of Buddhidhan's house. She sent him the message that Bhupsinh's friend Rajsinh was here to meet him and wanted a word with him in private. Surprised at the unfamiliar name, Buddhidhan came out and stood before her.

'Rajsinh, please come in,' he said, and took Rajba into the drawing room. He looked closely at the attire, the face, and was startled. Bewildered he said, 'What's this! You! Here, at this time?'

Imitating a man's demeanour, Rajba sat up straight, her hand reaching to touch the dagger at her waist, but from habit, it petulantly came to rest on her hip instead. She thrust her chest out, but her shapely form only became more apparent. Moreover, she could not conceal her eyes and knew she was caught out. 'Buddhidhan, you have done me wrong. Bhupsinh finds solace in Sadashiv Pant's house. You promised to help me, but failed to keep your word. Does this befit our affection?'

'Rajsinh, I understand your pain. Bhupsinh is the reason for our relationship, and it would benefit neither of us to form an association independent of him. Bring Bhupsinh back in hand—my loyalties are with both of you. Bhupsinh should be the one to give you the succour you need,' he said with brazen courage.

'And what of *your* assurance, Buddhidhan? Your word? Your promise?'

'I am very sorry. A word wrongly given cannot be kept. I must break this promise, because I am bound by a greater one.'

'And what of me?'

'I have thought well of you, Rajba, and for you, too.'

'Are you certain of this? Be careful.'

'Yes. I am certain.'

'Think again.'

'I have considered it well. Godspeed,' Buddhidhan said, somewhat shaken, and got up.

'I know what you think,' Rajba said abruptly and she caught hold of his arm, forcing him to sit back down on a bolster. She stood close to him, her body touching his. Who knows from where she found the courage. A Rajputani, and so brazen! Freeing his hand and visibly squirming from her touch, Buddhidhan said, 'Raj, this is enough. Send for me through Bhupsinh, and I will come.'

'Why, are you afraid of him?' she laughed disdainfully. Then, bending over him, she put both her hands on his shoulders and stood very close, her chin touching his.

'I am afraid of God. No one else.'

Realising she would not get her way, the Rajputani stood up straight, her eyes rolling in anger. 'So be it. Be afraid of your God, Buddhidhan. Come when Bhupsinh calls you. But *I* will hold you to your word, or I am not a true Rajput. All right, I will be on my way now,' and she pushed him aside in hauteur and left his house.

Buddhidhan brooded over the incident for a moment, then returned to his business as if nothing had happened. He stopped visiting Bhupsinh's house altogether. If the paths of the two friends ever crossed now, their salutations were perfunctory. Word of this trivial matter spread from ear to ear all the way to Suvarnapur. The world believed that something had caused a breach in Buddhidhan and Bhupsinh's friendship. Queen Gossip provided thousands of explanations to people's serpentine tongues.

Buddhidhan's chief concern now was to find ways of separating Bhupsinh and Sadashiv Pant, and to ensure that the Garasia was once more beholden to him. He clearly felt that he had erred in fostering familiarity between the two. But he had learnt his lesson: he resolved to no longer trust anyone, not consider anyone innately good, and never to allow his affairs to slip into the hands of others. He needed to wield influence over the Garasia to make him an instrument of his own success, but he decided not to count even Bhupsinh as his own.

Moreover, he now understood that he could not allow Bhupsinh to veer off the right path, because it was difficult to rein in a man who was in the wrong. It is possible to control him perhaps; but to do so one would have to stoop to his low, wicked ways. If Buddhidhan had given in to Rajba's entreaties, for instance, Bhupsinh would have become a puppet in his hands. But this prospect did not appeal to his conscience, and it slipped away like mercury without leaving a trace.

One day, on his way to the Sahib's office, Buddhidhan found Bhupsinh walking ahead of him. Sadashiv Pant's house fell on the same road. Ramabai was standing at a window on the first floor. She came down and opened the door. Bhupsinh entered the house, and the door closed behind him. Witnessing this scene, Buddhidhan sighed and walked away. As he sat in his office, his mind was not at ease. Just then Buskin Sahib called out to him, and Buddhidhan got up to go.

The Sahib was seated on his chair, holding a quill between his teeth. Removing the quill, he said, 'Buddhidhan, do you know in which year the Ruler of Suvarnapur had responded to the Garasia?'

Thinking a while, Buddhidhan turned to the Shirastidar and replied, 'Pant, you took all these documents home to study three, four days ago. The answer is in there, and the letter also bears the date of the response.'

The Sahib said, 'Send someone home and have the documents brought over.'

The Shirastidar submitted, 'Sahib, I will look for them in the office today. If I can't find them here, I will bring them over from home tomorrow.'

'Not at all. Either send someone, or go fetch them yourself right away,' the Sahib commanded.

'Buddhidhan, will you please send someone to my house?' the Shirastidar asked.

Buddhidhan found his opportunity. There was an office clerk called Narbheram, a wily, witty, jealous, garrulous and brazen mimic. He hated the Dakshinis and taunted Sadashiv Pant bitterly, ridiculing him behind his back for the freedoms he allowed Ramabai. But

Narbheram had proven himself useful to Sadashiv Pant in other ways, which is why the Shirastidar tolerated his mockery and believed Narbheram to be his man. Buddhidhan now chose Narbheram to locate and bring back the documents. On reaching Pant's house, the clerk found the door firmly shut. Instead of knocking or calling out to anyone, he bent down and peeped through the keyhole. He saw Bhupsinh inside the house. Without drawing any attention to himself, he turned back. On his return, he whispered this juicy news into Buddhidhan's ear. Buddhidhan told him to inform Sadashiv Pant. Narbheram went and stood before Pant. Concealing the glee in his heart, his face twisted in sorrow and anger, and he made as if he were at a loss for words. But of course, he told him all eventually. Sadashiv Pant's face turned ashen. His head in a whirl, he sought Narbheram's advice. Narbheram said, 'It is best you ask Buddhidhan. He will know what to do. Personally, I think this wicked Bhupsinh should be exposed and beaten up.' Narbheram thought, Now you're caught, my boy! Bhupsinh is after all a man. It is you and your wife who will be exposed and derided. Before the frightened and distressed Shirastidar, Buddhidhan maintained a grave and concerned mien, and yet appeared disinterested. 'Tell the Sahib that the document could not be found. Take his permission, and let us go to your house.'

All three thus headed to Sadashiv Pant's house. Since a Rajput Garasia was involved, they also kept a few soldiers with them, anticipating a brawl. Looking in from the keyhole, they saw Bhupsinh going up the stairs. Narbheram signaled even the passers-by to stop. On his advice, the group climbed into the neighbour's house and went up to the room adjoining the one in which Ramabai and Bhupsinh were. A wooden partition separated these two rooms. The three of them and the soldiers looked through the gaps in the partition. Sadashiv's eyes were red with anger, his lips quivered and he looked like one possessed. 'I will kill or be killed,' he grimly announced. Standing behind him, Narbheram was beside himself with glee. He whispered to Buddhidhan, 'Good! Much liberty is being taken. This madam is suitable for the Sahibs!' A crowd gathered outside the window. Their noise attracted Ramabai's attention and she alerted Bhupsinh. The Garasia was startled at first, then began to seethe with anger. He twirled his moustache, and anticipating that the crowd would come up the stairs, he took Ramabai under one arm and drew his sword half out of its scabbard with the other, declaring, 'What can these effete men do! Even if Sadashiv himself comes here, I will pocket him and keep you in my house as a co-wife with Rajba. My sword is unyielding!'

Sadashiv was frightened. His anger drained away and he fell pathetically into Buddhidhan's arms. Buddhidhan felt genuine pity for him then. 'Sadashiv, you are no match for him. For the time being, forget what you have seen. You will either be killed by the Garasia's sword, or be poisoned by your wife. Come, let us tell these people that nothing is amiss so they will disperse and this melee will cease. Take a few months leave from the Sahib and go back to your native place. We will tell him we could not find anything worthwhile in the document. Once at your native place, do what you will with Ramabai. Do not endanger your life here.' The bystanders noisily dispersed and went their own way. Ramabai had opened the window partially to ascertain that they were actually leaving, and she recognised Sadashiv by his turban.

Once the coast was clear, Bhupsinh quietly left for his home. There, he started ordering Rajba around as if he were her master. But Rajba was more than piqued. She had been told about the incident at Ramabai's house, and she had decided she would create a scene and make sure that Buddhidhan was sent for.

'Thakurani, fire the hookah.'

'That's all I am good for now! For other things, you have someone else,' Rajba retorted and burst into tears.

'What's all this?'

'As if you don't know! Reclaiming the garas is hardly on your mind. You abandoned the friendship of a man like Buddhidhan and took up with a cunning fellow like Sadashiv and ...'

'And what?

'Just that you no longer have any need of me. Of course—how can I compete with the beauty of a Dakshini!'

On the one hand, this dialogue commenced. On the other, Sadashiv Pant sought leave. But since there was no one who could replace him immediately, Buskin Sahib hesitated to let his Shirastidar go. Sadashiv Pant now considered Buddhidhan as his own man; so he requested him to take over his responsibilities. Buddhidhan, as if he were doing him a favour, agreed to step in. Even the Sahib approved of this arrangement. Buddhidhan ascended a step on the ladder towards his ultimate goal.

Bhupsinh was left friendless. Ramabai had left. Rajba was playing hard to get. Bhupsinh had squandered away his money over Ramabai and Sadashiv Pant, and was now desperate for his inheritance. Thinking of his garas, he also thought of Buddhidhan and how he needed him again. But Bhupsinh would have chosen death over swallowing his pride. Rajba was equally obstinate; she had a message sent to Bhupsinh's maternal family. Bhupsinh's maternal uncle sent back word saying, 'Befriend Buddhidhan—he has become a Shirastidar. Such cowardice and debauchery are not becoming of you.' Since Bhupsinh now spent more time at home, Rajba would also keep nagging him saying, 'With Buddhidhan, there is no question of pride. He is our well-wisher. It is because you went astray that he parted ways with you. He will be pleased to know that you are now reformed. He now has an office and will be of use to you'. Eventually, the Rajputani got her way. Tired of her insistence, the apathetic Bhupsinh started visiting Buddhidhan again.

Then, Rajba died of a sudden illness. Buddhidhan therefore resumed visiting Bhupsinh's house without a care. He even helped Bhupsinh financially, and the two became friends again. Buddhidhan was however careful to ensure that the resumption of their friendship did not become public knowledge.

By then, Buddhidhan had been in Lilapur for five years. Saubhagya Devi had a daughter who was a year old. Their next door neighbour was a Bengali traveller whose wife had an unusual name, which they had all taken a fancy to. Buddhidhan's mother had thus named the little girl Alak Kishori. Sometime after, a boy was born to them. His birth-chart determined that his name was to begin with the letter 'p'. He was named Pramaddhan, to rhyme with Buddhidhan. The infant would lie in his grandmother's lap quite idle and inert; so his father felt that his name was well chosen. Content that Buddhidhan had obtained the position of Shirastidar, his mother died at peace, surrounded by her beloved son, daughter-in-law and grandchildren. The house seemed painfully empty after her death, and the couple mourned her deeply. In time, as the son became engrossed with his new office and the wife got busy raising their two children, their grief became a thing of the past. Even so, Buddhidhan often felt that his children would not be raised very well, having been denied the care and upbringing of his loving, intelligent and wise mother. He had no time for them. And Saubhagya Devi, while virtuous and devoted, was not worldly-wise; she had never had to worry about things while her mother-in-law was alive. The old woman had trained her well when it came to household work, and she was now quite adept at it. But she had had no opportunity to learn about child-rearing. She didn't even remember how she herself had been raised by the old woman, so how was she to act on her own? She was simple, good-natured, and of average intelligence. She believed the world was full of good people, like her husband and mother-in-law. Virtue and right conduct came naturally to her, and she believed that the wheels of the world turned on their own, without requiring a nudge and a push. Buddhidhan considered himself fortunate for having such a wife. He had never before seen such joyous days. He was now the Shirastidar of Lilapur, and his conjugal life was blissful. After the day's work, he would sit with his wife and play with his children, then watch them sleep as he spent pleasurable hours with Devi. She would gently touch his face to wake him up every morning when the cool breeze wafted in through their widow. They would wake up quietly so as to not disturb the children. In his pensive moments, it would often seem to Buddhidhan that such beautiful, blissful days would never ever return. In his joy and gratitude, he would embrace Saubhagya Devi or his children.

Sadashiv Pant found a good job in his native place. Buskin Sahib sent him a certificate of good conduct, and he made Buddhidhan's position as the Shirastidar permanent, following which, his prestige climbed in the native states. In the belief that Buddhidhan and Bhupsinh had drifted apart, Buddhidhan's appointment was appreciated in Suvarnapur as well, where he now cultivated relations with the ruling clique. The new Shirastidar visited Suvarnapur on work from time to time, and the administrator and his coterie began to accord him both respect and money. Dushtarai took the lead in praising and pleasing him, and Buddhidhan was now seated next to the Karbhari Shathrai in the Suvarnapur palace assembly. Every so often, Buddhidhan extracted bribes from these corrupt men, believing that he did no wrong. In fact, he used this opportunity to cultivate relations with the palace retainers so as to be able to closely follow the machinations of the royal household. In this undertaking, he freely used the money he had accumulated. Shathrai, however, still had some misgivings about Buddhidhan.

Rana Jadsinh had no legitimate heir. He claimed one Parvatsinh to be his son. Shathrai kept Parvatsinh under his thumb by threatening to divulge the identity of his real parents. Parvatsinh was tired of such harassment. Garbaddas, the son of the previous administrator, was a state official. He had cultivated a relationship with Parvatsinh. Garbaddas engineered many a petition and complaint against Shathrai to the British Agent. He also fomented disaffection in the palace through various queens and palace servants. Even this faction had made a few overtures towards Buddhidhan. Parvatsinh was the main impediment in Bhupsinh's way to the throne.

Pretending to be a well-wisher, Buddhidhan informed Shathrai about the palace intrigues against him, after which he secured Shathrai's trust. The Karbhari now began to solicit Buddhidhan's advice even in personal matters and obtained bribes for him from the palace as well.

Ultimately, Shathrai succeeded in removing Parvatsinh from the line of succession, and in having Garbaddas dismissed, to boot. However, Garbaddas continued to trust Buddhidhan, not knowing that it was he who had betrayed him in the first place. From then on, Garbaddas not only confided in Buddhidhan, he also kept him apprised of Shathrai's activities. Shathrai trusted Buddhidhan and believed that his relations with Garbaddas were purely instrumental. Buddhidhan, on his part, thought it no sin to cheat these two rogues, reasoning that since his goal was noble, using wickedness against the wicked was perfectly justified.

With Parvatsinh's removal it became imperative for the ruling clique to foist a new prince upon Jadsinh. Rana Jadsinh was a debauch and an addict who consumed various narcotics and intoxicants, including chemical preparations. As a result of these excesses, he had lost his virility. His queens did just as they pleased. But if a queen were to give birth to a son, she and her paramour would wield more power, which would reduce Shathrai's influence over the palace. This was not acceptable to him; so Shathrai had set in motion schemes to find a false heir who would remain under his influence. Buddhidhan was aware of these plans, but the administrator had not yet confided them to him.

While it was not possible for Buddhidhan to openly associate with Bhupsinh, he had learnt from experience that it was disastrous to allow Bhupsinh to come under anyone else's influence. He also did not want to be seen as openly opposing Shathrai and his cohorts, but he knew he required an instrument with which to achieve this end. When Garbaddas visited Lilapur on work and met Buddhidhan, the two of them went to meet Bhupsinh. No false heir could be produced without the queen's connivance. Garbaddas informed them that attempts were being made to include Jadsinh's chief queen in this plot. Parvatsinh was no longer a contender for the throne; hence Garbaddas thought it beneficial to act as Bhupsinh's secret informant. Buddhidhan's plan succeeded: Garbaddas sought his counsel in all matters, and was therefore incapable of wielding independent influence over Bhupsinh. His allegiance, moreover, had been secured.

Rana Jadsinh's chief queen was of high birth, and she resented the machinations of the Karbhari. However, she gave in to temptation, and soon it became known that she was pregnant. Garbaddas and Bhupsinh sent many petitions to Buskin Sahib, claiming that the pregnancy was pure fabrication. Shathrai's coterie congratulated themselves on the success of their scheme, but fear lurked within. Shathrai was required to visit Lilapur once. To test Buddhidhan, he raised the issue of Garbaddas' petition. Buddhidhan replied, 'Let him go to hell. Dogs often bark behind an elephant's back. It is another matter that truth is on our side this time. But there might come a time when we would be required to do what is being alleged. We have to protect our interests.' Shathrai did not show his cards on this occasion, and left Lilapur suspicious of Buddhidhan; but his suspicion did not last long.

Bhupsinh's garas was still in the keeping of the Rana's Darbar. As Rana Jadsinh's Karbhari, Shathrai contended that the Darbar had incurred large expenses for the marriages of Bhupsinh and his siblings, and on the death ceremonies of his parents, all of which had been paid for from the revenues earned from the garas. They also argued that due to drought, the yield from the lands was negligible. The administrator further contended that it was Bhupsinh who owed substantial sums of money to Jadsinh, and hence that his garas should remain in Jadsinh's possession until such time as the debt was recovered.

Bhupsinh, on Buddhidhan's advice, sent a petition to Buskin Sahib asking for the reinstatement of his garas. Buddhidhan showed that petition to Shathrai, and received at least fifty thousand rupees from the Suvarnapur palace in exchange for a promise to help keep the garas from Bhupsinh. He leveraged the newfound confidence of the palace and used it to understand how the Karbhari forged state treasury accounts. He also convinced Buskin Sahib, forged the documents himself, and ensured that the garas would remain with the

Darbar for the next five years. Meanwhile, Bhupsinh knew that the fifty thousand rupees were in reality to help him secure the throne of Suvarnapur; so whilst appearing disgruntled in public, he was secretly satisfied with these developments.

Shathrai was convinced that Buddhidhan was no friend of Bhupsinh's, and that he was open to being bribed. This set his mind at ease. Henceforth, whenever the new Shirastidar of Lilapur visited Suvarnapur, the Karbhari of Suvarnapur would invite him home for meals, and they would talk freely. Other palace functionaries also developed familiarity with the new Shirastidar. In time, Buddhidhan came to know the Karbhari's family intimately, and learned to fathom their minds. Also, Narbheram, who usually accompanied him, took great delight in finding the fissures in the family of Karbhari Shathrai.

Shathrai had one daughter named Khalaknanda, and a daughter-in-law, Rupali. Every evening, a soldier named Jamal Khan was deputed to carry a lantern and accompany Khalaknanda to her in-laws'. Jamal Khan could sing, draw, and was quite a dandy. Sometimes, en route to her in-laws' house, Khalaknanda would stop at Jamal Khan's and spend a few quiet moments with him. Sometimes, she would disguise herself as a man and go gallivanting around town at night, arm in arm with the soldier. Rupali, Dushtarai's wife, had found her own way. Dushtarai was the Faujdar, the police chief, and was required to travel to different villages. A Rajput soldier, Merulo, would stay in the house with Rupali. Merulo would also occupy Dushtarai's bedroom whenever he was away.

None of this had escaped the busybody Narbheram; he had witnessed some of these scenes himself and had heard of others. He apprised Buddhidhan of the same. The paramours of both these women had become the confidants of their husbands. Shathrai trusted Jamal Khan implicitly, as Dushtarai trusted Merulo. As the day neared for Jadsinh's chief queen to announce that she had delivered a prince, the onus of finding and securing a suitable baby boy was assigned to these trusted men. Jamal Khan and Merulo saw each other as rivals. This responsibility only deepened their mutual animosity. Jamal

Khan located a Muslim boy, while Merulo found a Koli one. Shathrai trusted Jamal Khan, and chose the Muslim boy to be prince since he was good-looking; Merulo was disappointed.

On Buddhidhan's instructions, Garbaddas had cultivated relations with both these men. One day, an angry and disgruntled Merulo sat talking with Garbaddas and blabbered about what had happened. Cajoled and provoked by Garbaddas, he revealed more. Garbaddas rushed to Lilapur to consult Buddhidhan. It was decided they would waste no more time and not let this opportunity slip away. A petition was made to Buskin Sahib, and Bhupsinh sought an escort and the authorisation to intervene. Accompanied by Garbaddas and mounted soldiers, Bhupsinh rushed to Rana Jadsinh's palace. Showing the Sahib's authorisation, the contingent entered the palace and sought a private audience with the Rana. Bhupsinh reasoned with Jadsinh, 'The Sahib knows everything. If you are implicated in this matter, you will lose your throne. Why worry about who will rule after your death? It will bring you no glory if the throne goes to a Muslim, and not your own cousin. It will bring you no merit in the other world either. And if you were to have a legitimate heir tomorrow, you would still have to give the throne to this boy who is not your own blood. The Sahib has sent us. You are answerable to him. You decide. This is your responsibility.'

Jadsinh was frightened at the mention of the Sahib; the letter was signed by him as well. It stated that the ruler should pay heed to Bhupsinh and provide him a satisfactory explanation. Jadsinh replied, 'I know nothing about all this. I will ask the Karbhari and send my explanation. I do not love sons of Muslims and Kolis more than my own cousin Bhupsinh. I will do all that is in my power.'

Garbaddas asked, 'Can all this be settled tonight?'

Jadsinh replied, 'Bhai, who knows with these things? I will inform the Karbhari. What more can I do?'

Garbaddas: 'Can't you do anything about this yourself?'

Jadsinh: 'Myself? Do you want me to do police work? Go and meet the Karbhari.'

The party rode back as fast as they had come. Suvarnapur was in a state of panic. Shathrai rushed to the palace. He was not satisfied with the Rana's explanation. He knew that the matter would not end there. Lilapur was not far from Suvarnapur. Garbaddas reached Lilapur, met Buddhidhan and said, 'You know that the Rana is incapable of doing anything himself. He blurted out something about Kolis and Muslims. There is substance to the charge. We came back because we knew that staying there was not to our advantage.'

Soon after, Shathrai's messenger rode in, conveyed his salutations to Buddhidhan, and sought information. Buddhidhan said, 'I cannot say much in this matter. The Rana said something about a Muslim or a Koli child, and also said that the Karbhari knew everything. The matter is for the Sahib to decide. It would be best if Shathrai were to abandon this plan.' The messenger returned. Garbaddas took two thousand rupees from Buddhidhan and gave it to Merulo; with his help, they found the house of the Muslim woman and posted a few riders there to keep a watch over her. Garbaddas, Bhupsinh, and a few soldiers hid near the queen's palace.

Shathrai was frightened. He knew there would be an enquiry if matters were prolonged any further; his dirty ploy would come out as his own men had turned traitors. He feared the consequences of the Sahib's enquiry and distrusted the Rana in this matter. But the queen's pregnancy had already been announced, so he conferred with his clique. That night, they decided to announce after a couple of days that the queen had given birth to a still-born daughter, procure a dead infant, and bury her. They also decided to postpone procuring a male heir till matters had cooled down.

Meanwhile, Rana Jadsinh received a letter from Buskin Sahib which said: 'I am most distressed about this matter. I must state that I have reason to believe that you were also a party to this scheme, alongside the Karbhari, Shathrai. This time, I have decided not to inform the Government about what has happened. But you must be warned that if any such attempt is made in the future, it will not be in your interest. Moreover, you are instructed to inform the Government

Agent of any future pregnancy at the beginning itself. Any laxity on your part in carrying out this instruction will strengthen suspicion against you, and the Government will be duly apprised of the same. It is hoped that your Karbhari will take cognizance of this, and comply. A copy of this communiqué will be kept in a special file in the Agent's office.'

All those involved in the scheme were deflated by the letter. Correspondence ensued back and forth, but fear was etched in their minds. Buddhidhan received information about Shathrai's activities from Garbaddas, and he used the money that Shathrai had given him to infiltrate his own house. Before the matter of foisting another heir could be resolved, Rana Jadsinh suddenly died, owing either to some illness or intrigue. This information was immediately relayed to Lilapur, and Suvarnapur was placed under the Agency's control. Locks of flesh and blood in the form of guards were posted at the queen's palace, the treasury, and the state offices. Wheels were set in motion to get Bhupsinh anointed the ruler of Suvarnapur. Officers and guards began to congregate around Bhupsinh's house, which was a mere hovel. Shathrai took to visiting Buddhidhan often in a bid to have his crimes pardoned. Garbaddas' influence increased. Buddhidhan could sense his star rising and smell prosperity in the offing, but he did not lose his composure. He remained industrious. He was not tempted; he did not commit haste, and he did not lose sight of his goal. Only Bhupsinh and Buddhidhan knew that the latter's fortunes were tied to the former's ascendancy. Everyone else saw him only as a Shirastidar for all times to come.

Buddhidhan met Bhupsinh with a letter of felicitation from Buskin Sahib. Addressing him with just the words, 'My Rana! The King of Suvarnapur,' Buddhidhan's voice choked and tears of joy rolled down his cheeks. Bhupsinh was overcome with gratitude. He embraced Buddhidhan warmly and said, 'Buddhidhan, this day has come only because of you. I will never forget what you have done for me. Yes, I am now the King. And you are my Minister. Hardship will become a memory of the past as we both look to the future.'

Buddhidhan retained his poise in face of the new king's emotional outburst, and his own memory of the intense desire for revenge. He did not want revenge to cast its shadow on auspicious beginnings. He did not want the Sahib to harbour any suspicion that the new ruler would use his authority to settle old scores. Nor did he want the worst fears of the old guard to come true and present them with an opportunity to commence new intrigues. These and other similar cogitations flashed through Buddhidhan's mind, and he took immediate remedial measures. He advised Bhupsinh, 'You should call upon the Sahib tomorrow and inform him of your intention to found an English school in Lilapur in memory of the years you have spent here. You should also tell him that you intend to commemorate your ascendance of the throne by establishing a 'Buskin Garden' in Suvarnapur. You should tell him that you intend to keep all the present palace officials in service, but also suggest that you need an honest, trustworthy and neutral person as an advisor. You should tell him: If you have come to trust Buddhidhan, depute him to me, or give me someone else.'

Bhupsinh did as he was counselled. Buskin Sahib had formed a favourable opinion of Bhupsinh over his dealings with the garas, and had sympathy for him. Hearing such noble thoughts from him on this occasion, Buskin Sahib was well pleased. The Sahib sent the Government a most favourable report on Bhupsinh and agreed to provide him with all support. He also agreed that Buddhidhan could join the new Rana's service, if that was what Buddhidhan desired. On receiving Government clearance, Bhupsinh's coronation was celebrated with much pomp and ceremony in Suvarnapur. On Buddhidhan's advice, representatives of newspapers in Bombay were invited to witness the occasion, and well looked after. Buddhidhan met them as a neutral person and praised the new Rana. Newspapers, both English and vernacular, printed long and glorious reports about Rana Bhupsinh's coronation. They praised Bhupsinh's wisdom, and the world believed it to be true.

As soon as a replacement for him was found in Lilapur, Buddhidhan took up the position of Hazoor Secretary, that is Principle Secretary to the Rana of Suvarnapur. Garbaddas was another trusted man of the new Rana. Buddhidhan secured a position for him in the accounts department. Positions of the other officials remained undisturbed. As time passed, Buddhidhan's position was renamed 'Counsellor', and his pay was increased. Things inched back towards normalcy. If any intrigues smouldered, the Counsellor wisely doused them before they could catch fire. Small incidents did occur—there were internal rivalries and jealousies to deal with—but they were not apparent to an outsider.

The Counsellor worked quietly, astutely, without intruding in anyone else's business, guided everyone on the right path, reasoned with the Karbhari, and as a result, when the administrators met, there was no trace of discontentment to be seen. His prestige increased from day to day. He restored the temple of Rajeshwar Mahadev built by his ancestors. People looked upon him with hope. When he had occasion to go to Bombay, the Counsellor made it a point to call upon the British officials there. He accomplished his mission and received their praise. He kept in touch with priests and pretended he had faith in their rituals and observances. These were considered the Counsellor's finest qualities, and as his influence over the Rana became apparent, they came in for even greater praise.

So, these were the circumstances when the Rana and his Counsellor visited the Mahadev temple that day, some three or four years after Bhupsinh's coronation. We had left the two of them in conversation at the Rajeshwar Mahadev, where Alak Kishori and Kumud Sundari had been confined in the same courtyard as Navin Chandra. We were distracted briefly by details about Buddhidhan's past, and so lost focus of our main story. Dear reader, if you did not find this distraction necessary and useful, wipe it out now from your mind's eye and pretend that it never happened. Forget the past and flow with the present, as it unfolds in the following chapter.

6 Intrigues in Rajeshwar

> One who is unattached achieves his ends while maintaining his silence.
>
> —Bhavabhuti

Suvarnapur's administration appeared to be slumbering, moving almost of its own volition. All except the Rana and his Counsellor were somnolent. Those who observed the state felt that this slumber was, in fact, the natural order of things, but those who remained wakeful desired this condition.

Buddhidhan, the real manipulator of this apparent somnolence operated from behind the scenes. Each of the actors involved believed that their actions were autonomous, and that he, Buddhidhan, was one of them. The people believed that the Counsellor had the Rana's ear; they did not however suspect that he was key to all the Rana's decisions. But this perception and this sense of calm was also contrived by the Counsellor. The fire of revenge that had consumed him during his years of impoverishment still raged unabated within him; but even Bhupsinh himself was unaware of this. The Rana believed that Buddhidhan was subject to his wish and will, and thus showered him with unsullied affection. Buddhidhan had meanwhile turned Bhupsinh and his administration into mere instruments for his festering rage. However, it is also true that despite this, over time, Buddhidhan had come to grow a selfless devotion and friendship for

Bhupsinh. Buddhidhan's ambition and desire for glory had taken root as well. Even so, this was not enough to calm his desire for retribution. In fact, this was daily stoked by the very sight of his enemies. For Buddhidhan, Bhupsinh's hatred was a mere instrument to actualise his own animosity. He would do nothing, would remain unseen, act only through his instruments while others would act as directed by him. Buddhidhan would remain distant and indifferent like the sun and the moon, while the sea below him rose and fell in tides. He observed things unfold as desired by him. This was characteristic of the Counsellor; this was his strategy. For four long years, Bhupsinh, an instrument himself, could discern neither the means nor the fruit thereof. He became increasingly restless. This, too, was a part of the Counsellor's strategy, and he was satisfied that it had taken root.

Bhupsinh sat leaning against a bolster on a golden carpet. From where he sat, he could see the Shivalinga. No longer impoverished, the expected changes had occurred in his attire, his person, his face and disposition. In the past, a Garasia weary of the Karbhari's machinations had required the help of a similarly poor advisor. Now, a Rana having exhausted his patience with his Karbhari sought help of his Counsellor. But the wants of the past were different from the needs of the present. Earlier, he had to plead and please an equal: his want was greater, and friendship was based on self-interest. Now, this was replaced by a certain impatience—he could now command, and their relations were guided by mutual affection and a sense of duty. This change was apparent; yet the affection of old often shone through.

'Buddhidhan, you have done *nothing* all these years! How long do I have to bear this petty rascal Shathrai? How long do I have to address the man who gave me so much misery as my Karbhari? Should we not simply behead those who fed off my garas? I won't rest as long as you don't resolve this matter!' Having raised himself up in excitement, Bhupsinh now sat back and glared at Buddhidhan.

Buddhidhan sat next to the Rana, his feet turned away in respect from his ruler. He smiled and said, 'Ranaji, be patient. You have become king—shouldn't your enemies also get something under your rule? Do some good unto the wicked.' He removed his turban and sat back quietly.

Bhupsinh laughed out aloud, 'Nice, very nice indeed! This is new. Do some good unto the wicked! Be kindly to the insolent and cause offence to a friend—this befits politicians like you. We are proud people. We could give life to the living and kill the dying. But you deal with friends and foes alike. Sweets and vegetables being sold at the same price can happen only in the city of the blind. Even a schoolboy knows this.'

'So be it. Give the order. It is in your power to dismiss the Karbhari tomorrow itself.'

'Oh stop fooling around and tell me what it is you intend to do.'

Both became grave. Then Buddhidhan began his discourse. 'Ranaji, desires can be fulfilled both through haste and through patience. A weed that grows fast withers away soon. A tree has deep roots. For example, how deep are Shathrai's roots? At the time of your coronation, all the officials owed their allegiance to him. He had his men in the palace. He is known both in the Agency and in the Bombay Government. The newspapers praise him. Russell Sahib, who replaced Buskin Sahib, trusts him. What ploy has he not tried to make me his confidant. If we had removed him outright, that boil would have become a festering wound. He would have tried a thousand machinations and caused all manner of trouble. He would have used all his power in the state and in the British Government to obstruct us. He would have destroyed your prestige before it could take root. What all would he not have done. And that would have been the outcome of haste.'

'Yes, that is certainly true,' replied a subdued Bhupsinh. Buddhidhan, like a dexterous snake catcher, realised that the hissing snake was caught in his pincers.

'Ranaji, we need time and patience before we can destroy him root and branch and cast our own roots deep.' The Rana looked dejected and slumped onto the bolster. Buddhidhan continued, 'But we have overcome these obstructions. Our preparations are almost over. The outer shell of the building is ready and all the bricks are firmly in place. Now only the surface work remains to be done—only the plastering remains.'

Bhupsinh sat up and listened attentively. 'All right, let us move ahead then.' Buddhidhan abandoned the allegorical mode and laid out details of his plan before the Rana, who became immersed in this narration which appealed to his self-interest.

'Our relations can no longer be concealed. People know about it since I joined your service. Naturally, Shathrai does not trust me, but he is a sweet-talker. We have not yet attacked him openly; hence his mistrust is not complete. And it is good that it is so. I do not openly meddle in his administration, therefore his machinations are subdued; but this will not last forever. We have made sure that his intrigues are rendered ineffective. Narbheram has been posted as his secretary. He indulges in mockery and participates in derogatory talks about me. The Karbhari trusts Narbheram completely. But you know well that he is our man. He has befriended Merulo; so we now know all that Dushtarai tells Rupali about his father's and his own plans.

'Shathrai and his brother Karvatrai, who is the chief judge, and son Dushtarai, who is the police chief, have tyrannised the poor people. Hitherto, we have chosen to look the other way, which has made them even more brazen and unrestrained. If they do not collapse under the weight of their own sins, a gentle nudge from us will do. It is for us to decide when to give that push. People are seething with anger at their unchecked oppression. People feel that the King is good, but that his Minister is wicked; their sentiments will catch fire when we fan them. And this would be a powerful justification, both for the people and for the Sahib, when we finally remove the Karbhari. No one will find fault with you, and everyone will be ready to kick the fallen.

'The Karbhari liked our advice that an elephant remains untroubled by a barking dog, and so he refused to pay any money to the Bombay newspapers. When the Karbhari was away in Bombay, a few newspaper men had visited Suvarnapur. Merulo, spurred on by Narbheram, insulted them. Some of our people live in Bombay.

We give them respect and honour. But Shathrai's pride is like that of Ravana. He behaves most arrogantly with such visitors, and they hate him after just one meeting. At times, Narbheram does not allow them to meet him. Other soldiers imitate Narbheram. If you want to know for yourself the outcome, here, read this newspaper. Once a thing is printed, no one can separate truth from fiction. In due course, I will demonstrate the impact that such writing has, both on the government and the people.

'Russell Sahib is not a military man. Unlike Buskin Sahib, his mind is not easy to fathom. It is not in his nature to insult someone or even call a spade a spade. You and the others believe that the Sahib trusts Shathrai. But Russell Sahib is a deeper man. The incident of the Muslim woman's son is recorded in a special file, and the Sahib knows about it, as is evident from this letter from Lilapur which you can read at leisure. The people's complaints have reached the Sahib. He will bring this up with you when you meet him. I will dwell on this and tell you tomorrow how you can apprise him of facts without openly denigrating the Karbhari. At present, the Karbhari is responsible for all that happens, or does not happen, in the administration.

'The chief judge, Karvatrai has done injustice to a bania. I have thought of a ploy to send the bania to the Sahib. It will not benefit the bania, but the matter will be placed before you by the Government, which will be good for us.

'Gradually, we have removed all the old officials from the court and the palace, and sent them elsewhere on higher salaries. You know well that the new functionaries are trusted men. Shathrai has tried to make them his cronies, we know this. You are aware what use we want to make of Garbaddas. The time has come for it: we can use him whenever you desire. We will take this up after your meeting with Russell Sahib.'

The Rana stretched and relaxed his limbs once this 'report' was over. He stood up looking pleased. Buddhidhan also arose and said, 'We have all the means for the action to begin. All we lack is a man with an English education.'

'That is all right, look for one. But make sure that Shathrai does not stick around for another three-four years.'

'Ranaji, please be patient. The world knows when a child is born; it takes nine months, but no one knows what happens inside the mother's womb. How long did you have to wait in Lilapur before you got the throne?'

'True, but that was God's will.'

'That matter was also in your hands: you could have had Jadsinh killed, just as Shathrai got Parvatrai killed.'

The Rana had no further arguments. 'So be it, bring on the delivery. But the fact of birth is known to all: pregnancy cannot be concealed.'

'But Ranaji, this child is going to be born without a pregnancy!'

The Rana was disarmed once again. 'Very well then. Whatever you think and do is fine.'

The Counsellor followed his King as they walked out. 'Ranaji, it is only a matter of a few days now.' He moved closer and whispered something into the Rana's ears. Bhupsinh was visibly delighted, turned around and patted the Counsellor on the back. He came out of the temple.

'Your kindness is upon all, your Grace!' shouted the ushers. The King sat in his carriage, the wheels moved, the horses trotted along, and the soldiers drew their swords. The procession left. Buddhidhan watched them go, and when they could no longer be seen, he turned back. He climbed up the steps of the temple and stood there with a hand on his heart, and his eyes over the horizon, murmured: God! I do nothing; it is only You who acts. God, I have never harmed anyone—not without reason—and will never do so in future either. Even You punish for a valid reason, don't You? His heart was thus consoled and the thorn in his conscience removed. Cleansed, he suddenly became aware of his surroundings. He looked around and shouted for Murkhdutt.

Murkhdutt came out running. He was cooking when the Rana arrived and thus had to stay put inside his room for the whole hour that the Rana was inside the temple. He had realised that Navinchandra was in the courtyard, and that he had sent the women from the Counsellor's family there. Frightened, he had gone to the window that looked out over the pond and, holding on to its iron bars, had raised himself on his toes to look out. Fortunately, Navinchandra had not stayed long in the courtyard. He had bathed in the pond and when Murkhdutt saw him, he was wiping himself dry. The priest thought it unwise to shout to him, so he picked up some pieces of dry cracked flooring and threw them at Navinchandra. His hand did not pass through the iron bars and hence these pieces fell short of Navinchandra. At last, one such piece hit Navinchandra on his back, and he was startled. He turned around, looked up and saw Murkhdutt. He went up to the window. Murkhdutt softly told him about the visit of the Rana, the Counsellor, and the Counsellor's family, and warned him to remain where he was and not go either to the courtyard or into the temple while they were present. 'If you want to see the Rana, leave from the other side and stand near the gate.' To pass the time, Navinchandra asked to take a book from his belongings. Murkhdutt was surprised that this man should, like a scholar, ask for a book!

Navinchandra washed and hung his dhoti to dry, using it to shield his face from the sun. He liked the feel of the winter sun on his body. He sat down and opened his book to read, once in a while looking up to gaze around him. Murkhdutt went back to his cooking. He had just finished when the Counsellor called him. He rushed out with a, 'Yes Sir!', his voice resonating inside the temple dome.

Buddhidhan asked, 'Has no one come today?' Murkhdutt replied, 'Alak Behn and Bhabhisahib have come.'

'Where are they?'

'In the courtyard. Please come in, I locked them in there when the Ranaji arrived.' The priest ran ahead, followed by Buddhidhan.

'Aren't there any travellers in the dharamshala?'

'Yes Sir, there is one. He must be somewhere near the pond.'

The lock and the door were opened.

7 Pleasure Garden

Flowerbeds of mogra, rose and champa had recently been planted in the courtyard behind the temple. In that garden was kept a bare and rickety string cot belonging to Murkhdutt. When alone, he was given to lying on it and singing rustic songs or reciting verses in his crude speech. Alak Kishori and Kumud Sundari now sat on one side of this cot. Their companions sat on either side of them in attendance. Alak Kishori plucked some flowers and offered them to the others.

'Bhabhisahib, which flower would you like?' she asked Kumud Sundari.

'Whichever you choose to give me.'

'No, you select one.'

'Whichever you give me is the one I will like.'

'If you do this in all matters, it will be hard on you!' laughed Alak Kishori.

'I accepted the good brother you gave me. Why would I need to choose now?'

'Then take this sephalika—it has your delicacy and your complexion.' Kumud Sundari smiled and took the flowers tenderly. Her extended arms resembled a river of clear sparkling water, and the flowers were like white lotuses floating in it.

Alak Kishori: 'Vanleela, have you ever seen hands as beautiful as those of my bhabhi?'

Radha: 'Behn, she is *your* bhabhi; how could she lack in anything!'

Vanleela: 'You have given her flowers, but you should string them and adorn her hair with it—these are the days of spring.'

Radha: 'The spring is new, and so is she!'

Alak Kishori: 'Yes, we will string these flowers together and tie them around her bed. We would make a veni of roses for her hair.'

Vanleela: 'And tie some mogra and champa on her wrists.'

Alak Kishori: 'And bhabhi, then you must dance for my brother.'

Krishna Kalika laughed: 'Only courtesans dance to seduce.'

Alak Kishori: 'Die, you wretch! Watch your words! Shame on you.'

Dark and pockmarked, Krishna Kalika was shapely. But her intelligence was limited and her conduct was lax, so this rebuke was wasted on her. She considered Alak Kishori a little too smart and over wise. She thought she had said nothing inappropriate. But Kumud Sundari's face fell at that comment. She felt slighted. She realised it was only because of the lowly company she was in. She thought about her relationship with Pramaddhan; fulfillment of bodily passion was the basis of their relationship. Pramaddhan was the provider of comfort, and if that were true, Kumud Sundari asked herself, What is wrong with what was said? She remembered the books she loved. Sarasvatichandra would have satisfied all her wants, all her desires. She felt a profound discontent. Sarasvatichandra's virtues came to mind, and suddenly overcome with emotions, her eyes became moist. The women assumed she was hurt by Krishna Kalika's comment, so they chided Kalika, and pleaded with Kumud. Kumud Sundari wiped her tears and said she was not hurt by the comment. But she could not explain the real reason for her tears, so the women continued to believe that she was hurt by Kalika's words.

Sarasvatichandra and Kumud Sundari had met only once, many moons ago. She was intimate with Pramaddhan, knew his every desire. And yet, just as the moonstone melts at the touch of the moon's rays, she too melted and shed melancholy tears every time she thought of her moon, her Chandra. It had never occurred to her if Sarasvatichandra was handsome or attractive, for it was through his letters and his words that she had grown infatuated with him. Pramaddhan was handsome, quite a dandy, and committed to opulence and sexual pleasure. And yet her attraction for Sarasvatichandra had remained undiminished. A woman should not be superior to her husband in age, beauty, learning, intelligence, wisdom, wit, and in her ability to experience aesthetic delight. Such a woman experiences the pain and inadequacy of an incompatible marriage. She remains discontented with her husband. She fails to respect him, feels no affection for him, and cannot unite her heart with his. If she is not endowed with virtue, she may even come to despise him. But God had endowed Kumud Sundari with virtue; she had been raised well by her parents and cultivated by education. The very air she had breathed at Vidya Chatura's house had been different from the atmosphere at Buddhidhan's. She felt affection for her husband and her in-laws. She wished them well and did not wish to harbour any sense of distinction or being apart from them. But there was a limit to her endurance. Like a fish out of water, Vidya Chatura's daughter flailed in a house bereft of learning. With a great effort of will, she had calmed herself and regained her poise. But Krishna Kalika's barb had brought Sarasvatichandra back into her consciousness. His last letter was still tucked inside her blouse. She could not take it out in plain sight, but her mind went to it and conveyed her desire to her heart which began to beat faster at the touch of the hidden letter. A shiver coursed through her body; her hair stood on end and she broke into a cold sweat. But Kumud Sundari alone was aware of this. She forced gaiety upon her face. The gaiety that had been disrupted returned as the women resumed their banter. The string cot felt rough against their soft skin, so they all got up. Vanleela and Kumud Sundari walked towards the pond, their fingers intertwined. Alak Kishori put an arm around Krishna Kalika and they strolled around the flowerbeds. Radha stood on one side, playing with the branch of a mogra shrub.

Alak Kishori asked Krishna Kalika, 'Now tell me the truth: yesterday, I made a face at Khalaknanda and Rupali when they were walking about accompanied by Jamal and Merulo. Did they comment on it later?'

'No.'

'Kalika, you whore, speak the truth!' Alak demanded, playfully pinching her dark cheek.

'Fine! Let go of me. Why do you pinch me so! Is it only your family which rules over Suvarnapur!' Krishna Kalika responded with a dismissive shake of her head.

Alak Kishori caught hold of her with both hands and pressed hard. 'Tell me, you imp!'

'She responded by the same token.'

'What did she say?'

'Khalaknanda said: This lass pretends to be so virtuous. I will break her pride.'

'The whore! Who is she to break my pride! What else?'

'Rupali said: This is like a sieve laughing at the husk!'

'I see. Who are they to talk about me? One can only draw water when there is water in the well. How can they talk about me when I am faultless?'

'Some speak the truth; others tell lies. Who can ascertain truth from lies?'

'I will pull out their tongues if they keep this up.'

'She is the Karbhari's daughter.'

Alak Kishori pouted and said, 'Good; we shall also see how long the Karbhari lasts.'

'But behn, we must not be so proud. Whatever we may think, Khalaknanda is after all from an influential family.'

'All right, then. I will never speak to them again.'

As this conversation was taking place, on the other side of the garden, Kumud Sundari and Vanleela walked leisurely. Vanleela was humming softly to herself ...

> *Dejected, the passionate woman cries*
> *and pleads with her husband*

Feeling deeply dejected and spurned herself, Kumud Sundari was lost in her own thoughts. She drifted away from Vanleela. Walking by herself, she came to lean against the temple wall and looked out towards the pond. She repeated Vanleela's song. And then of their own volition, two couplets sprang from her heart.

O' Moon, why have you abandoned the horizon?
In darkness, your lotus withers
Whatever came over you, O' bee?
How could you abandon your lotus?

Her imagination was afire; its flames leapt around, changing hues, adding dashes of colour to her visions. Her mind and reason were bedazzled; her heart was in a frenzy; her senses, her eyes and ears abandoned her. Though awake, she was in a dreamlike state—and in her mind's eye, she saw Sarasvatichandra. One moment he seemed to be standing below a tree in a large forest. The next moment, he was in a village, resting on a peasant's cot, weary and fatigued. Then again, she saw him roaming through the streets of a city, solitary, unknown and unrecognised. Soon after, she had a vision of him lying ill and uncared for in a dharamshala. She felt that he was very near her, albeit in disguise, and his eyes almost seemed to rebuke her.

Kumud Sundari often fell prey to this waking dream-state. But this went against her wifely virtues, and she wanted to remedy it. After having come to her marital home, Kumud had become emaciated, and she felt weak even in the mind. Some believed that newcomers took time to adjust to Suvarnapur's water. Medicines, remedies and nutritious food were given to her, but to little effect. Buddhidhan believed that his daughter-in-law yearned for her parental home. He had given instructions that she should be engaged in fun and games and taken on pleasure trips. Buddhidhan also knew that Vidya Chatura's house was that of a reformist, and that its women were used to a certain freedom of movement. Alak Kishori followed all his instructions wholeheartedly. But Kumud Sundari knew well what ailed her. She asked Pramaddhan for some books to be procured from Bombay. She believed that if she were to immerse herself in these books, she would be rid of the ghost of Sarasvatichandra. The books had not yet arrived;

as she waited impatiently for them, she often found herself in these trance-like states. Today, however, these images had a different force, a different urgency to them. No one could have imagined the churning of her heart as she stood petrified against the temple wall, barely able to breathe. Vanleela walked towards her, singing a song.

When did you become a foe, my friend?
You awakened me from my sleep
And tore me away from my beloved

She stopped singing as she neared Kumud. 'Bhabhisahib, look at this!' she suddenly said aloud. In Kumud Sundari's preoccupied state, the song registered before Vanleela herself did and its impact lasted longer than her call.

'Bhabhisahib, oh do come and look!' Vanleela entreated.

Staring distantly at this 'friend turned foe' and returning to the present reluctantly as if from afar, Kumud asked, 'What ... What did you say?'

'What a strange sight! There is someone sleeping here right on the edge of the pond, with an open book on his chest. What all people do! Taking a *book* to the pond of all things!'

'Let him be. What is it to us? Why concern ourselves with an unknown man?'

'But what if he were to turn on his side, bhabhisahib, or get up and fall straight into the pond?!'

'Wake him up then.'

'Bhai! O bhai!'

Navinchandra woke up, and looked up in the direction of the voice.

'Move carefully. I woke you up just so you wouldn't fall into the pond if you were to turn on your side.'

'That is most kind of you, behn,' Navinchandra said, and sat up. For a fleeting moment, his eyes met Kumud Sundari's. And, as if there was nothing uncommon about this sight, Navinchandra looked away. He was about to pick up his book when the ushers shouted out that the Rana was about to leave the Rajeshwar Mahadev. Navinchandra hurriedly got up to see the Rana depart, leaving his book and the two women behind.

Poor Kumud Sundari! Her eyes trailed him as he walked away. Even as she and Vanleela turned to go back, her body pulled her in one direction, her eyes in another. This man so resembled the one whose image had possessed her mind for long now. Was this Sarasvatichandra? Did his wanderings bring him here? No, no ... That is unlikely, how could that be. Has he come here to see me in this pitiable condition? No, he would not ridicule my suffering. But, whether he accepts it or not, it *is* him. So be it. A deep sigh of dejection escaped Kumud. What is our relation now? I must purge my mind of these thoughts. Whether it is him or someone else, what is it to me? God has willed that I be with someone else: he is my truth; all else is deceit. And Kumud Sundari walked off with Vanleela almost against her own will. But, she thought again, it would still be nice if it were him. I have no interest in him now. Marriage has determined for me the object of my affection. But if he stays here, I might be able to hear him speak to someone else. If this man is indeed him, his learning will not remain concealed for long. At some point, his speech will spring forth, and in this land bereft of learning and culture, his sweet nectar-like words will reach my ears.

No. Even that would be wrong.

Why? What is wrong if relations are not physical, if bodies are not involved?

But how can I be so sure that this man is him?

He had the same face. And he had a book.

But anyone can have a book.

Who knows what all of this means! I only know it would be good if he stays on here. I would take delight in his wellbeing. And I would be cured—what more do I want? If this is the extent of our relationship, what could possibly be wrong? I will neither speak nor move with him. I won't even look at him. I will only hear him speak to others. I would be free of worry if I just knew he was all right.

Kumud Sundari's thoughts thus came round full circle as she and Vanleela walked back to the others. Seeing them, Alak Kishori came towards them. She looked at Kumud's face closely, put her hands on her shoulders and asked, 'Bhabhisahib, what is wrong today? You seem so pensive. Pain and suffering are not for you. Leave it to the karbharis to plot and plan and build and destroy in their heads. Tell me, are you longing for your parents, or craving for my brother?'

'God knows. I do not know why, but I feel most fatigued today.'

Just then the temple doors opened. Buddhidhan entered, followed by Murkhdutt. Murkhdutt had the lock and key in his hand.

Alak Kishori, Kumud Sundari, Vanleela and Krishna Kalika entered together, and stood facing the Counsellor. Radha, who was still wandering about in the garden, saw the book lying near the pond. She picked it up. Whose is it? Who kept it here? she wondered, leafing through its pages. Then she hurried to join her group at the temple. She went and stood next to Kumud Sundari, leaning against her with one hand on her shoulder. Just then, asking, 'Where is Radha?' Alak Kishori turned around and saw her. Kumud had just taken the book from Radha's hands.

'What is that book?' Buddhidhan asked. Kumud Sundari kept her eyes lowered on the pages of the book and shyly replied, 'Radha had this book in her hands. It is called *The Pandit: Kashividyasudhanidhi*. It publishes articles in Sanskrit and English and also reprints sections from old books. My father also subscribes to it and receives a copy every month.' The rest of the women stared at her, uncomprehending.

Radha: 'It was lying there on the embankment, so I brought it with me.'

Murkhdutt: 'It belongs to the man who has come to live in our dharamshala, Navinchandra. He must be looking for it.'

Buddhidhan took the book from Kumud Sundari, and asked that Navinchandra be brought into the courtyard. The priest ran out. Navinchandra was looking for his book. Murkhdutt called out to him, 'Come! The Counsellor has asked for you. It is a good opportunity to make your introduction. Your book is with him. Come.' Both went into the temple courtyard together. Navinchandra greeted the Counsellor with a namaskar; Buddhidhan responded solemnly. The women stood at a distance. Kumud Sundari was trembling inside. The book had made her suspicions even stronger. She stood right at the back of the group so she could look at his face without being seen. She believed that if her suspicions were true, he would not be able to bear her gaze.

Buddhidhan asked him, 'Where are you from? There must be some purpose to your visit here.'

Navinchandra: 'I come from Bombay. I wanted to see the native states for myself.'

'Are you a trader in Bombay?'

'Among us, there is a saying that Goddess Annapurna does not let anyone go hungry. I wished to experience that for myself. I was a student in Bombay; now I am a seeker of experiences.'

'Then you must find yourself a trade.'

'Trade gives you one kind of experience. I desire the whole gamut of experiences that life can afford.'

Buddhidhan found the man quaint and allowed himself a smile. 'And how do you propose to accomplish this desire?'

'I can observe without speaking. I can keep to myself what I hear. I can experience all colours without being stained by any.'

Buddhidhan suppressed a laugh with some effort. 'Is this your book, then?'

'Yes, sir.'

'What have you studied?'

'Some English and a little Sanskrit.'

'Where did you study?'

Kumud Sundari eagerly awaited his response.

'In Bombay.' The answer left her unsatisfied.

'Here, take your book. What is your caste?'

'We belong to the same caste.'

'As long as you are here, please eat at my house.'

'As you please, sir.'

Kumud Sundari's innermost desires were fulfilled; but her sense of duty towards her husband was not.

Buddhidhan liked to collect interesting men around him. He was happy that one more was added to that collection. Alak Kishori was given the responsibility of looking after the new guest, a responsibility she accepted. The priest was asked to bring the guest over to the Counsellor's house at dinner time.

Throughout the conversation, Kumud Sundari looked intently at Navinchandra. Sometimes, he withdrew his gaze as if her look pierced him, but at other times he looked at her unblinking. And still other times, he looked away as if completely indifferent. In this examination, Kumud Sundari forgot her own confusion. She climbed into the cart with the other women, softly murmuring the couplets about the moon and the lotus to herself. Buddhidhan sat in his own coach and went away.

8 At the Counsellor's House

Navinchandra started taking his morning and evening meals at the Counsellor's house. Shathrai's household was uncaring of its guests, their attitude being: 'Dump the guest in the godown.' Those who ate in the Karbhari's house felt as if they were fed scraps, like dogs. Shathrai would neither talk nor sit with his guests, and they invariably felt slighted. As a young man, Buddhidhan had also felt unwelcome in Shathrai's house. However, if one did not accept the Karbhari's invitation, and this came to his notice, one would also be considered swollen-headed. Sometimes, Shathrai would taunt his guests or ridicule them so, it would singe his visitors. Buddhidhan had always looked for reasons to steal away from that house. But this was in the past. Buddhidhan did, however, still remember it. And so he took care to ensure that no one felt slighted under his roof. He had therefore trained his children as well as his servants in the art of humility and civility. Navinchandra ate alongside Buddhidhan. There was not the slightest discrimination. Buddhidhan treated even a wandering wayfarer as an equal, in thought, word and deed. The honoured and loved Counsellor of the Ruler of Suvarnapur conversed interestedly with his guests, encouraged even the quiet and the reticent to speak up and engage in debates. In such discussions, he betrayed not a trace of pride and arrogance. Pramaddhan would also join in at mealtimes and ensure that the guests were comfortable. Saubhagya Devi, Alak Kishori and Kumud Sundari would quietly sit in a group and roll betel-nut leaves.

In Shathrai's house, Buddhidhan had observed very different demeanour. Khalaknanda and Rupali would walk around noisily, talk loudly, laugh with the servants one moment and scold them the next. They were wealthy, wore ornaments in excess and behaved ostentatiously. But their sense of their own importance extended only to such display. Neither of them knew how to look after or manage the household. They never covered their heads. Sometimes their unkempt hair would come loose. At times their backs were uncovered, and they moved around the house without wearing a blouse sometimes. Petticoats seemed cumbersome to them, and the women did not care what happened to their garments when they sat down, got up, or moved about. Unknown men around the house did not feel the need to caution them, and if they did, felt ashamed in pointing such things out to women. The men of the house fooled around with other women and neglected their own household. As a result, visitors to the Karbhari's residence could cultivate undesirable proximity with these women. Buddhidhan had observed this, and he felt a strong revulsion. He took care to ensure that such goings on would never transpire in his own house. In his caste, it was not customary for women to cover their faces. But the women took care not to appear before elderly men.

Navinchandra was not considered an elder; he was a caste-fellow, and so the women could sit with him as he ate but they did not participate in conversation with him. Navinchandra was also quite shy. He did not interact with the women directly and placed no burden upon his hosts. His civility was endearing, his reticence charming, and within a few days, the Counsellor's family came to consider him as one of their own. Buddhidhan had at their first meeting found the young man rather strange; but his opinion changed with time. Navinchandra would sit and converse with Pramaddhan before and after meals. Pramaddhan thought well of his 'English knowledge' and said as much to his father. Pramaddhan also learnt that Navinchandra often wrote for major English newspapers in Bombay. However, Buddhidhan did not immediately believe this about someone who seemed to be a complete vagabond.

One evening, Navinchandra arrived as usual at the Counsellor's house for dinner. Buddhidhan was still busy at the palace and had not yet returned, although it was well past dinner time. Navinchandra sat with Pramaddhan in one of the drawing rooms. Some six or seven others who had come to meet Pramaddhan were also around. Pramaddhan lounged in an easy chair at the centre of the room. One of his hangers-on removed his pagri while another helped him with his angarkha, and a third helped him remove his jacket. A fourth person praised him, while a fifth chimed in, and the sixth abused Pramaddhan's foes and competitors.

Just then, the post arrived. All the letters were placed in Pramaddhan's hands as he presided over the group. He opened the English newspaper first. He hurriedly scanned it, and said with evident joy and excitement, 'Navinchandra, your article has been published!' He had asked Navinchandra to write a piece so he could convince his father about Navinchandra's abilities.

'Is it published? Read it out aloud,' one friend said.

It was read out. Meanwhile, the master of the house finally arrived, and the party of hangers-on dispersed with alacrity, leaving only the family members at home. Pramaddhan and Navinchandra went into the dining room. There, Alak Kishori sat upon a wooden bench, leaning against a wall, with five or six other women surrounding her, gossiping. Saubhagya Devi sat on the floor near the brazier; old Dayashankar's wife Jamna Kaki sat with her, warming her limbs. Kumud Sundari stood at a window by herself, resting her hand on the ledge. Alak Kishori now got up from the bench and went and stood with her sister-in-law, as Pramaddhan and Navinchandra sat down together side-by-side, their backs to the two women. Alak embraced Kumud fondly and whispered into her ears, 'Now I am warm, bhabhisahib; your body is quite warm for a winter night!' Kumud managed a faint smile. With every passing day, she felt a little less inhibited in Navinchandra's presence.

Buddhidhan came in, and the food was served. Over dinner, Pramaddhan spoke of Navinchandra's article. Buddhidhan said, 'Yes, I know of it. The Sahib's Shirastidar was here; he read and praised the article. It is quite well written. Navinchandra, if you desire your gamut of experiences, stay here in Suvarnapur. We need someone who can write English. I will put it to the Rana at an opportune moment.'

It was late by the time everyone finished eating. It was decided that Navinchandra would stay the night at the Counsellor's house. A bed was made for him in Pramaddhan's drawing room. He lay down to sleep. Buddhidhan and Pramaddhan retired to the adjoining drawing room. Alak Kishori did not return to her husband's house as it was already late. Her mother and sister-in-law advised her to send her in-laws a message that she would not be returning that night. At least let them know, they said. 'What is the need?' Alak replied, 'They will come to know anyhow,' and she did not send the message. Pramaddhan was not yet ready for bed, so the sisters-in-law sat around the brazier, talking.

Buddhidhan had received much unusual news that day. The father and son sat conversing in the drawing room.

'Pitaji, is there any news of Shathrai's clique?'

'I think there has been a breach in our ranks. We need to ascertain who has done it, and how.'

Just then, a man dressed as a soldier sought permission to enter the room. It was Narbheram. He acted as a confidant to Shathrai, but in truth, he was one of Buddhidhan's most trusted men. He sat facing father and son, and submitted, 'Buddhidhanbhai, our task has become more difficult.'

'How so?'

'Until recently, Shathrai was in the dark about your relations with the Rana. Now the Karbhari knows that the two of you meet often, that you had gone on a hunt with him. He even knows that you met in the Rajeshwar Mahadev.'

'Is that all?'

'He removes anyone he suspects—that is his way.'

'Then what?'

'He has fabricated letters between you and Rajba. He plans to show them to the Rana.'

Buddhidhan saw red. 'Who is going to show him the letters?'

'The Rana's old attendant, Mahva.'

'I see.'

'I myself wrote those letters,' said Narbheram, and took out some fifteen-twenty letters and tossed them into the Counsellor's lap.

'When are they to be presented to the Rana?'

'After your return from the palace.'

'Let these remain with me for now. I will have them sent to you by noon tomorrow.'

Buddhidhan's trust in Narbheram was reaffirmed. He had appointed trusted men both inside the palace and elsewhere; some were known to be his people while the identity of others had remained a secret. But he had not yet had the opportunity to put all of them to the test. Narbheram, however, had acquitted himself with a sterling performance. The Counsellor felt a newfound affection and gratitude towards him. But loss accompanies gain: as the saying goes, the uncle got married but the aunt became a widow. Buddhidhan trusted the Rana, but knew that he had to be very cautious. He had the Rana's ear; but if something about Rajba were to take root in Bhupsinh's mind, it would be difficult if not impossible to uproot, and all his ploys would come to naught. To this day, the Rana himself informed Buddhidhan about all palace intrigues. But now the Counsellor felt the need to appoint one of his own men to keep an eye on the Rana. Who should that person be? Garbaddas? No. Narbheram? Yes. Moreover, he reasoned, this appointment would also be a reward for Narbheram's loyalty. All these thoughts flashed through the Counsellor's mind much like lightning brightens up the entire sky in a fraction of a moment. This also clarified for him some other machinations that he had not quite been able to fathom. He had enough ammunition, but his conscience did not allow him to deploy it before his adversary made the first move. His resolve to fight back became stronger. The moment of doubt was over—now was the hour of decisive action.

'Narbheram, a critical moment is upon us. Once the letters are placed before the Rana, he will pretend to trust Shathrai, and be angry with me. He will ask Shathrai to appoint a trusted man in his service. Can we ensure that Shathrai forwards your name?'

'Yes, that can be done. Today, Shathrai trusts no one more than he trusts me.'

'All right. Does Garbaddas visit him often these days?'

'Oh yes—I forgot to mention that. Rupalibai has ensnared him.'

'Correct. But keep a watch over his movements. These days, Garbaddas is playing a double game; he pretends to be a confidant of both parties.'

'And what would he gain by doing so?'

'Well, if the Karbhari and the Counsellor destroy each other, he could be the next Karbhari. Garbaddas thinks he has the Rana's confidence and trust.'

'And what will you do about this?'

'We will deal with it. For the present, just keep watch on the plots he hatches.'

'Very well. I will take your leave.'

'All right; but you should come and see me more often.'

Narbheram left. Buddhidhan's eyes followed him—his soldierly disguise was perfect. The Counsellor smiled at the sight. Then he turned to his son. 'Pramad, be extremely careful about any food that might be sent from the Karbhari's house. We should accept it, but bury it deep in the ground.'

'Why? Is he likely to poison us, you think?'

'It is said that Rana Jadsinh was murdered. And we know well that the Karbhari had Parvatsinh killed. Then how can we trust him? Now go to sleep.'

Pramaddhan was stunned, and went away without another word.

Buddhidhan got up and paced up and down alone in the drawing room. He put a finger on his lips as he talked aloud to himself. May your face blacken, Karbhari. Finally, you have shown me your true colours. I did not attack you so far because you are a caste-fellow and also a relative. But, so be it. Let us fight this out. So far, our enmity has been disguised. Henceforth, it shall be an open one. Garbad, even you are trying to play smart. I did that once, too. But there is a difference; I did not get anyone killed. I fear God. What can I do if someone was killed without my having occasioned it? I cannot be blamed for Parvatsinh's murder. No. But you, Garbad, you have gone one up on me. Plotting my death now, are you? If the Rana slips out of my hand, it will be difficult for me. It took me five-seven long years to extricate him from Ramabai's clutches. Now he is besotted with Kalavati, and there appears to be no escape from this. Buddhidhan, if this happens, Bhupsinh will never be yours.

Buddhidhan stood in his drawing room like a Brahmarakshas in a forest. His mind was aflame; his heart beat fast as his thoughts spun round and round. Murderer, would you murder even me! May you be destroyed root and branch, Shathrai! And where did you find Kalavati? Now that I know of your intrigue with Rajba, I understand your game with Kalavati. It is you who got the Rana besotted. It is a ploy to create a cleavage between the Rana and me.

Rajba. That old incident came back to Buddhidhan. He saw Rajba, passion raging in her eyes, clasping his hand in hers. And suddenly he was frightened. He broke out in cold sweat and shivered. He sat down on the bolster. A woman dressed as Rajsinh stood before him. She leaned against him, and he felt her hands on his shoulders and chin. The Counsellor of Suvarnapur stared fixedly at the vision with bulging eyes and felt he was going to faint from fright.

Just then, a door flung open and Saubhagya Devi entered the drawing room, smiling. The evil vision vanished the moment his eyes fell on his Devi. Besotted, the devotee gazed upon his goddess in blessed relief.

'Dearest, you will soon become the Karbhari, and we will lose you. You will pass your nights just like this and will have no time for me. When we were young, we used to talk till midnight. But now all you care for is your Karbhar. I now have a co-wife, even without you having married again!' Devi came and sat down next to him, her body touching his. She caressed his neck. Then, putting an arm around him, she led him to their bed chamber. Though parents of an adult son and daughter, Buddhidhan and Saubhagya Devi were still young of body and mind and not yet subject to the thoughts and aspirations of the old.

Buddhidhan was murmuring in his sleep. 'Shathrai, if you had resolved to kill only me, I would not have met with success. But you intend to kill even the Rana, which makes my task easier. The Rana will always be under my influence. You believe that once you remove Buddhidhan, you will control the Rana; and if he escaped your clutches, you would sacrifice him as well. Good. Excellent. But Dushtarai visits Kalavati ... which is also fine.' Saubhagya Devi woke up hearing her husband's blabbering. She pulled him closer to her and contentedly closed her eyes again.

The comets of dreamland may at times become manifest through such delirious speech. The only witness to this was an inanimate lamp. In the grip of his dream the man attempted to turn sides, but his wife, even in her sleep, did not let him turn away and pulled him closer yet. And their creaking bed, like a sad bard, sang their song, but alas to a deaf bedroom. The long winter night thus became shorter.

9 The Consequences of Intoxication

Upon his return from Lilapur, the Rana's generosity had allowed Buddhidhan to build himself a large and beautiful house. The gate opened onto an enclosed space, followed by a courtyard. On either side of this courtyard were spacious rooms. On one side, a room was divided to make a kitchen, a room for storing water, and a dining space. On the other side, the younger women held court. An enclosed passage, another room, and a store-room were to be found behind the main courtyard. Saubhagya Devi's seat was in this enclosed passage. The front courtyard was partitioned from the inner living space with wooden planks. There was an English style 'waiting room' in the outer courtyard. During the day, the servants and soldiers of the family sat on the platform or *otalo,* and slept in this courtyard at night. A window of the women's quarters opened on to a side-street. Pramaddhan's bed chamber was above the women's quarters. The floor above the courtyard was a large one. This space served as Buddhidhan's drawing room. Pramaddhan had a drawing room adjacent to his bedroom, where he sat in the company of his friends. Buddhidhan's bedroom was on this level. A window opened from his room onto his drawing room.

The second floor was constructed above these rooms and it had an extended terrace, with partial enclosures encircling the rooms on it. These rooms had windows opening onto the terrace. Navinchandra's bed was made in Pramaddhan's drawing room. Pramaddhan saw to Navinchandra's comfort and then proceeded to the Counsellor's drawing room. Navinchandra was about to extinguish his lamp and go to sleep when he heard voices from either side of him. On one side, he could hear the Counsellor, Narbheram and Pramaddhan in Buddhidhan's drawing room. On the other side was Pramaddhan's bedroom, and since he was with his father, this is where the sisters-in-law sat chatting. The books that Kumud Sundari so wanted had finally arrived from Bombay a few days ago. Not satisfied with the solitary pleasure of reading them, Kumud read out parts of them aloud to Alak Kishori. She translated captivating passages from English and Sanskrit books for Alak, who listened to her meekly and attentively.

'Alak behn, listen, this is most interesting. A woman forsaken by her husband laments her loss. Her words are haunting. Listen: "The peace which others seek, they find, as the heaviest storms do not last forever; for the heavens grant even to the guiltiest minds amnesty for what is past".'

'What does it mean?'

'It means, we feel guilt for our mistakes, but this burden does not last forever. There comes a time when we no longer feel the burden. Is this not amnesty granted by God?'

'Yes, of course.'

'The woman asks: "If the guiltiest of minds find amnesty, when will my God put an end to my sufferings? I am innocent: when will my sentence come to an end? I don't ask for more, just that I wish to know the worst that will befall me. All that is left after that is for my heart to burst open, if God wills it".'

'What does that mean?'

'She says that she wants to know what awaits her, even if it means knowing that she will never meet her husband again. She cannot give up hope, but knows that her hope will not be realised; and hence her mind knows no rest. She feels, therefore, that all hope is in vain and peace can only come once her heart breaks completely.'[1] Kumud Sundari felt a deep ache in her heart as she spoke these words.

[1] This paragraph is a discussion of William Wordsworth's 'The Forsaken'.

Alak Kishori said, 'It feels wonderful to be able to understand such things. But what you sang yesterday was even better. I understood its meaning; you had explained it to me. But please sing it once more, bhabhi.' Kumud sang again.

Oh! Were he present, fondly would he seek,
In secret whisper, that inviting cheek;
Woo thee in close approach, his words to hear,
And breathe these tender accents in thine ear.
Goddess beloved! How vainly I explore
The world, to trace the semblance I adore.[2]

Explaining the meaning of the verses to Alak Kishori, Kumud said, 'This is from Kalidasa's *Meghdoot*. I had spoken to you about it yesterday. I have translated that passage for you.'

'Oh, you are so romantic!' Alak Kishori exclaimed, enveloping Kumud Sundari in a tight embrace. She looked at her sister-in-law's face, brought her lips close to her cheeks and teased, 'Shall I be naughty, just like the song you sang? I would have definitely married you if you were a man, and not stayed away from you for even a day! Bhabhi, when one reads and understands words like this, how can one not be romantic? You do not speak about the things we do, but you understand them so much better. You are wise as a swan, dear bhabhisahib! You sing, and I will listen.'

Navinchandra had extinguished the lamp and lay in bed. In the adjoining room, Buddhidhan and Narbheram spoke frankly, while in the bedroom the sisters-in-law spoke softly. Although soft, their voices could be heard in the adjacent room. Neither group was conscious of Navinchandra's presence, and hence did not lower their voices. Nothing could be seen through the door, but voices carried in the quiet of the night. Navinchandra was familiar with all these voices except Narbheram's. His ears were drawn to both conversations. He

[2] H. H. Wilson, trans. 'The Megha Duta, or The Cloud Messenger of Kalidasa', 2nd ed. (London: Richard Watts, 1843), 91.

rose from his bed and moved from one door to the other, placed his ears close to the door and listened intently. He did not intend to pass on these secret conversations or use them wrongly. He found the act of curious eavesdropping quite innocent.

While the conversation between the sisters-in-law pleased and delighted him, he was astounded by the Counsellor's conversation. Kumud's poem, her song, her craving, melted Navinchandra's heart. If the lamp could discern his expression, there certainly would have been cause for gossip. But that state lasted only briefly, and then his desire to learn the intrigues of statecraft drew him to the other side. He was surprised that Buddhidhan, who appeared happy and carefree, was actually neck-deep in worries. He remembered his own reading: 'uneasy lies the head that wears the crown.'[3] Only the Karbhari knows his suffering; and even gold has impurities; such maxims took on new meaning for him. Navinchandra thought that the Counsellor was dissatisfied with his present position, and that he desired the post of the Karbhari. He felt that Buddhidhan's desire was based on selfishness alone. He was astounded that one made so many enemies, played such intrigues, and associated with such persons to obtain the Karbhar. 'The head of the avaricious reels in constant vertigo!'—he grasped the import of this adage anew overhearing Buddhidhan's soliloquy. But he did not understand the part about Rajba, and was taken aback by Saubhagya Devi's words. This set him thinking that the craving for sexual pleasure does not leave one even in advanced age; and that a man driven by worldly ambition becomes incapable of experiencing, of enjoying the everyday pleasures of the household. He also mused that a man married to money forsakes his wife.

The Karbhar, all these murders, these intrigues—Why? How can one mind bear such terrible burdens? The 'whitewash' is only superficial; their insides are filthy. This is how God creates us: a beautiful body is nothing but a lump of meat. Dawn breaks out from an earth drowned in darkness. One should not ask about the history of

[3] Author's note: *Henry IV*, Part II, Shakespeare.

the powerful, or else scandals would tumble out. The educated remain discontented despite hard work, riches elude them; while the likes of the Karbhari and others roll around in wealth. But such sentiments are misplaced. The worries, the intrigues, the wily ways, the dirty acts, and this whitewash all add up to some nominal prestige and some money—neither of which sustains and nourishes. Karbharis, keep your pleasures to yourselves!

Perhaps, Karbharis who are learned are not faced with similar problems. Let it be. It is all the same; only the patterns differ. Reformed Karbharis will experience the pain of reformers. And all their wives would have the same complaints as Saubhagya Devi. The poor Karbharis and leading businessmen of Bombay—all of them lead lives of such miserable drudgery!

Karbharis, you run the state, but look at your deeds! The foolish dance to your tunes, while you become one with the wicked and profit from them. It is not that you are not possessed of intellect or good conscience. Those who claim so are ignorant. But the very air you breathe is contaminated. How could that not pollute your mind and conscience? How contaminated are even the most learned minds? My experience in such matters is limited. What I witnessed today is the first lesson of my experiential learning. What all am I yet to witness, God alone knows.

But, Kumud Sundari, whatever it may be, you ought not to be seen in this land. O Lotus, you belong to a lake. Vidya Chatura's daughter—Who *are* you? And these people? Have these lowly beings become any better than you because of their Karbhar? Even beautifully arranged rows of crows on the mountain tops would not compare with swans. Royal swan, you are a child-woman. 'Of the meritorious ones, the reason for their worship and reverence is not their seniority or age or some insignia of prestige that they bear, but their virtue.'[4] How do your days here pass, an immaculate beauty like you, in this dirty, sullied land?

[4] From Pandit Jagannatha's *Bhaminivilasa*, sixteenth century.

Divine, sublime, royal swan
Raised in Mansarovar, how do you live here?
Pure lotus bloom, the wasps hovering around you
Sup of your nectar, and drink your fragrance
The wind carries your scent and pollen,
Scattering it across the mountains
You who were raised in Mansarovar find yourself
In a frog-infested puddle, my fallen swan
Raised in Mansarovar, how do you live here?

Your wellbeing is drowned by someone else's self-indulgence. You never knew this would happen, did you, Sarasvatichandra? You did wrong! Your learning is worthless!

His mind was afire, as if the unrest of his heart had passed like electricity to his mind. Navinchandra, a vagabond wayfarer, slept in a large bed made for him in the drawing room of the Counsellor of Suvarnapur. He shivered in the cold, covered himself with a thick blanket, and exhausted by his emotions and excitement, finally surrendered himself to sleep. All members of the Counsellor's family slept, and it felt as if Suvarnapur itself was asleep. Kumud Sundari's body lay with her husband; her heart trailed the body, and finally she too succumbed to a tormented sleep. Alak Kishori slept in the room above the courtyard. The doors of the room were shut. She was in deep slumber. In her dream-state, her husband timidly asked her, 'Why did you sleep there?' She carelessly replied, 'Whether I sleep here or there, what is it to you?' Even before this dream was over, another joined itself with the previous one. Alak saw herself enacting the scenes from *Meghdoot,* that she had heard Kumud narrate, with Krishna Kalika. When Krishna Kalika responded to her amorous play, she scolded her.

The Counsellor's house was peaceful for about an hour. Some windows opened out onto a street outside the house. A handful of men had been observed loitering around there since eight or nine in the evening. Krishna Kalika had timidly apprised Alak Kishori of this; but the Counsellor's daughter had paid scant regard to it.

She did not realise that small incidents can sometimes have large consequences.

Some time ago, Alak Kishori had made a face at Khalaknanda and Rupali while they were sauntering about with their paramours. She had also told a few of her female companions her reasons for doing so, and had then forgotten about the incident. But Khalaknanda had not forgotten. She was also a proud daughter of a Karbhari, and not much younger than Saubhagya Devi. She saw Alak Kishori as an upstart. Some women had told her that Alak Kishori was encouraged by her mother. Hitherto, no one had the courage to say anything to Khalaknanda's face; but they did tell her what Alak Kishori had to say about her. Imprudent as she was, Alak Kishori had also haughtily said that her father was going to be the new Karbhari. So the rivalry between the Karbhari and the Counsellor had now filtered down to the women and children of both families.

Saubhagya Devi was a pious woman. Her daughter had inherited this quality. But there was a difference: Alak Kishori was self-righteous about her piety, and openly showed her disdain for the debauched women of the Karbhari household. She ruled over her husband, but did not care for any other man. Khalaknanda and Rupali were so incensed by this slight that they were determined to crush Alak Kishori's pride. Rupali suggested a plan that Khalaknanda agreed to. They incited Jamal Khan, who gladly accepted the challenge; he believed that no one could check him. He thought he would kill two birds with one stone. He was dazzled by Alak Kishori's beauty and wanted to possess her just as he had Khalaknanda. He was now being presented with this very opportunity. He hatched a foolish plan to abduct Alak Kishori on her way to her husband's from her father's house. To this end, Jamal Khan had been loitering around the Counsellor's residence, along with three-four accomplices. Alak Kishori did not return to her husband's house that evening. They waited till midnight, and by one in the morning, his accomplices had left the scene.

Jamal Khan was also about to leave for home, when a plan came into his seething mind. Nothing could be worse than returning empty-handed, he thought. All this anticipation, this excitement would come to naught. All my brazen desires will go waste if I do not lay my hands on this fair damsel tonight. Every day, I chase thieves. Tonight, I shall be a thief myself. And he decided to scale the walls of the Counsellor's house. Going around to the back of the house, he looked up at the roof, and saw a way in. He twirled his moustache as if in preparation, and began to climb. My friends proved effete, thought Jamal Khan. If they had stayed, they too would have shared in the fun. But leave them be to their fate. Good that they are gone!

It was a dark night. Cautiously, climbing on all fours, he reached the roof. An owl hooted as it suddenly flew into his face on soft and silent wings. A bad omen, he thought, and threw a tile at it in anger. Come on, Jamal Khan, he reassured himself, What's a bad omen to a Miyanbhai! He was now on the roof of the Counsellor's house. Standing up, he looked around and saw no one. But far away, he espied a shadowy figure. Must be a thief, he thought. Let's catch the bugger. But what do I get anyway? Forget it. I will get Alak Kishori. What a name! Alak Kishori. Alak Kishori! *Alak Kishori*! All right, this is all very well, but how do I enter the house? He slowly climbed down to the terrace. A window had been left open. He crouched and entered the room. Fortuitously for him, even the door to the staircase was left open! Jamal Khan came down the steps as if it were his own house, and soon, Shathrai's lowly Musalman soldier stood before the bed of the Counsellor's daughter.

A castor-oil lamp burned in a niche. Like a tigress on a river bank, Alak Kishori lay resplendent upon her bed in the full bloom of her youth. The blanket she used to cover herself with had been flung aside, as if the cold dared not touch her. Her carefully arranged clothes had fallen out of place. The pleats of her sari unfurled between her legs like a rivulet flowing through the crevices of a hillock. The lamp threw her face and bosom into relief. The lamplight flickered, revealing glimpses of the beauty hidden in shadows, suggesting enchanting possibilities. The vision was captivating. Her long arms stretched out on either side of her, like wings. She looked fierce even in her sleep. It was as if the image of Ma Chandi about to slay the demon Mahishaasura was sculpted on the bed. Jamal Khan could not muster the courage to even touch Alak Kishori.

Womankind, if you are determined, your splendour and radiance are immeasurable. Men lack the courage to take advantage of your vulnerability and violate your virtue. A single chaste, fiery glance from you is enough to keep the evil intentions of men at bay. This power is uniquely yours. Its use is a matter of your discretion and will. Alak Kishori's eyes were shut. But like a serpent protecting precious jewels, her serpentine eyebrows protected her virtue. The Turk stood petrified—his arrogance and lust had no power over his movements now. An attack on virtue takes time.

The Khan, though dandily dressed, was in attire which did not hamper his plans. He wore a beautiful Delhi-style cap of black velvet embroidered with zardozi over which he had draped a cloth that concealed his face. He had groomed his moustache and beard with perfumed oil. Being winter, he wore a woollen jacket with silver buttons, cut foppishly. He wore his dhoti tight and carried a small dagger tied at his waist. His shoes were English in style, but of local make. He had put kohl in his eyes, perfumed cotton in his ears, and sprinkled rosewater on his kerchief. He had washed and brightened his face. He was confident the damsel would find his youthful charms irresistible and become instantly infatuated with him. Khalaknanda had however warned him that this might not be, and had urged him to use force; he was prepared to, if she resisted. He believed that a mere woman was powerless before a man. He also carried a small thick black stick. Thus attired, arms crossed over his chest, legs grounded far apart, he stood close to the sleeping Alak Kishori's bed, stupefied. He looked at the gorgeous form of this woman sleeping without a care before him, and his moist eyes shone with carnal passion. The awareness of place, time and power aroused him, and his mind and body were aflame with a terrible yearning. The lines between rapturous pleasure and unbearable agony grew blurred. Allah! What beauty! This divine face ... these rosy cheeks ... Allah! This is unbearable! Khalaknanda is nothing in comparison to this one. Come, my beautiful!

He extended an ardent hand, and saw himself confidently climbing into her bed—but his courage failed him. He just kept standing there and staring at her, trying to think of his next move. His desire was aflame, but his joy was abject; his sensuousness stilled, his eyes glazed over, his legs trembled and he felt feeble from head to toe. There was no one there to prevent him from jumping onto the bed. But the sleeping Alak Kishori's face was flushed with such radiance that the lecherous wretch could not bear her resplendence—he could not approach her fire.

God knows what is happening, Jamal heard himself say, but I haven't the audacity to step any closer. He had entered the palatial house of the Counsellor all by himself. If the Counsellor comes to know, what will become of me?

Then Alak Kishori turned on her side. Her face was now turned away from him. All his qualms, his hesitation suddenly evaporated. His lust raised its fierce hood again, and Jamal Khan remembered Khalaknanda's command. He silently removed his shoes and climbed into the bed. He lay against her side, unmoving and hesitant initially. But not for long.

The Counsellor's daughter woke up startled as if she had been singed by fire. Reacting even before she was fully awake, she flung away the offensive hands and feet which assailed her and leapt out of bed. This happened in the blink of an eye before she was even fully possessed of her senses. She tucked in her sari at her waist and glared at the beast in her bed with raging eyes. She screamed in wrath and fear, 'Who is it? Wake up! Pramadbhai! Bapuji! Wake up! Thief! Thief!'

Jamal Khan composed himself, sat up and said, 'My beloved, it is me, Jamal. Do not be afraid. I am so besotted with you that I had to visit you on this dark night.'

Kishori was somewhat less frightened, but her legs still trembled. '*You*!? Jamaliya, you rascal! Get up and get out, or I will teach you a good lesson. Do you take me for your Khalaknanda!'

'Bai Sahib, do calm down, my sweet beloved.'

'You beast! I will cut off your tongue if you say more. I'm calling everyone,' and regaining her courage, she walked to the window. Recognising danger, Jamal braced himself. Persuasion didn't work. So he caught her by the arm to stop her from approaching the window, saying, 'Wait ...'

'Leave my hand!' Alak Kishori pulled herself free. But he caught her again and clasped her neck, 'Why are you doing this, my love? Just wait ...'

Alak Kishori looked full at him, her eyes ablaze. She held his gaze briefly, then freeing her neck from his loathsome grasp, she drew herself up to her full height and clenching her teeth and her fist into a tight ball, she punched Jamal full on the mouth. She looked down, almost expecting Mother Earth to say, 'Oh good! Well done!' Jamal was momentarily dazed, his mouth stung by the unexpected blow. In anger, he grabbed her from the back. He was a powerful Musalman. She could not free herself from his grip, but did not lose courage and started screaming for help. Jamal pressed his hand over her mouth, but she screamed louder whenever his grip relaxed even slightly: 'Bhai! Bapuji! Ma! Help me! O Help!' There was an intense scuffle. Who knows from where Alak Kishori found the strength to not succumb. She tried to hit him hard on the chin, the face and the nose with her head every chance she got. Sometimes she succeeded; other times he fended off the blows. At some point Jamal Khan started chasing her around the room. Neither accepted defeat.

Below them, there was a huge commotion in the house. Alak Kishori's first scream had already roused the family. Each one tried to determine the source of the cry. Buddhidhan's first thought was that Shathrai's men had breached his house with murderous intent. Navinchandra heard the cry, 'Thief!' Startled awake, Kumud Sundari hurriedly woke up her husband. They thought the house was on fire. Saubhagya Devi recognised her daughter's voice and she rushed out onto the terrace. The servants ran out into the courtyard, looking up in the direction of the floor above and questioned each other about the source of the commotion. Those asleep on the first floor assembled on the terrace. Pramaddhan opened the door to the staircase. Gathering at the entrance to Alak's room, people shouted, asking her to open the door. Saubhagya Devi banged on Alak's window to force it open. Next to his wife, Buddhidhan shouted, 'Alak, don't be afraid! We are here!'. Kumud Sundari stood behind everyone else, shaking with fear. Navinchandra tried to make his way to the front through the sea of servants. Buddhidhan, helped by a few servants, tried to force open Alak's door. Pramaddhan, accompanied by a few others, climbed down to find another way into her room. In the meantime, Kumud shouted, 'That window up there is open; he must have climbed in from it.' Navinchandra heard this. He had learnt to climb and jump in the gymnasium. He looked at Kumud, tied his dhoti between his legs, and climbed up nimbly onto the roof. He saw the staircase, Alak Kishori's lit room and heard all the noises coming from it.

Inside the room, pit against the strength of a Musalman soldier, Alak Kishori was visibly tiring and running out of breath. But somehow, with tremendous effort, she kept dragging Jamal nearer to the lamp. The evil Turk realised that the others were closing in on him and that there was no way out. He was grimly resigned to face whatever consequences there may be. He also realised that those on the outside were unable to find a way in. This made him more brazen, and he became unrestrained and utterly vile. The use of physical force only heightened his sexual pleasure. Then suddenly, like a lamp dispelling darkness, an idea providentially came to Alak in a flash and she knew she was saved. As they neared the oil lamp, she swiftly pulled at Jamal's dhoti and set it on fire. As it caught fire, he let go of her. Sensing victory, Alak ran towards the door, but she didn't reach it—throwing off his burning dhoti along with his dagger, Jamal Khan leapt onto Alak before she could reach the door and pinned her down. Alak was completely helpless now. Her strength, her will to fight deserted her as she realised her subjugation. She lost the capacity to think and became numb. Her body was defiled at many places. Her sari had come undone during the scuffle and lay upon the floor, pleading with

Mother Earth for succour. Jamal climbed on top of her like a tiger on a cow. He caught her arms and said, 'Beloved, do not be afraid.' The moon was eclipsed by shadows. As she fell, disconsolate, Alak let out a heartrending wail: 'Hai! O Ma! He has killed me!' No one had heard such an anguished cry before. Their desperation mounted and the commotion around the window increased palpably, if in vain. The evil beast knew that no one was capable of breaking into the room; there was no one to stop him now. Alak's tired hands were locked in a desperate struggle with his around the knot that held her petticoat in place. A moment's delay and her virtue was certain to be violated, a permanent blot on God's hands. Saubhagya Devi was hysterical and prayed fervently to the Goddess.

God is the final refuge of the helpless. Buddhidhan had always staunchly believed this. Either the merits he had accrued or Saubhagya Devi's prayers were responsible for what followed. Just at that critical moment, Navinchandra rushed down the staircase and landed a fierce kick on Jamal's back, stunning the soldier. Then he grabbed the cloth around Jamal's neck and pulled so hard that Jamal feared he would choke, and he let go of Alak Kishori. Navinchandra dragged him further away from her; but Jamal put his hand between the cloth and his neck so the noose would not tighten, then he turned around and broke free from Navinchandra's clutches with a mighty heave. Navinchandra shouted out to those outside, 'Don't worry! I have saved behn!' Her family members could breathe again. But in this interlude, Jamal Khan saw his chance—and he flew at Alak Kishori, who had barely regained some of her composure. At this renewed attack, she screamed in panic and dismay: 'Navinchandrabhai, save me!' and she ran and clung to him from behind. Navinchandra stood between them, shielding the doe-eyed one from the tiger's paws. Jamal Khan was disappointed and could see no way out. Suddenly, he spotted his dagger and rushed to grab it. At the same moment, Alak Kishori let go of Navinchandra and made a dash for the door. Those on the outside were pressed against it and nearly tumbled into the room when she opened it. The Turk had leapt up the staircase, but

Navinchandra grabbed his leg and Jamal Khan fell hard, but as he fell he managed to plunge his dagger into Navinchandra's shoulder.

Saubhagya Devi was the first to enter the room. Her daughter rushed into her arms, crying, 'Oh, Devi!' Saubhagya Devi embraced and consoled her daughter who was sobbing uncontrollably. Buddhidhan and Pramaddhan stood close by, giving her strength. The servants caught hold of Jamal, who was sprawled on the ground. They kicked him in rage and held him so tight he could not move. Blows and kicks rained upon him mercilessly and he bore them in silence. Wounded by the dagger, Navinchandra lay inert upon the floor. He had lost much blood and had fainted. In all this melee, no one had noticed him. Only Jamal glared at him triumphantly even as he was being thrashed, saying to himself, Rascal, you deserved it! He looked longingly at Alak Kishori, and cursed the owl. He took solace in knowing he had touched her. In the struggle between the high and the low, the latter has nothing to lose; even in defeat, and even a slight gain to the low is like a two-fold loss to the high. When pure water meets filth, the filth is not cleansed; even if it is, it soils the water. This is as God wills it.

Jamal Khan was dragged onto the terrace and brought down to the courtyard. When questioned, he brazenly said that it was Alak Kishori who had invited him up. This further enraged everyone. After more thrashing, the soldier came to his senses and told them who had sent him, and why. Saubhagya Devi sat on the threshold of the room above, as Alak lay sobbing into her lap with relief, still shaken by what had happened. Kumud Sundari and Pramaddhan were by her side, while Buddhidhan paced around the terrace, deep in thought. Even through her sobs, Alak Kishori heard Jamal Khan's disclosure—and realised with shock that what had happened was the consequence of her own haughtiness. This heightened her distress no end.

All this while, Navinchandra lay unconscious and unnoticed, his blood flowing unchecked. Kumud Sundari searched for him everywhere but could not locate him in the commotion. Finally, she saw his deathly pale body lying on the floor. Seeing him in that state, terrible inauspicious thoughts filled her mind, tormenting her tremendously, but she could not share her feelings with anyone. In the end, her heart won out over social stricture. 'Oh God! Is this Navinchandra who is lying here?' she said aloud for the others to hear.

Hearing Kumud, Alak Kishori, too, forgot her woes, sorely repenting that she had allowed herself to forget even for a moment the timely kindness of the stranger. She got up and hurried towards Navinchandra. 'Oh Devi! He has a dagger wound and it bleeds! Come soon, Devi, oh come fast!', Alak urged her mother. The others gathered around. Kumud Sundari brought out the lamp and held it close to the body; she saw the wound and the spilled blood. Horrified and grief-struck, she quickly wiped her tears before anyone could see them. Keeping the lamp near the staircase so it would light the room better, she sat down next to Navinchandra's body, facing her sister-in-law. Looking intently at his unconscious face, unnoticed by anyone else, Kumud lightly touched his forehead.

Buddhidhan came in from the terrace. He at once instructed Pramaddhan, 'Go, quickly bring me a clean piece of cloth and tincture iodine.' He ordered a soldier, 'Go fetch the vaidya.' Tincture iodine, bought in Bombay, was kept in the house, but Pramaddhan was clueless as to its whereabouts. He rummaged about, asking, 'Where is the tincture? What is it like?' His sister got up. It was she who managed the household. She found the bottle, asked her brother to read the label, and brought it out; but they still could not find a clean rag. The houses of the rich have many fine cloths and garments, but no clean rags. While they took time searching for one, Buddhidhan grew angry. 'How long does it take you to find a rag?!' He looked at his own fine dhoti and thought of tearing it up. But before he could do so, like Draupadi had done for Krishna in *Mahabharat,* his young daughter-in-law tore a piece from her new sari, and hearing the cloth rip, Buddhidhan looked up at her. Buddhidhan and Pramaddhan applied the tincture to the wound and dressed it. The vaidya also arrived meanwhile. All this went on through the night. Regaining partial consciousness, Navinchandra moaned in pain. It was decided that he should be confined to bed in the Counsellor's house for a few days until he had recovered his strength completely. He was lifted and taken to another room. Quite naturally, all his care became Alak Kishori's responsibility.

Attention now turned to Jamal Khan. They had to ascertain his real intent and determine how best to use him at an opportune moment. If his deed were made public, it would disgrace the Counsellor considerably. There was a Rajput soldier named Samar Sen whom Buddhidhan trusted completely. They had come in contact during Buddhidhan's Agency days. The Rajput was immensely grateful to the man who had shielded him from the wrath of Buskin Sahib, and had hoped to return the favour some day. Buddhidhan had made him a caretaker and given him a room in a large building owned by the palace. The building had a cellar. Samar Sen was now ordered to take Jamal Khan there and keep him confined in secrecy.

Kumud Sundari was still uncertain if Navinchandra was Sarasvatichandra. But her heartfelt desire wished this to be true. She carefully preserved the torn garment.

'Bhabhi, go and take rest now. Devi and I will do what needs to be done,' Alak requested Kumud. Kumud was duty-bound not to show even the slightest attachment for a man who was a stranger to her. With herculean effort, she tore herself away and went and stood, forlorn, at the door of her room. Pramaddhan got up saying, 'Everyone is there. What more can we do now?' and he gently led her inside. They spent the rest of the night in bed. She lay beside him, but her mind was in the adjoining room. The time her husband spent in sleep, she spent in silent and fervent prayer. Sleep finally came; and morning dawned, too. She arose singing the *Gajendra Moksha,* and was overjoyed to see that Navinchandra had fully regained consciousness.

10 Instruments of Intrigue and the Warcraft of Karbharis

Navinchandra's care became Alak Kishori's responsibility. Murkhdutt visited often and asked after him. The vaidya administered medication. The servants performed their tasks. Saubhagya Devi stayed downstairs but came up once a day to ascertain his well-being. Pramaddhan read him the newspaper and looked in on him every time he would pass by. He would also sit and chat by Navinchandra's bed in the company of his friends. Buddhidhan visited him daily and spent some time talking with him. He had instructed the vaidya to report Navinchandra's progress to him daily. Kumud Sundari never missed an opportunity to visit him whenever he had someone else for company. She would come in, keep her distance, and return feeling glad at the progress made by the patient. She would often sit in the adjacent room and listen to Navinchandra converse or make polite talk with visitors. If those visiting Navinchandra were not strangers, Alak Kishori would sit by his side, nurse him, chatter away innocently, and include Kumud or others in the conversation. At times, the sisters-in-law, their guest and Pramaddhan would play a game of dice. In a short time, the guest became one of the Counsellor's family. His health improved. He no longer felt he was an outsider in a stranger's house. These were pleasant times of peace and quiet for the Counsellor's family. This was also around the time that the palace intrigues were at their height; and Navinchandra felt it was his misfortune that he was unable to witness this first hand. Rumours flew thick and fast; some even found their way to his chamber.

Since the incident with Jamal Khan, Buddhidhan had lost his equanimity. He imagined its roots to be much deeper than they actually were. Jamal Khan was held captive in the cellar. A clandestine search for him had been mounted. A worried Khalaknanda had incited her brother and compelled him to take certain actions. Buddhidhan had foreseen these events and was eager to turn the outcome to his favour. He could now clearly see on the horizon the advent of the day when he would need to confront Shathrai openly. The spark that Shathrai had lit by insulting the piety of his mother and Saubhagya Devi still smouldered within him; Shathrai's intrigues had stoked the fire which burnt like live coal. The insufferable insult to Alak Kishori had added fuel to it, and fanned by Buddhidhan's intellect, this fire of enmity now encircled Shathrai's family and his Karbhar. Buddhidhan could also see his sun rise to its zenith. Kindly Dayashankar had taken the words spoken in anger by the young son of a poor widow to be the ranting of a sick, delirious boy. That affectionate man was still alive, though old and decrepit. Buddhidhan felt that what Dayashankar had laughed at was about to be realised, and it gave him pleasure. If only mother were still alive, what a support she would have been! At times, he felt that her absence would be the only blemish on his ascendant joy. But the thought that he would finally be able to complete his mother's shraadha would make the son emotional. His mind was in a whirl and each day caused new ripples. This sea of emotions was made stormy by the insult to his beloved daughter. That night, as Jamal was being beaten up, when Alak Kishori lay numb and sobbing in her mother's lap, Buddhidhan had been pacing up and down the terrace like a tiger, eyebrows raised, one hand twirling his moustache, muttering aloud, Beware Shathrai! I am no longer weaponless! In that commotion, no one had heard him or seen his expression in the dark.

One morning, Buddhidhan woke up early. Usually Saubhagya Devi always rose before him, but that day she continued to sleep. He sat up in bed and looked at her face. He felt that his debt was still unpaid as her insult remained unavenged. Her delicate lotus eyes, her long black hair spread across the pillow, her glorious forehead, her full lips and fair delicate checks roused him. Her appearance had changed over the years, but her beauty remained undiminished. Buddhidhan was overcome with affection for her. But he felt that his affection, too, was a charade as long as the insult remained unavenged. He decided there and then to remove this blot for good and raised his hand in promise, speaking softly so as not to wake her, 'Devi! Don't take me to be a coward. Now when you hear a battle cry, you shall see my hand raised!' He laughed and cupping her face gently in his hands, he bent over her and kissed her on the lips, and the nectar spread into her soul through them. She woke up smiling, and responded passionately to his kiss. Buddhidhan felt this was a beautiful and auspicious beginning to his campaign. He got up with renewed vigour and enthusiasm to set about his mission. This forceful stream merged with his ever-growing desire to obtain the Karbhar.

On the other side, Shathrai had also decided to eliminate Buddhidhan. He had been a Karbhari for many years and his power had remained unchallenged. He was determined not to tolerate this thorn in his side anymore. He no longer feared Bhupsinh, but he had grown to fear Buddhidhan. This fear was deep-rooted. So long as he feared the Rana, the fear of the Counsellor had remained suppressed. Shathrai considered Bhupsinh insignificant, but Buddhidhan was potentially death itself. Shathrai was determined to annihilate him. He was also prepared to deal with Bhupsinh if he foiled his plan. Shathrai had already begun his preparations.

It is known that one scabbard cannot contain two swords. So long as Buddhidhan and Shathrai remained deferential to each other, the situation remained under control. But ambition breeds opposition. Their hostility was hitherto concealed. But times had changed, and Buddhidhan felt that his foundations were now deep and secure—a structure could be built upon it. Shathrai had fathomed Buddhidhan's anxiety; he felt that Buddhidhan's cunning was precisely what would play Bhupsinh into his hands. Shathrai felt he could easily drive a wedge between the two. The Karbhari was a past master at intrigue and adept in the use of various machinations. His conscience never impeded his actions; he had much wealth and many supporters. Shathrai also believed that Bhupsinh's benevolence, Buddhidhan's own God-given intelligence and the fruits thereof, a few truly devoted men, and some money were all the means at Buddhidhan's disposal. He believed in fact that he could crush Buddhidhan as easy as a bed bug.

Shathrai's brother Karvatrai was the chief judge of the state; appeals against his judgment went to Rana Bhupsinh. The Counsellor sat in on the appeals alongside the Rana, and his opinion prevailed. Appeals were heard in the afternoon. This also gave the Rana and the Counsellor an opportunity to spend time together. Initially, Buddhidhan did not intervene in the process. But as the time for open conflict neared, more and more of Karvatrai's judgements were reversed. As a result, the bribes that Karvatrai received also started drying up. Shathrai sought to remedy this situation.

Dushtarai had brought a courtesan named Kalavati to Suvarnapur from Bombay. She was delicate, slender, fair and beautiful. She also sang melodiously. One day, she was invited to the palace for a performance. The Rana liked her singing. She soon became a regular feature of the court, and on the suggestion of some courtiers, began to stay back after the performance. The Rana did not object. In this small group, the appreciation moved from her singing to her shamelessly exhibited body. The foolish Rana would listen to this talk with interest, gazing enrapt upon her while she sang or danced, as if she had possessed him. He could not say much as he feared Buddhidhan's censure. One day, in Buddhidhan's absence, Kalavati's beauty was much appreciated and a palace servant named Mahvo, who was one of Shathrai's men, took upon himself the task of ensuring that the courtesan would soon present herself in the Rana's service. The Rana did not object, and one afternoon Kalavati was brought to the palace. The palace was defiled, the body of the ruler of Suvarnapur became impure, and his mind corrupted. The people of Suvarnapur now had to contend with a lowly debauched woman as the consort of their Rana. Bhupsinh started having an aversion to the task of dispensing justice every afternoon and presiding over courtly matters. The hangers-on fathomed this. The Rana's personal secretary Nichdas broached the subject with him: 'Ranaji, God has not made you for such drudgery; let the Counsellor do that work.' But who would tell the Counsellor this? Nichdas apprised Shathrai of this situation.

In Buddhidhan's presence, Jagabhai, the court bard, found occasion to sing this poem:

> *O great and benevolent Rana Bhup:*
> *Your virtues and beauty are unmatched,*
> *To the care of your people night and day*
> *You devote your time, money and all,*
> *You have forgotten the simple joys of leisure and pleasure*
> *O great and benevolent Rana Bhup, you must now become a lion!*
> *You must hunt daily and in beautiful dense forests, roar!*
> *Be the King of the forest, O Rana, for what more need a ruler do?*

The bard stood with folded hands and said, 'O benevolent Ranaji Bhup, Saviour of the poor, the likes of me must deal with daily drudgery. But to see *you* toil thus—how can this be!'

Buddhidhan was astonished and looked at the bard with suspicion. The bard did not meet his gaze.

Shathrai: 'But Jagabhai, he has to rule, a king cannot be idle. Should he not dispense justice?'

Jagabhai: 'My lord, if the Ranaji has to break his head over such things, what is a trusted and capable Counsellor for?'

With incidents like this, the grounds were laid, and Bhupsinh became less and less interested in matters of court and governance. In the afternoon he would send a message to Buddhidhan saying, 'You begin—I will join in.' He would eventually make an appearance, to put his signature on a few documents. Buddhidhan observed all this. Shathrai had not yet displaced him in the Rana's affections, but the die was cast. Buddhidhan came to know that Kalavati visited the palace every afternoon, so he inquired into her past. She spent afternoons with the Rana, and Dushtarai spent nights with her. The Rana spent the money, so Dushtarai enjoyed himself for free. Merulo too was happy. He boasted to Narbheram, who informed the Counsellor. Gradually, the Rana became brazen, and an attendant named Raghi Khavasan remained in attendance while the Rana was alone with Kalavati. Raghi served Kalavati, and became their favourite.

Raghi was having an affair with Mahva. He was cunning but felt helpless in face of his desire for Raghi; he would tell her everything. Mahva was debauched, while Raghi was greedy for money and ornaments. Raghi was foolish and playful, but she recognised Mahva's vulnerability and managed to cheat him, scold him, rob him and have her way with him. The palace gave them ample opportunity to do as they pleased; such are the houses of the high and the mighty. In Shathrai's house, Raghi Khavasan was feted. Taking the lead, Narbheram would quietly counsel her: 'Bitch, you should be around to serve in every possible way when the Rana and Kalavati are alone together. This will earn you money; and someday you can also become a queen.' Raghi took him seriously, and we know well what the outcome of that would be. Raghi felt beholden to Narbheram, and told him everything she heard. Even then, she did not divulge what Mahva had told her. One day Narbheram said: 'Bitch, Mahvo can be said to be truly devoted to you only the day he brings you the nose-ring that the queen gave his wife. Otherwise, you are just a keep.' Raghi said excitedly: 'Of course he will!' However, there was no way Mahva's wife would give him the nose-ring. Mahva made excuses and reasoned with Raghi, but she did not budge. Narbheram would goad her in glee, 'You deserve it. My Mahvo, my Mahvo, you would keep singing. But he proved otherwise. Time alone is the true test of things.'

Raghi could not break off relations with Mahva, but a wedge was driven between them. She now began to confide in Narbheram even things that Mahva would tell her. The Rana had a one-eyed usher named Ranjit. Before Merulo, he had been Rupali's paramour. When the affair became known to him, Dushtarai decided to kill Ranjit. This was long ago, even before Buddhidhan had moved to Lilapur. In those days, Buddhidhan occasionally visited Shathrai's house. It was here that he had come to know of Dushtarai's intentions; Buddhidhan had then warned Ranjit and showed him a way out of this difficulty. Accordingly, Ranjit had met Shathrai and pleaded, 'Sir, my enemies have spread lies about me to Dushtarai. Have mercy on me and transfer me out of here. If not, I will have to resign.' Dushtarai could not divulge the real reason, and so he had let Ranjit go, saying, 'Wretch, let him rot elsewhere'. This transfer eventually led to his becoming an usher. Ranjit was still grateful to Buddhidhan and remained a close supporter. Buddhidhan, through Samar Sen, taught him the next step: Ranjit flirted with Raghi, which resulted in their affair. Raghi Khavasan was also the favourite of the queens. Mahva's secrets now began to tumble out one by one.

And thus, through his intellect, the Rana's court, the queen's quarters, the palace intrigues, all became transparent before Buddhidhan. The Counsellor now believed he knew all that Kalavati did and said. So far, Shathrai had used her only to corrupt the Rana, for circumstances were not yet ripe for more. Then, she began to say things like, 'We are condemned for our profession. But aren't there women worse than us in the Rana's harem? I have heard rumours—only God knows their veracity—who can talk about the queens? I have heard things about Rajba ...,' and gradually Kalavati became increasingly brazen in her utterances.

Finally, Buddhidhan went to the palace one morning with the letters that Narbheram had obtained for him. He threw them into the Rana's lap and said tearfully, 'I thought of Rajba like a mother. I tremble at these letters. Read them. Shathrai will send them to you through Mahva. If you have even a sliver of doubt, I will resign, and will remain content to see you rise.'

The Rana was moved. He got up and wiped his old friend's tears. He said, 'Buddhidhan, I have absolute faith in you. I owe my present to you. Let these forged letters be brought before me. I will hang the one who brings them. Why don't you finish off Shathrai right now?'

Buddhidhan took back the letters and advised, 'Take the letters that Mahva gives you. Pretend that you believe them all to be true. Show that you utterly detest me and are entirely willing to do Shathrai's bidding.' And giving the Rana some other necessary instructions, Buddhidhan went home.

That afternoon, when Mahva presented the letters to the Rana, Bhupsinh appeared duly outraged, he roared and vowed to destroy Buddhidhan. He called for Shathrai and confided in him. Shathrai was secretly overjoyed, and promised to ensure that the Rana would never have to see Buddhidhan's face again. The Rana said, 'Prepare someone who can take over the Counsellor's responsibilities. Ensure that Buddhidhan remains in the dark until we have succeeded in our plans.' The Karbhari thought for a while and said, 'Appoint Narbheram as your Hazoor Secretary. That was Buddhidhan's first post as well; he will not suspect this appointment, and Narbheram will soon learn on the job.' This was done.

The cycle of the new moon of Chaitra began a few days later. It was decided to bring everything out in the open on that day when the full court was assembled. Shameless Garbaddas had taken it upon himself to prove that Buddhidhan had accepted bribes in judicial work. Mahva's brother Khodo had worked for a time in the postal department at Lilapur. It was decided that he would make Rajba and Buddhidhan's letters public. He concocted a story about how he had come to be in possession of those letters. Narbheram was to provide testimony in this matter. It was decided that the enraged Rana would then order Buddhidhan's arrest and the confiscation of his house. The Rana was told that he should depute Karvatrai to judge the charges against Buddhidhan. Dushtarai whispered to the Rana, 'Once Buddhidhan is arrested, we will present all three women of his house to you. They are very beautiful.' The Rana shuddered, but managed to hide his discomfiture. On their way back from the palace, Shathrai advised Karvatrai: 'Why should you have to do all these things? The Political Agent might poke his nose into this matter. We will persuade Ranjit, Mahva and the others to finish him off. People will think he committed suicide. We will tell the Rana that even in death, Rajba was saved from public disgrace. This will work—short and swift.

Buddhidhan dead, the Rana in Kalavati's clutches, and we will arrange a son for one of the queens; what more could we want?' They plotted to keep a few pregnant women in the service of the queens so that a son could be easily foisted on the throne when the need arose, and the mishap with Jadsinh's queen could be averted. Shathrai was certain that the Creator had destined that son Dushtarai would follow him as a Karbhari. A queen with an imposter son: both queen and son would remain under his thumb. The child's birth was thus celebrated even before the wedding!

The first day of Chaitra was also Rana Bhupsinh's birthday. The full court assembled twice that day, once in the morning and again in the evening. It was decided that Buddhidhan would be stripped of his post and power during the morning assembly. He was to be arrested as soon as he emerged from the palace. Dushtarai was made responsible for this part of the plan. He was told, 'Your soldiers should walk with him for a time and accord him full respect and honour; he should be allowed to move about freely. He should be taken out from behind the palace.' The rear part of the palace had a large garden with a maze. The meandering lanes were covered with creepers which created dark spaces, where birds were kept. During Jadsinh's reign, queens, palace servants, officials and courtiers all had their places of assignation in the maze. Behind the maze stood a Shiva temple. Women worshippers were lured, coerced, tricked, and even abducted and brought into the maze. Rana Jadsinh had himself taken part in the debaucheries of his courtiers and committed immoral acts here. During Bhupsinh's reign, Buddhidhan had put an end to all these activities. This route was now used only by Kalavati. At the centre of the maze was a shallow pond. It was decided that Buddhidhan should be led towards this pond, where Ranjit and Mahva would attack him from behind, throw him into a ditch and strangle him to death. His body should then be thrown into the pond; thereafter Ranjit and Mahva should retrieve him and pretend to revive him. It should be declared that disgraced beyond redemption, Buddhidhan had committed suicide, and his body should be cremated immediately, they decided. It was also decided that Shathrai should make a show of excessive grief and mourning.

Raghi divulged the entire plan to Ranjit, who naturally forewarned Buddhidhan. But Buddhidhan doubted Ranjit. The Rana was, after all, a Garasia—could he really be trusted to play his part? Moreover, he was also in Kalavati's clutches. And could his ever faithful fiercely loyal Narbheram be trusted not to change sides in such dark times? Mired in mistrust, doubts, fear and anxiety, the Counsellor lost sleep. He worried night and day about the fate that awaited his precious Devi and the children.

A broken hut, a wan wife,
Wasted children: Will I ever see them again?

Saubhagya Devi knew the *Sudamacharita* by heart. One day, Buddhidhan heard her and Vanleela sing stanzas from it. Overwrought as he was, his eyes welled up with sudden tears at the familiar words. He got up, washed his face and went back to work. Navinchandra observed all these happenings from his sick bed. He did not understand all of it, but was nevertheless surprised and he felt a growing empathy for Buddhidhan. Although emotionally distraught, Buddhidhan never once lost his patience. His genius did not wane, his intellect was not blunted. A lofty mind is not brittle; although delicate, it withstands worldly blows. It is aesthetically endowed and possessed of a refined sensibility which sharpens the intellect. Lofty minds are neither crass nor coarse; they are supple and subtle. A sword can suppress a cotton ball but cannot cut it down. If cut, it can be woven together again. An object that falls onto a hard rock either remains intact or shatters irrevocably. But when an object falls into water, the water parts momentarily and makes way for it, only to regain its original state. It is not that weapons do not wound the Gods, but their wounds heal on their own. Buddhidhan's inner core was not immune to attack, but it had over time become ever more alert, agile and resilient.

> Harder even than adamant and softer than a flower are the hearts of the super-eminent persons; who can correctly gauge them?[1]

When he thought of his family, Buddhidhan's heart was softer than a flower. When he thought of his worldly engagements, it became harder than stone; it hissed like a snake when gripped by revenge and turned into a raging ball of fire when confronted with the evil of Shathrai and his group. As he considered the future, his heart prepared for the ultimate sacrifice. Now that war was inevitable, he became hungry for battle. Taking stock of his enemy's position, he grew eager in anticipation as he saw that his heart's oldest desires were about to bear fruit. Buddhidhan was pleased that his rise was imminent, and his mind opened itself to receive the rays of the glorious rising sun.

As the first day of Chaitra drew closer, the Bombay newspapers published a series of articles on Suvarnapur. The newspaper columns were full of stories about Shathrai's administration, his tyranny, the urgent need for reform, his disastrous influence over Rana Bhupsinh, and rumours about Kalavati. The English newspapers did not accept articles from readers, but their letters to the editor were printed. The Karbhari camp read these articles and accused the Counsellor of inciting the newspapers. Narbheram pointed out, 'This must be shown to the Rana. It is unbecoming of the Counsellor.' Shathrai agreed, and Narbheram began to present and read out these newspaper clippings before the Rana daily. The Rana appeared angry; several times, Narbheram almost felt that the anger was genuine. The Rana was hurt by references to Kalavati.

Buddhidhan had managed to get some articles inserted, and he had kept the Rana informed about this. But the Rana was surprised by Buddhidhan's capacity to create this big a storm. Buddhidhan had also told him that he was not the one behind the Kalavati story, but he

[1] M. R. Kale, trans. *The Uttararamacharita of Bhavabhuti*, Act II, Verse 7, 5th ed. (Motilal Banarsidass, 1934), 19.

realised that on this matter, the Rana did not trust him. This was one reason for Buddhidhan's own mistrust of the Garasia.

The populace of Suvarnapur also sent petitions and pleas to the Rana. Narbheram did not allow them to be placed before Bhupsinh, and kept Shathrai informed of his actions. Shathrai's trust in Narbheram was now sealed.

It so happened that a bania had sent a petition to the English Sahib regarding an injustice done to him by the judge Karvatrai. The Government had sent that petition to the Agency, which in turn had sent it on to the Rana for remarks and clarifications. Narbheram, who was the Huzoor Secretary of the palace, sent this petition to the Karbhari. Acting at Shathrai's behest, Narbheram put the bania in the dungeons, and got him to sign a letter stating that injustice had been done to him by the palace. The letter was sent to the Government, while the bania remained imprisoned.

Buddhidhan had arranged for copies of the petition, the letter and newspaper clippings to be sent directly to the Sahib. He sent the bania's wife to Lilapur, from where she filed another petition. Buskin Sahib had been transferred to a different province. Buddhidhan corresponded with him regularly and updated him on the challenges he faced. Buskin Sahib promised to mitigate his troubles. He also assured Buddhidhan that he would write to Russell Sahib and intercede on Buddhidhan's behalf. Buskin Sahib's wife was soon to return from England. She was to pass through Lilapur. Buddhidhan, along with Pramaddhan, met her. Madam Sahib arranged for his meeting with Russell Sahib, and Buddhidhan acquainted him with the goings-on in Suvarnapur. Satisfied with his explanations, Russell Sahib said, 'When the need arises ask me; I will protect you.' Buddhidhan also met Russell Sahib's wife, whom he presented with sweets and dry fruits. As Bhupsinh had changed his mind about meeting the Sahib after Kalavati's entry in his life, acting as the Rana's emissary, Buddhidhan presented the Sahib with a letter from the Rana. In his response, the Sahib praised Buddhidhan.

Suvarnapur palace had appointed an advocate as its representative in Lilapur. This advocate sent false and exaggerated reports to the palace daily. He wrote with great flourish that he had spent two hours with the Sahib where the Karbhari and his administration were praised, and so on and so forth. He also reported the Counsellor's meeting with the Sahib to Shathrai, in which he stated that the Counsellor had not been accorded any honour or respect by the Sahib. Shathrai was pleased. Buddhidhan had no interest in dispelling these rumours. Both the English Madams had gifted the Counsellor signed portraits. He showed these, along with Russell Sahib's letter, to the Rana and expressed his satisfaction at the honours accorded him. The Rana was reassured that Buddhidhan's prestige in the Agency was intact, and that he could have his way there. The Counsellor believed that by demonstrating his influence over the newspapers and the Sahib, he would continue to wield power over Bhupsinh. He was right.

Buddhidhan had no intentions of attacking Shathrai directly: his ploy was to lead Shathrai into the grave that he had dug for Buddhidhan, and for this the wheels had already been set in motion. On the day of the assembly, he needed to shield himself from intrigue. Therefore, he had also ensured that Dushtarai's police would come nowhere near him that day. He could not take anything for granted in these difficult times. It fell to Navinchandra to ensure that on the eve of the first day of Chaitra, the English newspapers would print favourable stories about the Counsellor. Navinchandra was now strong enough to sit up, and accepted the responsibility enthusiastically. He was eager to witness the court assemble on the first day of Chaitra, health permitting; Buddhidhan was also in favour of his attendance at the palace.

Narbheram was charged with ensuring that Dushtarai would be required to rush home at the critical juncture. The idea was that in absence of their chief, his men would hesitate before attacking Buddhidhan. Should this not happen, Buddhidhan had also kept a team of soldiers in readiness to subdue Dushtarai's men. Samar Sen's older brother Vijay Sen was the commander of a troop. In times of peace under the British rule, the army rotted and was used only for ceremonial purposes. Whenever the court assembled and canons were fired in celebration, a troop of soldiers remained present at the palace, with their swords drawn. It was decided that Vijay Sen and his men would be present at the palace. Vijay Sen was unaware of the tumultuous events that were to take place that day. Buddhidhan had ordered Samar Sen to remain close to him during the assembly, and had briefed him on the instructions to be passed on to Vijay Sen, if the need arose. He also arranged for some trusted Rajput soldiers and Arab guards to be posted at his house while he was at court. They were instructed not to allow any stranger to enter the house until Buddhidhan returned from the assembly, and also to be wary of Dushtarai's men. The womenfolk were asked to remain confined to the house while Buddhidhan was away. These were routine arrangements, but the instructions given appeared extraordinary to the family. They had no inkling of what was to come, and many conjectures were made as they prepared to carry out their part of the instructions. Everyone awaited the outcome of these strange events.

This was the scenario on the dark last night of the month of Falgun. They waited for the new day to break to see what would unfold before it ended. Buddhidhan tossed and turned all night as if he slept in an airless room on a hot summer night. He stared at the ceiling continually. Even the comfort of Devi's bed gave him no respite that night. Finally at two o' clock, his overwrought mind and body succumbed to sleep. He slept rigidly, not so much as turning sides. Whether to ascertain if a heart gripped by the machinations of statecraft had any place for her in it, or to capture that heart for herself we do not know, but the sentient hand of the sleeping woman came to rest on the chest of her lifelong companion as he dreamed uneasily.

11 In Readiness for Court

The much awaited first day of Chaitra dawned at last. From early morning on, the homes of the courtiers were abuzz with activity. Shathrai bathed and dressed for the court. Narbheram was the first to arrive in attendance. Soldiers gathered noisily outside the Karbhari's house. Shathrai relaxed on a mattress, leaning against a bolster. A servant brought him his jacket and helped him into it. Shathrai called for a mirror, admired his reflection and sat twirling his moustache. Narbheram was pacing about. He watched the Karbhari and muttered to himself: Look at him gaze at his face in the mirror; his heart is bereft of compassion and righteousness. 'Oh God!' he sighed aloud and walked away shaking his head.

A group of policemen huddled outside Dushtarai's quarters. The Faujdar sat on his bed, while his wife fetched his clothes and helped him dress. As he got ready, Dushtarai flirted with Rupali, bragged about his own intelligence, and mocked Buddhidhan's fate. He spoke with much excitement and anticipation, 'Tonight, Alak Kishori, Kumud Sundari and Saubhagya Devi will be subjected to some fine treatment, and I will prove just what kind of a man I am.' His degenerate wife took delight in her husband's licentiousness as if she had attained the height of good fortune.

There was commotion all around. Everyone was busy chatting, roaming about aimlessly, showing their power, or obeying orders. Narbheram sought out Merulo. The soldier was busy folding

Khalaknanda's clothes. Narbheram sat down on a large upturned copper pot, untied the knot of his tuft and said: 'So, you are folding behn's clothes today.'

'Of course, one has to do it.'

'True, she is 'behn' after all.'

'How can that be denied.'

'Yes, these are your lucky days, you are a Krishna among the gopis. If you don't take advantage, you'd be a fool. Jamal has disappeared. So now you have two instead of one. Any news of Jamal?'

'Wretched Turk. Who knows where he rots. Good riddance!'

'But you changed the topic. You didn't tell me about your behn.'

'*Behn*? She might well be a sister to others, Narbheramhai, but I am clear about these things. Those older than I are like mothers to me, and those younger are sisters.'

'And those of the same age?'

'Those I can take. If Jamal can take her, I can, too.'

'Isn't Rupali jealous?'

'How can she be jealous! Am I jealous that now she has Garbaddas as well? She has two, so I have two!'

'Garbad, that rascal has it good.'

'Narbherambhai, what can I say. Garbad played mischief. Our Karbhari is busy with his administration, and the Faujdar is busy policing. Garbaddas would come to meet them when he knew that neither of them was home. He would wait for their return. The Karbhari was using Garbaddas to beguile and mislead Buddhidhan and had given him a free run of the house; so we had no authority to turn him away. He would sit alone in the drawing room, look out of the window, or waltz around the terrace.'

'What were you doing at the time?'

'I was busy with ... you know. Garbaddas took advantage of that. Sometimes Khalak—behn only to her brother—would be at her in-laws', and Rupali would be alone at home. She would come out into the courtyard with her hair open, and he would be standing on the terrace, looking down.'

'This was planned on purpose?'

'No, my dear sir. It all began unintentionally. Rupali is used to doing that, it is a habit with her. One day, Garbad could no longer contain himself and he coughed to draw her attention. What followed you know. The comings and goings began after that.'

'How do you know so much?'

'Some I witnessed. The rest she confessed, a bit by persuasion and a bit by coercion.'

'Then you will have fun today.'

'Of course! Important men will fight over the Karbhar in court, while men like me will take care of the 'Karbhar' of their homes. Rupali on one side, and on the other, the naughty one. But Narbherambhai, tell me how long will the assembly last?'

'They will be in the court till noon. You are the master of all you survey till then. Don't you know how long they will be gone?'

'I know about the evening assembly, when Alak Kishori and the others will be arrested and brought to the palace. This means I am the master of the house till noon.'

'Today all the soldiers will also be at the palace. Don't worry. I will be the first to come. I will warn you in advance.'

'I am grateful.'

'If fortune is not with you, you might be in for a surprise before noon.'

'My dear sir, with gopis on either side, this Krishna will carouse. At such moments, I am not one to be frightened even by Shathrai. One should keep doing what one is doing. I am a match for the best of them.'

'Lech! Two women, together!'

'Why not? These sisters-in-law may rule over the town; before me, they are meek as goats and cows.'

When elders are debauched, others in a family are also corrupted. Children and servants closely observe the conduct of their elders. If the elders are respected, so is their conduct, be it moral or immoral. That is considered best and is therefore emulated and perpetuated.

Their merits and sins affect not only their families but also those around them. How else could a lowly servant exercise such authority over the Karbhari's own daughter and daughter-in-law? God grants heaven and hell in this world itself. This is exemplified by the homes of Buddhidhan and Shathrai. With these thoughts, Narbheram took leave of Merulo.

Meanwhile, the entourage gathered. They hurriedly wore their footwear, and the procession left for the palace with due ceremony. Narbheram sought out Dushtarai and walked alongside him. Soon, the two were walking ahead of everyone else. Only a few soldiers stayed back as guards. Rupali watched them leave from a window. Dushtarai turned back once, looked up at her, and smiled. His chest, and his mind, swelled with pride. As the procession moved out of sight, Rupali came down. Merulo was working on the floor below. She came and hugged him from behind. In a while, Khalaknanda joined them. They both laughingly embraced Merulo from either side, rocking back and forth. Unmindful of the scene back home, Shathrai and party moved towards the palace, intent upon Buddhidhan's destruction. The certainty of this fact filled their minds, and their arrogance brimmed over.

Narbheram: 'So, Faujdar Sahib, you are in full force today!'

Dushtarai: 'Of course!'

'Now your writ will run large, as it did in Jadsinh's time?'

'Why not! Let us see.'

'But will you be able to turn the court into a house of pleasure as before?'

'That day, too, shall come.'

'Why not make an auspicious beginning today itself?'

'How so?'

'There will be a dance today at court.'

'So?'

'Won't your Kalavatibai go in for a change of costume? You should follow her into the room. You have all the authority.'

'No, no, not today. There will be time for that.'

'Courage, that is what you need. My dear Sir, be brave! He is gone. Finished. The Karbhar is yours. Make a beginning. But then, you know best.'

'It would be bad if the Rana gets to know.'

'Forget it, what does that Garasia understand! All he can do is smoke his hookah.'

'So, should I take the plunge? What is the problem in any case? It has been years since I took the liberty.'

'No problem. I will keep the Rana engaged.'

'Good. And what if father comes to know?'

'Oh, I have not seen anyone as cowardly as you! Didn't your father do the same in his youth? Everyone is naked in infancy.'

'Fine. Then watch me.'

'So be it.'

'All right then, see what I do today. But don't forget to play your part.'

'Of course, Faujdar Sahib!' Narbheram said, muttering to himself, In case of any trouble, I will say what the fox said to the elephant: Please hold on to my tail! The crafty rascal. Reason fails before greed. As if it is your father's rule! You will know for sure today. Go you wretches, you cunning asses! Narbheram bit his lower lip pensively. The Karbhari, judges, administrators and soldiers ambled along. Narbheram moved amongst them like a fly.

Buddhidhan's home was also bustling with activity. He had got up at four that morning, having slept only for two hours. He bathed, performed his ritual worship, and paced up and down his drawing room. Saubhagya Devi woke up early, bathed, marked her forehead with three lines of sacred ash and a red bindi at the centre, and commenced worship of Lord Shiva before sunrise. She had arranged silver utensils around her, lit two ghee lamps on either side of her and incense sticks which filled the room with their fragrance. She sat cross-legged on a low wooden stool with a woollen, multicoloured seat. She was the very embodiment of a chaste, pious woman. The sight of her reminded Navinchandra of Mahasweta from 'Kadambari,' and he looked at her radiant face reverentially, as if she were a goddess to be worshipped.

Kumud Sundari had studied English, but in matters of religion she was still a child. She was untouched by reformist ideas about faith or worship. She observed her mother-in-law offer puja, and was awed and attracted by the grandeur of the setting and the glory that Saubhagya Devi brought to it—it appealed to Kumud's aesthetic sensibility. And so she had begun to learn the ritual of sun worship from Devi. Alak's mind was not in such matters; Saubhagya Devi was happy that her daughter-in-law seemed keen on worship. Kumud Sundari had not yet learnt the full ritual, she therefore helped Saubhagya Devi by preparing the paraphernalia for the puja. Saubhagya Devi felt content and fulfilled that her daughter-in-law served her, just as she had served her own mother-in-law. The ritual was completed hurriedly as Buddhidhan had to leave soon. The puja over, Kumud Sundari got busy preparing breakfast for the men since the assembly was expected to be a long one. Navinchandra also woke up early. He brushed, bathed, and not having much else to do, sat on the terrace watching the auspicious beginnings of the day in the Counsellors' house. Busy with arrangements, Kumud breezed in and out of the courtyard with a lamp in her hand, and occasionally looked up at the face, standing distant and above it all, which seemed at times to be looking down at her.

Samar Sen arrived in the courtyard with some other men, adding to the noise and bustle. The servants busily cleaned and swept the house and obeyed a constant flow of instructions from Saubhagya Devi and Kumud Sundari. Pramaddhan sat by the side of a lamp and did the work assigned to him by his father. Having finished it, he came down and sent a man to fetch Dayashankar Kaka and some other relatives. Meanwhile, Alak Kishori arrived from her in-laws' house, escorted by a guard. She, too, immediately busied herself with household work.

Buddhidhan's drawing room began to fill up with people. Dayashankar walked in, stick in hand, slowly climbed up the stairs and sat down on a couch. The headmaster of the school arrived wearing English 'boots and stockings', sat on a chair and began to read the previous day's newspaper—it had an 'article' by Navinchandra, although written anonymously. Shastri Maharaj climbed the stairs reciting sacred verses, sat with Dayashankar and began to chat with him. The Qazi entered looking sombre, greeted all present with courtesy and sat down next to the headmaster. The City Judge who had recently passed the District Pleader's examination joined in. He was an honest and frank man who often clashed with Karvatrai. Other officers used him when they had to send blunt messages to superiors, like the Rana, the Karbhari and the Counsellor. His intellect was pure and he did not like employing devious means; this made him quite unsuited to working in a princely state. The City Judge had acquired this position on Buskin Sahib's recommendation, and he also had Buddhidhan's protection. This was why, while all other state officials had gathered at Shathrai's house, he had chosen to come to Buddhidhan's instead. He was a genuinely carefree man. People knew they could get their work done by him as long as they praised his honesty and independence. His name was Tark Prasad. Corrupt and unctuous officers considered this straightforward man stupid and called him Dahyabhai. However, Dahyabhai had considered the situation quite thoroughly and come to his own conclusion: truth would eventually prevail and evil would be defeated. Shathrai would be destroyed and Buddhidhan would rise. This calculation also motivated his steadfast loyalty to Buddhidhan's faction. On arriving, Tark Prasad greeted each present appropriately and slumped into an easy chair. Buddhidhan's son-in-law, Vidurprasad also arrived. Sitting next to Tark Prasad on a chair without armrests, he engaged the Judge in conversation. He worked in the accounts department as an assistant to Garbaddas. He had also worked a short while in the police department, as also in the department that dealt with the cousins of the rulers—the Bhayats. Vidurprasad was a meek man; but sometimes, at his parents' instigation, he harassed Buddhidhan and sought things that were beyond his station. He did not care if Buddhidhan faced any difficulty in meeting his demands. The moment one demand was met, he would come up with another.

If Buddhidhan ever did him a favour, he was given to saying, 'So what? What is so unusual about it?' He never allowed a sense of gratitude to enter his mind. But he was docile and submissive before Alak Kishori and therefore remained more or less quiet. Vidurprasad was a considerate man in some ways, but took interest in talks that degraded his father-in-law's family, even though he was ultimately a well-wisher. He was a capable man, but made many mistakes in his work; Buddhidhan often spoke about them in the house. On such occasions, Vidurprasad accepted without protest Alak Kishori's verbal lashings at night. Even his parents would go quiet when their proud daughter-in-law stepped into the house. They quibbled only behind her back. Dayashankar's son Jaymalshankar joined the gathering. With monetary help from Buddhidhan, Jaymal had studied English and had passed the Matriculation examination from Bombay. He was a well-built, impressive-looking and practical man. He was related to Shathrai on the maternal side; he was given a post dealing with the petty expenditure of Bhupsinh's palace. Shathrai had given him this position—on Narbheram's suggestion—knowing that Buddhidhan would not object to the appointment.

Jaymalshankar had been sent by the Rana to fetch Buddhidhan. He now sought the Counsellor out and whispered into his ear, 'Bhai Sahib, Kalavati spent all night in the palace and went home only at four in the morning. Ranjit asked me to tell you that she talked about Rajba all night, and that the Rana is fuming. You know well whether or not the Rana can be trusted. After Kalavati's departure, he sent a note to Shathrai. Who knows what he wrote in that note? He was heard muttering, "These can't all be lies," and he spoke about "Ramabai" or some such person, and said that even she had told him the same thing.'

Buddhidhan heard Jaymal's warning and sent him back to the palace with the message that he would follow shortly. He could not decide whether the Rana was being devious with him or with Shathrai. But he had no time to deliberate upon this now. He had deliberated and plotted enough. Suddenly, another thought came to him. In the short time that he had observed Navinchandra, Buddhidhan had realised that his guest was trustworthy. Navinchandra had no dealings with Shathrai and no selfish motives in the palace; and for this reason, Buddhidhan found he could trust him even more than Narbheram. He sent for Navinchandra and Alak Kishori the moment Jaymalshankar had left. 'Get the breakfast ready soon and send it up here,' he said to Alak and sent her off. The Counsellor then placed a hand on Navinchandra's shoulder, looked him straight in the eye and said, 'Navinchandra, I need to assign you a responsibility today. It is a matter of absolute trust and must be kept secret. It is as if I am placing my most invaluable jewels in your custody. You are learned, appear to be high-born, and I consider you honest in every respect. I believe you will remain steadfast in these qualities even when I may no longer be around.'

Navinchandra was surprised. 'It is not proper for one to speak about oneself; but yes, have the confidence that the trust reposed in me will not be wasted. I am grateful for your generosity, and am bound to you. For me, any service rendered to you is the same as an act in the name of God.'

'You know that tumultuous events are expected to take place at the palace today.'

'Yes, but I do not know the details.'

'Details you will know later. For the moment, you should know that today either Shathrai will prevail, or I. God willing, the outcome will be good. But times are strange. At the court, if you should perceive that I am in any danger, or upon a sign from me, you should rush home and take my entire family to Lilapur, rent a house and stay there. Alak Kishori knows where my money and jewellery are kept. In that matter, you should seek Dayashankar Kaka's advice. On reaching Lilapur, you should meet Russell Sahib and inform him about my situation here. You should also write to Vidya Chatura and act as per his counsel. Pramad is still childish; it is your responsibility to look after him and guide him. I have kept carts waiting for you in the house adjacent, in case the need arises. You should take Samar Sen with you or the armed escort sent by him. Do not trust Shathrai, his son, or any stranger for that matter. And you should march out fast; their thoughts are utterly evil and depraved. I believe it will not be beyond your capacity to accomplish this.' The Counsellor looked at the young man anxiously.

Navinchandra was too astonished for words. This scenario was beyond his imagination. He would never have thought that in a strange land, someone could repose so much trust in him, and in such circumstances. But he quickly regained his poise and said: 'Have no fear: this is the first time that God has tested my virtue and lineage. I shall not fail.'

The Counsellor's hand moved from his forehead to his eyes and face, and suppressing a deep sigh, he said, 'Navinchandra, I leave in your custody my dearest, most precious jewels. Never before in my life have I been through such trying times.'

'Bhai Sahib, consider me a brother—a son in fact. I touch your feet. I feel no distance from your family. What more can I say? Deeds are better than words. Your wealth to me is like offerings made to God. Devi is like a mother to me, and Alak is my sister.'

'I have other friends, but their interests are tied to the State. Shathrai is a wealthy and powerful man.'

'Bhai Sahib, you have trusted me completely; I am not unworthy of your trust. No one can buy me with money. I will share a secret with you, too: my father is a millionaire.'

The Counsellor seemed unconvinced. Navinchandra saw this, and felt a tinge of sadness. 'I have this ring as proof. Take a look.' He had tied a diamond ring to his janeu thread and hidden it in the folds of his dhoti. He took it out. Buddhidhan took the ring in his hand and stared at it; the diamond was worth at least seven or eight thousand rupees. 'Bhai Sahib, I also know a few other things which are supposed to be secret. I know that Shathrai intends to kill you. I know about Kalavati.'

Now it was Buddhidhan who was startled. He squared his shoulders and looked Navinchandra full in the face: 'What!'

'Bhai Sahib, please do not be startled. I will tell you later how I came to know of these matters. I know a lot, but haven't said a word to anyone, not even Pramadbhai—God is my witness. I can keep secrets. I have not made use of any secrets that I know. I say this only to prove that I am worthy of your trust.' Buddhidhan fell deep into thought. Seeing him in a quandary, Navinchandra continued, 'If you have any doubts about me, I am not keen to take on this responsibility. I am a foreigner, a wanderer, a free bird. If you prefer, I am ready to leave for someplace else this very moment, and no one will ever know about it. You can assign this responsibility to anyone else you please.'

'No, no—it isn't like that. Come, you are like a brother to me. This is your responsibility. But remember that the teeth do not have to be told to protect the tongue.'

'Please do not worry, Bhai Sahib.'

Alak Kishori called them for breakfast. The son-in-law joined them; Dayashankar also came in and sat down on a stool. Not wanting to frighten them, Buddhidhan had not yet spoken to the women about the political intrigues of the palace. But it had now become imperative to do so. He told them what he had said to Navinchandra, and requested them to do exactly as they were asked. They were taken aback and apprehensive, but there was no time to waste. The Counsellor went to his bedroom to change his clothes; Saubhagya Devi followed him.

'Devi, there are some papers in this box. If it becomes necessary to leave for Lilapur with Navinchandra, open it once you are there, and do what is written in these notes.'

'But what is all this?' Devi demanded to know.

'Nothing. Do not be afraid, Devi. Until I return, let Dayashankar Kaka not leave the house.'

'You have never kept anything from me till date. Have I done something wrong that you no longer trust me?' Devi asked, wiping anguished tears from her eyes.

'No, no, it is nothing. I will tell you everything later. Is this the time to talk? It is just that the assembly will be stormy today and ...'

'I see from your face that you are very afraid of something.'

Buddhidhan made an attempt to laugh, 'No, what should I be afraid of! I have told you what it is, haven't I?'

'Yes, there is a scare. But my heart tells me that all will be well. I am not afraid; it must be something else.'

Just then, Alak Kishori entered the room. Buddhidhan said to Alak, 'Be brave, if the time comes to leave with Navinchandra. Look how brave your sister-in-law is.' Pramaddhan came to inform them that everyone was ready, and that messengers from the palace had come asking after them twice. Saubhagya Devi sent Alak Kishori to fetch kumkum.

Dressed for the palace, Buddhidhan emerged from his room and as he hurriedly made his way down the stairs, he met Alak midway. 'Victory to you, father! I met you halfway. Let me apply the tilak. Today, triumph will be yours!' And Alak put a tilak of red kumkum paste on his forehead. Everyone assembled in the courtyard and put on their footwear, eager to leave. Navinchandra was ready, too; Buddhidhan had asked Pramaddhan to lend him appropriate clothes for the occasion. The Counsellor now took Navinchandra by the hand.

Vanleela was on her way to her maternal home. But hearing rumours of intrigue from her husband, she had called Kumud Sundari to the door to talk about it. They stood talking on the threshold. Vanleela left, and as Kumud Sundari entered the house, she ran into the Counsellor and his entourage on their way out. She shrank to one side and allowed them to pass before entering the house.

'Navinchandra, the omens are auspicious. We met Alak Kishori on the stairs, and now Kumud Sundari near the door,' the Counsellor said.

'Yes, the omens are auspicious. Let us proceed.'

Everyone congratulated the Counsellor on the good omen, and they all proceeded for the palace.

And yet, Buddhidhan's mind was full of misgivings. Will I ever get to see this house again? Will I meet my family again, or is this the last time we are together? I could not even embrace Devi as I left. Oh God! What is to happen? Will I ever meet my Alak and Kumud again? My son Pramaddhan ...? Such thoughts crowded his mind as he looked at the beautiful women of his household gathered at the door to see him off. But the body moved on and dragged the mind with it. And as he left his home behind, he became immersed in thoughts about the palace. Buddhidhan, who was born poor, could see many obstacles between him and the Karbhar. He could also see the various means and instruments he had employed to remove them. He was accompanied by his strange party, all differently attired, preoccupied in their own thoughts. En route, they met Shathrai and his entourage. They all walked together, and yet they were visibly distinct. With them walked Navinchandra, a part of the procession, and yet distanced from them all. He attracted everyone's gaze, and yet remained unrecognised. He observed this whole new world with new eyes.

12 King, Palace and Administration

The moon behind the western mount is sinking;
The eastern sun is heralded by dawn;
From heaven's twin lights, their fall and glory linking;
Brave lessons of submission may be drawn.[1]

Rana Bhupsinh's palace was situated at the centre of a sprawling garden, which was encircled by a high wall. The wall, built to resemble the ramparts of a fortress, was about ten yards high. The lime-wash on the wall had gone black in some places and was patchy in others. Masons on raised platforms were busy repairing it. A canopy of green leaves could be seen protruding over the wall. Some trees in the garden had dried up or shed their leaves; their bare brown branches grazed against the green leafy ones, as if to render them barren, too. Some mango trees were in bloom; they glistened and swayed in the morning sun. Like a white bud emerging from dense foliage, the upper stories of the palace could be seen rising from amidst this green copse. The palace was better looked after than the garden or the walls. The original palace had been a two-storied building. Bhupsinh had added two more levels to it and they were visible from the garden. The upper stories were smaller than the original two floors, with a view to giving stability to the structure. The third floor was smaller than the second

[1] Arthur W. Ryder, trans. *Kalidasa: Translation of Shakuntala and Other Works*, Act IV, Verse 2, Reprint (New York: J. M. Dent & Co., 1912, 1920), 41.

floor, while the fourth was the smallest of them all. The fourth floor contained only one large bed chamber. It had been decorated in what Buddhidhan imagined to be 'Bombay style'. The walls of the bedroom were made of small pieces of glass. Each piece was smaller than the width of two palms and was set in a rosewood frame. Some were square, some oval, while others were hexagonal in shape. Deep red curtains covered the glass walls and were kept open at some of the windows. The openings in the curtain were square or triangular in shape. Some pieces of glass were coloured and reflected the sun's rays. The reflection dazzled the eyes of those who gazed at it even from outside the palace walls. The palace looked like a lissome Kathiawadi woman who insisted on wearing skirts and silken blouses even after girlhood was left far behind. The surrounding walls were like the block-hemming of a flared white chaniya. The trees reached beyond the walls like a blouse with red patterns and gathers that came down to meet the skirt. Their green branches and round tree tops resembled breasts straining against a tight blouse. The upper floors of the palace were like a head emerging from the torso, and the glass palace shone like two sharp, gleaming eyes. Like a piece of jewellery in the parting of a woman's hair, a parrot came and sat atop the glass palace. The coloured glass looked like tattoos on the woman's face.

The palace, a solitary imposing figure, stood under the blazing summer sky. The procession which approached it in the heat of Chaitra was drenched in sweat, their faces red in the heat and their clothes wet with perspiration. They walked faster as the palace came closer. The approaching shade gave their legs new vigour. Just like a child playing in the heat runs home to the mother when hungry, leaving its playmates behind, the men thought of the Rana as they left town and neared the palace. Their minds craved intrigue and hungered for the fruits of their machinations. The courtiers now rapidly made their way towards the palace, like a king's chariot surging ahead, leaving the others behind. The crowds of citizens thronging near the palace made way for the courtiers.

The palace gate was large enough to accommodate the approaching procession. Its two thick doors were covered with strips of metal. There was a room on top of the gate for the palace drummers who made announcements regarding the passage of time, important events and ceremonial days for the citizens. A raised platform on which canons could be placed ran along the length of the wall. There were steps leading up to the platform from several points. The room above the gate had doors that led to it. Behind the doors were two large platforms where the soldiers sat, slept, chatted, polished their swords, lined up their guns and guarded the palace. Today, they stood in line near the gate and saluted the officials as they entered the palace. Two soldiers on horseback moved between the palace and the gate and passed on instructions.

Beyond the gate, there was a thick cover of trees and bushes on either side of the avenue and waterways filled with clean, sparkling water. Sparrows and pigeons quenched their thirst, splashed and dipped into these canals and flapped their wings dry. The rhythmic drone of the wheels that drew out this water filled the air. The bare feet and dark, stout, sweat-soaked bodies of the labourers and gardeners toiling in the garden and the waterways were not incongruent with the surrounding garden. Navinchandra, raised amidst the artificial landscape of Bombay, realised as soon as he entered the gate that man had not tried to impose his artifice over God's creation here and traditional wisdom was not yet forgotten. He could see descriptions that he had read in old books come alive before his eyes.

All around them, guava, pomegranate and custard-apple trees were to be seen in abundance, laden with fruits. Flowers of many different colours, shapes and fragrances filled the eyes and nostrils with God's munificence. Parrots, peacocks, cuckoos, sparrows and pigeons flew from tree to tree, pecking at the fruits. The flapping of their wings and their sharp calls filled the ears. Navinchandra recalled with pity the landscaped gardens of Bombay that delighted only the eyes. He grew contemplative. Amidst the tall, solitary trees, the lonely statuesque palace and the endless coppery sky above, Navinchandra was filled with the sense of his own insignificance, his smallness, and he was duly humbled. He understood the desires felt by Raja Dushyant in the forest abode. Cowper's description of the deep, long whistle of a soaring kite came back to him. He could feel the sense of quiet take possession of the others as well. He suddenly felt very lonely, and the absence of his parents and the home he had left behind in Bombay seemed to crush him like an immense weight.

Remote, unfriended, melancholy, slow,
Or by the lazy Scheldt, or wandering Po;
Or onward, where the rude Carinthian boor
Against the houseless stranger shuts the door;
Or where Campania's plain forsaken lies,
A weary waste expanding to the skies:
Where'er I roam, whatever realms to see,
My heart untravell'd fondly turns to thee;
Still to my brother turns, with ceaseless pain,
And drags at each remove a lengthening chain.

Eternal blessings crown my earliest friend,
And round his dwelling guardian saints attend:
Bless'd be that spot, where cheerful guests retire
To pause from toil, and trim their ev'ning fire;
Bless'd that abode, where want and pain repair,
And every stranger finds a ready chair;
Bless'd be those feasts with simple plenty crown'd,
Where all the ruddy family around
Laugh at the jests or pranks that never fail,
Or sigh with pity at some mournful tale,
Or press the bashful stranger to his food,
And learn the luxury of doing good.[2]

He murmured softly to himself: Oh, Kumud Sundari! I shunned you. But you came even closer. Am I now to be charged with your well-being? Home. Friendship. Love. Can these ever be forgotten? The

[2] Author's note: 'The Traveller', Oliver Goldsmith.

beauty of a pure mind. Beauty imbued with knowledge! Is my craving for you inevitable? No ... No!

Suddenly, the drummers began to beat their drums, and Navinchandra looked up, startled. He saw the flag flutter proudly atop the palace, and the procession came alive. His reverie broken, the surrounding scenes rushed into his consciousness. The traveller remembered where he was. Never before had such thoughts come to anyone whilst walking through the palace gardens of Suvarnapur; and if they had, no one would have had any inkling of it. No one was capable of comprehending or fathoming his thoughts; and for the world that was Suvarnapur, this was best. With this realisation, his mind became quiet again.

A path with trees on either side led to a circular grove. From its centre, a path led to the royal palace. The palace faced the east, but it also had entrances on other sides. At the eastern entrance, Vijay Sen and his troop of soldiers stood with their swords drawn. An old but powerful elephant also stood there. His large domed head swayed from side to side as he looked at the passers-by with grave but curious eyes. The small bell hung around his neck tinkled when he moved his head. The horses were acquainted with him and stood quietly beside him without fidgeting, but their ears would perk up every time the little bell rang. The grandeur and intelligence of this animal greatly impressed those entering the palace. Rana Bhupsinh had just arrived at the court riding upon this beast. Matangraj, the elephant, had served many rulers previously and was also familiar with the Karbharis. He raised his ash-smeared trunk and lowered his head as Shathrai and Buddhidhan approached him. Shathrai walked past him. Buddhidhan went up to Matangraj, patted him on his trunk, spoke kindly with his keeper to inquire after the elephant's health, and rejoined his group. Matangraj looked at Buddhidhan. Navinchandra noticed, and was surprised, and he entered the palace with his mind crowded with all kinds of thoughts.

The court was to assemble on the first floor of the palace. A wide staircase, covered with an embroidered carpet, with a brass balustrade led up to the first floor. Removing their shoes in a heap on the ground floor, the procession climbed up and entered the palace stateroom. The stateroom was immense—enough to accommodate between fifteen hundred and two thousand persons. An expensive woollen carpet covered the floor. A gold and silver-plated throne was placed at one end of the stateroom. Its armrests were shaped after lions; silk cushions with gold embroidery had been kept on it. A thick intricately patterned carpet with gold embroidery covered the area in front of the throne, extending almost halfway across the hall. The sun's rays filtered through large, multi-coloured windows into brass-lattice doors, filling the huge hall with light. On the opposite wall were artificial windows of similar colour and shape. There were also large cupboards that created a similar effect. In the alcoves of the windows, plain glass tables were placed on which figurines, bone china and other such fine objects were kept. The walls of the stateroom were sky blue, painted to resemble the curtains of a playhouse. The roof was decorated with bright red paint, glass chandeliers, and other bits and baubles. A curtain with gathers made from embroidered cloth hung from the skirting of the roof. Seen from below and around, the stateroom resembled an enormous bed—it stupefied the mind and induced an infatuated sleep; those caught in this delusionary slumber saw dreams of regal grandeur, forgot their reality, and thus struggled fiercely with the desire for power.

The Karbharis and officials gathered in the stateroom. Some moved around, some stood at the windows, some looked into the mirrors, some looked up, some looked down, some joined in chatter, some moved about busily in preparation for the assembly, some stood, some sat, some waited, some reflected, some stared, some strained their ears, some looked on stupefied, some asked for news, some gossiped, some passed on information, some predicted the outcome of the day's events, some pondered their own future, some conjectured the future of others, some were enthused, some were anxious, some were dejected, some tried to hide their sentiments, some tried to gauge those of others, some veiled their animosity and spoke affably, some saw through this, some were taken in by it, some matched wits, some spoke bluntly, some were intent on revenge; and all of this was reflected in the myriad glass bulbs, the cut-glass, the shining brass, and also in the eyes, ears, words and minds of all those who observed, heard and thought to a greater or a lesser degree; some reflections were big, others small, some clear, others hazy, some shallow, others deep; their form and colours were different and so was their constancy. This entire scene made a profound impact on Navinchandra who stayed close to Buddhidhan all this while, and for that reason attracted the attention of everyone present. As if he were at an exhibition of English goods, or watching statues that moved and spoke, or in a marketplace where a foreign tongue was spoken, Navinchandra stood aloof and distanced from it all; he was like an ascetic in a world of householders. He looked intently at all this activity and grandeur, astonished, observant and analytical. He likened himself to the multi-faceted, multi-hued glass that refracted the sun's rays, and smiled at his own comparison.

The humble, ordinary denizens of Suvarnapur crowded onto the rich woollen carpet, pushing and jostling, and settled down noisily. Some stood and stared like rustics, some stood apart gravely, some came forward as if they had a rightful place at court, some saluted court officials, some excitedly pointed out known officials to their kin, some puffed up with pride when some official returned their salutations. Thus, the people, who should have been the ones to be saluted and honoured by the rulers, who should have been the boon-granting Kamdhenu of Kings and all their officials, they surrendered their pride to officialdom and became meek and enthused and awed in the face of such majestic splendour. Navinchandra's eyes were focused on their simple enthusiasm. When he turned around, he saw Shathrai and Buddhidhan standing at a far window by themselves, talking and smiling at each other like old friends. He was astonished.

Suddenly, there came a solemn call from the hall adjacent: 'Your kindness be upon all, Your Grace!' The assembly was as startled as a muster of peacocks surprised by thundering clouds, and then everyone scrambled to their appointed places. Shathrai sat to the right of the throne. Next to him sat Karvatrai, followed by Dushtarai, after whom the other officials and functionaries took their place by rank. Some even took a place higher than their rank, leaving others to grumble. Buddhidhan took his seat to the left of the throne, and Pramaddhan sat next to him. Navinchandra sat behind Pramaddhan. Samar Sen, his sword tied at his waist, stood behind the throne to the left. The group that had accompanied Buddhidhan, including the school headmaster, also took its place. The Bhayats sat at some distance behind the Counsellor and his son: their beards and moustaches were shaped differently; they wore headgears woven in golden thread and had daggers and swords at their waists.

Just then, Kalavati walked in with a party of musicians. She shone bright as a jewel, her lips stained red with betel leaf juice. She and her musicians sat in the centre of the vast stateroom. The assembly was entranced, their eyelids grew heavy as if they were about to surrender to sleep. They gazed at Kalavati with lascivious eyes, as if where she sat was in fact a bed, and she the lone waiting woman on it. At that moment, there were scarcely two or three people there who saw anything else. Navinchandra observed the movements of the assembly's eyes. Jaymalshankar whispered something to Buddhidhan, who leaned back to hear him. Narbheram, who sat behind Shathrai, looked intently at Jaymal and Buddhidhan.

'Dushtarai was in Kalavati's room checking on something,' said Jaymal, sounding out of breath.

'What for?' the Counsellor asked, concealing his eagerness to know.

'I do not know, but he was fooling around with her.'

'Right here, in the palace?' the Counsellor asked, as if surprised.

'Yes. Narbherambhai and I were with Ranaji at the time. Narbheram was reading out today's English newspaper to him. Suddenly, he saw something through these new, English-fashioned louvers, and stopped reading the newspaper.'

'Then?'

'Ranaji asked, Why did you stop? What are you looking at? Narbherambhai pretended that nothing was the matter and replied,

Nothing at all. But Ranaji insisted on knowing and he looked through the louvers himself, and then he lost his head.'

It was as if nectar was poured into Buddhidhan's ears, but nothing in his outward demeanour betrayed this. 'Did Ranaji say anything?'

'His hand went to his sword and he rushed to the door, his eyes breathing fire.'

'Oh!'

'But Narbherambhai went and held Ranaji back, whispered something to him, and sent me away from there.'

Buddhidhan thought it over briefly and said, 'All right, go take your place.' In a little while, he signalled to Jaymal again, called him close and said, 'Go up to the top floor window and look out for the horse-carriage that is to come from Lilapur. The moment you see it approach, come and tell me. No one else should know about this.'

'Very well,' said Jaymal and quietly left the assembly. Narbheram did not understand what had transpired and stared at Jaymal's receding back. He returned his gaze to the Counsellor and then, like everyone else, focused his eyes on Kalavati and the two courtesans who flanked her on either side. He engaged Shathrai and Karvatrai in a conversation about which of them was more beautiful.

Just then, the door behind the throne opened and chants of 'Maharana, your kindness be upon all!' and suchlike rang out. The assembly stopped looking at Kalavati and turned towards the Rana instead, like a gust of wind. It was as if the entire stateroom rose up as one man—all the surrounding mirrors attested to this, as did the hearts and minds of those present. Two thousand persons bowed low in greeting. Salutations rained and countless hands went up to as many foreheads in greeting.

The Rana's garments were woven of gold and silver threads. He wore diamond and pearl ornaments. The gold handle of his sword was studded with a diamond. His crown, worn over embroidered headgear, was also bedecked with diamonds. The Rana's body was redolent with perfumes. He was a feast for the senses. He walked in regally, looking joyous, his chest thrust out. He looked at Shathrai, smiled at him, and took his seat on the throne. Everyone else took their seats as well. The royal ushers crowded in behind the Rana. On either side, servants fanned him with gold-embroidered fans. On one side stood Vijay Sen, his sword drawn. He served as the Rana's bodyguard. This was the tradition of Suvarnapur palace at times when the court was in session. On the other side stood Ranjit, with the golden regal standard. Roses and other flowers, perfumes, rosewater, paan wrapped in gold and silver foil were placed in front of the Rana in large plates of silver. A sarangi player set the tone and Kalavati began to sing in her sweet, melodious voice; mridangam and sitar accompanied her. Spring was nearly over, but she sang spring compositions which were the Rana's favourites. She also sang a *Hori*, usually sung at the time of Holi.

I will not live in your city
Krishna robs me in broad daylight!

The assembly was delighted, captivated not only by the singing but also by the ardour of the beautiful courtesan. The soulful notes of the sarangi and the chords of the sitar moved them. The gathering was entranced. Kalavati came to the last stanza:

No one dare question his tyranny
There is no justice in this city

The Rana, seething inwardly, composed an unpoetic response to Kalavati's song in his head:

Then don't live in my city
Whore: in broad daylight, you cheat me!

Jaymalshankar returned just as Kalavati was singing the last lines. He whispered something into Buddhidhan's ear. In a few minutes, the assembly heard a horse-carriage screeching to a halt and was jolted out of its trance. Russell Sahib's Shirastidar, Ramchandra Rao, entered the hall accompanied by a soldier. The singing stopped as people made way for him to pass. Buddhidhan got up to receive him, and Shathrai stood up to shake his hand. The Rana accepted the Shirastidar's salutations while remaining seated. Ramchandra Rao took his seat between the Rana and his Counsellor.

The Rana enquired after the Sahib, and Shathrai asked the purpose of his visit. The Shirastidar replied, 'I will tell you after the assembly has dispersed. It is nothing urgent.'

Kalavati took advantage of this interruption, got up and went to change her costume. In the meanwhile, a soldier had come up to Ranjit and whispered something to him. Ranjit called Dushtarai to a corner and said, 'Bhai Sahib, do forgive me, God knows I am true to my salt. But do you know your Merulo? Do you know him at all?'

'He is better than you.'

'Indeed. Bhai Sahib, this opportunity will never come again. He knows that you are stuck here, and he is at home with ...'

'Rascal, I will cut out your tongue!' Dushtarai would have hit him if they were not in court.

Ranjit fixed Dushtarai with his good eye and said, 'Bhai Sahib, this has to be done right now. Go home quietly, and see with your own eyes. If I am lying, put your sword to my neck.'

The Faujdar returned to his seat, but his mind was in a whirl. He fumed and fretted, but could not betray his emotions. Peace eludes those who doubt. He decided he must go home under some pretext. But nothing could possibly be more important than what was to happen in the assembly. Dushtarai took his father's leave, saying that someone at home had taken very ill, and promised to return soon. In his anxiety, he forgot to take any soldiers with him. The soldiers were engrossed in the courtly spectacle, so they did not see him leave, and no one offered to accompany him. The Faujdar left the assembly alone.

When Kalavati went in to change her costume, her place was taken by other courtesans. Some of them sang better than her, but the courtiers naturally praised the Rana's favourite. These courtesans sang beautiful tappas and thumris much to the delight of the citizens. But the courtiers chose to neglect them and loudly talked amongst themselves instead. The singers felt angry and insulted, but were helpless. They sang even louder and more melodiously in the hope of catching the Rana's ears.

Buddhidhan quietly asked the Shirastidar for the Sahib's letter, and read it. Shathrai asked for it, too. Buddhidhan gave it back to Ramchandra Rao and signalled that it should be sent to Shathrai by the 'long' route. The Rana asked for it, read it, and handed it to Shathrai. Karvatrai also leaned forward to read it. Ramchandrabhau had been sent by Russell Sahib to ascertain facts about the bania who was Karvatrai's victim; he had to examine and report if the bania was still imprisoned and what his family's condition was. The Sahib had written to the Rana to request him to facilitate Rambhau's mission. The letter was read and discussed in whispers. Shathrai returned the letter to Rambhau, and looked around for Dushtarai who had not yet returned. Narbheram realised that Shathrai was worried. Buddhidhan and Narbheram exchanged a pointed look. Shathrai would have liked to give the task to Karvatrai, but Karvatrai was himself the object of inquiry. So he finally decided on Narbheram. Leaning close, Shathrai spoke into his ear, 'After the assembly, we have to take up the matter of Rajba. But *this* obstacle has to be removed before that. Go out, write a note to the jailor that the bania should be released immediately. He should be given money and frightened into giving suitable answers to Rambhau. See to this, and return soon. Meanwhile the assembly will also wind to an end, after which Rambhau can begin his inquiry.'

'Whom shall I send the note with? Can Jaymal be trusted?'

'Yes, send him; he is one of our own. You be where you are required to be.' Narbheram got up and left, but not unnoticed by Rambhau. The Shirastidar had been Buddhidhan's subordinate in Lilapur, and had good relations with the previous Shirastidar, Sadashiv Pant. Buddhidhan had therefore cultivated his acquaintance. There were two or three contenders for the position of Shirastidar when Buddhidhan left the post. Rambhau was the likely choice and Buddhidhan had supported his claim. Shathrai was in favour of another candidate. When Rambhau had still occupied a low post, Shathrai and men from his office had ill-treated him. Rambhau had taken this insult to heart. Therefore, while he might have accepted bribes from Shathrai, he still wanted to get even with him. Rambhau did not see the bribes as any favour done unto him. He believed that Buddhidhan would also pay him, if he became the Karbhari. Moreover, bribes were paid because they needed favours from him. Buddhidhan knew Rambhau well and he also knew how to keep an upper hand in their dealings. Buddhidhan had cultivated proximity with Russell Sahib, which allowed him to exercise authority over Rambhau. Buddhidhan had also used his relations with the Sahib to Rambhau's advantage. This apparent selflessness had helped Buddhidhan forge closer ties with the Shirastidar. This Dakshini brahmin was sharp. The moment he saw Narbheram leave the court, he became restless.

He addressed Shathrai, 'Karbharisahib, I will go and complete some personal work while the assembly is underway. I wish to return to Lilapur soon, upon fulfilling the Sahib's order.'

'Very well.'

Rambhau discreetly asked Buddhidhan, 'Who supervises the functioning of the prison?'

'Tark Prasad,' Buddhidhan whispered in response.

Rambhau got up and said, 'Ranaji, I seek your leave. I will take Tark Prasad with me for company.' No one could say no. The judge got up to leave with Rambhau.

Shathrai and Karvatrai were both worried. They felt the bania should have been made to disappear without a trace, but the time for that was over. In hindsight, this appeared to them the best solution, and they sorely regretted the missed opportunity. What will be will be. We will deal with what comes. But doesn't this Dakshini brahmin love his money! This thought emboldened Shathrai, who appeared quite at ease now.

All this while, Navinchandra had been deep in conversation with the schoolteacher. The teacher pointed out and described all the officials of the state to him. The state of Suvarnapur was divided into twenty revenue divisions called mahals. Each mahal had officials such as the mahalkari or mahal administrator, the judge and the faujdar.

Suvarnapur was also the administrative headquarters of a mahal, and the officials who governed it resided in town. Moreover, it was also home to city officials such as the city judge, the collector of taxes and the head of city police. Official titles were a hotchpotch of Peshwai, Mughlai and English administrative titles. The titles did not give an indication of either the position or the responsibilities of these officials. For example, Dushtarai's title was Faujdar, but he was the 'Police Commissioner' of the entire state.

'The man seated next to the Karbhari is his brother Karvatrai. He gets paid two thousands rupees per annum. He has been in service for fifteen years. Their father had left them nothing. Today he is worth at least ten lakhs.'

'How so?'

'My dear sir, it is not our tradition to speak of such things. Now look, the one next to him is Dushtarai's father-in-law. His house shines and glitters because of his daughter, Rupali. It is considered acceptable among us to seek a position when one gives one's daughter in marriage. He has served the son-in-law well. He exercises the greatest influence and is wealthy. God has made the use of intelligence redundant for him. At present he is an official in the recovery of dues department.'

'Who is that?'

'That fat man? He wields a lot of power. People dread him. He is the Karbhari's brother-in-law; he knows everything there is to know. To begin with, he was in the police department where he tyrannised people, both for money and for women. Buskin Sahib pressed for his removal and considering him unfit for the police department, he was anointed on the seat of justice. My dear sir, he always wished well for both parties. He never fails to return a favour. The Counsellor has made him in-charge of this mahal; now he milks both the king and his subjects.'

'Is there no one to check him?'

The schoolteacher chuckled. 'Why, would your elder brother pay heed if I were to complain against you to him? Who has the guts to lodge a complaint?'

'But irregularities and wrongdoing in the administration of a mahal would surely come to light very easily?'

'No, dear sir, no. You have no experience in such matters. If the Karbhari's cook were to be made assistant Karbhari, he would be praised from the very first day. He would receive appreciation. But if some rascal were to acquire a position on his own steam, his shortcomings would be revealed immediately. Such a man cannot be capable. All right sir, do you know that man?'

'Yes, he is Narbheram. I know something of him. Tell me about his past.'

'He and the Karbhari work together to malign the Counsellor. Narbheram can plummet to the lowest level to flatter. That is his skill.'

'But there will be many like him.'

'True. But he was sent by Buskin Sahib. The Rana trusts him to an extent, and therefore, the Karbhari gives him some respect.'

'Hmm.'

Many officials were thus described and discussed in a similar vein. Tark Prasad had been quietly listening to them talk, when he was abruptly summoned. As he got up to leave, he put a hand on Navinchandra's shoulder and said: 'Now listen to my short description. All those who sit here, grave and sombre in their red pagdis, have committed such vile deeds that their punishment, if they were ever to be brought to justice, would range from monetary fines to hanging. These gentlemen who hide behind fine clothes are corrupt, thieves, debauched, deceitful, murderers, and possess many other such fine capabilities besides. They enjoy power and are entrusted with the protection of poor, innocent people, whom they devour. They mislead the world, keep the Sahibs happy through their petty politics and retain their authority. Power of money and status is the key to their success. I have said little, but you will have grasped all you need to know.' And Tark Prasad gave Navinchandra a sly smile as he left in company of Rambhau.

Navinchandra felt like someone who suddenly discovers that the person who was sitting by his side was not human but a ghost. His attention now shifted to the singers. They sang unhurriedly. At times they clapped, they swayed, opened their mouths wide, made faces, lowered their eyelids in feigned coyness, rolled their large eyes, winked and gesticulated to the rhythm of their song. The assembly sat still as if in a trance, like people in a painting. Navinchandra observed the goings on, his mind preoccupied with thoughts of what the schoolteacher and the city judge had just told him. His eyes moved from face to face. He looked at Buddhidhan and felt sorry for him. The tales of the *Arabian Nights* he had read seemed to be coming true before his very eyes, and he felt like Aladdin trapped inside the demon's palace.

Kalavati now made her grand re-entry into the assembly, and the other courtesans stopped singing. She was dressed like one of Lord Krishna's gopis of her imagination. She wore a broad skirt of blue silk with deep red patterns brightly embroidered on the hemming. The skirt was gathered in at the waist by drawstrings. A gauzy odhni bright as moonlight covered her head, coming down to her slender waist. Shiny anklets and fish-shaped toe rings gleamed on her feet. These and other tiny ornaments as well as her finely cut nails shone like seashells as she began her dance, to the accompaniment of the sarangi and the mridangam. Her entire ensemble gave the impression of sparkling foamy waves. The ornaments, her fair knees, the taut veins of her feet, her nails and her heels drew attention to themselves. The gaze moved to her costume only when other parts of her body were still. Her hair was like dark clouds on the horizon. Gold, diamond and pearl ornaments adorned her neck and her supple arms. She sparkled like a sky studded with stars. The sight of her fair glittering body produced a haze before the mind's eye. Her large kohl-lined eyes came alive as she met the gaze of the assembly. Her anklets, her swirling skirt, her odhni, everything danced in rhythm as her delicate feet moved rapidly before the stunned audience. She was like lightning in a still sky. Her movements, swift and fluid, were akin to a small fish swimming in the quiet waters of a lake. She was the only one who moved. The audience sat still. She seamlessly danced into their mind's eye, arousing fierce passions that she herself did not feel. Her flat, delicate stomach revealed itself ever so slightly as she whirled and twirled, her breasts heaved and shook, and the assembly stared at her transfixed, their passions enflamed, their breathing heavy. Her charming lotus-like face swayed like a snake's hood, the sweet poison of her breath spread all around her. The assembly surrendered its manhood to her, and she played with them as if they were children or puppets. They waited impatiently for her song. Her eyes widened, her lips quivered, and the desires made manifest and aroused by her dance now tumbled out as a song.

Let me go, O' let me go now, Ghanshyam,
It is evening now, my Lord
I came in the afternoon
An aeon has since passed
My mother-in-law will scold
My husband will ask questions
People will sully my name

She sang, quite impervious to the emotions embodied in the words of the song. But the assembly was captivated, and swayed to her melody as one. Bhupsinh appeared to be entranced like everyone else, but inwardly his displeasure mounted. Watching Kalavati, he thought to himself, Bitch, go, leave now! Why wait till tomorrow? She was singing the last stanza of the song.

Daya Pritam says, Listen, O' beloved we must stop here
Let me go, O' let me go now, Ghanshyam.

The Rana could no longer keep up his façade—he got up abruptly as if possessed by a ghost and stormed out of the door through which he had entered. The assembly was astonished and anxious at this unexpected turn of events. The ushers shouted their customary calls which were drowned out by the sudden flurry of movement and commotion. People got up, made way, came together to enquire, and generally made noise. Buddhidhan, Shathrai and other principal court officials hurriedly followed the Rana. In the rush, rank and prestige were forgotten. The spell was broken, the mood interrupted. Kalavati stopped her song and dance and stood still as the entire hall milled around her and her accompanists. Some pushed past them, while others were careful not to brush against them. In the melee, Navinchandra somehow managed to hold fast onto Buddhidhan's hand and follow him out, wondering what came over the Rana suddenly, but he had no time to indulge his thoughts as he was shoved and jostled and pushed and dragged along by the crowd.

They followed the Rana down a flight of stairs to his personal drawing room. The room was large enough to accommodate a hundred to a hundred and fifty persons. A chandelier hung from the ceiling, the walls were adorned with mythical figures painted in the Jaipur miniature style, and there were paintings in the English and Chinese styles as well. There were mirrors with golden frames. There were 'wall sets' containing two or three frames. A mechanical music box was kept on a beautiful semi-circular table. On one wall hung a full length coloured portrait of Rana Bhupsinh. Facing the portrait, a bolster and embroidered square cushions were kept on a mattress. Bhupsinh sat down and, leaning upon the bolster, stretched his legs out. He sat there, biting his lips and frowning. His hookah was brought to him; it was intricately inlaid, one side was made of silver, the other of gold. He began to puff on it pensively. Others sat around him in silence on the carpet.

'Maharaj, are you not feeling well?' Shathrai asked with folded hands. They waited tensely for his response.

The Rana removed the hookah pipe from his mouth and blew smoke. He seemed agitated and preoccupied. He drew another puff and said, 'Yes. I wish to be left alone.' Everyone got up to leave and hurried towards the door.

'Kamdar, you stay back', he said to Shathrai.

Shathrai turned back. Buddhidhan saw this, and he looked at the Rana—their eyes met for a fleeting moment, and he went out with the others. The Rana and Shathrai were left alone in the drawing room. Shathrai sat facing the Rana.

'Kamdar, I wish to take up the matter of these letters.'

'Ji, very good. But what happened to you suddenly?'

'Don't you know there is a limit to a man's patience! How long can I carry this doubt in my head?'

Shathrai was pleased. 'Ji, you are absolutely right. It must be resolved. Such behaviour is unbecoming of Rana's trusted advisor.'

'Is everything in place? There is no need to make it known to all; after all the disgrace is mine as well. You go and send in the Counsellor alone.'

'Everything is in place. Narbheram has gone out; he will be back soon,' and Shathrai got up to leave. The Rana looked at him; Shathrai appeared perturbed and sympathetic to the Rana's distress, but he was of course delighted at the turn of events. In a while, Buddhidhan came in alone. He was acutely apprehensive, even frightened as he entered. Never before had he experienced such a state. But masking his fear, he put on a grave mien and waited for the Rana to relate to him his conversation with Shathrai. He needed to show courage. As soon as Buddhidhan entered the drawing room, the Rana burst forth. His conversation with Shathrai was either swept aside, or the Rana deliberately chose not to mention it. The Counsellor could not fathom the reason.

'Buddhidhan, your counsel for patience must be drowned in a well now. I cannot contain myself any longer and wait for the assembly to be over. My mind is not in my control.'

'Why, Ranaji? What could be so serious?' Buddhidhan asked with evident concern, but the cause of his concern was something quite different.

'This man, your Dushtarai, was flirting with Kalavati in my palace—behind *my* back!'

'Oh! When? Ranaji would recall what I had said: a courtesan cannot have only one paramour.'

'Yes, yes. What all will I have to recall, Buddhidhan? So many of your predictions have come true, but we are barely in our right mind to reflect on them at this moment. I would have finished both of them today—this fellow Narbheram stopped me. I still doubt if he is your man. How long can I tolerate if that bitch sings in my assembly? Buddhidhan, I want to finish them off, I tell you, there is murder on my mind. I could not bear to sit a moment longer in the court. You must act fast. That is why I got up. Any further delay, and you and I shall not get along.' The Rana spoke agitatedly, and he puffed on his hookah, kept shifting on his seat, unfolded his legs and folded them again—his unease was all too apparent. Buddhidhan's hope was restored, but a shadow of doubt still lingered. The Rana had still not told him of his conversation with Shathrai.

'Ranaji, the resolution you seek from me is very much within your grasp. I am here to carry out your wishes.'

'Yes, that is so, but what do you intend to do? Where is that rascal Dushtarai?'

'Shathrai is also anxious; he has sent messengers to fetch him.'

'All right, but what have you decided?' the Rana pressed him for an answer.

Buddhidhan hesitated for a fraction, he was still not fully confident of the Rana. 'Maharana, you have yourself read the letter brought by Russell Sahib's Shirastidar, Rambhau. Other skeletons will also tumble out. I hope that a remedy for Shathrai will emerge from them.'

'How?'

'You are aware of the discussions I have had with the Sahib. How can I be certain before I know of the contents of his letter? But Ranaji, rest assured your wish will triumph.'

'But Kalavati's bluff has to be called today! Both of them will be made to ride a donkey—that is for sure!'

'You take that up on my signal.'

'But, today itself, Buddhidhan.'

'Yes, of course, Ranaji.'

Just then, an out of breath Mahvo rushed in through one of the side doors. The Rana was enraged. 'Mahvo, you rascal, don't you know that I have asked to be left alone?!'

'Ji Maharanaji, I know, and that is why I came in. I am your servant; I would not want that your disgrace be made public. It should be dealt with in secrecy.'

Buddhidhan looked up in fright. He saw Mahvo carrying a bundle of letters. Mahvo flung them at the Rana's feet and stood with folded hands. Rana's eyebrows were raised as he skimmed through the letters. Buddhidhan calmly asked, 'Mahvo, what is it?'

'Bhai Sahib, what right do wretches like me have to speak when the letters are with the Rana? Are you yourself not a confidant of the Rana?'

'Very well,' said Buddhidhan and turned towards the Rana. He recognised the letters. Mahvo looked on with supreme disdain as he saw that the Counsellor's authority was paralysed.

The Rana threw the letters at Buddhidhan, and snarled, 'What vile ploy is this, Mahvo? You should be hanged! Have you no shame in bringing such a charge against my trusted Counsellor? Have you no fear? Do you think I am so naïve and foolish as to be deceived? Buddhidhan, my friend, have no fear about the letters.'

Mahvo smiled ingratiatingly and said, 'O Saviour of the poor, we poor are always wretched. Would I have the courage to bring before you forged letters? The Counsellor is your trusted man. He has done me good as well. But your kindness has been immense. If I did not believe that my duty towards you is foremost and paramount, I would not have done anything to harm the Counsellor. God alone knows the mental agony I have endured while doing this.'

Buddhidhan stared at Mahvo during this little speech. 'Mahvobhai, it is quite unnecessary to state how faithful and loyal you are to the Rana. That you also remember my kindness speaks well of you. The good deeds of the past must for now be put aside. But do be fair to me, and furnish proof that I am indeed the author of these letters. Do also tell us as to how you came to be in possession of them.'

The Rana, who had been biting his lips in anger, now banged his fist and thundered, 'Enough! I need no proof from you, you wily rascal!

I am not going to believe your fabricated lies. Such brazen depravity! Go, go and blacken your face, miserable wretch. Shathrai! Kamdar!'

Shathrai rushed in. 'Kamdar, have this rascal Mahvo arrested at once and hand him over to Dushtarai. Where *is* he?'

'He is on his way, Ranaji.' Shathrai sat down next to Buddhidhan and asked him softly what the matter was, but before he could answer, Bhupsinh thundered, 'Kamdar, look at these poisonous letters! This worthless lowlife has taken on our own Counsellor! Incredible! If Dushtarai is not present, call a soldier, take this wretch away! Who is guarding the door?' This was the first time ever that the Rana had to himself shout for a soldier; the officials waiting outside cringed.

'Ji, Huzoor!' Vijay Sen entered the room, and holding Mahvo by the arm, took him away. The Rana slumped back on the bolster, exhausted.

Buddhidhan protested, 'Ranaji, this is not right. You should view the proof that Mahvo has. To you I may be innocent, but I must be so for the world as well.'

'Forget the proof. What was done is correct. To glorify the wicked is to make them swollen-headed. If we seek proof from them, they assume even greater airs and participate in other intrigues,' Shathrai said solemnly.

'Ranaji, my plea must be accepted.'

The Rana sat up straight and said in a low voice, 'Shathrai, the Counsellor is right. There is a reason why I scolded Mahvo; the lowly should not be given much importance. But I have heard such rumours from other sources as well. I do not believe in them. But Buddhidhan, do not take it amiss, I too am human. If not today, I may doubt you tomorrow. That would not be good; yes, I think we must do as you have suggested.'

'Ji, Ranaji.'

'Kamdar, have the matter examined. Meanwhile, I will go to the queen's quarter. The queen knows something about the matter which I must now ascertain for myself.'

Buddhidhan was unsurprised by this deep-rooted conspiracy of Shathrai. But he knew that the Rana trusted the queen, and that worried him. The Rana got up with an air of finality and walked towards an internal door. As soon as the door opened, there was a loud crack, like a gunshot. Bhupsinh hesitated and looked around in surprise and alarm. 'Oh! God save the King!' Shathrai and Buddhidhan shouted as they rushed towards the Rana. Suddenly, the floor beneath the Rana's feet gave away, and he fell through it. But Buddhidhan ran and caught the Rana firmly in his arms, and both of them managed to come out and stand aside on secure ground. In seconds, the floor began to cave in from all sides and the hole widened to expose a large tunnel, four or five feet wide. The marble came loose and fell into the gaping cavity. The beautifully inlaid marble floor looked like it had been ravaged by an earthquake. The heavy wooden frame of the door balanced on the gaping hole like a bridge. Others now rushed in, excited, frightened, apprehensive. Suggestions, possibilities, theories flew thick and fast. 'Intrigue! Treachery! Trap!' shouted Buddhidhan as he encircled the Rana with both arms. Samar Sen, Vijay Sen, Pramaddhan, Jaymalshankar, Navinchandra and others who had come with them swiftly encircled the Counsellor and the Rana. Samar Sen and Vijay Sen drew their swords and stood prepared on either side. Navinchandra waited for a sign from Buddhidhan. The palace soldiers rushed in. Shathrai, who knew nothing, was momentarily stupefied. His eyes searched desperately for Dushtarai. 'What ever happened?' he asked and rushed to the Rana's side. Karvatrai and other officials followed him.

'What are you staring at! This is a crime against the State! The work of some vile traitor! Maharana, God preserve you! Ranaji, are you hurt? Vijay Sen, commence an investigation at once! Remove this debris and go into the tunnel, be careful, and keep your weapons in readiness ... Be careful, the floor is caving in!' Buddhidhan shouted out instructions like a man crazed, but all the while he held on firmly to the Rana. The effect was dramatic.

'What is it, Buddhidhan? Let go of me! What has possessed you? Let them all go to hell. What is that? A light inside the tunnel?' Bhupsinh, recovering from his initial shock, tried to enter the tunnel. But Buddidhan was adamant and forcefully held him back, 'No, no, Maharanaji! The fate of Suvarnapur cannot be endangered at any cost. Please stand back. There are many others to do this. Kamdar, you come along with me!' Buddhidhan ordered Shathrai who was standing there looking dazed. Bhupsinh was glad to see Buddhidhan's loyalty for him being exemplified, he was reassured. He looked at Shathrai, his mind crammed with doubts. Meanwhile, Vijay Sen, Samar Sen and other court officials were hard at work like labourers trying to remove the heavy debris. A path was soon cleared, and they entered the tunnel through a narrow gap in the floor. Inside the neatly dug tunnel that lay before them, they now saw two figures dimly silhouetted by the light of a lantern. Jamal Khan and Ranjit. Jamal held the lantern, while Ranjit's sword was drawn. 'Catch them! Arrest the traitors! Bring them up!' loud shouts were heard from inside the tunnel, which were echoed by those anxiously waiting on the outside. As the news spread like fire, many others now rushed to the spot, guards, court officials, townspeople. Soldiers and palace guards caught the two and dragged them out of the tunnel. People were surprised to see the duo, especially Jamal Khan, who was himself a soldier in service of the palace Karbhari. They began to thrash them.

As he watched all this unfold before his eyes, Shathrai was too crestfallen for words. He observed Buddhidhan, as if from a great distance, and submitted to the overwhelming numbness that was coming over him. The Rana knew quite well that Jamal Khan was Shathrai's confidant. Questions flooded Shathrai's mind, but no answers. How will I explain Jamal's presence? Will the Rana believe me? Can the Rana's rage be contained? What will be the outcome of his wrath? I had searched for that wretched Jamal everywhere, in every possible nook and cranny. How, why, and on whose instructions did he resurface today? And of all places here in this tunnel? Where on earth is Dushtarai? Why has he not returned? Is all of this related to Rambhau's mission? Buddhidhan must have orchestrated all these events ... Who else but he could be behind this? Even as he searched in desperation for a last ray of hope, the wise, old and experienced Karbhari of Suvarnapur could see his fate sealed. Like the waning moon that disappears as the first rays of a new sun light up the skies, his heart could see no light, darkness enveloped him. He could no longer think clearly as an ominous foreboding and fear gripped his mind. Anticipating the impending disaster, his intellect was the first to take leave of him, and then his patience. He knew, his other faculties and people would also leave him. Like a fortune teller, he could read his own future. He felt weak. Dark thoughts clouded his imagination, he saw a macabre dance of the dead. All the sins of his past now caught up with him. He had failed to fathom the import of the Rana's order of having Mahvo arrested—the truth of it now dawned upon him in all its frightful dimensions. He could see all his wealth destroyed before him. He thought of his son Dushtarai, and his mind froze like blood in the veins of the dead. Even the tremendous excitement and commotion of his surroundings failed to stir him, and Shathrai slumped down exhausted like a yoked bull upon the nearest chair. The Karbhari of Suvarnapur, known for his formidable political acumen, his all-encompassing capacity for intrigue, his razor-sharp intellect to which even kings submitted, that Karbhari now sat impotent and numb. His mind blank, his virility drained, Shathrai looked and felt like an old man as he sat helplessly on a chair, his hands folded across his lap. He felt that all the means and resources available to him were now futile. Kaba had robbed Arjun of his bow and arrows.

Navinchandra, too, had been surprised to see Jamal Khan emerge from the tunnel. As the day's astonishing events played out, he could suddenly see things quite differently. Various fragments and pieces of the grand puzzle fell into place the moment he saw Jamal. Navinchandra now knew that he would not need to carry out the instructions that Buddhidhan had given him that morning. Shathrai had indeed planned for something, but the events had overrun his plans. Thinking of all this, Navinchandra recited to himself:

He comes full of desire but he will leave head shaven,
Name besmirched, rolling in dirt.

He was amused that such couplets came to him, and at such times. He had heard Vanleela sing parts of *Rukmani Vivah* to Kumud Sundari, and the verses had stayed with him. Kumud Sundari came to his mind, too. Like him, she too had witnessed the Counsellor spend many sleepless nights. All those sleepless nights are now about to bear fruit, he thought—what strategy, what intellect! Buddhidhan, you found an ingenious way of punishing the offender without any discredit to your own family. And Jamal Khan, if you had not done what you did, I, Navinchandra, would never have gained this invaluable experience. Buddhidhan, you turned adversity into opportunity, difficulty into possibility. From where did you learn this? Certainly not in school! Astonishing! Navinchandra's mind whirred and hummed busily with his thoughts and observations of people in positions of power and political intrigue.

The courtiers enthusiastically came together to beat Jamal and one-eyed Ranjit. The Rana had to intervene and stop them. Buddhidhan ordered: 'Samar Sen, take some men with you and trace the origin of this tunnel. But be careful. Ranaji, please hand over Jamal Khan and Ranjit to Vijay Sen. This investigation should proceed in complete secrecy—am I right, Kamdar Sahib?' Buddhidhan looked around for Shathrai.

Hidden behind the crowd, Shathrai responded from a far corner, 'Yes.'

'Come here, Kamdar! Why do you sit alone at the back? What is wrong with you today?' said the Rana, looking in the direction from which Shathrai's voice came. People moved aside to clear a passage between Shathrai and the Rana. The Rana walked towards Shathrai. Speculation was already rife ever since Jamal's capture from the tunnel, and Shathrai's subsequent and evident despair. Shathrai finally got up from his chair and walked in slow, dejected steps towards the Rana. It was not as if he was slow, or his walk unusually hesitant, but his face lacked all lustre, all hope. The preceding events had coloured the perception of observers and their minds had already arrived at certain conclusions. The courtesy shown by the Rana, and his cordiality, thus seemed artificial to many. The Rana held the Karbhari by the arm, and said, 'My most experienced, most devoted and loyal Kamdar, your help is of utmost importance now. You know (and Bhupsinh looked towards Buddhidhan) I can no longer trust my old confidants. But if you too remain despondent, whom shall I look towards? Now, do reveal the full intent of this play—call Dushtarai immediately.' As he spoke, the Rana neither let go of Shathrai's hand, nor did he remove his eagle eyes from the Karbhari for a moment. 'Oh yes, trusted and truthful Karbharis are required on just such occasions. Their true worth is recognised only at such trying times,' Bhupsinh said, twirling his moustache.

Each word that the Rana spoke singed Shathrai, each syllable uttered was like a snake bite. The sky and the earth collapsed into each other. Shathrai no longer knew whom he could trust, whom he could turn to. Then, suddenly, he saw the man. Narbheram had just returned and stood whispering in Karvatrai's ears. Karvatrai looked at Shathrai, and he felt sorry for him. The judge's capacity for intrigue was nowhere close to Shathrai's. Karvatrai was not as imposing as his brother, but had a stout physique. Shathrai's hair had greyed and signs of age were visible on his body. Karvatrai was young and strong; his moustaches were firm and black, he had dyed his hair to hide a few grey strands. He was more courageous, his mind was less rational compared to his elder brother and hence he had greater capacity to bear suffering. His eyes knew no shame; compassion and goodness were strangers to his heart. His intellect grasped no need to follow the path of truth and justice. But he loved his family, and he was moved by his brother's plight. He had seen and followed what others had seen, but he had not fathomed even half of what his brother had. He was bold and strong in his belief that nothing could possibly go wrong for him and his brother. Karvatrai now went and stood next to Shathrai in solidarity, and turning to the Rana, said: 'Maharanaji, our police will get to the root of this rebellion and the traitors will be duly punished. The dust of your feet is glorious. This task would be accomplished in a moment. The enemies of the Ruler of Suvarnapur are certain to be destroyed.'

'Without a doubt,' Shathrai spoke up; his brother's presence gave him the courage.

'Buddhidhan, call Dushtarai! Remember the words of the Karbhari. My enemies are certain to be destroyed!' the Rana smiled at his Counsellor.

The Counsellor returned his smile, and replied, 'Ranaji, you say your enemies are certain to be destroyed. But I know they already are.'

'But where is Dushtarai? Buddhidhan, words speak louder than deeds, at least those uttered in the presence of rulers.'

'Most certainly they do, Ranaji.'

Observers were perplexed by these cryptic exchanges. Karvatrai sensed victory; he felt the Rana was about to bring up the matter relating to Rajba. Shathrai's understanding was quite the contrary; he glared at Buddhidhan, hatred evident in his eyes. He brought the small exchange between the Rana and the Counsellor to an end. 'Maharana, at this moment, we need to act, not talk. We must get to the root of this. My brother and I, along with some other officials, must leave the palace at once. Buddhidhan, come with us. We must investigate; your presence will be useful.'

As an escape route flashed before him, Shathrai felt the blood flow back into his veins. He felt he must quickly escape the Rana's clutches, and leave him with Kalavati and Narbheram. If matters went out of hand, Bhupsinh could be killed, or Shathrai himself could flee Suvarnapur with his family and wealth. This was his new plan. In any case, Buddhidhan should not be allowed to stay with the Rana.

Sharp enough to recognise that Shathrai was clutching at the last straw, Bhupsinh did not allow him to get away. 'No, Kamdar, I cannot let you go. I am deeply disturbed by today's incidents. You must stay with me and give me solace.'

The Karbhari had thrown his dice. He was disappointed that the outcome was not to his liking.

'Kamdar, call Dushtarai. Why do you not follow my command?'

Before Shathrai could formulate his response, Karvatrai said, 'Ranaji, Narbheram has just returned from home. His news is that Dushtarai is unable to come, his physical condition does not permit it.'

'Oh! What happened to him? He was here a while ago? Has there been some treachery at your house, too?'

'Ji, Ranaji, there is some such matter,' Narbheram replied. Shathrai and the others were startled.

'What is the matter? Narbheram, what has happened?'

'I cannot speak of it. Please forgive me.'

'Will you not obey my command?'

'Here is the man who can speak!' and Merulo rushed in, breathless and wounded, his arm covered in a bloodstained bandage. He fell at the Rana's feet, howling, 'Tyranny, cruelty, O Maharana! There is tyranny under your rule! Please save me, oh my saviour!' He wept loudly. The soldiers knew that Merulo was a favourite of the Faujdar, and one of them tried to lift him up. Just then, some noises in the tunnel drew their attention. Samar Sen and his troop could be seen herding Raghi, Nichdas and Khoda out of the tunnel. Everyone looked at them. Karvatrai could see his fate eclipse. He had lost heart after hearing Narbheram's report, but he put up a brave face. Merulo's presence frightened him about the home front. Samar Sen's captives scared him even more.

Dushtarai had rushed home. He was alone. He saw the soldiers posted at home chatting outside. He went in. The door was shut. He climbed up on the first floor and looked down into the courtyard. He was blinded by what he saw. Some game was on. Merulo was dressed up like a Muslim man and Rupali and Khalaknanda were dressed as his wives—they were acting out their parts. Having hitherto restrained themselves in the presence of others, they had now abandoned the last vestiges of shame. Khalaknanda heard some noises on the terrace and, startled, she hid inside. Enraged beyond belief, Dushtarai drew his sword and came down to the courtyard by another staircase. Taking Merulo by surprise, he cut him on the arm with his sword. Wounded,

Merulo promptly gave up all qualms and engaged his master in a fierce wrestling bout. He snatched away Dushtarai's sword. Dushtarai called out to the guards outside for help and opened the doors. The soldiers rushed in. But before that, Merulo wounded Dushtarai with his own sword and ran out from the back door, throwing the sword towards Rupali as he ran, shouting, that she should either save him or kill him. The sword fell in a corner. Dushtarai's wound was deep and he fell down. Khalaknanda saw her brother being injured, but feigned complete ignorance and lay down on a swing. Rupali was at her histrionic best, weeping and beating her breast. The soldiers considered arresting Rupali, but decided against it. They shut the doors and placed guards on them. They told her: 'Woman, we will tell the Karbhari of your deeds, we won't let you off.' Rupali went up, dressed up as a man, took Dushtarai's sword and jumped onto the roof of the adjacent house. The surprised neighbours followed her, but she managed to escape and rushed out onto the street, and a few streets later, she was indistinguishable in the crowd. She walked unhurriedly to Merulo's house. Merulo's brother was at home; she spoke to him, gave him all the information and sent him out to look for Merulo.

Narbheram had left the assembly on pretext of doing the work assigned by Shathrai, but he followed Dushtarai instead. Narbheram wanted to witness the fun and also report it back to the Counsellor, who would find the information useful. He met Merulo on the way, who was trying to run away. Narbheram stopped him and advised: 'Go to the palace this instant and lodge a complaint against Dushtarai. Their sun is about to set; you would be believed. If you hide, you will only prove your own guilt.' Narbheram taught him what he should say to the Rana. Merulo said: 'I will first go home and only then to the palace. No one has seen me except Dushtarai, who is about to die. The one who has seen me will not report me. I should go and alert my brother.' He met his brother on the way. Both of them went home and met the waiting Rupali. Merulo sent her off with his brother to a village that was within the territory of another state. He then proceeded to the palace. Narbheram went to the prison, but found Rambhau and

Tark Prasad already there. These two had travelled by a horse-drawn carriage. They found the bania in the prison. Rambhau was quick to gauge things. Narbheram heard him and rushed back to the palace. Shathrai was busy talking to the Rana, so Narbheram narrated the events to Karvatrai. He told Karvatrai he had met Merulo who was going to lodge a complaint against Dushtarai, and also the events that had led to Merulo's injury. Karvatrai was sorry to learn of the family's disgrace; he certainly did not want his family to be shamed in court. Merulo was about to complain about Dushtarai, which could not be countered without divulging details. A thief was about to punish his guards, and Karvatrai did not know how to counter Merulo's charge, since Narbheram had not told him that Merulo had grievously injured Dushtarai as well.

People were stunned to see Merulo wounded. They asked him about the cause of the wound. Shathrai was clueless. He went up to Merulo, still believing him to be the family's confidant.

'Kamdar Sahib, you can no longer save me. My complaint is against the Faujdar.'

Shathrai drew back as if stung.

'Ranaji, I have eaten the Kamdar's salt. It is not right for me to badmouth his family. But I have no option left. I came to know some secret matters relating to the palace and the court in which the Faujdar was a party. He came to know that I knew. He believed I would not be able to keep his secret. See what he has done to me. He would have killed me if I had not run away. I am afraid to go back home, hence I have come here seeking refuge.'

'What was that secret?' asked the Rana.

'Oh Maharanaji! How can I speak of it before you? Such things happen. It is nothing but some intrigue. But, my Provider, I am not as lowly as Mota Bhai Dushtarai took me to be. Please protect me until my complaint is resolved or till such time as I leave for my native village. Please ensure that I am under the protection of your trusted men so that the policemen do not harass me. I do not want anything else. I am a poor man.'

'But what was the secret matter? How do I know if you are right or wrong? Such a rascal—you evaded my question!'

'Maharanaji, I will tell you if you insist, but only you.' Merulo looked at Shathrai as if frightened.

'The Kamdar, too, has a right to hear your lies, so speak up. A lie, and you will be killed.'

'Ranaji, I have invited trouble for myself. Please forgive me, Kamdar Sahib, I have no option but to tell. Ranaji, there was something about a tunnel to be built between that pond in your garden and Kamdar Sahib's office room. It was to be built on the Kamdar's orders. I came to know of it. Kamdar Sahib, I tremble, please do not be angry. Oh, even Jamal is here! Ranaji, Jamal knows all about it! Please ask him. Let me go, my provider. Please do not ask me anything more. Jamal will tell you everything.'

'Lowly rascal! Vijay Sen, take him away!'

'O Maharana, is it your way to punish those who seek justice! I made a mistake. Never again will I complain. You are our provider. You protect us. Please let me go home. My house is better than your prison. The policemen will harass me, but let that be. But I have done no crime to deserve imprisonment.'

The Rana was surprised at Merulo's courage and loquaciousness. 'Fine. Go home. Vijay Sen let him go. Investigate his complaint, and report back to me.'

Merulo happily saluted the Rana and left.

'My dear Kamdar, so do you see how cunning men can be? People who work for us, be it at home or in the state, must be faithful and rooted; or else, you have seen the result. He did not hesitate while placing a charge against my trusted officials. How could he break into his master's house? How could he have the heart for it? What is even more surprising is that he ate your salt, but has none of your qualities.' The Rana looked at Shathrai gravely.

Meanwhile, Rambhau and Tark Prasad had returned from the prison. Shathrai realised he could no longer bribe Rambhau. Rambhau had met the bania in the prison and had all the facts in his possession. If Russell Sahib alone had to be tricked in this matter, it could have been done by bribing Rambhau. Shathrai realised that the Rana would be eager to take advantage of the matter. He sighed deeply and thought to himself, When the sky bursts, it cannot be patched up. Things were different when Rambhau had left the court earlier today. I was still the Karbhari. But the situation is now changed—Shathrai, the time when you could get things done with money is past.

Formally accusing Shathrai and Karvatrai in the matter, Rambhau said: 'Ranaji, Russell Sahib holds you in high esteem. But such Karbharis would cause you immense harm. It is true that he has been Karbhari for long now—but he is like an old disease. The Sahib knows well about the tyranny and cruelty in your state. He has said nothing hitherto and hoped for reform. But his hope has proved to be false. If the Sahib were convinced that no reform is possible, he would have taken different measures. He is convinced that the Karbhari does not allow complaints and pleas to reach you. You are not the one to tolerate tyranny if you were aware of it. If the Sahib were convinced that you do not have any able person in your service, he would most certainly recommend some outsider. But he knows well that you do have able and honest officials for whom the interest of the people is paramount. But the Karbhari has rendered them ineffective. However, the Sahib also believes that when you realise the true condition of your state, these officials will be ascendant and people will be happy. I am not authorised to say anything more. I place before you all the complaints that the Sahib and the Government have received about your administration. You are requested to have the matters properly investigated. The Sahib has sent these English newspapers which describe good and bad officials of your administration, and has left the comparison to you. He generally does not rely upon newspapers, but in this matter, his views match with those of the newspapers. Hence, the Sahib has sent them. Please have them read to you by some honest, English educated person and acquaint yourself with the details. And yes, I am asked to communicate a message from the Sahib. He believes that one should not fall behind the times. You must bear this in mind.

You should employ English educated persons who can help you keep abreast of our times, persons who know English statecraft, laws and ethics. The Sahib's letter deals with other issues also. I have nothing more to report as his representative. But I have a personal request. It is not a secret and hence it is not improper to mention it in the presence of the assembly. I am a well-wisher of your state. I am unfit to give counsel but if you will be so kind as to hear me, I wish to say that rarely is an officer as good and just as Russell Sahib posted in the native states. His advice is worth its value in gold. Your Counsellor knows the Sahib well, and would be able to speak with greater eloquence and experience and substantiate what I have said. The Counsellor has worked in the Agency, he has served you, and the Sahib is well acquainted with him. The Agent Sahib is pleased that you trust the Counsellor. He believes that so long as such individuals are part of your administration, both the people and you will benefit. The Counsellor would tell you the advantages of accepting the Sahib's advice. Ultimately, it is within your powers to accept or reject all such advice. The good and evil results of your actions are also your responsibility. We can only advise. You hold the reins of the administration. The results are a prerogative of the Gods. I have nothing more to add. Kamdar Sahib, pray do not blame me. I am merely a messenger.'

The Shirastidar's solemn speech came to an end. The assembly had frozen while he was speaking; it remained frozen like an image a little while longer. Rambhau took out wads of papers and newspapers from a cane basket carried by a soldier and gave them to Buddhidhan who stood beside the Rana. The officials looked at each other quizzically, whispered questions and guessed what the letters had in store for them and others. Finally, Rambhau handed to the Rana a square envelop that contained a letter from the Sahib. The Rana immediately opened the envelop, read the letter and responded after some thought: 'Ramchandra Rao, there is no need to say that the Sahib is my well-wisher. His affection is evident in the letter. The Sahib's advice is proper; there have been incidents today itself that prove that his assessment is correct. My eyes have opened. I am sorry that I bestowed my trust on one who was unworthy of it. Please go to the rest house and have your meals. I will send my response within an hour or two.' Rambhau saluted the Rana and left.

Shathrai could not look up. Buddhidhan looked at the Rana intently, awaiting orders. Other officials were also eager to hear the Rana's decision. Rana Bhupsinh scratched his forehead, smoothed his moustaches and began: 'Buddhidhan, I am confused. Kamdar, I am very sorry. Your fate is beyond my control until all these papers and newspapers are read, the matters examined and the root of rebellion and treachery found. But yes, it is time for me to remove all illusion. Kamdar, you and your cronies are vile, wicked and faithless—of that I have now no doubt. I know well that the letters given to me by Mahva, intended for Buddhidhan's destruction, are forged. I know the author of those letters, and I also know that you are the source of the intrigue. You must be punished for it. I am very sorry. I am also extremely angry. How different can people be! Buddhidhan is of one kind, and you Shathrai are quite another. Have I done any less for you? Have I deprived you of anything ever? Have I not trusted you enough? No, the fruits of my deeds cannot be such!' and the Rana shook his head gravely. 'I have no more compassion left for you, Shathrai. Buddhidhan, you have counseled me thousands of times to be kind, to be liberal, to forget enmity and be good. And I have curbed my instincts and submitted to your advice. But no longer. The very men you were trying to save from my wrath have perpetuated such vile treachery to cause your downfall! Thank God that He showed me the right path, or else what would have become of you? But this demon did not even stop at that. This stupid fool, in my own palace, tried to ... But no, it is not worth mentioning. Is there anyone so blind who cannot see what is apparent to all? Officers, if you are wise, learn your lessons. Your ruler is not blind like others—he sees with his own eyes. Russell Sahib is naïve. He thought that Shathrai had truly deceived me. He does not know that I knew everything all along, but that I deliberately kept quiet. I have not been in the dark about the tyranny and cruelty faced by my poor people. Shathrai would have ceased to be a Karbhari long ago, but for Buddhidhan. But enough is enough. His evils have caught up with him. He is crushed under the weight of his own sins. Buddhidhan, I will no longer accept your advice on this matter. Vijay Sen! Vijay Sen! Arrest the Kamdar and his brother and keep them as under trial prisoners under your charge. Arrest Dushtarai as well, and keep the three of them separate. Be on your guard. None of them should be allowed to escape or talk to anyone else. Your own life is at stake here. Lock up their houses and place your guards there.'

Buddhidhan suddenly fell at the Rana's feet and said with folded hands, 'O Saviour of the poor! I have a humble request to make!'

'Get up! What is all this drama? Get up and ask. Have I ever denied you anything?' The Rana caught Buddhidhan's hands and tried to lift him up.

'No, Ranaji, no. I will get up only after you hear and accept my plea. Shathrai is my caste brother and also a distant relative. Please do not send them to prison, their religion cannot be observed in prison. You cannot be like them, Ranaji.'

'All right, all right. Vijay Sen take them to some other place, but keep a strict watch over them. Ensure that they are provided with food and drink. Anything else? Shall I arrange for sweets to be sent to them? Tell me, Buddhidhan!'

'No, Ranaji, you are most kind. All else can wait.'

The Rana ordered: 'Vijay Sen, arrest that bitch Kalavati and drag her to the prison. I want to see her dragged though the dusty streets in her silken and embroidered garments, her ornaments strewn on the streets to be found by beggars. Vijay Sen, I want to see a man who is the most wicked, the darkest among the dark, the ugliest among the ugly and the filthiest among the filthy, an outcaste, rub dust, ash and black soot all over her body, face and hair. Detain all the others involved in this treachery. All of them will face an investigation and be duly judged.' The Rana then asked Jaymal to come closer, and whispered to him, 'I am going to assign you a difficult task. I do not want to see the queen's face. Take her to the old palace and keep her there.

'Officers, you know that today is my birthday. The day did not begin joyously. That does not matter. My people have been freed from suffering and tyranny. They would celebrate. That is for me a matter of festivity. Moreover, the court will assemble as scheduled at five in the evening. I will give you enough reason to celebrate. The Counsellor and I will together plan as to how that is to be effected.

'Shathrai, we are about to part ways. I am sorry that we had to see this day. But do not incur the wrath of Gods by putting the blame on me. The kingdom of God allows each one of us to earn merit by our good deeds.

'Buddhidhan, come with me. You are the only one who can show me a way out of this morass.' The Rana took the Counsellor's hand, and they walked away together. Before leaving with the Rana, Buddhidhan signaled to Pramaddhan and Navinchandra that they should go home.

Shathrai had no strength left to formulate a response even in his mind. The clothes on his body were the same, his body was the same, he was the same man. He had entered the palace of Suvarnapur in full glory that morning like the midday sun; but the sun had set when he was about to leave the palace. He was dethroned. But pride shone on his face like the last flicker of a dying lamp. A pride that was incongruous to the moment, barren, bereft of light and impotent. No one noticed his pride. Everyone looked at this Karbhari whose power and glory had waned. He took his leave of the royal palace where for years he had ruled uninhibited over kings. Officials and people had believed his authority to be eternal. He would not return to the palace. Shathrai felt a terrible void. The palace suddenly seemed like a dense and dangerous forest. Shathrai emerged from the palace, forlorn, and looked around with vacant unseeing eyes. The pride and glory of being the royal Karbhari, that had once been his, accompanied Shathrai upto the gates of the palace garden, and then turned back in search of the man who would take his place. A single tear glistened in his eye. He almost had to run to keep pace with the new guards that Vijay Sen had posted. For the first time, he was required to keep pace with the soldiers, instead of the soldiers keeping pace with him. His condition was like that of an impoverished and failed student. People pointed fingers at him, some with pity, and this momentary attention passed on to discussion about impending changes in the administration. People seemed to rejoice at his fall. His only companion was his brother Karvatrai. Finally, they disappeared from the sight of onlookers. He was soon out of people's minds as well. Talk about the tumultuous events of the morning turned to eager anticipation of the court to be held that evening.

People had entered the palace noisily. They emerged from it in silence, as quiet as midnight. No one said a word. Each face looked grave and pensive, as if they had emerged after a reading of the *Ramayana* or the *Mahabharata,* or were returning from a crematorium having consigned a body to flames, having collected the ashes and dried their eyes. The only sound was the crunch of their feet. They had followed Shathrai to the palace; they left it without him.

Navinchandra and Pramaddhan were among the last to leave, accompanied by two or three soldiers. Their faces looked peaceful and free of fear. The group that had come with them also left for their respective homes. As Navinchandra's eyes trailed after Shathrai, these words rose to his lips:

Time ordains both strength and weakness:
For one in the spring of his youth
Time turns the sweet call of the swan
Into the harsh cry of the peacock.

Yes. Time ordains both strength and weakness. Time alone arbiters between power and the loss of power—nothing else but Time can do this. Man, your pride is incongruent. Shathrai, it is not that your conspiracy has failed, but your time has been defeated, mused Navinchandra as he walked.

They had barely reached the gates of the palace garden when Samar Sen came running, and breathlessly urged, 'Pramaddhan, Bhai

Sahib has called for you! Navinchandrabhai, please go home quickly; Bhai Sahib and Pramaddhan will be there soon. Ramsen, accompany Navinchandrabhai.'

Samar Sen and Pramaddhan went off in one direction. Navinchandra and Ramsen went another way. New thoughts swirled in Navinchandra's mind like sparrows flying overhead, and he walked at a brisk pace.

13 On the Way

Navinchandra was among the last to leave the palace. A guard walked behind him. They walked back in silence like two shadows on the long desolate road surrounded by vast fields under the blazing summer sky. Navinchandra was exhausted, and ravenously hungry. It was noon; the road was fiery hot. The unrelenting sun beat down upon him, draining his tired mind and body. He was drenched in sweat. Sweat poured in streams from under his pagdi. His eyes and cheeks were red with the heat. Why are you in this state, Navinchandra, he asked himself. Images of the inviting cool and quiet of the Counsellor's house, still far, were suppressed by the tumultuous and fiery scenes he had just witnessed at the palace. He had seen, experienced and learnt a great many things, both at the Counsellor's house and at the Suvarnapur palace assembly. The one in search of experience had been presented with rich learning opportunities. Yes, that could not be denied. But the satisfaction and pleasure of having learnt from these new experiences were not uppermost in his fatigued mind just then. He thought of home. He was hundreds of miles away from home, and yet all at once thoughts of his parents and friends filled his mind, bringing a rush of memories in their wake, and a sharp yearning. From the road, he could see the point where the river Bhadra met the sea. For an instant, he felt a strong impulse to take a boat. He became oblivious of his surroundings, of the presence of fellow travelers; he did not know where the road led or why he was walking upon it. 'His eyes were in his heart, and that was far away.'[1] His heart was at home, and home was in his heart. Nothing of Suvarnapur, not one object, not one individual had come to belong in his mind. And yet, there was one person in Suvarnapur who had a place in it. Kumud Sundari, the daughter-in-law of the Counsellor's family, occupied a central place in his world. Kumud Sundari, why are you here? Navinchandra, what is the matter with you? You remembered home when you entered the palace gardens. And now again. Why? Why do you think of Kumud Sundari and home inseparably? These and other similar questions rose sky high like tidal waves in his mind. Some incidents of the Counsellor's family interspersed his thoughts. Navinchandra, are those events responsible for the present condition of your mind? Dear reader, you should be acquainted with those incidents.

While he was recovering from his injuries at the Counsellor's house, Navinchandra had observed and experienced much. He had been wounded trying to protect Alak Kishori's virtue; Alak was immensely grateful for this. She had sat by his bed, attending to him, till his wounds had healed and he had fully recovered. She had no respect for her husband whatsoever. She treated the whole world with derision, and her husband was no exception. She showed no deference to anyone except her parents. She did not however believe her mother to be intelligent. She wielded power over her friends. She did not consider anyone, including her husband, to be her equal. She did not know what it was to love someone as an equal. But yes, Alak Kishori was capable of affection. She was true to her word and compassionate. It never occurred to her that any one could be worthy of deference or respect, that she could set aside her arrogance, be that of money, beauty, virtue, wisdom, intelligence, status or family, and be amiable, be affectionate and cultivate an equal friendship. This quality was dormant in her father. Buddhidhan's daughter, and not the son, had inherited this quality. Her brusque and haughty demeanour was on account of it. She had been able to protect her virtues because of this

[1] Author's note: 'The Gladiator', Lord Byron.

quality. Whenever she looked at any man, her inevitable response was: Who is he? How dare he compare with me? Who am I, and who is he? Do I succumb to anyone? Is anyone fit to be my equal? Her pride had thus remained undiminished. Ultimately, it was two individuals who vanquished her pride. Affection that she had hitherto given to none, she gave to her sister-in-law. Kumud Sundari drew warmth unasked from her; Alak felt affectionate towards Kumud. One reason was Kumud's gentle and loving disposition; the other reason was that she was Alak Kishori's choice. Alak would become effusive and sentimental whenever she was with her sister-in-law. People would laugh at her. Her mother, too, would laugh at her daughter's exuberance. Alak Kishori knew this, but she disregarded what others said. She even scolded her mother: 'What is it to you? I will be what I like with my sister-in-law! You do what you have to do.' She could even forget her own beauty in the presence of Kumud and sat meekly when Kumud read out passages from books and explained them to her. Alak was not even conscious of not being haughty around her sister-in-law. Kumud allowed Alak to run the household, was deferential to her in public and followed her around; this satisfied Alak Kishori's ego, and her affection for her sister-in-law deepened. But those who observed them closely realised that it was Kumud who ruled over Alak, and that it was she who followed Kumud. It was Kumud's subtlety that did not allow Alak to realise that she was under Kumud's influence. Alak's pride melted before Kumud.

The other person who robbed Alak Kishori of her pride and hauteur was Navinchandra. She was beholden to him. She never left his bedside. She looked after his medication and comfort and all his other needs. She sat by his side even when he had visitors. Her friends also sat in Navinchandra's room. Concerned, her mother advised and cautioned her: 'It is good that you care for him, but it is not good for you to sit by his bed all day long alone, or in the presence of visitors. People will gossip. After all, he is a man and a stranger. Have a servant sit there with him, and you supervise from afar.' In response, Alak snapped at her, made a face and said, knitting her brows, 'Oh, I know how people are. Who cares about people! As if they are the only ones possessed of wisdom and virtue! They can ridicule me all they like. I don't care!' Resigned, her mother could only respond, 'All right. Do what pleases you.' So Alak continued to sit by Navinchandra's bedside, freely mocking people and their interfering, over wise nature. She also received her visitors in his room. Kumud, shy as she was, would always hesitate to enter Navinchandra's room, though her room was adjacent to his. Alak would often drag her to his room, saying: 'Bhabhi, he is like a member of the family. Why should you be shy of being in his room? He is educated, and so are you. Sit here and read something nice. I will listen to you read, and so will he. He could even explain things that you may not understand. And since I am there, it shouldn't be a problem for you.' She would catch Kumud by the hand and make her sit. Kumud experienced thousands of inarticulate desires. She read when forced to. She listened, but not once did she allow herself to smile, converse or engage with Navinchandra in any way. In all the days she spent there, not once—not even for a moment—did she gaze straight at Navinchandra. If either she or Navinchandra wished to say or ask anything of each other, they did so through Alak Kishori.

Even as Alak tended to him night and day, Navinchandra was aware that such overzealous care, even if sincere, was contrary to social conduct. He also recognised that by her insistence, Alak had put Kumud in a difficult situation; but he felt helpless in the face of his illness and Alak's stubborn disposition.

Gradually, women began to gossip about Alak Kishori. It was blown out of proportion by those jealous of the Counsellor's growing power and influence. People enjoy gossiping about prominent families. Vanleela told Kumud about it, but Kumud treated it with disdain. Vidurprasad too heard the whispers and braced up to confront Alak Kishori, but was duly subdued after she lashed out at him angrily. He was subdued, but not convinced. One day Garbaddas was invited to their house for a meal. Alak Kishori bathed before entering the kitchen to cook. The bathing area was dark. Garbaddas took advantage of it and made a pass at her. In response, Alak threw a ladle full of boiling dal on his face and ensured that the lecherous man never entered their house again after that day. Garbaddas stopped harassing women. Vidurprasad was convinced of Alak's chastity.

Alak Kishori's unfettered conduct thus emerged unscathed and victorious. She was so proud of her chastity and autonomy that she was unafraid of associating with those of loose morals. She would say: 'A buffalo has to bear the burden of her horns—if others have low morals, what is it to us?' She had among her friends some unchaste women and some who were brazenly sensuous. And Alak Kishori was particularly fond of them for this reason. Alak's sensuality and physical desires may have remained unexpressed with her husband; but with her friends, she was completely frank and free. They also reciprocated her emotions. This was the reason for Alak's excessive fondness and partiality for Krishna Kalika. No one had the courage to tell her to give up the company of such friends.

This base association did not remain fallow for long. Krishna Kalika became infatuated with Navinchandra. But she could not, on her own, fulfill her desires. So she decided to make the Counsellor's daughter an accomplice. Alak frowned upon licentious behaviour. Let alone men, she did not permit any lascivious praise of women. Krishna Kalika saw that Navinchandra had made a pure and immaculate impression on Alak, and decided to use this to her own advantage. She would praise Navinchandra's good nature, his virtues, his learning. She also praised his handsome looks. Alak Kishori was overwhelmed by Navinchandra's chivalry in saving her from dishonour. She heard his praise with pleasure. Krishna Kalika surreptitiously introduced vile thoughts in her praise of him. One day she spoke of his physical beauty and moved on to talk about mismatched couples. Then, emboldened, Krishna Kalika said: 'Behn, you truly deserve a husband like Navinchandra; Vidurprasad is all right, but just so. It is like a crow that got the sweet dahitharu.' Alak Kishori scolded her for her foolishness, and the matter ended there. She too forgot about it.

After an hour or two, Alak went into Navinchandra's room. He was fast asleep. He had to be administered his medicines. She stood there, uncertain if she should wake him. His wounds were healing, but they needed to be dressed afresh and bandaged. His fever had subsided now, but he needed to be given medication. He was advised not to exert himself, and had gradually regained some of his former strength. His face looked brighter, his cheeks glowed. A fine film of perspiration glistened on the broad forehead of the sleeping man. Manmatha, the God of Passion, sat unseen and formless between Navinchandra's dark, manly eyebrows. His arrows pierced the heart of the helpless woman, who all at once trembled with an unknown desire. She, Alak Kishori who dazzled everyone who set eyes upon her, was herself dazzled. She watched in wondrous awe as his lips quivered in sleep and opened ever so slightly in a pout, as if ready to drink nectar from her lips. Alak could not fathom what was happening to her. She had never before experienced such emotions. She had not even heard of them. Whom could she have asked? Breathless and confused, she sat down on the floor by the side of his bed. She watched him breathe to a gentle rhythm. What was this man doing to her? Why did he seem so strangely transformed today? A vicious and potent desire possessed Alak, subduing even her pride and chastity. She stifled a deep moan in her throat. There was a mirror on the wall. In this mirror her face appeared adjacent to his. She looked up at their reflected faces. Krishna Kalika's words now rang through her ears. The mirrored image gave testimony to her words. She recalled how she had tightly held on to Navinchandra the day Jamal was captured. The memory of that touch tickled her imagination, she liked the sensation. Alak who had fought Jamal like Ma Chandi and robbed Garbaddas of his dignity, Alak who was fiercely proud and free now appeared powerless to resist the charm of the sleeping Navinchandra. She lost her capacity to think. The image of the sleeping man rode upon the turbulent waves rising in her heart like the full bright moon. Her heart churned. No one could see her turmoil. Fantasy is like a monkey. Krishna Kalika had stoked her imagination. The fantasy moved unbridled between her mind and heart, it petrified the pure and chaste Counsellor's daughter. It laid bare the wounds inflicted upon her by passion. She could no longer bear it. She mumbled, 'Har, Har, Shiv, Shiv' to calm herself, but to no avail. There are many who desire, even worship this state of inflamed uncontrolled passion. It gives pleasure to many. But it turned Alak Kishori frail and weak. There was no escaping its power. Navinchandra! Are you asleep? The virtuous woman could not plead for release. Tears rolled down her eyes. Just then Navinchandra turned on his side. As he turned, his hand moved and came to rest on Alak's shoulder, startling her. The sudden unexpected touch was pleasurable. She felt at last she was about to be freed from the terrible pangs of desire. Her lips trembled in a smile. But her conscience, too, fought to the last—she felt agonised that she allowed his hand to rest upon her, that she did not remove it. It was as if Alak Kishori's strong virtues propelled her hitherto unexpressed desires to manifest themselves even more strongly. She was not content with this slight touch and hungered for more. Desire, in the guise of gratification, exerted greater force. The touch did not bring a sense of release but of bondage and it sapped her mind and body. It spread through her like poison. This excruciating agony took the form of tears that refused to dry. Navinchandra's unsteady hand slipped further down and came to rest where all desires are harboured. Alak Kishori's warm tears fell on his hand. Sensitive to the wetness of tears, his hand moved. Pushed beyond endurance and willing to break all limits, Alak recklessly caught his hand in her own and pressed it to her wildly beating heart. Navinchandra opened his eyes partially, yet he remained in slumber. His eyes could not believe these dream-like scenes. What! Even *he* does not remove his hand? Did his mind, too, echo her desires, then? Or did he think it was a dream? What a great fall! Lowly company allowed this base fantasy to flourish. Fantasies of the mind became bodily passions. A body inflamed with desire permitted an illicit touch. A touch she had no right to, but one she accepted, allowed it to linger, to grow on her, to rest on a part of her beyond the scope of a stranger's touch. She held on to his sleeping hand when it moved as if by a divine command. Oh, most virtuous woman—you have lost your chastity by just this one act. Many times while administering medication, you inadvertently touched him. And still you were virtuous. But the touch of the same body makes you a fallen woman today. You are impure! One friendship, one fantasy. What consequences! Like you, has Navinchandra also become sullied? Did the Gods witness this? Did the walls register it? Did either of them realise that someone else had witnessed them? Or was it that others could see, but the two of them had been blinded? Strange are the ways of God.

Hitherto, Alak Kishori had never felt the need to close the doors of the room. Her mind was pure, so was her conscience. Like always, the doors were wide open, for she had entered the room with an entirely different mind. She had her back to it. Unknown to her, a pair of eyes watched her intently. Who?

Women, especially young women of the same inclination and age, are quick to form a friendship. Krishna Kalika and Alak Kishori were friends while Vanleela and Kumud Sundari had grown fond of each other. Vanleela was playful but wise, lustful but virtuous; she was fond of reading and singing, and though not given to vilification, she did enjoy watching others being compromised. She had learnt singing from Saubhagya Devi; she possessed a high-pitched voice and wanted to scale it up further. She was always ready for a lively debate in Alak Kishori's company. Vanleela visited Kumud daily. They would converse privately, play chess, sing to each other, and Kumud would read out interesting passages from books or poetry to her. Like always, after finishing her meals and household chores, that day too, Vanleela had come to meet Kumud. She had glanced into Navinchandra's room in passing, and seen his hand on Alak's shoulder. Startled, she had stopped to take a closer look, and then rushed to tell Kumud who had always scorned at the rumours.

'Bhabhi, you refused to believe them; now come and see with your own eyes!'

'Vanleela, you haven't changed. Let them be. Why should we bother about them? Don't we have anything else to do?'

'Oh, why such indifference! Can't we even look? Come on. They are so engrossed in each other, they won't notice us if we stood there for half an hour. Come!' and Vanleela caught Kumud's hand. But she had no clue how pained Kumud was, what turmoil it caused her heart and soul. Could Vanleela be speaking the truth? Oh learned Sarasvatichandra! What is this? What am I being told? Did you forsake me for this? Or are you in fact Navinchandra? Are you not Sarasvatichandra? You cannot be him. My Sarasvatichandra—though mine no longer—was pure. No, you *cannot* be him. Kumud Sundari freed her hand.

'Vanleela, you may go. I will not come.'

'What will you do here?'

'I will sing and play my sarangi.'

'Would you rather sing than see them? I never knew anyone like you!'

'So be it. You go on.'

Vanleela was surprised at Kumud's indifference and lack of curiosity. She went and stood near the door. Having rid herself of Vanleela, Kumud returned to her place. Her eyes brimmed over with tears. It was as if she had seen her husband with another woman, or as if she herself had been violated. She flung herself on the bed and cried her heart out. Then as abruptly, she got up, wiped her tears and stood in the middle of the room. How can I allow you to be so disgraced, Sarasvatichandra? I will not let you tread this path. You have erred, but I shall reawaken your virtues. You will come to your senses. If you walk such a vile path, what will the world come to? How can my heart bear to see you like this? How will my heart hold? Can Gorakhnath bear to see his disciple Macchandra beguiled by lust? O Baba Gorakhnath, come to my aid. Give me your strength. Sarasvatichandra, why have you come to such a pass? Water, if you want to flow downhill, who can stop you!' Her eyes full of tears, she picked up the sarangi. She sat down on a chair that was close to Navinchandra's room, and began to sing. Her voice carried to the room adjacent.

She who resides in the heavens white
Fell down onto the Lord's head
Having fallen once, she fell again
Not being contained by the Lord
She fell onto the mountains
And thence further, even lower
Twisting and turning, she fell onto the earth
Gathering dust and grime in her wake
Sullied Ganga eventually entered the salty sea
She who falls is destined to meet such an end
A fallen mind is destined for dissolution

Never before was Kumud Sundari's song heard outside her room. Today, she broke free. Her voice opened up. Tears flowed down her cheeks as she sang. Her sarangi was wet with tears. She poured all of her pain into the song. Sapped of her strength, as she sang the last lines, she fainted, and the sarangi fell to the ground. Kumud's lotus eyes closed and her mouth parted slightly, revealing her pearl like teeth. Her arms hung limp, her body became lifeless and inert, her tears dried on her pale face; only her tender breasts, witnessed by the lifeless walls of Pramaddhan's bed chamber alone, moved to the rhythm of her beating heart. There was no one to see this. In a house full of people, you were alone. There was no one to care for you, Kumud Sundari.

In the next room, Navinchandra had woken up, but he was still in-between sleep and wakefulness and incapable of recognising either state. Alak Kishori's touch had induced a pleasant dream. This was his first ever experience of such a touch. Even when his eyes opened, he felt he had woken from one dream into another. He gazed at Alak Kishori with partially open, dreamy, playful and lusting eyes, as if she were a part of his dream. He did not withdraw his hand, and for a moment, he was filled with pleasure. Just then Kumud Sundari's soulful song wafted into his ears. As his ears sensed the sublime pleasure of music, the pleasure of touch numbed. His eyes shut again. Kumud's song carried her pain as well. They suffused his heart. This was the first time he had heard Kumud sing; the timbre and melody of her voice was divine like that of apsaras. He was enveloped by a pure joy. To Vanleela's eyes, it appeared as if Alak Kishori and Navinchandra were engrossed in each other, their steady gaze fixed upon each other. They were still as an image. Vanleela had no doubt that their desire was mutual.

Suddenly, both the sarangi and the song stopped. As Kumud's sarangi fell with a sharp thud, it broke a string and let out a long shrill sound, mingling with her broken voice and a heart-wrenching sob. It jolted Navinchandra out of his dreamy state. He was now fully awake and alert. He gently freed his hand from Alak's clasp, and looked at her with sad yet censorial eyes. Then, in a voice that redeems one from purgatory, he said softly but clearly: 'Behn Alak Kishori, I am like a brother to you.'

Shamed beyond words, Alak could not meet his eyes and looked down, silently beseeching mother earth to swallow her. Like a drop of water evaporates from a heated pan, her passion, her desires vanished. She neither knew how to respond nor could she move a limb; she just sat there frozen with her eyes glued to the floor. There was only one thought in her mind: Oh God! What have I done! Her head throbbed painfully. She could not look up at him. She told herself, I should either bite my tongue and take my life this instant or stop breathing.

Navinchandra saw her turmoil. He solaced her and said, 'Behn, do not be so distressed. Even Brahma erred once. Do not make the same error again. I know your conscience is pure. I am not a simpleton. What has happened cannot be undone. Put it out of your mind. Your dharma was upheld; praise the merciful God for it.'

Alak Kishori was overwhelmed and speechless with emotion.

'Behn, get up. Please give me my medicines.'

'Bhai, you are truly my brother,' Alak found her voice at last and mustered the courage to speak. 'Navinbhai, the blessing you have given me today is far more valuable than the time you saved me from dishonour. Oh, how I have fallen and tainted myself! What have I done! My life is futile. I am worth less than dust.' She looked up at him, her eyes brimming with tears.

'Behn, do calm yourself.'

'My virtue has been compromised, and by my own hand. I cannot bear the shame of it! What face will I show the others now?'

'People know nothing. God alone was witness. He is most compassionate.'

'True; but this disgrace, this ignominy is beyond endurance—I, *Alak Kishori*, fallen! I can no longer live.' And she ran out of his door, weeping.

Vanleela had seen Navinchandra withdraw his hand and also heard the words that gave testimony to his purity. But before she could hear Alak Kishori's response, her attention was diverted. She heard the sarangi fall and rushed to Kumud's room. She saw that Kumud had fainted. 'Bhabhi, what happened?' she cried out as she rushed to her aid. Saubhagya Devi had seen Vanleela crouching at Navinchandra's door. Pained and angry, she had come up to admonish her daughter, to ascertain for herself the truth of the rumours, and to find out details of the matter from Vanleela. Saubhagya Devi was also worried about the family's prestige. As she came up, there was no sign of Vanleela, but she saw Alak tearfully leaving the room and stared after her in surprise; she felt that perhaps she had erred in thinking ill of her daughter. Alak Kishori was also startled to see her mother at the door, and scared that she had witnessed what happened. Saubhagya Devi was about to ask her something, when Vanleela shouted from the next room, 'Oh someone come and help! Devi, Alak behn, come, look! Bhabhi has fainted!'

'What!' cried Saubhagya Devi and she ran; in her haste she stumbled and fell, but before anyone could come to her help, she picked herself up and rushed again. Alak Kishori forgot all about her distress and hurried after her mother. Her mind was numb and so were her feet. Navinchandra forgot his illness and wounds, jumped out of bed and rushed to Kumud Sundari's room. This was the first time he had entered her room. He stood behind everyone else, perplexed and anxious.

Kumud was still slumped unconscious on the chair. Everyone crowded around her. Saubhagya Devi asked, 'Vanleela, what happened?'

Vanleela was scared. Kumud had fainted while she was at the door of Navinchandra's room. What was she to say if asked where she had been? She replied, 'Who knows. She was singing and playing the sarangi, and suddenly she fainted.'

Navinchandra came forward. It was his responsibility to plead patience with the women and find a way of reviving Kumud Sundari. He looked at Kumud's face, remembered her song, and guessed the reason for her condition. Concealing his anguish, he said, 'Devi, do not worry. Please help me lift her and put her on the bed. She will revive soon. Alak behn, call for some rosewater.' Alak Kishori hurried out, and on her way, she instructed Samar Sen: 'Send someone to fetch father and another to get the vaidya.' Vanleela followed Alak and said, 'I think bhabhi had an epileptic fit. At my home there is a bottle of medicine we had got from Bombay. Have that fetched as well.' One person was sent to get that. Samar Sen stood guard at the door but his attention was on Kumud's room.

Saubhagya Devi held Kumud's head in one hand and caressed her face with the other, entreating her to open her eyes. 'Kumud! Kumud, my daughter ... Oh do say something! Why are you so silent?' Navinchandra turned his face and wiped his tears unnoticed. He said, 'Devi, let us lay her upon the bed. She will not speak now.' Saubhagya Devi was aghast. 'She won't speak? Will Kumud never speak again? Navinchandra what makes you say such things! She is the light of my house!' she said, almost delirious. Alak returned with the rosewater, followed by Vanleela. Navinchandra splashed seven or eight handfuls of it on Kumud's face. The others watched anxiously. Like the lotus bud that opens each morning, Kumud Sundari stirred ever so slightly. 'Devi, look, bhabhi moved!' Alak said. But in vain. Kumud Sundari did not regain consciousness even after half a bottle of rosewater was poured. Navinchandra was helpless and again said, 'Devi, let us lay her upon the bed and wait for the vaidya.' Alak Kishori and Vanleela lifted Kumud from the waist and legs, while Navinchandra supported her head and back. Saubhagya Devi tried to give them a hand, but she felt as if she were lifting Kumud's dead body and she fell backwards in horror against the wall. She cried out, 'Hai! Oh, my dearest Kumud!' Navinchandra's face came close to Kumud's as he supported her head and shoulders with both arms. His tears rolled down his cheeks and fell onto her eyes and face; he was unable to wipe them.

Slowly and carefully they lowered her onto the bed. Saubhagya Devi came and sat by her, she kissed Kumud's face, ran her fingers through her hair, weeping. Navinchandra put on a brave act and tried to console the women. Devi's breath seemed to momentarily revive Kumud, and she opened her eyes, but they remained unseeing and vacant. She had not regained full consciousness, and blabbered intermittently in her delirium: '*You are my life, you are my second heart/You are the moonlight to my eyes and the ambrosia to my limbs/You flattered your guileless wife with hundreds of such loving expressions/Why talk more of this?*'[2] Then her voice cracked and she fell back unconscious. No one understood what had happened. They were shocked. Navinchandra gave up his attempts to comfort them. He got up and went and stood at a desk that had some books and drawings kept on it. Making a valiant effort to stop his tears, he murmured softly to himself.

Damn me! My wanton ways
Made her leave in anger.
What will she do, what will she say to me
For deserting her this long?
I have little use for wealth or people
Or my life or my house.
Damn me! My wanton ways
Made her leave in anger.
I brood on her brow curving
Over her anger-shadowed face,

[2] Kale, *The Uttararamacharita of Bhavabhuti*, 34.

Like a red lotus
Shadowed by a bee hovering above.
Damn me! My wanton ways
Made her leave in anger.[3]

She is gone, he said, and wept like a woman. It mattered not that he was in a house of strangers. His eyes fell on some drawings kept on Kumud's table. She had drawn them. One drawing depicted a scene from the third act of *Uttararamacharita* in which Sita looks at Ram with moist yet admonishing eyes. Another depicted Dushyant looking at a flower-bedecked Shakuntala approach him. A volume of Shakespeare was on the table in which the pages of *All's Well That Ends Well* and *The Winter's Tale* were marked with book markers. Navinchandra observed what was before him, and grew pensive.

Meanwhile, unconscious Kumud kept murmuring snatches of songs. 'Oh learning, Oh Sarasvati, you have slipped away ...' And then: 'Oh bee, why did you fly away?' There was a pause. Then, as they listened, the two songs merged into one another.

Your name has slipped away
You have slipped away from me
But not from my heart
You have not slipped out of my heart
Why, bee?

Navinchandra turned around and looked at her unconscious face. Kumud was laid on her back. Her thick black hair lay about her head like the spread feathers of a peacock. The flowers strung in her hair were now crushed and dishevelled. Everyone sat around her in silence not knowing what to do. At last the vaidya arrived, followed by Buddhidhan and Pramaddhan. Alak Kishori narrated the sequence of events. The vaidya began to administer to Kumud. He diagnosed

[3] Barbara Stoler Miller, ed. and trans. *Gitagovinda of Jayadeva,* 1st Indian edition (Delhi: Motilal Banarsidass, 1984), 82–83.

that she had an epileptic fit. His efforts bore fruit. Kumud regained consciousness.

Buddhidhan asked Alak Kishori, 'Don't you take her for outings these days?'

'No, we have not been able to go of late.'

'That is the cause. Take her out. Take the carriage and go today itself. Is there any difficulty?'

'No, none whatsoever.'

The elder's command was obeyed. Ever since Navinchandra had entered their house as a guest, Kumud Sundari had never looked at him directly in the eyes. Later that day, just as she was about to climb into the carriage, she looked at him, breaking her own self-imposed rule. Her eyes betrayed anger, pity and anguish. From that day on, whenever she met his gaze, there was a silent censure in her eyes.

After this incident, Navinchandra's mind wavered between the strong desire to return home and to wander away to newer places. He had resolved that he must leave Buddhidhan's house. He was held back only by his curiosity to witness the much anticipated fallout of the palace intrigues. On the morning of the palace assembly, Buddhidhan entrusted him with a great responsibility, and Navinchandra felt that his desire to leave was unlikely to be fulfilled soon. However, as soon as he stepped out of the palace, the thought came back to him. His wanderlust resurfaced and it excited and intensified his imagination; even the grand spectacle of the palace assembly paled before it. The afternoon heat made the restless images in his mind even more vivid. In the distance he could see boats out on the sea, and was drawn to them like a drunken man to a beacon. As he walked under that merciless sun, many thoughts flooded his mind.

Sarasvatichandra, do you realise what delirious Kumud Sundari babbled? 'Sarasvati ... You have slipped away from me, but not from my heart ...' Oh! It was cruel, cruel on my part, and callous!

My beloved has turned heartless
The signs of love have turned

This tender heart will be torn apart
O' foolish, ill-fated one

Oh God! Whose sin is it? Sarasvatichandra, do you realise what you have done?! A pure and virtuous woman—sacrificed in the fire of her husband's stupidity, lasciviousness and debauchery. A virtuous woman unable to forget her past. She cannot forget the one to whom she gave her heart, and she cannot commit adultery, either of the mind or the body, forsaking the one she is married to. A strong-willed child-woman. Your desire for the man you wanted as a husband is so intense, and yet you wouldn't even look at him! What self-control! Man, of the two, you are the woman; Woman—you are the man. Your sarangi restored him to his senses when he foolishly desired a woman not his own; you steadied his mind by your sublime song. What power! Oh Kumud, I was about to defile myself! Can a man know what difficulties lie ahead of him? I am a sinner. But, if you really are a sinner and a weakling, why did you then let go of her? Poor, wretched Alak Kishori! How can I berate you? Was I in my senses that I could admonish you? And Kumud—your eyes were filled with rage!

Her glance is straight; her eyes are flashing red;
Her speech is harsh, not drawling well-bred
Her whole lip quivers, seems to shake with cold;
Her frown has straightened eyebrows arching bold.[4]

Undoubtedly, your heart is shattered—your song, your drawings, the books you read, your speech, they all point to that. Oh sweet and melodious sarangi! Your strings play the same mournful tune. The ways of God are indiscernible. What happened? Why did I lapse, even if for a moment, even if not fully awake? How did you fathom that? Why were you required to endanger yourself to save me from deluge? Oh sinful mind! Your debasement became manifest. Is learning not sufficient to uplift the base instincts? What if Kumud had not warned

[4] Arthur W. Ryder, trans. *Kalidasa: Translation of Shakuntala and Other Works*, Act V, Verse 23, Reprint (New York: J. M. Dent & Co., 1912, 1920), 59.

me? Would all my learning have been to no avail? Are the instincts of the illiterate and the learned, the cultured and the uncultured similar, then? Yes. Yes, most certainly they are. Alak Kishori you are illiterate, but it is you who became my teacher. You do not want a blot upon your virtue. Neither do I.

Why is the mind subject to passions? Food tempts even those who have delicacies to eat; even the wealthy cannot refrain from stealing from others. Is the desire for flesh similar? Is lust so powerful that it subjugates the intellect and turns man into a beast? If it is so, then what is human volition, human will? Why did King Pandu allow his lust to overpower him in full knowledge that it would result in his death? I learnt the true meaning of King Pandu's story through this one incident with Alak Kishori. Just as a matchstick is fire itself, lust lurks within each person, ready to manifest itself at every opportunity. It must be so for everyone. It must have been so with Alak Kishori. Does not this wise, sagacious, accomplished exponent of political intrigue, Buddhidhan, also submit to his instinct at a mere touch of his woman? And Saubhagya Devi, I have witnessed the power you wield over the mighty Counsellor. You are pure and virtuous. Your virtues remind me of Saibya.

Covering her head with her sari,
Her face acquires a demureness of its own
She speaks a few words softly, intoning them sweetly
She walks slowly, with eyes downcast
O goddess mine: these are the
Marks of a pure and noble lineage

Saubhagya Devi, you are an embodiment of virtue. You are pure. O Arya woman, your pious image is etched in the minds of all whom you meet. I have read virtue described, but I never could comprehend the power and attraction of your piety. Travel to England, wander in America, the vineyards of Persia, or roam around in Armenia, it is impossible to find a woman as virtuous as the Arya woman. But even in this our land, you are becoming imaginary and rare; the arrogance of English knowledge has wrought destruction upon you. Saubhagya Devi, you embody the Arya woman. You are as revered and lovely to behold as the land of our country. How fortunate is Buddhidhan to have a jewel like you. Buddhidhan, enshrine this woman in your heart and hold her dearer than you do your power.

But the question is: Why does the most pious and pure Saubhagya Devi desire Buddhidhan? Navinchandra suddenly laughed out aloud. Oh, the celebration of the body! It is so wrong to make assumptions about a person's instincts from their outward appearances. Imagination misleads—it is not good to have a very active imagination. A person obtains an M.A. degree, fills his mind with lofty 'philosophy', and his hands per chance come to rest upon a woman's breasts, and he behaves as if he is mindless! Is this not illogical? If someone else were to paint this picture before me, I would certainly dismiss it as improbable and laugh it off. If such a thing happened once, it could not be said that it would never happen again. Vanleela was at some distance from me; unknown to her my eyes were drawn to her. I turned my gaze away, but I did feel an attraction, I wanted to look at her. How can I dismiss this experience? But for the experience, would I even admit to it? Even to myself? What could be the reason for dismissing it even as a probability? It is like this: a man observing constellations in the sky falls into a ditch; lofty imagination is not well grounded. A man crossing the seas does not count every wave he rides upon. Those who reflect on the condition of the country, the world and its Creator forget the existence of hunger and passions. But hunger and passions catch us by the ears, grab us by the neck and bring us back to our senses and reality. One is forced to put the book aside and eat. Even the likes of John Mill and Wordsworth had to marry. Did they marry only for companionship of the mind? They might well respond to such a query in the affirmative, but that is deceit. I, Sarasvatichandra, have come to that recognition today. If it were only about companionship of the mind, why do they marry at all? Why are they not satisfied with conversations alone? Love, we are told, is companionship of the mind, marriage a union of minds; but these definitions are partial. I realise this today. Alak Kishori, you are my teacher in this. If I had known this four months ago, Kumud Sundari, I would never have put you in such a state. But what has happened has indeed happened. Can it be undone? I cannot marry. Is it possible for me to not submit to passion again? I should not keep the company of those who pander to the senses. I should stay miles away from women. I must leave Buddhidhan's house. This would also make Kumud Sundari happy. If I am no longer around, she will eventually forget me. But where shall I go?

> *Who can say 'Thus far, no further' to the tide of his own nature?*
> *Who can mould the spirit's fashion to the counsel of his will?*
> *Square his being by enactment—shape his soul to legislature.*
> *Be himself his law of living: his own art of good and ill?*[5]

Oh heartless poet, are your cruel words true? Oh heartless poet, is it true that instinct is more powerful than will? Do desires of sensual pleasure rule over a man, dance over his head and chest and beat him into subjugation? Oh why are our senses not in our control? Does desire have more force than intellect? Cannot the intellect rule over the body? Navinchandra sighed deeply. Tears rolled down his cheeks unrestrained and unseen, and were dried by the harsh sun.

He had not yet covered half the distance to Buddhidhan's house. The road forked ahead of him. He took the path they had taken that morning. Ramsen, walking behind him, stopped him and said, 'Bhai, take the other route, from that lane.'

His reverie broken, Navinchandra asked, 'Ramsen, didn't we take the other road in the morning?'

'Bhai, this is a shorter route.'

'Oh, is that so? Fine. Let us go.'

And he lapsed back into his cogitations. If marriage were only for the sake of the body, Kumud Sundari should be content with Pramaddhan and Sarasvatichandra's memories should not haunt her.

[5] Author's note: 'The Story of a Soul', James Brunton Stephens.

If marriage were to mean nothing but bodily union, and if Kumud is still haunted by memories of Sarasvatichandra, it would imply that her chastity is compromised.

His thoughts were interrupted once again. In the lane they had turned into, there was a small, beautiful house. The windows on the first floor were open. Glass chandeliers and mirrors could be seen from outside. Flowerpots and decorative plants had been kept on the otalo. The door was open but the latticed door behind it was shut. A fair complexioned, beautiful girl of fifteen or sixteen opened the latticed door as Navinchandra and Ramsen approached the house. Navinchandra did not so much as glance at her and walked past, preoccupied. She seemed hurt by this. Ramsen said, 'Bhai, you go on ahead or else wait for me.' He went up to the girl, spoke to her in whispers, then hurried back and joined Navinchandra. 'Bhai, did you see her?' Navinchandra turned back in surprise and asked, 'What?'

'Nothing. That was Padma's house.'

'Who is Padma?'

'Don't you know her? Since you are friendly with Pramaddhan, I assumed you knew her.'

'Who is she?'

'She is the courtesan, Padma. Didn't you see her? How beautiful she is! Come, let's go if you wish to see her, we can eat a paan made by her.'

'No, what do we have to do with her. Now I understand; we took this route because of her.'

'Yes. I had to give her a message.'

'What message would you need to give her?'

'Nothing important.'

'There must be something. Do tell me.'

'All right. But only if you can keep a secret. Or else I will lose my job.'

'You will not lose your job; why would I need to tell anyone? Do tell.'

'Pramaddhan visits her in the company of friends.'

'Pramaddhanbhai!?'

'Yes, Bhai, please do not tell anyone. He visits her even in the afternoons.'

'Does he have no affection for Kumud Sundari?'

'No, no! He loves her a lot! He goes mad even at the mention of her name. But Bhai, she is there every day. What is the use of all this wealth if he has to look at and be satisfied with the same thing every day?'

'Are there other such places that he visits?'

'No. Come, let's go in. She will be hospitable; after all you are a friend.'

'Is Buddhidhanbhai aware of all this?'

'No, sir, no! It would be death for Pramadbhai and all of us. Buddhidhanbhai would not even look at other women.'

'Are you certain of that?'

'Yes. Without a doubt. Only those blessed with great fortune would have Buddhidhanbhai and Devi as parents.'

'Then why has Pramadbhai become wayward?'

'Bhai, he was raised by the likes of me. We took care of him, and now he spends some leisure time here. Hence, he is pleased with us. His friends also have fun, and we too earn some money in the bargain.'

'Does Kumud Sundari know?'

'She knew nothing until recently. A few days ago, she went to the Rajeshwar Mahadev. That fool Murkhdutt blabbered something.'

'How does Murkhdutt know this?'

'On some nights, Pramaddhan takes Padma to the Rajeshwar Mahadev for fun and frolic. So Murkhdutt knows. A few days ago, Bhabhisahib visited the temple and she saw Padma's blouse drying in the courtyard. She asked Murkhdutt about it. The fool got frightened, lost his nerve and blurted out that Pramadbhai had come for a visit, and that Padma must have forgotten to take it.'

'Did she not throw a tantrum?'

'That is what is so surprising! If it were any other woman, all hell would have broken loose. But Bhabhisahib took the blouse home, gave it to Pramaddhan without any fuss and told him that someone had left it at the Mahadev temple, and that he should return it to whom it belonged. Pramadbhai was really scared and said he knew nothing about it. Bhabhisahib said: You are resourceful and wield power. Find out to whom it belongs, or else keep it with you.'

'And then?'

'Pramadbhai has not been able to visit Padma of late because of all these palace intrigues.'

Navinchandra heaved a deep sigh. They had come out of the lane and were back on the main road.

'Bhai, please don't tell anyone,' pleaded Ramsen.

'Why did you bring me into this lane?'

'I came to give her the good news that she will now find a place in the palace. I told you, I thought you knew all about her.'

'You made a mistake; not I.'

'Navinbhai, you are most generous. You are not innocent of these things. Have mercy on a poor man. What more can I say?'

'You needn't worry. I won't speak about what you have told me. At any rate, no one will know that you have spoken about it to me.'

Conversation stopped, and Navinchandra became immersed in his thoughts once again. Kumud Sundari, pure, virtuous and innocent Kumud ... This is the height of torture! Sarasvatichandra, this is all your doing. Your sin. Unthinking adventurer, you have tormented her! How unfortunate are the children of the high and mighty. Blameless Buddhidhan. Pious Saubhagya Devi. The foremost consequence of your power is that your son was raised by servants. A child raised by servants is bound to go wrong. How much attention can the father pay? Pramaddhan is not by nature wicked. He has been spoilt by servants and friends. Life in the households of the powerful tends to be unnatural. Those who run the politics of the state have darkness in their homes.

But look at the power of the virtuous! Even this lowly servant recognises what good fortune it is to have them as parents. What really separates me and Pramaddhan? What is the difference between the learned and the illiterate? His conduct is impure, but there is impurity in my thoughts. The disease in me was stymied before it could spread. He continues to be debauched, perhaps more so now. Is that not the difference between knowledge and the lack of it? But how did such vile thoughts even enter my mind? Only because I came here. One must associate with equals. Yes, certainly the company of the higher is to be desired. Just as the lowly benefit by association with the high, the high are degraded by association with the lowly. I have already experienced the fruits of proximity with Alak Kishori. I walked with a servant and he brought me to a prostitute's house. And a past association with Kumud ... She saved me from a great sin just by playing her sarangi and singing. Yes, I must now leave Buddhidhan's house ... It is time.

They had reached the Counsellor's house. A messenger came up to Navinchandra and handed him a letter. He opened the letter as he entered the house.

14 Destiny Fulfilled

Before leaving for the palace, Buddhidhan had left two faithful soldiers to guard the house. Saubhagya Devi bathed again, smeared sacred ash on her forehead, lit silver lamps and incense sticks and sat down to pray before the household deity. She recited the verses that her mother-in-law had taught her. Old Dayashankar sat in the courtyard enjoying the mild morning breeze of Chaitra. Alak Kishori and Kumud Sundari sat with him, listening to his reminiscences of the palace, the Rana, Shathrai, stories of Buddhidhan's youth, his mother, and legends surrounding the Karbhari family. Dayashankar, like Sanjay of *Mahabharata,* satisfied their curiosity with great verve and pleasure, recalling the days of Buddhidhan's long illness, his pledge, the plight of his widowed mother, and adolescent Saubhagya Devi. The two young women heard the stories, and felt the hardship and suffering of days gone by. Even their worst enemy should not have to see such days, they said. This re-telling brought back painful memories for Saubhagya Devi. She remembered the affection of her dear mother-in-law, and could no longer concentrate on her puja as tears streamed down her eyes. She wiped her tears, got up and joined Dayashankar in remembering the old days. She said, 'Dayashankar Kaka, Mataji should have been around to see such good days. There can be no one like her. I weep every time I am reminded of her affection and her patience. It was her lot to suffer. She hardly knew any happiness. She was born only to raise and nurture us.' And so it was on the day of the big assembly, as events in Rana Bhupsinh's court unfolded according to Buddhidhan's plan, such were the noble and uplifting scenes unfolding in his household.

After the Jamal episode, Alak Kishori had sobered down. She had also matured greatly after the incident with Navinchandra. She had become less haughty in the company of the kind, intelligent and sensitive Kumud who had also turned Alak's mind more and more towards Vidurprasad. Stories of the suffering and humiliation that her own parents had endured had mellowed Alak further.

Vanleela had clearly heard Navinchandra say: 'Behn Alak, I am like a brother to you.' She was convinced of Navinchandra's purity. This had removed a thorn from Kumud's heart. Vanleela repeated to Kumud the lines she had sung in her delirium. Kumud could imagine the intense agony she must have caused Navinchandra and felt that her conduct had been heartless. She knew that her attraction and infatuation for him was contrary to her conduct as a chaste wife. Aware of her own weakness, and battling conflicting emotions, Kumud had counselled Alak. She realised her folly and resolved to curb her desire for Navinchandra. The episode of Padma's blouse also served as a lesson for her—Kumud realised that in some ways it captured her innermost desires; if she did not crave for Sarasvatichandra, her husband, too, would not have sought Padma's comfort. Kumud became determined to banish the man who possessed her mind and soul. This was difficult. She focused her attention on the good qualities in Pramaddhan and made a conscious attempt to make place for him in her heart. Dayashankar's stories made her feel emotionally attached to the Counsellor's family. For the first time, Kumud Sundari felt proud of her marriage to a scion of this family. She felt a new energy in the belief that if she were to purge her mind, she would be able to reform her husband as well. A new light enveloped her as the noon sun blazed outside, penetrating the darkness within.

The family was destined to receive the bounty of good fortune. Though unaware of it, they could feel the soothing presence of divine grace in their midst. The Counsellor's family thus prepared itself to be worthy of this bounty. Alak Kishori's conscience was duly purified. Her haughtiness gave way to humility, her arrogance to maturity, and her indifference and contempt gave way to a newfound regard for her husband. Kumud Sundari's conjugal disaffection and discontent, known only to her, had the potential to destroy the family. By her own firm resolve and sincere efforts, even this was being gradually replaced by affection for Pramaddhan, and a certain inner quiet. Was this not a sign of good fortune, too? Was it any less significant or valuable than Buddhidhan being entrusted with the Karbhar? All of this contributed to the bliss that Buddhidhan and Saubhagya Devi were about to experience, and enhanced the glory of Buddhidhan's triumph.

It was about ten in the morning. The sun was already sharp. The women and Dayashankar moved out of the courtyard. Dayashankar went into the drawing room to repose in an armchair. Saubhagya Devi sat on the swing in the shade, moving gently to and fro, eagerly awaiting news of her husband. Kumud Sundari went up to her room. Alak Kishori went to the kitchen to instruct the cooks about preparation of food for the day, and then went up to join Kumud.

'Bhabhi, what will be the outcome at the palace assembly today?' Alak asked Kumud.

'It will all be good, I feel, and besides, our worrying about it is not going to help matters. Oh, it is ten already! Someone should be coming from the palace soon. Perhaps Navinchandra.' Kumud blushed despite herself as she uttered the name.

'Bhabhi, Navinchandra will come only if things go wrong.'

'Oh, is that so? Then the news must be good.'

'Navinchandra is a good human being,' Alak said, smiling. She had already forgotten the past. Alak's heart was transparent. In many ways, she was childlike in her simple-mindedness, and the incident and agonising shame over which she had resolved to take her own life was barely a blur in her mind now. She lived in the present. She no longer felt any desire or attraction for Navinchandra. She remembered only his goodness and purity.

Kumud Sundari did not respond.

'Bhabhi, he has been here for so long. No one knows why he came here, or why he left his home. What do you think?'

'Ask Devi about it. They decided to send us to Lilapur in his care. They must know something about him,' replied Kumud, eager to change the subject. She calmed herself by looking at Pramaddhan's photograph. 'Behn, I feel that news from the palace will be good, and that your brother will come to tell us so. Although, he may not come if he is detained by more important work.'

'Oh, you are crazy about your husband! You bring my brother into everything!' laughed Alak.

'Look who is telling me!'

'I am certainly not as bad as you!'

'All right. But is it wrong to be crazy about one's husband?'

'Of course! All day long you think of nothing but him.'

'Tell me, what can be more important for a wife than her husband?'

'That is true. But do we need to talk about him all day long?'

'Some time ago, you weren't even ready to admit this. Every time someone mentioned your husband, you would snarl.'

'That is also true. But it is no longer so. Do I do that now?'

'No. Did I say that you do! Did you hear what Dayashankar Kaka had to say?'

'Yes, my hair stood on end just listening to him. How Pitaji and Devi have suffered!'

'That bitch Khalaknanda insulted our grandmother, and that wicked Dushtarai sent such a vile message! Did you hear about that?'

'Oh yes. Today, they will all get the fruits of their deeds.'

'Pitaji harboured that insult for so many years. But today will be his day.'

'Bhabhi, it is so hard for him. He worries so much, constantly; it shows on him.'

'Now tell me, Alak behn, is Deviji wrong when she worries about Pitaji all the time?'

'No, of course not. How can it be wrong?'

'Is it ever wrong for a woman to worry about her husband?'

'No. It can never be enough.'

'Now you have got it right. So tell me, is it wrong if you think and talk about Vidurprasadji all the time? It is perfectly good and desirable to be crazy about the husband. Those who are not are in fact guilty in the eyes of God.'

Alak Kishori blushed. Kumud Sundari was stunned by her own words: '... guilty in the eyes of God'. She looked at Pramaddhan's photograph. Kumud felt a sudden surge of blissful relief along with the realisation that Sarasvatichandra now belonged to the past. She gazed at Pramaddhan's photograph with longing.

'Bhabhi, you are right. In that book you have given me, Lalita says: "Whether good or bad, naming him my beloved husband, I give solace to my mind. Such are my thoughts. But my heart refuses to fall in line. Restless, I yearn to be with him." Perhaps I have mixed up the lines. But Lalita desires Nandkumar even though he is undeserving of her.'

'Yes, she cannot take her mind off her husband.' Even Kumud felt that the example of the fictional and semi-literate Lalita was worthy of emulation.

Alak said with a mischievous glint in her eye, 'Yes, henceforth even I shall yearn for my husband and think of him all the time!'

'You and I and all other women will craze for our husbands! We shall settle a new village for crazy women like us!' Both of them burst out laughing. Buddhidhan's household was being purged of impurities. Kumud was changing Alak.

Just then Vanleela came up. She hesitated for a moment, but entered the room nevertheless.

'Come in. Why did you hesitate, Vanleela?'

'How come you are here at this time?' asked Alak.

'I have come to tell you all the gossip. Merulo has wounded Dushtarai, and Rupali has run away disguised as a man! Khalaknanda is hiding and cannot be traced!'

'What!' Alak stood up and excitedly caught hold of Vanleela's shoulder. Kumud remained seated but looked at them with curiosity. Vanleela relayed all that she knew without pausing to catch her breath.

Krishna Kalika and Radha joined them with the news that Jamal had been found and captured in the palace. They all went to Saubhagya Devi, and the gossip was recounted to her with undiminished interest and fervour. Then Vidurprasad arrived with full details of the day's events at the palace. Alak Kishori's joy was limitless. She could barely restrain herself from dancing about the house. Kumud was most impressed with her father-in-law's brilliance, and felt proud to be a part of the Counsellor's family; the family's victory was a victory for Kumud as well. Joy brought sobriety to Saubhagya Devi. God had willed victory for her husband and defeat for his enemies—Saubhagya Devi seemed overwhelmed by this and could only weep in joy. The entire story was retold to Dayashankar. The listeners were no less interested in the narration on account of repetition. All of them moved to the drawing room. Vidyurprasad's narration became more detailed as his audience increased and he held them captive for quite some time. This was a novel experience for Alak Kishori; never before had she felt captivated by Vidurprasad. Time passed in excited chatter.

Then Navinchandra arrived, shoving a letter into his pocket. While the group eagerly turned to him for more details, Kumud's attention was instantly drawn to the letter in his pocket. She was curious to read the handwriting on the letter. She reasoned that the letter would throw more light on him and his antecedents. She felt there was a chance her curiosity may at last be satisfied. She had resolved with all her strength to put him out of her mind. But seeing Navinchandra, she felt her resolve weaken.

Navinchandra had made up his mind to leave. As he entered the house, he wanted one last glimpse of Kumud Sundari. He looked at her once, twice, thrice, but his desire was undiminished. Kumud Sundari, this is our last meeting, he said to himself as he was besieged by questions from his onlookers. His thoughts interrupted his responses and narration, but no one noticed. He was overcome by emotion with the thought that he would no longer be able to even look at Kumud; and that she was given in marriage to a man who visited Padma. Kumud saw these images fleeting before Navinchandra's eyes, the pain and turmoil on his face, and the letter peeping out of his pocket. What could it possibly be? she asked herself. Hitherto she had remained firm and not responded to his searching eyes. Her resolve weakened with every passing moment. There was no way out of this predicament.

Krishna Kalika had failed in her attempt to make Alak Kishori an instrument of her lust. She now stared at Navinchandra. She saw the two pairs of eyes gazing intently at each other, and was singed by envy. She pictured the pleasure that Kumud Sundari would have received from Navinchandra, and determined to bring that pleasure to an end. She quietly drew Alak Kishori's attention to this union of eyes.

'Rand! I will skin you alive if you ever mention this again!' Alak Kishori shoved Krishna Kalika away and became engrossed in the conversation again.

Just then, a big ruckus and uproar was heard from outside. Everyone rushed to the windows. They saw a terrified Khalaknanda running in the street, chased by an angry, abusive mob that pelted stones at her. Shathrai's house had been seized. His daughter had been driven out from it. Buddhidhan had ordered that Shathrai's house and women of that family should not be touched or harmed. Khalaknanda's husband's family had refused to shelter her. People who knew of her licentious and evil deeds ran after her. Those delighted at the fall of Shathrai and Dushtarai joined the mob. They clapped and jeered at her. There was no compassion in any eye for the plight of the former Karbhari's family. Khalaknanda had nowhere to go. She should have run away with her sister-in-law Rupali, she felt. It was too late now. There was no escape for her. Frightened for her life, she ran around the streets, pursued by the stone-throwing, abusive mob. She cried out for help, stumbled and fell several times, got up and ran again. Followed by the mob, she reached Buddhidhan's house.

Alak Kishori and the others watched the scene from the window. Alak Kishori taunted, 'Devi, look at this wretched rand! Neither Jamal nor Mahva can save her now. You bitch, you deserve it!' Saubhagya Devi glared at her daughter to hear such words from her tongue. She came downstairs and stood on the otalo; the other women followed. Seeing them, Khalaknanda became even more frightened. Her defeat was total. She felt that the mob that was following her like a pack of bloodthirsty hounds would incite Saubhagya Devi to revenge. She knew that Alak Kishori would want to avenge the Jamal episode. There could be no better opportunity. Shathrai's daughter burned within; fear brought back memories of her many misdeeds. She remembered how she had insulted Buddhidhan's mother all those years ago, and the vile suggestions she had made about Saubhagya Devi, a young bride then. These and countless such misdeeds danced before her eyes like a rotting carcass infested with vermin. She made an attempt to run away from Buddhidhan's house, but it was foiled. She was exhausted from all the running. Someone pushed her and Dushtarai's sister fell flat on her face at Saubhagya Devi's feet. A man pushed his way to the front of the crowd, shouting, 'Beat up the rand!' and he put his foot on her back. A policeman, once close to Dushtarai, stood watching the spectacle; he made no attempt to stop the man. In a moment, people would have started kicking her.

As Khalaknanda fell, Alak Kishori incited the mob, 'Yes! Beat her up! Thrash the rand! She deserves it!'. She provoked them by reminding them of Khalaknanda's misdeeds. Ramsen came forward, eager to obey Buddhidhan's daughter. Krishna Kalika, Vanleela and Radha silently enjoyed the farce. Dayashankar Kaka tried to stop Alak Kishori, but she did not heed him. Vidurprasad and Navinchandra also tried to restrain the people, but in vain.

Finally Saubhagya Devi stepped forward and spoke up in anger: 'Alak, stop this at once! Do you want us to be like *them*!' She told the people commandingly, 'Turn back. Go home. What harm has she done to you? You kick a woman! Aren't you ashamed! Ramsen, take her away.'

The mob retreated a little but kept up the excited cacophony of murmurs and whispers. 'She is the Counsellor's wife, Saubhagya Devi. Devi is right, we should let the miserable bitch go. But how can we let her go! She deserves a beating and worse! She has ruined so many lives! Well said, Alak behn! She truly deserves to be punished! Oh, *she* is Alak Kishori? Yes, and that one there is Pramaddhan's wife, Kumud Sundari.'

Alak argued with her mother, 'Devi, I will not listen to you today. You will never change! You know perfectly well that this woman deserves no compassion. Ramsen, hold the bitch tight by her hair!' Ramsen could not decide whom to obey. The other soldiers were keen to obey Alak Kishori, but it was not a small matter to disregard Saubhagya Devi's wishes.

In desperation, Saubhagya Devi turned to Kumud Sundari. 'Kumud, this girl will not listen to me. You only talk some sense into her.' She knew of her daughter-in-law's persuasive skills and of her daughter's soft spot for her.

Kumud came forward, gently put a hand on her sister-in-law's shoulder and said, 'Alak behn let her go. Why flog the dead?'

'So you, too, are on Devi's side,' Alak said half accusingly.

'Of course. Has she said anything wrong?'

'You heard what Dayashankar Kaka recounted for us this morning.'

'If anyone has the right to bear a grudge, it is Devi, not us.'

'No, she would never bear a grudge. She is the kind who would bless even those wanting her dead.'

'Why do you hold a grudge?'

'Why shouldn't I! Should I forget what that bitch did to me—using that lowly Jamal? And what about the insult to Devi? She is *my* mother!' Alak barely stopped herself from saying: To you she is mother-in-law, but to me she is mother. But Kumud heard what was left unsaid and continued regardless in a voice at once gentle and firm: 'I don't deny that, do I? You can feel hurt and angry, and so can I. Even so, what Devi says is right. We must follow her advice. You will get what you want in the end. Alak behn, please do as I am asking of you. I will explain all this to you later.'

Alak Kishori softened a little and said, 'All right. Ramsen, do what Devi wants you to. But bhabhisahib, you are making a mistake. How will Khalaknanda ever realise the consequences of her evil deeds?'

The man who was standing with his foot on Khalaknanda moved away. Ramsen and some other soldiers of the Counsellor made a cordon around her. Khalaknanda now stood up. Alak turned to her mother, 'Devi, now tell us, what should we do with her? If you permit me, I will tell father and have her beheaded.'

'Yes, yes! She deserves death! Have her beheaded!' shouted the mob. 'Alak Kishori, prove that you can do it!', someone shouted and hurled a sharp stone at Khalaknanda that hit her on the back and she screamed in terror and pain. The sight of her blood incited the crowd even more.

'Ramsen, what are they doing! Stop them!' said Saubhagya Devi with a weary and pained expression.

Then, several voices in the crowd addressed the Counsellor's wife: 'Devi, do not compel us to speak up. The misdeeds of this bitch are so vile we are ashamed to mention them. She had no compunction in committing those deeds, but we hesitate even to speak of them before you. Behnji, your revered mother-in-law is no more, or else she would have told you all about this woman here.' Khalaknanda was an accomplice of her brother Dushtarai, the Faujdar. She had ensnared many sisters, young daughters and wives in her vicious net of vice; she had lured them, cajoled and threatened them and brought them under her power to satisfy her brother's lust. Many innocent and pure women had become her unsuspecting victims. Saubhagya Devi had never concerned herself with anything that did not concern her husband. Hence, such vile words and deeds had never before fallen upon her pious ears. She was stunned beyond belief. She had remained completely ignorant of the venomous power that Khalaknanda had wielded. She had forgiven Khalaknanda's insult of her years ago.

Irate and impatient, Alak Kishori said, 'Bhabhi, Devi refuses to say anything. You tell me, what do you want me to do?'

'It is not as if you do not know what Devi wants.'

'Of course I know what Devi wants! She would want us to rescue this rand, take her into our home, give her shelter and feed her. That would make Devi really happy!'

Helpless in face of her daughter's wrath and acerbic taunts, Saubhagya Devi again turned to wise Kumud: 'Kumud, you tell me, would such a thing be wrong?'

Kumud looked at Alak and softly said, 'Behn, a daughter must do what the mother wants.'

'No. I do not understand such things. And I see that you too have joined Devi,' Alak retorted in anger.

Kumud calmly replied, 'No, that was just an aside. Devi, I think Khalaknanda should be kept under guard at some safe place. We can give her food. Let Pitaji deal with her when he returns.'

'Yes, that is all right.' Alak, who revered her father, did not find anything objectionable in Kumud's suggestion. Devi welcomed it. The mob was satisfied as well. Khalaknanda did not look up or meet anyone's gaze; her eyes remained fixed on the ground. Following Alak Kishori's instructions, Ramsen and two other soldiers took Shathrai's daughter to an unoccupied house in the neighbourhood. The mob dispersed noisily. As Khalaknanda was taken away, Alak Kishori taunted her, 'Rand Khalki! See, this is the difference between your administration and ours. Go. Take your black face away from this place!' And she turned her back on her and entered the house followed by her friends. Saubhagya Devi quietly asked Kumud to send a woman servant to cook and care for Khalaknanda and keep her company while she was watched over by male guards. Kumud immediately made arrangements. As mother and daughter-in-law entered the house, a tearful Saubhagya Devi took Kumud's hand and said, 'See how the wheel turns, my daughter. What power she had once. You were not even born when she was young, haughty and beautiful. How her youth and beauty have frayed. And how she has come to this pass today. Such is the will of God!'

Kumud Sundari was drawn to her compassionate mother-in-law. She was the last one to enter the house. Everyone else was already on the first floor. Navinchandra had dropped the letter on the staircase. Kumud saw it and picked it up. Everyone was busy talking about Khalaknanda, debating what would have been the best thing to do. They could hear foot falls. Someone looked out and saw a group of men approaching the house. The officials and functionaries of the state knew that Shathrai's long rule had finally come to an end, and that Buddhidhan would be the new Karbhari of Suvarnapur. All those wanting to be in attendance, and curious about the happenings at court, now gathered outside Buddhidhan's house.

Alak Kishori asked, 'Why are all these people here now?'

Various explanations were provided. Finally Vidurprasad said, 'What can they do but stand in attendance before the new Karbhari? The house of the Karbhari has changed.' Vanleela said, 'Alak behn, you will now have to vacate this room. This will become an office, and the officials will wait here.'

The soldiers opened the doors for the officials, and the women moved to Navinchandra's room. The officials climbed up. Dayashankar closed the door after the women. He recited to himself: 'Welcome Lakshmi, wealth and glory. You bring friends and relatives. Some say I am a cousin, the other says I am a bosom friend.' Vidurprasad chuckled listening to him, and went out to receive the officials.

The rustle of the heavily starched and ironed clothes of the officials, the squeaking of their footwear, their hushed murmurs, the respect with which they uttered the name, 'Buddhidhanbhai', all these sounds fell on Saubhagya Devi's eager ears as she sat on the swing. Years ago, during the reign of Rana Jadsinh, the son of a poor widow would sit right at the back of the assembly, near the pile of footwear. He would come home and meekly narrate the stories of Shathrai's power and influence to his mother and young wife. Those scenes played before Saubhagya Devi's eyes now. She compared those days with the scenes that were unfolding before her right now. She did not despise the old days, she was not bitter, and yet she was overjoyed at the turn of events. Her face was wet with tears of happiness. When she pictured the high office that her husband would adorn, a shiver of pleasure ran through her body. The sound of all these officials reverentially taking her husband's name gave her a pleasure akin to bathing in a lake filled with nectar. She tried to imagine her husband resplendent in his new glory, his new stature, his newfound power, and still as affectionate and attentive towards her as before. Her waiting eyes yearned for his return. Drawn by the scent of a shift in power, these officials had gathered together, just as a sign of rain draws peacocks. Saubhagya Devi had remained a steadfast companion through Buddhidhan's worst years. She sat alone today, feeling blessed at her good fortune. Today, her bliss was replete. Today, nothing marred her joy.

A little while later, Buddhidhan appeared at the doorstep. His eyes instantly searched for Devi, their eyes met, and conveyed the shared joy and good fortune. They smiled at each other. He climbed up, followed by his retinue, as Saubhagya Devi went into the kitchen. Her daughter held court there. There were many more hangers-on than usual. Alak Kishori's splendour and power were a sight to behold.

Only Kumud Sundari was not there.

15 Sarasvatichandra

The women went down as the men trooped up to the drawing room. Kumud Sundari went to her room to examine the letter that Navinchandra had received. She had also received a letter that day, from her younger sister, Kusum Sundari. The letter was about Sarasvatichandra. Kusum Sundari had sent it to Vanleela, who was related to the sisters, with strict instructions to hand it over to Kumud in secret. Vanleela had done so. Now alone in her room, Kumud read the letter. And she was filled with sorrow. Kumud had resolved, with a tremendous effort of will, not to let her mind waver from Pramaddhan. But as she read of the suffering and ignominy endured by Sarasvatichandra, she found her resolve melting.

Sarasvatichandra's father Laxminandan was a wealthy merchant of Bombay. He was reputed to have assets worth ten to twelve lakhs of rupees. He was not educated beyond what most ordinary merchants are. Sarasvatichandra's mother Chandralaxmi was a wise and virtuous woman. Her good conduct and nature had influenced Laxminandan as well. Chandralaxmi's mother-in-law Ishwarkaur was a bitter woman. She could not bear her son being under his wife's influence. Ishwarkaur ruled over the household, and did so with intent to slight the daughter-in-law. Chandralaxmi was large-hearted and disregarded the mother-in-law's insults. Laxminandan loved her all the more because of it. Things changed with Sarasvatichandra's birth. The old woman softened up, and her regard for the daughter-in-law increased. Chandralaxmi died when Sarasvatichandra was four or five years old. On the same day, Laxminandan was betrothed to an adolescent Guman. Sarasvatichandra was raised by his father and grandmother, till such time as Guman came to live in the house. Laxminandan had a photograph taken with his son in his lap, and Chandralaxmi by his side. As a wealthy resident of Bombay, he could dare such an act. When Ishwarkaur came to know of it, she had fought with the daughter-in-law for months for this brazenness. She naturally did not think that her son was at fault. There is a saying among the village folk that a dead buffalo is worth more than a living one. Ishwarkaur realised the virtues of her daughter-in-law once she died. She cried a lot. She had the photograph brought out; Laxminandan kept it in his room. Ishwarkaur would point out Chandralaxmi in that photograph to young Sarasvatichandra. And then Guman entered the household. She was from a lowly family and harboured ill-will towards the stepson and her mother-in-law who doted on him. Guman's mother had taught her that it would be wrong for her to love the stepson.

Sheth Laxminandan was wealthy as well as influential. He was a well known patron of scholars and learning. There were many who had benefited from his patronage. His home was a meeting ground for scholars of diverse fields; men of letters and academically inclined young people would gather there for discussions and debate. He was well liked and respected by them. The Sheth's sensibility, too, had been cultured and refined by his association with scholars. And thus it was that infant Sarasvatichandra played in the laps of scholars. They inculcated in him a love of learning at a young age. His bright face was reminiscent of Chandralaxmi's luminosity. The clerks and servants who wished to curry favour with Guman tended to ignore Chandralaxmi's son. Children of the wealthy are most often deprived of a cultured upbringing. But God granted this boon to the fortunate son of Laxminandan who was thus saved from the curse of being raised and influenced by servants.

At a tender age, Sarasvatichandra became friends with an extremely poor and intelligent boy named Chandrakant. Chandrakant had a great thirst for knowledge. They both studied together. This mutually nourishing friendship grew deeper over the years. Sarasvatichandra formed other associations as he grew older, which proved short-lived; but his friendship with Chandrakant remained steadfast and solid as a rock.

Sheth Laxminandan, owing to the company he kept, had learnt to speak and write some English. He was a member of the Reformist Society of Bombay. He managed the business and running of a few weaving mills. He was also involved in several public and private philanthropic activities. His philanthropy was motivated by self-interest; he was eager for public applause. He cultivated contact with English merchants and officials and invented occasions to invite them home and play host to them. In return, they bestowed him with honours. He was invited to the Governor's evening parties. Such news never failed to make its way to the newspapers. The famous and learned editor of *The Bombay Light* Bulwer Sahib, the editor of *Gurjar Vartik* Uddhatlal, Bombay's favourite city poet Tarang Shankar, the impoverished and upcoming writer Shanti Sharma, the famous Marathi patriot Virrao Dhampate, and well known Parsi public speaker Shamsherji were among his friends. Sheth Laxminandan was honoured with the title of 'Justice of Peace', courtesy an influential officer of the Secretariat who was known to him.

All this power and influence also accorded the Bombay merchant prestige in the native states. Whenever the Minister of Ratnanagari, Vidya Chatura, came to Bombay, he preferred to be Sheth Laxminandan's houseguest. They were also caste fellows. Vidya Chatura was deeply impressed by young Sarasvatichandra's intelligence, his quest for knowledge, his humility, civility, his pure conscience, his friends and mellow nature. The Minister grew fond of the boy's radiant and smiling face.

The son of a wealthy merchant should ideally have been betrothed in infancy; but for some reason, four or five years went by without Sarasvatichandra's marriage being fixed. Once Guman arrived, she consistently spurned all marriage proposals for the stepson without consulting Laxminandan. Ishwarkaur tried hard to find a match for her grandson, but all proposals fell through because of Guman. Finally, Ishwarkaur spoke to Laxminandan. He told her there was no need to tie down the boy at such a young age. When Sarasvatichandra was about fifteen years old, Guman gave birth to a son, whose marriage was fixed immediately. Laxminandan did not consider this either objectionable or unusual. But his mother lost her head and lashed out at him in anger; and so he was shamed into finding a match for his firstborn. Around that time, Vidya Chatura was on a visit to Bombay and was Laxminandan's guest. He observed that Sarasvatichandra had progressed well in his studies, his intellect had matured, that he was fond of reading, and had acquired a refined sensibility and was appreciative of all the arts. His attachment and regard for the boy grew. Vidya Chatura was in search of a good match for his daughter. He felt it would be inappropriate to broach the matter directly with a man as prominent as Sheth Laxminandan. Instead, he sought his mother Ishwarkaur's advice. The grandmother was delighted; Laxminandan, too, gladly accepted the proposal. Guman felt insanely jealous, but the men decided between themselves without consulting her. Ishwarkaur's joy was boundless. A family like Vidya Chatura's and a girl like Kumud Sundari were worth more than the wait of fifteen long years. She expressed her joy all the more effusively in Guman's presence and showered love and blessings over her precious grandson. Guman seethed inwardly, but kept quiet. Ishwarkaur wanted an early marriage. She often wondered, Why does Vidya Chatura delay the marriage? Will I have the good fortune to bless the couple? She also sent messages to Vidya Chatura. Not eager for an early marriage, but anxious not to displease the old woman, the Minister made vague promises.

Sarasvatichandra's studies progressed well. He passed his M.A. at the young age of seventeen or eighteen. The following year he passed his legal examinations. Thereafter, he passed many examinations, wrote prize-winning essays for which he was awarded scholarships and medals. In every field he emerged at the top. University professors and well known scholars loved him. It was said that he had an original mind. His aesthetic ability was regarded to be of a high standard. Combining learning and wealth, he had all the good qualities of those born high, but none of the ills. He was tall, fair, well-built, and handsome to look at. His face was bright, his features delicate. His friends were given to saying that even if Sarasvatichandra were not learned or wealthy, his well-proportioned body, handsome and masculine bearing would have attracted others to him.

As Kumud Sundari grew in age and maturity, she heard with interest her parents talk about Sarasvatichandra. Vidya Chatura and Sarasvatichandra regularly corresponded with each other through letters. Vidya Chatura often discussed Sarasvatichandra's letters with his wife Gunasundari. Kumud wondered what this man was like, who came in for so much praise from her learned and affectionate father. Vidya Chatura also made it a point to talk of Sarasvatichandra when he knew Kumud was certain to be listening. He wanted her impressionable mind to develop a genuine affection for her husband-to-be; his wish was fulfilled. It also gave rise to unknown desires and passions in adolescent Kumud. In the first blush of her youth, she was anxious to see the man she was to wed, to get to know him. Such anticipation excited her imagination. One day, she saw one of his letters to her father. Vidya Chatura had left it on the table. She so wanted to read it. But how could she, without her father's permission? Should she be brazen and ask him for it? Ultimately, curiosity got the better of her. There was no one else in the room. She went up to the table. Her eyes searched out the letter from a pile just as the first rays of dawn pick out a white lotus about to bloom. Her small fair hand emerged from the folds of her soft sky-blue sari and picked up the letter. She anxiously looked around for prying eyes, smiled, concealed the letter quickly in the folds of her sari and walked back to her room as if nothing had happened. For a moment she felt like a thief, but the thought did not stay with her long. She read the letter once, twice, thrice, and yet she was insatiable. Sarasvatichandra's beautiful handwriting, his poetic language, his articulate and mature thoughts captivated her. She came under his spell. Excited, she pressed the letter to her chest. Her eyes had the vacant look of one looking into the distance. She murmured, My beloved, my dear, my life, you write so beautifully! Oh why won't you write to me? In anticipation of a response, she eagerly began writing him a letter. But she suddenly felt bashful and could not decide how she should address him. She considered and rejected many adjectives. Finally, her letter began with: 'My Chandra' and ended with 'Yours, Kumud'.

The letter—her heart itself, her anticipation and waiting—reached Sheth Laxminandan's house. Laxminandan picked it up from a pile of letters. He was surprised by the handwriting. He gave it to a servant. The servant showed it to Guman and then brought it to Sarasvatichandra as he sat talking to Chandrakant. The servant, as instructed by Guman, waited to find out the sender's name. Sarasvatichandra was surprised by the unfamiliar handwriting. He tore open the letter, and was pleased to see the sender's name at the bottom. He handed the letter with a smile to Chandrakant without telling him who it was from. He waited to see what his friend's response would be.

Chandrakant read the letter wide-eyed and said, smiling, 'Bhai, this is indeed your good fortune. Among us, it would take another lifetime to find such a wife!'

Sarasvatichandra laughed aloud. 'Chandrakant, tell me is this really such good fortune?'

'Then what else! Do Hindus ever find such rare gems? Bhai, this match is truly a divine blessing. You should thank God for it.'

'Your ideas have not progressed. Your English education makes you believe that the sum total of life is a good wife. The worldly efforts of men are not subsumed in a wife, Chandrakant.'

'I truly cannot fathom this ascetic trait in an aesthete like you!'

'But I have not spoken of asceticism.'

'What else is this! See the one I have at home, and then tell me how different our fortunes are! This letter itself is proof.'

'You are dissatisfied with your wife. Ganga bhabhi is simple-minded. Why such disaffection on account of her?'

'You are the only one I know who has one measure for himself and another for others. You are not satisfied with a woman like Kumud Sundari, and you accuse *me* of disaffection! Bravo! Bravo! You are not happy even after receiving such a loving letter from your adolescent bride-to-be, and charge me of disaffection. I am quite happy Ganga is mine! But do think about what I've said. Here, read the letter at least.'

Sarasvatichandra got up and, walking about the room, said with a smile, 'Chandrakant, do you really believe that I do not value this letter?'

'I am only going by your words.'

'If anyone knows my mind, it is you, Chandrakant. If you, too, make such a mistake, I cannot blame the others.'

'Was all that you said a lie, then?'

'No, what I said was true. And so is this. A body without a soul is useless; our body is more than the soul. How can one's fortune be measured solely by whom one is married to?'

They chatted and argued amiably for a long time, after which Chandrakant went home. He was as well educated as Sarasvatichandra. But being poor, he could study only because of his friend's help. Sarasvatichandra closed the door of his room, picked up the letter and read it again. What can an adolescent bride-to-be write to her chosen husband? Dear reader, pay attention. It was a short letter.

> My Chandra,
>
> I do not know what to write. I write because I could no longer contain myself. I wanted somehow to reach out to you, and hence this letter. You would laugh at this worthless piece of paper. But you are Chandra—you are the moon in the sky. It is the duty of the moon so high to nourish the Kumud that grows upon the earth. So the world says. And why should I not believe the same? I do not know what more to write. What if I should ask for your photograph? It is not I but my heart which has dictated this letter. You have inspired it. I have nothing more to say.
>
> Yours,
>
> Kumud.

Solitude opened Sarasvatichandra's heart and softened it somewhat, made it tender. He believed that women were unnecessary in his life. He considered marriage a lifelong encumbrance. He saw a life without progeny as the epitome of renunciation. He preferred a love of the mind and its pursuits and believed that only fools desired bodily pleasures. He felt it was possible to keep the mind free of desires. He felt that worldly life was lowly, worthless and barren. He did not wish to hurt his affectionate grandmother by going against the worldly norms, and so he had accepted the marriage with Kumud Sundari. He was indifferent to Kumud's virtues and follies. But mercury encased in glass does not remain unaffected by the temperature outside for long. His passions, buried under ascetic inclinations, came to the fore under the power of her unsullied beauty. His cold heart was drenched by the waves of simple affection that Kumud had unleashed. His desires, hitherto caged, flew out like freed birds as soon as Chandrakant left. Faced with her letter, his distance, his resolve melted, and he slumped into a chair, gazing intently at the delicate curves and whorls of Kumud's words, running his fingers over them. What is this? What is this, Sarasvatichandra? What strange power is this? How you would laugh at me, Chandrakant, if you could see me now! He gazed at the writing on the letter for a long time. He was no longer ashamed to admit the salience of women. Then he began to write a response to Kumud.

> Beauteous, beloved Kumud,
>
> Your letter has become most precious to me. It is true that the moon in the sky remains unaffected by the lotus, but your letter has proved to me that the two of us are mutually dependent and share the same ground. If I had to describe your influence over someone as hard-hearted as me, I would describe it through this verse.
>
> *O Vaidarbhi! You are blessed with so many virtues*
> *That even Naishadha is drawn to you*
> *Why should one praise the moon just because*
> *It makes the ocean turbulent with tide*

> Dear Kumud, my friend Chandrakant knows how stone-hearted I am. But I cannot even begin to describe the turmoil in my heart after receiving just one letter from you! I was too ashamed to bare my heart even to him. He still thinks I am cold and unfeeling.
>
> What if you should ask for my photograph? I am sending it, without your having to ask for it. And I will come to you—to gaze upon you.
>
> Dear Kumud, I dislike verbose, convoluted expressions of love. I do not know you at all, and yet I am compelled to write such a letter. My mind, hitherto self-content, now eagerly anticipates your response. Is this what people call love? Is this what is known as self-emanating, born of the mind? Is this desire? Desire has implanted itself even in my cold heart. Is it not true?
>
> Yours forever,
>
> Sarasvatichandra.

Sarasvatichandra began to realise that human experience was constituted quite differently from knowledge and thought. This realisation was both exhilarating and unnerving. His carefully nurtured ascetic resolve melted and it was as if he was born anew, body and soul. His mind was possessed by a single thought: Kumud is mine, and I am hers. The romance of love triumphed over his ponderous knowledge and ideals. Sarasvatichandra found a reason to visit Ratnanagari, and was received affectionately by Vidya Chatura. He recognised Kumud at first glance. After Vidya Chatura left for the palace, Kumud, driven by curiosity, desire, love, stealthily walked up to Sarasvatichandra's room. It did not even occur to her then to seek her mother's consent.

Sarasvatichandra was seated at a table with his back to her, writing a letter to Chandrakant. He remained unaware of her presence. Kumud pressed herself against the wall and stood to the right of the table. She was in his line of vision, but engrossed in writing, he did not look up. Tongue-tied, painfully shy, Kumud constricted herself even more, wanting to disappear into the wall. Her bangles tinkled softly against the wall and, startled, Sarasvatichandra looked up. He looked at her, elated. The famous scholar of Bombay, the son of wealthy Sheth Laxminandan, the toast of learned men, suddenly turned speechless before this delicate rose petal-like figure that stood before him, shrinking in her own skin. For long moments, neither of them could utter a word or blink; the world outside of them seemed to blur and vanish as they forgot all else, except for the eyes that remained intensely riveted upon each other. The girl was a mere adolescent. But even the scholarly man of letters was in the same state of speechless ecstasy. Then, as if awakened from a daze, Sarasvatichandra mumbled, 'I have written a few books ...' and he handed them to her. Kumud took the books from his hands and pressed them to her heart; her searching eyes withdrew, now fixing themselves upon her toes and his. She said nothing. During the exchange of books, their fingers had fleetingly brushed against each other; they were both acutely aware of this. His face lit up like the sun breaking through rain clouds. Her cheeks flushed a slow red just as the eastern horizon flushes crimson with the rising sun. She could not lift her eyes. The youth at last found his tongue and something to say.

'God willing, you will come and live in Bombay very soon.'

No response.

'Have you seen any of these books before?'

Silence again.

'You wrote me such beautiful letters, and today, not a word out of you!'

She stood mute like a statue.

'Kumud! My dearest Kumud!' Sarasvatichandra got up from the chair.

Hearing him speak her name, a sharp thrill coursed through her body as she had never before experienced. Her face turned a deep warm red, her knees felt weak. She mustered all her courage and said, barely audible, 'You are here for a very short while, isn't it?' Her voice was soft as the tinkle of tiny silver anklets and sweet as a sarangi. These few words escaped her pearl-like teeth and along with her sweet-scented breath etched themselves upon Sarasvatichandra's mind and heart. He felt an intense joy flood his being. His eyes came to rest upon her gentle and radiant face and he slumped back into the arm chair as if inebriated. They conversed for a brief hour or so, she standing before him while he sat in his chair. The hour passed much too quickly, and the spell was broken when young Kusum Sundari called for her sister. Sarasvatichandra remained seated for a long time after she left the room, with his eyes closed, trying to ascertain for himself whether these magically beautiful moments that had just passed were for real or part of a daydream.

He spent a few days in this dreamlike state, after which he returned to Bombay and immediately wrote to her. In response to his letter from Bombay she wrote: 'After you left, the poem "He stole my heart" keeps playing upon my lips. I recite it to myself and your image comes before me. I understand now what love is. My father has fixed the date of our marriage for the next month of Magha. My excitement is boundless. I cannot wait.'

Many such letters were exchanged. Some may feel it is useless to write letters without a purpose. One writes, I am going crazy without you, the other responds, I am possessed by you! Sombre people say that 'the toys of children and the coquettishness of lovelorn lovers' are similar. But wealth, prestige, power and suchlike which are dear to others are worthless to lovers who deepen their love for one another only by its constant expression and reiteration. Who between the two sides is right? The things that fascinate both groups are similar in nature: they are products of the imagination; they guide thought, word and deed. They are powerful and dear to those who hanker for them, but despised by those who have rejected them. They give joy as well as sorrow. They are real for those who believe in them, but a mere momentary mirage for those who do not. What is the difference between a heartfelt infatuation and the hoarding of wealth that one is certain to leave behind, or hankering after prestige or glory and the desire to commit to memory what is certain to be forgotten and craving for those who are certain to die? Sarasvatichandra's mind which had once shown ascetic tendencies was now under the sway of entirely new emotions. He discoursed endlessly with himself about what he could see was changing within him everyday, and why. He could not understand that if asceticism was also a form of desire, why should he then shun this other powerful desire which he now experienced? Why cannot both exist simultaneously? Why should the soul remain untouched by the world if the body does not remain untouched? Sarasvatichandra also discussed these and other existential predicaments with Chandrakant, and wrote about them in his letters to Kumud. One responded as a worldly wise practical man would, while the other responded as a young woman deeply and irreversibly in love. He learnt much from both, and educated both in turn. He was immersed in a heady emotional and spiritual churning of sorts. Searching for answers to his own questions, Sarasvatichandra found himself shedding his old ideas like a snake sheds its skin, and being born into a new one. He wanted to possess Kumud Sundari's tender, impressionable mind and heart. When Chandrakant reminded him of his earlier ascetic predisposition, he would say that renunciation meant being completely immersed in one thing, and shunning all else. And by that logic, he was still an ascetic. But the dreamlike state he was in did not leave him. His letters to Kumud were a reflection of his thoughts. Just as the reflection of the sky remains in the waters of a river, Sarasvatichandra's thoughts were reflected in Kumud's nascent mind. He was ever present in her mind, consciously and unconsciously. On one hand God set up this play, while on the other, He laid out an entirely different one. Human beings desire one thing, God wills something else.

Guman's son was no longer an infant. As a young bride, Guman had seen the affection that Sarasvatichandra had been given as a child. She wished similar affection to be showered upon her son Dhananandan. But for several reasons, her wish did not come true. As Sarasvatichandra matured in age and learning, the scholars who had previously collected around his father now sought his company. Over the years, they had become self-sufficient and were no longer dependent on the Sheth for patronage or money. They were grateful to him, but were no longer drawn to him as bees are to flowers. Moreover, wealth and status no longer enamoured and enticed them as easily as before. These scholars had more occasions to associate with Sarasvatichandra. Sarasvatichandra had become a lawyer of the Bombay High Court after passing his law examinations. He was studying to be a Council Barrister, albeit he did not intend to use his learning to secure a livelihood. He viewed the position of the Council Barrister as ornamental. He assisted his father in his business alongside his studies. Sarasvatichandra was acquainted with many learned and influential men of his times and was a member of several societies. These gave him the opportunity to make new associations.

What was advantageous for the son was disadvantageous for the father. Sheth Laxminandan's associates were newly wealthy men or those who sought wealth. The scholars preferred his son's company; and so in scholarly circles, Sheth Laxminandan came to be known as 'Sarasvatichandra's father'. Guman was never fond of her stepson; now she had even less reason to be so. She seethed in jealousy. Guman saw Sarasvatichandra's rise as detrimental to her son Dhananandan. In time, Sarasvatichandra passed the Council Barrister's examination. Laxminandan was full of praise for his elder son, and made him a partner in his business. Guman's woes multiplied. Old Ishwarkaur would fan Guman's jealousy by unabashedly expressing her joy at her first grandson's achievements. Much to Guman's fury and vexation, even her little son was drawn to Sarasvatichandra; he would seek him out and climb into his lap, despite her instructions to the contrary.

Guman would berate Laxminandan at every available opportunity. But the best time was after dinner when he came to bed, tired. She would say whatever she liked, and the man would meekly submit to her tongue-lashing, shamelessly accepting all the untruths he was told. Her inflammatory words had greater impact on his tired body and mind. She found something new to complain about every day. She had an inexhaustible supply of tears, taunts and rage. Her similes were more evocative than Kalidas, her power of narration tighter than that of Bana! But just as Guman had her faithfuls amongst the servants, Ishwarkaur had them, too. All that Guman said about Sarasvatichandra to Laxminandan was reported to Ishwarkaur, who would relate it to the grandson, who would, without any feeling of rancour or rage, pacify her. In a short time, Sarasvatichandra developed good business acumen. His courteousness impressed outsiders as well as those who worked under him. They all called him 'Bhai' and submitted to him with affection and respect. Soon, he began to take on the responsibilities of his father. This gave Guman one more reason to be unhappy. Complaints about 'Bhai' erupted like so many ants on Guman's bed.

'Wonderful! No one heeds you in this house anymore! It is Bhai's rule inside and Bhai's rule outside. Whatever Bhai wants happens. I am of no consequence at all, but that is hardly new. But you? You were once worshipped like a god; now they treat you like a stone. Are you at all concerned? They barely acknowledge your presence. Such is my state when you are around, who knows what awaits me later! Bhai will become the master of the house and we shall be his servants. Whom shall I blame? When you are so meek, to whom shall I take my complaints? Mark my words, Bhai will reduce you to a sorry state one day. You trust him so easily because he is your son, but these English educated sons are not true even to their parents. He will capture the house, the jewellery and the business—and leave you with nothing to do but count beads! You will be subservient to him. And who will care for poor me and my Dhan!' she sobbed. 'If you were so uncaring, why did you marry me! I would have toiled and ground grain for others and filled my stomach somehow. But I would not have seen such days at least. Nothing moves here without Bhai. No one can be so submissive even to one's own son.

'Listen to me. He knows the law—everyone will support him. Journalists and High Court judges are his friends. He will know all your tricks and then capture the business. If you object, he will file a complaint and seek his share. Beware, wake up before it is too late. There is still something to be salvaged. Instead of him giving us a share, you give Bhai his share and settle the matter so that we don't have to worry about tomorrow. But I know, you can never love us as much as you love him. For you he is made of gold, and we of ash. Are you at all concerned about what will happen to me as a poor, wretched widow?'

Over time, these nightly discourses had their impact. They broke Laxminandan's resistance just as waves break a rock and turn it into sand. During the day, Laxminandan had little time to worry about such matters. But at night, despite his resolve not to listen, these complaints would raise their ugly head. He despised his wife for it; but he neither had the time and energy to ascertain the truth, nor the courage to shut her up. All these things were said behind Sarasvatichandra's back, which gave him no opportunity to explain himself. As termites eat through wood, ultimately, the woman bore a hole in Laxminandan's head and made him powerless. The son through his generosity, courtesy and ability wielded authority; but the father could not see this. Instead, he imagined the worst possible picture as painted by his wife. He began to believe Guman.

One evening Laxminandan came home exhausted. He was hugely relieved not to find Guman in the bedroom. He slumped into an easy chair and asked a servant to bring him his food. He put his feet up and relaxed. Suddenly, he found Guman facing him. Oh God! What new war will she wage now, he thought nervously. She stood there in silence. Laxminandan began to eat. Even when tired and irritated, the Sheth thought of his son and couldn't help but ask, 'Is Bhai back? Has he eaten?' A demonic power does not forgive even a single misstep. Sheth Laxminandan realised that his innocent question was about to unleash a barrage of abuse. He knew he had invited trouble. Guman burst forth: 'So much affection for Bhai? Bhai has come home and eaten without worrying about his father. The father can think of nothing but Bhai. Bhai does not even bother about you. He is engrossed in reading his wife's letters—even before they are married! You don't bother about the one you married. People are wrong when they sing: Happy are those who marry the twice-married!'

The English charge that Hindu women enjoy no freedom. But was Guman any less free if she could scold an elderly man as wealthy and powerful as Sheth Laxminandan? A clerk, who had come in to deliver a telegram from England for Laxminandan, went back considering this question. The Sheth had just finished his meal. Guman went in to keep his soiled plate while Laxminandan read the telegram. She returned and stood leaning against a window railing; then she took out a letter.

'Whose is it?'

'Have a look. It is Bhai's letter to Kumud. Did you ever write such things to me?' Guman said, handing him the letter stolen from Sarasvatichandra's desk. Laxminandan took the letter and looked up at her incredulously. For once, he was both perturbed and enraged. 'Where did you get this letter from? How could you do this? And you have the gall to give it to me! Are you not ashamed?'

Guman was not the least put out and calmly replied, 'I know I should not have given his letter to you. I also know that I should not have read it. I have brought it only to show you Bhai's true character. I have not stolen it. The wind brought it to my room. If I return it now, he will accuse me of prying. Therefore, I gave it to you. You do what you like with it. We also married, and I am only a few years older than Bhai. But it is not proper to write such letters before marriage. It is not as if he is the first one to get married.'

Laxminandan's anger subsided. He read a few words of the letter, then said, 'Let him write what he wants, what it is to you? He is young. He has not written it to someone else's wife, has he!'

'That is true. But if I am at fault, I am treated as an elder, but when Bhai does something wrong, he is just a young boy! I gave it to you for a reason; read it if you want to. Who bothers about me in any case!' Guman left the room in a feigned huff, sobbing. The Sheth did not bother about her and went back to his telegram, muttering to himself, Oh why on earth did God create women? *Why?* They are so stupid, so utterly stupid—stupid from head to toe! The Sheth knew that Guman was stupid, but his natural affinity for her convinced him that she was not wicked or malicious. He was inclined to pardon her stupidity, though he found her most tiresome at times.

Guman realised the Sheth was in no mood to placate her. She re-entered the room on pretext of some work. Sheth was preoccupied with the telegram. She tried to draw his attention by opening and closing the doors noisily, and feigning as if she were suppressing sobs. The Sheth looked up and soothingly asked, 'Why are you standing there? Come, come here. Now stop crying. Do not do such things in future, all right? What is there to cry about? See, what did you gain by bringing his letter to me?'

Guman came in and sat on a chair facing him, her eyes red with crying. The Sheth took pity on her. He got up, closed the door and came and sat next to her, trying to placate her. Guman saw that her plan was coming to fruition. At first she played hard to get, then meekly said, 'What is it to me? I gave you a letter. But this Kumud is truly a match for Bhai. By mistake the postman gave me a letter addressed to Bhai, and I opened it, believing it was for me. But just see how clever this woman is! Her roots are deep. Simple men like you won't understand a woman's character. We do. Bhai has become her captive already. If she has such a hold on him now, what would she not do later? We will have no place to go to. We will also have to be subservient to her. Bhai also writes to his father-in-law. You were only telling me the other day how cunning these people from the native states tend to be. Moreover, those who have received an English education remain faithful to no one. They will show their true colours at the right time. Now you run the business. So you should be in control outside, and I should rule over the house. Instead, we have a different story. And you still trust Bhai!'

Guman spoke submissively without aggression. This softened the Sheth further. He said, 'All right. But is this such a big problem?' He read the letters because Guman wanted him to. Then he remarked, 'But what is so objectionable about these letters? They are what all young people write to each other.'

'You will hand over everything to Bhai. Have you ever considered what will happen to my Dhan and me?'

'Oh. So is that what it is?'

'Yes. Is that not a problem? For you it is all very trivial.'

'All right. That will be taken care of,' the Sheth placated Guman, made her laugh, fooled around with her for a while and went out.

Sarasvatichandra's thoughts were all about Kumud Sundari. She played on his mind constantly. As the day of marriage came closer, his joy increased manyfold. He controlled his father's business. He knew that no questions would be asked if he were to spend money from its accounts. His mother Chandralaxmi had received close to a lakh of rupees from her parents and from Laxminandan in jewellery and money. Sarasvatichandra inherited it when he became an adult. He preferred to spend money from this amount rather than spend his father's money. His father owned two or three bungalows on the Walkeshwar hill. He was given one of them for his use. The bungalow had a large drawing room. Sarasvatichandra decorated it to his taste, for which he spent five to six thousand rupees. He had a large portrait of Kumud painted and had it framed in an intricately carved ivory frame, spending another three, four thousand rupees on it. Sarasvatichandra liked to gaze at this portrait for long hours in company of his friend Chandrakant. Chandrakant often reminded him of his former ascetic nature and teased him. Sarasvatichandra's response was always laughter. He believed that his love and devotion for his wife was true, praiseworthy, and considered it his moral duty to further this emotion. Thoughts are guided by disposition. To top it all, Sarasvatichandra got an exquisite diamond ring made. A large diamond, pure as water, set in an intricate gold base. The base could be opened by pressing a key, supported by a tiny hinge. On the inside of the base was painted a beautiful image of Sarasvatichandra's face, which could be seen only when the base was open. The ring was for Kumud. It cost five thousand. For this millionaire's son who did not hesitate before spending fifteen or twenty thousand rupees, this expenditure on the love of his life was paltry. Chandrakant teased him on his face, but secretly he admired

Sarasvatichandra's devotion to Kumud and sincerely wished his friend good luck. Oh, the wealthy are most fortunate! A mind so pure and noble despite so much wealth! Such deep learning, such prestige, and the blessing of a union with such a loving and beautiful woman! And so much love and devotion! My good friend is fortunate indeed! May God protect his luck! Chandrakant did not know that the wheels of fortune can turn in a moment. In the game of dice that is life, luck and misfortune are two sides of the same dice.

These stories travelled to Guman, who naturally related them to Laxminandan, furnishing proof that Bhai in his infatuation would squander all the family wealth on his wife. Laxminandan had never spent money on such things; even he felt that his son's expenditure was unjustified. Guman said, 'We know of this expenditure—it has been spent from the wealth that you have entrusted to him. But we do not know where else he has spent the money. How can we know? This is the outcome of your trust.' It never occurred to the Sheth that Sarasvatichandra could have spent the money from his own inheritance from Chandralaxmi.

Ishwarkaur knew of Guman's machinations. She would tell Sarasvatichandra, who would listen to her without comment, and try and solace her as best as he could. But he was pained by Guman's evil doings, and by his own father's unsteady mind. Ishwarkaur was convinced that Laxminandan would disinherit Sarasvatichandra someday. She could do little about it, but she had about a lakh of rupees which she wanted to give to Sarasvatichandra. Sarasvatichandra smiled at the suggestion and said, 'Grandmother, God will take care for me, as He does for everyone else. If we were to implement this suggestion, parents would become even angrier and the conflict would escalate. The best option is to will this money to the younger brother. The money will remain with you for your lifetime, the parents will be happy, and these hurtful schemes and machinations will also stop.' Ishwarkaur was not convinced. She was certain that neither Laxminandan nor Guman would be grateful to Sarasvatichandra; moreover, this was too small a sum to turn Guman benevolent. Ishwarkaur knew that her grandson was quite capable of charting his own course. But she was sad that the most worthy son of the family was likely to receive nothing from the ancestral wealth, and felt helpless as Sarasvatichandra himself opposed her plans. Ishwarkaur called Chandrakant and sought his assistance.

Chandrakant approved of the old woman's plan, but he knew it would be extremely difficult to fructify. There was a time when Sarasvatichandra had different plans. He wanted to give away Chandralaxmi's wealth for activities dedicated to the country's progress. His father's wealth was ancestral property. He wanted to renounce his claims over it. His desire was to mingle with the common folk without donning the saffron robes of a mendicant. He wanted to travel across the length and width of the country in search of new experiences, and God. He wanted to spend three, four years as a wanderer, then settle down someplace and use his experience and knowledge for the social and spiritual uplift of the people. Sarasvatichandra realised that the reformist classes would decry his actions, and also that his father would be terribly pained by it. He was not going to be deterred by any direct or indirect criticism that might come his way while adopting a path he strongly believed in. But Sarasvatichandra abandoned his plan knowing how his father would feel. Chandrakant knew of these plans. He knew from his own knowledge that Sarasvatichandra himself was the biggest obstacle in actualising his grandmother's plans. Chandrakant was a pragmatic man; he had known extreme poverty first-hand, he knew the pain, the ignominy and desperation of poverty. He loved Sarasvatichandra even more for his self-sacrificing tendencies. But he was afraid that these very inclinations would someday lead this gem of a man to an obscure life. He did not want his dear friend to abandon such wealth and adopt poverty. He was pained by the thought that his learned friend would invite the censure of the reformists because of his renunciation. The deep bond between Kumud Sundari and Sarasvatichandra had assuaged his fears somewhat. And yet he saw some strange similarities between Sarasvatichandra's fierce idealism, his strongly ascetic predisposition, and his intense love for Kumud. Chandrakant feared that someday Sarasvatichandra, accompanied by Kumud Sundari, would renounce the world. For all these reasons he was keen to put Ishwarkaur's plan into action. Chandrakant wanted a solution that could be kept secret from Sarasvatichandra, and one that was irreversible.

Chandrakant advised Ishwarkaur to appoint someone she trusted as an administrator of her wealth, who would manage her property and give her the profits accruing from it. After her death, the property would vest in Sarasvatichandra and his wife, and in case of Sarasvatichandra being without his wife, then in him alone. Chandrakant was certain that Sarasvatichandra would never use this wealth for selfish purposes. They could not decide who the administrator should be. Ishwarkaur asked Chandrakant to accept the responsibility. He accepted, as there was no other way of securing his friend's interest. A deed was drafted; some prestigious persons were called in as witnesses. Sarasvatichandra had no inkling of all this. Finally, when it was ready, Ishwarkaur summoned Laxminandan one day and handed him the deed in the presence of everyone. She chose not to explain her decision. She merely asked him to write his assent on the deed. She knew her son would have no option but to sign. Laxminandan read the deed, but appeared hesitant to sign. Ishwarkaur commanded, 'Bhai, sign the deed.' Wealthy, influential and prestigious Sheth Laxminandan saw a different facet of his mother that day—there was no plea in her voice. He had no option but to submit to her wishes. Laxminandan felt he was being punished for his subservience to Guman. His mother appeared to him then as a divine avenger. He signed the deed and handed it back to his mother. All those present solemnly signed as witnesses. No one spoke a word. There hung a photograph of Chandralaxmi near the door of Ishwarkaur's room. Laxminandan looked up at it and felt as if Chandralaxmi approved of his actions. He could almost hear her say, 'What you have done is worthy of my love.' Laxminandan felt that Chandralaxmi was content. Looking at her photograph, he remembered the love, the simple pleasures and joys that the two of them had shared in the past. And for a while, he forgot Guman. Then he got up and went to his room. He found Guman sitting there. Sheth Laxminandan felt like the aged King Dashrath must have felt as he left Queen Kaushalya's palace after proclaiming that Ram would be king, and entered Queen Kaikayi's chamber. Laxminandan put his hand on Guman's shoulder. Faced with the stark reality of his present, his blissful unsullied dream shattered.

'So you are back. What did she want?' Guman began her slow interrogation and got her husband to divulge everything. She was convinced this entire plan was hatched by Sarasvatichandra. She could now prove the vile influence of English education. The Sheth felt obliged to compensate her for the perceived injustice done to Dhananandan. Guman sieved his fatherly joy into doubt and despair. Where once stood a secure tree that generously showered affection, a weak and poisonous weed took root. How did my innocent son suddenly conceive of this deed? It must be the machinations of Kumud, or her father, reasoned the Sheth. He became convinced that his son had betrayed him, and sorely repented having signed the deed. He began to look at each of Sarasvatichandra's business decisions with jealousy and suspicion. The son's judgements were pure as gold, but to the father's clouded eyes they seemed impure as brass. There were differences in their thinking, as there are wont to be between the old and the new. Innocent and undoubting, the son acted in good faith, believing he still enjoyed the right of disputation, and that his view would prevail. But the Sheth cross-examined each act minutely, and saw only what he chose to see. He came to be haunted by the thought that, My son will take over everything and reduce me to nothing.

The Sheth devised a ploy to ascertain his suspicions. Guman's brother Dhurtalal exercised considerable influence over his sister. He had hitherto been unable to get a foothold into Laxminandan's house. He now saw that the fish was about to bite the bait and seized the moment. Guman's acerbic tongue was Dhurtalal's source of power. The Sheth reasoned with himself: I reposed full trust in my son, but Guman's charges are proving to be true. How can I not believe her now? My confidence in Sarasvati was false. The response of the haunted mind was the one that he chose to believe.

Sheth Laxminandan was the managing director of a cotton weaving mill. A few years ago he had entrusted this position to Sarasvatichandra. Laxminandan devised a plan to enrol Dhurtalal as an assistant to Sarasvatichandra and, over time, make them joint managing directors. He argued that it would protect Dhananandan's interests. If Sarasvatichandra could have seen through his father, he would have seen that the plan was to clip his wings. But that is not what he saw. His were the eyes of a trusting son. Sarasvatichandra knew about the sayings of worldly wise men that all machinations begin with a breach of trust and one person's goodness can be the peg from which the wicked gain a foothold. He was also told that one person's trust can be the source of strength for another. He had been cautioned that one should trust others only after they have proven their trustworthiness. But Sarasvatichandra had hitherto not felt the need to put these into practice. How can a loving and devoted son ever feel that, my own father is playing a treacherous game with me? Sarasvatichandra responded to his father with a pure conscience.

'Pitaji, Dhurtalal is our relative, and we should try and do him good to the extent possible. However, you are not unaware of his attitude and conduct. We can only deal with honest and sincere persons, or else we shall have to face the consequences. Monetary loss is insignificant, but we can ill afford the loss of trust and prestige or a loss to the shareholders of our mill. If you want him to join a business, we can easily accommodate him in any of our personal businesses, can't we? There are other ways to ensure Gumanba's happiness, an honest income for Dhurtalal, and no injury to our reputation.'

But the Sheth who had already made up his mind did not like this intervention. His suspicion deepened. 'Bhai, but I have decided. It must be done.'

'But there must be a good reason for it.'

'My wish is reason enough.'

'If that is so, your wish is my command. I only suggested what I thought was in the interest of the family.'

'That is all right. Make sure this is done.'

'Yes.'

For the first time, Sarasvatichandra heard a different tone in his father's voice. He could not fathom the reason for it. But he felt no need to dwell upon it further. It must be one of those things, he said to himself. He could never imagine that his father wanted to eliminate him from business. The Sheth thought: That was easy!

Around this time one day, old Ishwarkaur died while counting the beads. Laxminandan felt sad for a while, but not for long because of the grudge he bore her. He joined in with the laughter and chatter at the crematorium and did not think that his behaviour was unnatural. When he returned from the cremation, Guman was all dressed up to mourn, and he remarked on her attractiveness without any feeling of sadness. But for Sarasvatichandra, the loss was immense, and for a while he felt that with her passing away, he no longer had any more ties with the family. His grandmother had lavished much care and affection in raising him. He moved Chandralaxmi's photograph and a few other memorabilia from Ishwarkaur's room to his own. He would look at them and remember vividly his grandmother's stories, her affection. Forlorn, he sought solace at work. He never once thought about her wealth, and remained ignorant of the arrangement that she had made for him.

Laxminandan had set aside a large sum of money for Guman just about the time that Sarasvatichandra had joined his business. He had wanted to invest the money in some good shares. He had then trusted the elder son and sought his advice. Sarasvatichandra believed that women's wealth should not be invested in shares and had advised his father to instead invest it in secure government 'loans.' Laxminandan had accepted this advice. Sarasvatichandra had inherited Chandralaxmi's wealth, which was also invested in government loans. He decided to redeem the loan and invested the proceeds in shares. Those days, there were rumours of a possible

Russian aggression. The sale and purchase of government loans was stopped, and consequentially their market price also fell. The shares in which Sarasvatichandra had invested rose in value, from which he made huge profits. Laxminandan now suspected that Sarasvatichandra had deliberately misguided him. He had done one thing for himself and offered contrary advice for Guman. What could it mean? Love and trust prompt one to find benevolence even in a malicious deed, but disaffection and mistrust give rise to suspicion even in benevolent acts.

One day after lunch, father and son went to office in their two-horse drawn carriage. Guman had tutored Laxminandan. He was angry about Ishwarkaur's money, the imagined influence of Kumud's family on Sarasvatichandra, and the seemingly harmful advice he had given on the financial market. Guman added salt to the wound. The Sheth broached the matter in the carriage.

'Bhai, are you keeping track of the market prices?'

'Yes, the prices are good,' and he told his father of the profits he had made.

'But the government note is trading weak.'

'Yes, it will bounce back once these rumours subside.'

'And what if the Russians invade?'

The son laughed and said, 'Father, it will take a while.'

'You sold your government notes?'

'Yes.'

'Oh, I see,' Laxminandan looked at his son askance. 'Bhai, I am very disappointed in you. I must speak frankly with you.'

This unusual and illogical opening surprised Sarasvatichandra considerably. 'Of course! If you do not tell me, who will!'

'Listen carefully. For many days I have observed you but said nothing. You have changed, though I cannot fathom why. But it is my considered opinion that your views are no longer independent. Your marriage has been fixed to make you happy. But it is your duty to ensure that it does not lead to conflict within the family. Some youngsters become totally besotted with their wives, who never fail to take advantage of it. Such women are eager to destroy the household by using their husbands as tools. Those who influence their husbands before marriage will stop at nothing after marriage. But if the husband's heart is in the right place, such a situation will never arise. I am not suggesting that you are one of them. Only that if you are aware, you can be careful.'

If Sarasvatichandra had any intention to respond, it vanished. Laxminandan had crossed limits, but he could not do likewise. The only thought in his head was, My pure, innocent Kumud! He was profoundly hurt and angered by this vile and baseless allegation against her. Oh father! You do not know what you have said! It does not deserve a response. Dearest Kumud, in my heart and before God, your purity remains unsullied. This allegation in fact makes you shine forth even brighter. Sarasvatichandra had great reserves of forbearance, but only with regard to his own self. Every pore in his being felt outraged at this unjust accusation of Kumud, that too by his own father. My own Kumud! Why should I accept this vile and false charge against you? Is it not a crime before God? His face turned a deep red, but he somehow controlled his rage. He did not show the anguish he felt and allowed his father to speak without a pause.

Under Guman's inexorable and unforgiving influence, Laxminandan had completely lost his power to discriminate between good and bad, right and wrong, rational and irrational. He said everything he could have and more. He said he had faltered in his assessment of Vidya Chatura. He said Guman was vulnerable, and reminded Sarasvatichandra of his duties towards his stepmother. He accused him of being bewitched by Kumud Sundari and told him that men who submit to their wife and father-in-law are called effeminate. He expressed his displeasure at the huge sums of money that Sarasvatichandra had wasted in decorating the Walkeshwar bungalow and said he was worried about the future of a son as profligate as him. He charged Sarasvatichandra of profiteering from shares while ensuring losses for Guman. He also pointed out his own generosity in signing Ishwarkaur's deed, and said, 'But you should not have plotted such a thing against me.' He taunted him about Dhurtalal's inclusion in business, saying, 'You refused, but gave in only because I stood firm. You should be beholden to me, always.' He did not spare Sarasvatichandra's education and learning. 'You cannot earn a living simply by putting on airs of your English education,' he said. He said Sarasvatichandra was wrong to believe that he, Sheth Laxminandan, would cower before his knowledge of law. He said this and many such unbearable things. He picked holes in his son's business dealings to show that Sarasvatichandra lacked intelligence, experience, ability, judgement, in practical dealings and analytical faculties. He also gave him a long lecture on how his devotion to his father was found lacking.

Sarasvatichandra could not understand many of the things that were said to him, or even begin to gauge their intent. He was utterly and completely taken by surprise. He saw Guman's absolute control over his father and began to realise the extent of the situation he now found himself in. He witnessed the full force of his father's disaffection and the limitless injustice that was meted out to him, and recognised with sadness that his father was the epitome of weakness, insecurity and stupidity. He did not respond, since a retort would have been contrary to his understanding of his duties as a son, and of his upbringing. He knew that words were now futile. Even to reveal his mind was beneath his dignity and he chose to remain silent. He no longer pondered over his father's stupidity; his only concern now was the dilemma: What is my duty at present? What should I do now? He was so engrossed in this contemplation that Laxminandan's words no longer penetrated his ears. His face had turned red, he was drenched in sweat, he trembled with hurt, rage and indignation, his heart was filled with anguish and a bottomless despair, he could not think, his stomach was one tight knot, and hot tears gradually welled up in his eyes. No one saw him shed a tear. Sheth's interminable umbrage abruptly came to an end as he had nothing more left to say, and was exhausted besides. They reached office. Laxminandan got down with the air of a judge who had meted out just punishment. Sarasvatichandra followed him like a man just awakened from a ten-year long sleep. From now on, he was on his own. His head had turned.

Sarasvatichandra wrote a note and called for Dhurtalal. He spent the day familiarising Dhurtalal about all business matters. At the end of the day he took Dhurtalal to Laxminandan. Dhurtalal related the day's events to Laxminandan, who was happy at the turn of events. The next day Sarasvatichandra reported to his father on all the matters that he dealt with. Laxminandan was pleasantly surprised and asked what the matter was. Sarasvatichandra replied, 'Nothing. Just like that.' That evening he went home with his father and left soon afterwards, saying, 'Tonight I will eat and sleep at the Walkeshwar bungalow.' The home bustled with regular hangers-on and activities, but he remained indifferent to it. When the evening lamps were lit, he took the carriage and went out. He picked up Chandrakant on the way. The cool sea breeze on the Chowpaty beach did not assuage his state of mind. He felt no joy at the sight of the dark hills in the distance. He did not exchange a word with his friend on the way. As the horses pulled the carriage up the hill, Sarasvatichandra was suddenly pushed against his friend by this sudden movement, and it broke his reverie. They had passed by the colourful cosmopolitan crowds of Bombay, horse drawn carriages, lazy merchants, laughing children unattached to worldly concerns, friends sitting on the rocks with arms around each other, worshipful Parsis and European couples riding in free abandon—Sarasvatichandra's eyes had not seen any of them. The expression in them was peculiarly intense and distant. As if wanting to ask a question of the huge orange sun setting between the beacon at Colaba and the hills of Walkeshwar. As if searching for some spot far out on the limitless grey-green sea. As if wanting to measure the depths of the darkness now descending upon them. At last the carriage approached the bungalow. The purebred horses turned into the driveway, neighing. The coachman put aside his whip. The cool green of the darkening garden welcomed them. The gravel crunched crisply under the horses' hooves. The carriage came to a halt at the doorsteps. The two friends got down. They entered the newly decorated drawing room, and stood facing Kumud Sundari's portrait. Sarasvatichandra leaned upon his friend's shoulder and gazed at the portrait. He went up close to it, then turned around and led his friend to a couch covered with brocade cushions. He sat down beside him, rested his head on Chandrakant's shoulder and broke down. He wept and sobbed like a child.

Chandrakant was astonished and perturbed. He tried to comfort him, 'Bhai, Bhai! What is this! What is wrong? Have courage. What ever happened?'

'Chandrakant ... Chandrakant. No. There is nothing to be said. I am perfectly calm. What can happen? Nothing. Nothing whatsoever.'

'What is it then?' Chandrakant's heart beat faster.

'I will tell you.' Sarasvatichandra wiped his tears, sat upright and patiently narrated the incident with his father. He also told him that he had handed over the business to Dhurtalal. His head had now cleared. 'Chandrakant, I am ashamed that for a while I allowed my emotions to run riot. But what could I do? I had no inkling that things had come to such a pass. It is God's will.'

'Bhai, the fault is not yours. But you have acted in haste; it was not right.'

'Chandrakant, from today on, I shall treat my father's wealth like wealth gifted to a temple. I shall not touch it.'

'Calm down! Why say such things? It is not as if you do not have options.'

'No, I do not want any options. Sacrifice by one who has no options is like the chastity of an aged woman. My father believes that I relate to him for his wealth alone. He no longer cares for me. Nor does he trust me. It is good that he does not care for me. His mistrust I will remove. I shall bequeath all my wealth to Gumanba and Dhanbhai, may God grant them eternal wealth. Poverty is not too difficult for me.'

'Why do you persist with such unreason! Has God not granted you enough learning?'

'I do not wish to hawk my learning. I am not worried about a livelihood. I do not need wealth—it is useless for me. You know well that I remained a householder only for the sake of my father's love. That love no longer holds. So I am now a free man!'

'Who says wealth is useless?'

'I know your views. But the good of the country, the good of the people and the good of the self can all be attained without wealth. What can others do if we are found to be lacking?'

'You could practice before the High Court. Are you not qualified?'

'Fool, don't you know that I have always despised it! Do you really think I would soil myself in a world I find so repugnant just for the sake of filling my belly!'

'But what about engaging with the practical aspects of life? Aren't you running away from those?'

'Chandrakant, stop it. I do not want to have this debate.'

'But it is not as if you have to earn your livelihood. You have one lakh rupees. Your grandmother has left it for you, and Kumud Sundari.'

Sarasvatichandra was speechless. Chandrakant apprised him of Ishwarkaur's deed. Some of Laxminandan's long litany of accusations now began to make sense. Sarasvatichandra was greatly displeased, but there was nothing he could do. He had no right to gift away Kumud Sundari's share.

'Chandrakant, I do not care. I do not want that money.'

'You are mad, Sarasvatichandra! It is your own money. Set up your own household. Augment your learning, do good unto the world, give joy to Kumud, and be happy yourself! Can't you do that much?'

'But I cannot set up my own household. My father now believes that Vidya Chatura proposed the marriage only for his wealth. What can be done? The engagement cannot be called off on that ground.'

'You are being as wise as the God's bull. Vidya Chatura was impressed by you and nothing else.'

'Chandrakant, I desire to observe the pain and joys of poverty, experience the state of a vagabond, search out gems obscured by poverty and ignorance. I now have that opportunity.'

'But what will people say?'

'I do not fear opprobrium. Prestige and ignominy are both false measures of human effort; they are but dreams. They are not tangible objects that can be grasped.'

'All right. But have you even spared a thought for Kumud Sundari?'

'I leave her care to God. Her love, the outcome of a short acquaintance, will wane. She will forget me once she finds a good husband.'

'You are making a mistake. You will repent deeply if you hurt that young woman. You will commit a crime before God. She, too, is not going to be erased from your mind and conscience.'

'I know myself.'

'Indeed! If you really do, what else is needed! All you can then do is to aspire for the dreams of a deranged man. What others suppress, you not only articulate but also wish to experience. To me, this is a sign of pure idiocy and irrationality.'

'You have said enough.'

'Have I? I merely speak, but you are about to destroy everything! You became a barrister, gained so much learning, prestige, cultivated a love so profound and mutual, you have so much wealth and learning. Just think, what have you set out to do? This is the height of foolishness! Just imagine, what would *you* have said if some other barrister had brought this unto himself?'

'What else can I do?'

'You can and must put to good use the ability, the resources, and the virtue that is uniquely yours. Do not think like a cowardly ascetic and withdraw from the world just because it is difficult! Consider what would then happen to more ordinary mortals like the rest of us.'

Sarasvatichandra became pensive. He rested his head upon the couch. His half-closed eyes were for a while vacant. After a long silence, he reached out a hand to touch Chandrakant on the shoulder and began to speak in a voice grave and sad.

'Chandrakant, my dear Chandrakant! I cannot ever repay you for your friendship. A judge hears arguments of both sides before making up his mind. But a man takes an extreme decision privately; very rarely does he have friend to argue with. You have said much, you have even argued against me, but I know you have always thought for me, for my best interest. Nevertheless, my resolve does not leave me.

'Dear pure Kumud, I have had to hear words that abased you. And keep silent. Those words have left wounds in my heart which will not heal. I know my duty towards my father. But if in fulfilling that duty, I am required to torment or neglect my wife, this is not acceptable to me. A wife considers her duties to her husband primary as compared to her obligations to her parents. Once married, she accepts the husband's primacy. Why should the duties of a husband be any different, then? If a scripture says that I should torture my wife to make my parents happy, I reject such a scripture. One eye should be on parents and the other on the wife; more preferably, both eyes should look at them with equanimity—such is the duty of a son and husband.

A virtuous wife and a
Respected lord.
Are each to either all—kindred
And friends,
Wealth, love and life, and all
The heart should covet.[1]

'Yes, I think it is best that parents do not marry their sons if they want the son to neglect his wife and not share her joys and sorrows. My father wants me to be such a son even before marriage. After marriage, I would never have fulfilled his desires. It would have aggrieved us both. Marriage would have united Kumud and me. But what about my father? I am a son to him, but who is Kumud to him? Chandrakant, I know such logic can be nauseating. Kumud will never cease to reside in my mind. The beauty and purity of her heart has come to possess me, and it always will. I know well that separation from her would mean great suffering for both of us. But my father is my father and will

[1] H. H. Wilson, trans. *Malati and Madhava or The Stolen Marriage* of Bhavabhuti (Calcutta: The Society for the Resuscitation of Indian Literature, 1901), 74.

remain so. It is therefore best that this marriage does not take place. I will, for his sake, bear the agony. Kumud will marry someone else and forget me in time. A marriage to me will not make her happy. No one will let her be in peace—and hence ...' Sarasvatichandra was overcome with emotion; but he quickly regained composure and continued: 'You would argue that I should build our own house where Kumud and I would be happy. But why should that be necessary? If I have my own house, Pitaji would see me as a competitor—that thought itself is painful to me. Painful because it would make him unhappy and I would be forced to be party to his embarrassment. His happiness is also my goal.

'No. It is better to be unknown rather than to live apart from him. If it brings censure, it would be of my conduct. I am not afraid of that. Dhanbhai will ensure that my father does not miss having a son. The wedge of fear and envy in Gumanba's mind will also be removed. My father will regain his composure. Pitaji does not love me anymore, and so he will not feel the pain of my absence. I will not be worried on his account because he is a wealthy man. But I will never be able to forget him. It pains me that Kumud will always be present before me. And you, Chandrakant! How am I ever going to forget you! Chandrakant, the web of household obligations and service to the country, and your learning will help you forget me. If my father were to ever miss me, do comfort him, care for him. I will never forget you, Chandrakant.'

Chandrakant became emotional. He held Sarasvatichandra's hand in his and said, 'Dear friend, why do you say these things? Why are you being so cruel?' Chandrakant had practical sense. He hoped that by diverting Sarasvatichandra, his agitation and turmoil would subside. They talked of other things. Sarasvatichandra appeared quite calm. Finally, it was eleven in the night when the two friends parted. Sarasvatichandra ran after him with a bag, saying 'Chandrakant, take this bag with you. I will tell you in the morning what is to be done with it.'

'Friend, I think I shall also sleep here at the bungalow.'

'No, no! Go home, or Ganga bhabhi will curse me.'

'No, that she will not do. I do not trust your intentions.'

Sarasvatichandra laughed. 'Go now, don't be so suspicious. What will you do if my mind becomes uncontrollable?'

'You are audacious and impossible. That is why I'm concerned.'

'Now go home.'

'But you will be careful and not do anything rash.'

'All right. Send the carriage for me in the morning.'

Chandrakant took the bag and went home in the carriage, reassured that Sarasvatichandra would meet him next morning to give him instructions about the contents of the bag. Next morning, he waited for the carriage. There was no sign of it till eight. Chandrakant grew anxious. He hired a carriage and went to the bungalow. There was no one there except the gardener who told him, 'Bhai left early in the morning for a walk to Chowpaty.' Chandrakant rushed in the carriage to Chowpaty beach, a favourite spot of Bombay residents. A long paved road curves along the seashore. A little ahead, there is a railway crossing and station. Chandrakant saw Sarasvatichandra's carriage parked on the seashore. The coachman told him, 'Bhai went for a walk quite a while ago and has not yet returned. He gave me this note with instructions to give it to you.'

Chandrakant's heart sank. He read the note.

> Dear Chandrakant,
>
> You soothed and consoled me before going home. I felt calm. But I spent the night walking around the garden. I thought a lot. Ultimately, my thoughts prevailed over your counsel. I am putting it into action. Do not mourn the separation from me. All living things are destined to enter the darkness of death alone. To live an obscure life is to prepare for death. I have decided to abandon illusory light and to seek darkness without any remorse. I shall never forget you. At the right moment we shall meet again, directly or indirectly. I leave you behind, but can my heart go without you? Do not search for me. Console Ganga bhabhi. I will not be able to forget her.

> *Sooner or later, everyone will forsake me*
> *So if I were to leave you behind, dear friend*
> *It wouldn't be a fault*
> *The sun will set, the birds will fly away*
> *The night too shall pass*
> *And so shall the rising moon fade*

> I know that your deep affection would have tied me down and weakened my resolve. So I have decided to embark upon this adventure.
> Namesake of Sarasvatichandra. What else can I call myself?

A forlorn sigh escaped Chandrakant. He held his head in his hand and read the letter addressed to Sheth Laxminandan.

> Dear Father,
>
> If my action opens up the path of your happiness, it would not be considered a crime. But if you were to think of it as a crime, your son would not be further dejected in seeking your forgiveness.
>
> I have, as you desired, handed over the functioning of the mill to Dhurtalal. I have shown you all the records as well. Brahma lacks nothing. There is no reason for you to miss me. I pray to God that Dhananandbhai gives you every possible joy and satisfaction. Please use all your wealth for his welfare. If you have any occasion to remember me, that alone is wealth enough for me.
>
> I believe you will not object to my decision of adopting the path of renunciation. Hence, this decision. I will now lead a life of obscurity. It is not necessary to take leave of others prior to the act of renunciation. The renouncer has no one to take leave of. I have been innocent of any wrongdoing, my conscience is clear. But if Gumanba believes me to be guilty, please ask her to pardon me. Once I leave, you will have no more reason to feel distressed and wronged. You shall no longer feel cheated in your estimation of Vidya Chatura's family. May your bliss be eternal!
>
> Pitaji, do not worry about me. Do not grieve for me. Everyone must take leave sooner or later. Those who leave do not return.

Chandraba left; I too am leaving. She went one way; I am going another way. Just as you erased her memory, forget me as well. The wise are those who do not remember those who have left. From now on,

What does the world care for my sorrows and joys
There are so many souls upon this earth
Some distraught, some joyous
One cannot cry for them all
There would be no end to tears
So father, for one such as I
Why should you cry?
Do not remember me
Do not weep for me
Why these futile tears?
Why not forget one who has forsaken and left?
What does the world care for my sorrows and joys

Father, what more can I write. If you find anything missing from your house, do tell Chandrakant. He shall pay for it.
One who, for the sake of your happiness, wishes to be erased even from memory,
Sarasvatichandra.

Chandrakant read both the letters. A sea of sorrow engulfed him. He sat down on a boulder and said to Sarasvatichandra's coachman, 'Go and tell your Sheth, Bhai has left home. For good.'

The coachman was startled. 'What! Where did he go?'

'Who knows? Go tell him that he has left the city.'

'What has he written in the letter?'

'Just that.'

The coachman sped off and disappeared behind a line of trees on Charni Road. Chandrakant got up, took the hired coach and went to the railway station to make enquiries. No one could tell him anything. The station master, the ticket master and others crowded around him. They checked tickets issued on mail and passenger trains, but it told them nothing. Dejected, disheartened, Chandrakant returned home.

He sat alone at his writing table in the bedroom. He could no longer hold back his tears. He confided in his wife. 'Oh what shall I do now, Ganga? He is gone! Sarasvatichandra, what have you done? You can be angry with the Sheth, but what about me? What will happen to poor Kumud Sundari now? Where shall I look for you? Nothing is certain about these romantic idealists.'

The news spread like wild fire. After some time, Laxminandan's clerk came to fetch Chandrakant. Chandrakant once again read Sarasvatichandra's letter to Laxminandan and pondered over the statement: 'Please use all your wealth for Dhananandan's welfare'. He decided not to hand over the letter immediately to the Sheth.

Guman and Dhurtalal were with Laxminandan when the coachman brought him the news. Guman turned pale and Laxminandan looked stunned. Dhurtalal whispered to Guman, 'Make sure he hasn't walked away with things. He is cunning.' Guman gathered courage and told the Sheth, 'Get the house checked.' Laxminandan snarled at her, 'Checked? For what? My son has left home, and you want the house *checked*!'

'Look here, Bhai is not an innocent child. He is playacting to frighten us. He must be hiding somewhere just to send us on a wild goose chase. A man who owns two lakh rupees is not about to run away like this. Most likely, he must have gone to meet his father-in-law and bride-to-be. But first make sure he has not run away with things. This is just a ploy to secure my brother's removal. It is apparent even to me. Don't you smell a rat?'

Laxminandan turned red with rage and said, 'Careful! Today I am not going to listen to you. You may not care, but my heart is in agony.'

When Chandrakant arrived at the house, Laxminandan got up and took him to another room. Guman followed them, but he turned her away at the door, latched it, and came and sat with Chandrakant. He was overcome by emotions. The virtues of his firstborn son came back to him. He realised he had handed over charge to Dhurtalal in haste, and that he had been harsh on Sarasvatichandra and unjust. The anguish was evident on his face.

'Chandrakant! You know everything! Your face tells me that you know. Do tell me, what possessed him? I will not live without him! I will take poison.' Sheth Laxminandan suddenly looked old, and he beat his head helplessly upon the table. Chandrakant consoled him. He told him Sarasvatichandra had objected to the deed that Ishwarkaur had made, and that the deed had been drafted without Sarasvatichandra's knowledge. He also told him how much pain Laxminandan's words had caused his son. As he spoke, Chandrakant wondered what to do with Sarasvatichandra's letter. It would be dishonest not to give the letter to the Sheth. But once he gave it, he could not take it back; there would be a finality to the act. The Sheth could easily disown Sarasvatichandra if his mind changed once again, and Guman's ploy would then succeed. Chandrakant decided to deal with issues as and when they arose. He gave the letter to Laxminandan. As he read it, Laxminandan's emotions were somewhat similar to how King Munj felt when King Bhoj had sent him a letter written in his own blood. Tears flowed from his eyes. He understood his son's noble sentiments, and felt nothing but abhorrence and contempt for Guman and Dhurtalal. He put the letter aside and said, anguished, 'Chandrakant, you know where he is. Do anything, but bring him back. I cannot live without Sarasvatichandra!' Chandrakant picked up the letter and tore it up into small pieces. He said, 'Sheth, I told you that I do not know. And that is the truth.' The Sheth saw him tear up the letter, but he did not ask him why, nor did he think about it.

Chandrakant suddenly felt as if his heart would boil over and he spoke up fearlessly. His words tore into the father's heart. 'Sheth, you are an important and powerful man. But you should also be concerned about those under your care. If you want to arrange your son's marriage, you should also desire that the two love each other, and are happy. By accusing innocent Kumud Sundari, you thrust a dagger into your son's heart. God alone knows how much suffering you would cause them both. Is our society so regressive that parents cannot bear the son and the daughter-in-law to be in love? But what can you do? Such are the ways of God. One has not heard of a son reared by a stepmother to be happy. It is true that you desire your wife more than your son. Why would you accept that your son was without blemish? He was possessed by the thought that his father did not love him, and he left home. The man who always travelled by horse-drawn carriage, who never walked without shoes and socks, a man raised in the lap of luxury that you provided, is today roaming God knows where, alone, unknown and friendless. Where is the man who held sway over erudite audiences, a favourite of scholars and benefactor of so many like me? Sheth, his condition is like that of Dhruva. Oh God! What will Kumud Sundari's state be? Sheth, the light has gone out of your home. But what do you care.

'I must tell you a story. Listen. A man and his wife loved each other dearly. Their minds were one. A pair of sparrows made a nest in their house. The female laid eggs. Both the male and the female sparrow looked after the chicks with great love. One day the female sparrow died. The male sparrow brought another female to the nest. Together they pushed the chicks out. The chicks had not yet learnt to fly. They would have hit the floor and died, but for the woman of the house who caught them mid-air. The woman held the chicks to her breast and cried.

'Meanwhile, her husband came home. He asked her the reason for her tears. She did not reply. When he insisted, she finally showed him the chicks, told him what had happened and said, If such a thing can happen to birds, why not to us? There is no certainty about life. Today you love me dearly. But what would happen to my young children if I were to die tomorrow? It is this thought that brings me to tears. Her loving husband tried to console her, made her many promises, but the woman was not convinced. And the tears flowed unceasing from her eyes. What would happen to my children? She could think of nothing else. At last her husband told her that if such a thing ever happened, her children should bring him to this nest and remind him of this story. Would I ever forget our love?

'Days passed and that fortunate woman died. The man remarried. He had a son and a daughter from his first wife. The new wife slowly began to turn the husband away from the children. Every day she had a new complaint. She spoke ill of the children. But how could the motherless children speak ill of their stepmother? Ultimately, the new wife declared she could no longer live with the children, and the man would have to choose between them and her. How can a man love motherless children more than a new wife? The children can look after themselves, but where will the poor woman go? So the man called his children aside and told them that he did not want them anymore and that they should leave.

'The children looked pitiable. But who would take pity on them? Father, where shall we go? they asked. But alas, he was no longer a father to them. That demon replied, Why ask me? Go wherever you please. Go throw yourselves in a ditch! The orphaned children wept and left the house. That demon felt no pity for them. The girl was wise. Suddenly she remembered what her mother had taught her. She told her brother amidst tears, bhai, let us do what our mother taught us. Both of them turned back.

'Why have you come back? Go away! The man barked at them. Trembling with fright, the girl replied, Father, we will go away. But our mother had taught us that if such a thing ever happened, we should remind you of something. Will you listen to us? That heartless man took pity on them and agreed. The children reminded him the story of the sparrows and how their mother had wept that day. That demon melted. He remembered his past as also his promise. He wept and embraced his children and took them back into the house.

'Sheth, your condition is like that man. But Chandralaxmi did not teach any such thing to Sarasvatichandra. He has left home. You do not have the choice of assuaging his hurt. You thought that he loved you for your money? Even that relationship no longer holds. You are a father to him, but he is no longer your son. Yes, such is the truth. Do not worry that he has taken anything from you. Check all your valuables in the house. If you find anything missing, do let me know, and I will pay for it. Shethji, I must go now. You are an important man.

Pardon me if I have said things I should not have. I take your leave.' Chandrakant put his pagdi on his head and got up to leave.

Sheth Laxminandan caught his hand and made him sit down. 'Chandrakant! Chandrakant, why are you doing this to me? Please tell me where he is. You have brought me back to my senses. But I cannot bear to be separated from my son! I will go insane!'

'Shethji, there are others in your house who shall bring you back to your senses. Honestly, I do not know where Bhai is. If I had known, I would never have allowed him to go. I will with my own resources search for him. I will wander like him. I will do whatever comes to my mind. What is it to anyone? You enjoy yourself. A thorn from your side has now been removed. Stop worrying. I cannot endure this any longer. Please let me go!' Chandrakant jerked his hand free, opened the door and left.

Guman entered. The Sheth was delirious like a man possessed. 'What does the world care for my sorrows? One cannot cry for everyone! What? Does your pain mean nothing to me? Do not remember me, do not weep for me. Why these futile tears? For one such as I, father why should you cry? Oh, it is all my fault! It is all my doing. Chandrakant, bring Bhai back for me!' He looked up, Chandrakant had gone. 'Bhai! Bhai!' he screamed.

Guman, standing close to him, said, 'Bhai is gone.' Sheth got up and kicked her so hard that she rolled upon the floor and hit the door, howling. Dhurtalal and others rushed into the room. Brother and sister realised that Laxminandan was no longer under their control. Just like grass that bends to let powerful gusts of wind pass, everyone submitted to the Sheth's wishes, or acted as if they did. All his instructions regarding the search for Sarasvatichandra were apparently carried out. Many days passed, many persons were engaged in the search, much money was spent. But there was no trace of Sarasvatichandra. With every passing day, Laxminandan became less anxious, and Guman, freer from fear. She bribed the Sheth's men with money and promises to ensure that the search for Sarasvatichandra did not bear fruit. The Sheth was told that this stupendous effort had proved futile.

Meanwhile, Chandrakant did his utmost to find Sarasvatichandra. As his rage subsided, it was replaced by pity for Laxminandan. He recognised that the search mounted by the Sheth was feeble and persisted with his own efforts. One day Chandrakant received a letter from Bulwer Sahib of *The Bombay Light*. He immediately rushed to meet the editor. Bulwer Sahib received many letters from other towns. One of them appeared to have been written in Sarasvatichandra's hand. He showed it to Chandrakant. Chandrakant recognised the writing, the familiar language and thoughts. His joy was limitless. The cover had a postmark, it was marked 'Suvarnapur'. They decided to keep this news a secret between Bulwer Sahib and him. Chandrakant decided that he himself would go to Suvarnapur. Vidya Chatura and the Counsellor of Suvarnapur were related. He therefore decided to go to Ratnanagari, obtain a letter of introduction from Vidya Chatura and then go to Suvarnapur. In his excitement and anticipation, Chandrakant felt he was already in Ratnanagari.

Vidya Chatura and Gunasundari welcomed Sarasvatichandra's friend warmly. They were most curious to know about Sarasvatichandra. Chandrakant told them all about Sheth Laxminandan and Guman's doings. Affection and sorrow gave him the powers of a poet, and he lucidly captured the workings of his friend's noble, unselfish heart. Vidya Chatura and Gunasundari keenly felt his despair, and were taken aback by Sarasvatichandra's decision. Both of them felt he ought not to have taken such an extreme step. Vidya Chatura said, 'Chandrakant, I must say that the English education we impart has one major shortcoming: it makes rational thinking go asunder. We can also say that this is characteristic of Western knowledge itself. The West is motivated by a deep sense of discontent. All action and effort stems from it, furthers engagement with the world, and promises immediately recognisable fruits. This makes one impatient and eager to attain these fruits of action. In the natural course of things, such fruits are slow to come by, which goes contrary to this sense of discontent. One is never satisfied with one goal but must hastily pursue one goal after another, which makes the mind like that of a speculator. The impatient mind looks towards the future without any basis in its past experiences or any assessment of the future. It seeks ends without means. A mind discontented with the present grasps images of the future fleeting before it; but when the possible future lurking behind these fleeting images become clear, it shudders. Sarasvatichandra exemplifies this. Look how he wants to understand the world by renouncing it! Look how he wants to do good unto others by renouncing his own wealth! You will realise the worth of my words when you will yourself see the pitiable condition in which your friend is likely to be.

'The youth of today considers forbearance to be slavery and submission to others' thoughts cowardice. They seek independence to follow their own whims. For them bravery consists of expressing their ideas and actualising them. They mock at experience. They despise the lack of activity and consider the conduct of elders lowly. Many fathers would have spoken to their sons in the same vein as Laxminandan, but it is only your friend who took such a step. You men of Bombay should be forced to work among the most foolish and serve under acerbic, egoistic and malevolent superiors for a few years, tolerate their taunts and experience servitude. This would bring you all to your senses. I am not suggesting that such servitude is without its problems. But it is necessary to learn to be accommodating of other persons, of their experiences, and all kinds of situations in which one may find oneself. One must also learn to keep one's impulses under check.'

Chandrakant had seen much of the vicissitudes of life himself, and would not have allowed such proud words to go unchallenged. But he needed Vidya Chatura's help to find his friend. He also knew that Vidya Chatura had been hurt by Sarasvatichandra's decision, and needed a vent for his feelings. Various such considerations taught Chandrakant the virtues of submission and silence. He would not suffer even Lord Indra calling his friend a fool; but his eagerness and anxiety to meet his friend gave him the forbearance.

Vidya Chatura continued, 'Chandrakant, what has happened has happened. It is not good to brand those already scalded. Now you must search him out. This adventure would have taught him something. He would be better for the experience. The position of Chief Justice will fall vacant in my state in some months. He can be given that post. My younger daughter Kusum is not yet betrothed. I would be happy to arrange this match. It does not bother me that he is no longer wealthy. But I would insist that he takes up a profession. If he wants me to help him, I would do so gladly. But I can do nothing if he keeps wandering.'

Chandrakant attempted in vain to keep his temper in check. He said, 'Minister Sir, I am most grateful to you, but the wisdom that you desire in my friend he is incapable of. And that wisdom will elude him even more if this is your condition. Do not for a moment entertain the thought that he will abide by your condition in order to attain Kusum Sundari in marriage. I do not believe that suffering would soften him. Therefore, you should consider someone else. I am certain that the qualities you seek in him he will never acquire. All I need from you is help in my search for him. I would be grateful for it. You are also free to refuse. I must leave this evening.'

Chandrakant had lived in extreme poverty; but just as grass can grow from stones, he too had struggled to uplift himself, and with great effort, had overcome the burden of poverty. Sarasvatichandra had supported him, and that was no mean support. But Chandrakant did not seek help; he only accepted it when it came without his having to ask for it. Suffering and hardship were acceptable to him, but his pride and self-respect would never allow him to ask for help. He would never flatter his wealthy and more learned friend, nor did he think it necessary to say things that would please him. Sarasvatichandra loved Chandrakant even more for his fierce sense of autonomy, pride and self-respect.

Vidya Chatura, on the other hand, albeit most learned and occupying a high office himself, was raised to believe that he must always please his superiors. He considered it imperative to conduct himself in a way that pleased the powers that be, as long as such action did not invite the wrath of the Gods. He had cultivated the fine art of submission to the wishes of others and action in conformity with social beliefs. The office he occupied had also made him accustomed to receiving favourable responses. He was surrounded by people who took his every wish as a command. He did not permit obvious flattery, but those around him were past masters in that art. Hence, they wouldn't say this or that was a virtue and that he was an embodiment of it. Instead, they would gauge the qualities that Vidya Chatura most cherished in himself, and praise those. They would point out the expertise and novelty of his decisions and mock those who said or believed otherwise. This worked even better than flattery. Vidya Chatura, though weary of flattery, did erroneously believe that his thinking was acceptable to all, and perhaps even superior. A man so conditioned would naturally be astonished at Chandrakant's response. The minister thought Chandrakant was arrogant, childish and extremely discourteous. But there was nothing he could do. Chandrakant was not his subordinate. He laughed at him inwardly and thought, What can I do with him? What can be said to him? It would be pointless. And anyway, what is it to me? He will falter and learn from it. '*Advice should not be given to just any person. For, one with a good home was rendered homeless by an inconsiderate ape*.'[2] Vidya Chatura reasoned with himself, Why get into an argument with him? These Bombayites are like apes. And this one is educated to boot! Let them be. I treated that Parsi so well, and the fool went and published what was shared in private in the newspaper. This one is of the same mould. It is not my job to teach the whole world. The Minister of Ratnanagari had momentarily forgotten his diplomatic nature and spoken harshly. He now became his sophisticated self again and spoke kindly: 'Chandrakant, do not be upset. Your friend was once to be my son-in-law, and I am still fond of him. Even you would accept that he should not have done this. Let him be. What can he do if God willed something else? I said what I said believing that if you were to ever meet him, he may not listen to you, but my words might persuade

[2] A Sanskrit *subhashita*, an epigrammatic poem conveying a maxim, advice, or riddle, translated for this volume by Arindam Chakrabarti.

him. But, as you say, you know Sarasvatichandra far better, so do what you think is best. Whatever you need will be arranged by this evening.'

The storm subsided and the sailing was smooth thereafter. Chandrakant was pacified, and he apologised for his outburst. Vidya Chatura responded in the manner of a man who did not want the other to know if the apology was accepted or not and still wanted him to feel pacified. 'Do not worry, what was the apology for?' But Chandrakant was no longer listening and did not respond. That evening, he set out for Suvarnapur in a large coach provided by Vidya Chatura. As he lay down to rest, his thoughts were only about his friend.

The letter to Bulwer Sahib had been signed by one Navinchandra. They were not certain if this was in fact Sarasvatichandra. Navinchandra's father's name and address were unknown; but in the hope that a letter would somehow reach him, Chandrakant wrote him a letter. This was the letter that Navinchandra had received, dropped on the stairs, and which was picked up by Kumud Sundari.

Unseen by anyone, Kumud's sister Kusum Sundari had heard Chandrakant's entire conversation with her parents. This precocious young woman had written down Sarasvatichandra's story as told by Chandrakant in the form of a letter to her sister. She had not sent it by post, fearing that it might fall into Pramaddhan's hands. She had instead found a messenger who carried it to Vanleela, who had given it to Kumud.

Dear reader, now reorient your memory a little. We had briefly left Suvarnapur behind, if you will recall, to acquaint ourselves with the world of Sarasvatichandra, and had seen vignettes of Bombay and Ratnanagari. Now wake up from that dream and return your gaze to the world of Suvarnapur. The main protagonist of the grand play enacted in Rana Bhupsinh's palace returned home with pomp and glory. Officials had already gathered there to felicitate the new rising sun in his drawing room. An overjoyed Saubhagya Devi was anxiously awaiting her husband's return on the swing. As soon as Buddhidhan entered, their eyes met, shared the mutual joy and triumph, and as he went up to his drawing room accompanied by court officials, Devi busied herself in the kitchen where Alak Kishori, imitating her father's style, held court with her friends. Only Kumud Sundari sat alone in her room, reading the letter from her sister, and weeping silent tears. Dear reader, bring all of these images back into your mind. Behold! Even in a wakeful state you are adept at moving from one lucid dream world to another!

Kumud first read the letter from her sister. Her thoughts and emotions overwhelmed her. Dear Chandra, must you endure and suffer so much on my account? Is it no longer possible for me to address you as 'dear'? Cannot a husband remember his departed wife as dear? You were my beloved husband in the life that passed us by. You are no longer. I have submitted my body to my husband, as well as my mind. If it is proper for me to address God, my parents and other loved ones as dear, why then should it be improper for me to remember Sarasvatichandra as a dear one? You suffer so much for me. And we shared such a deep bond once. Kumud was well and truly caught in the web of love. She could no longer hold back her tears, which fell onto the letter. She put her head down on the table and wept copiously. Towards the end of her letter, Kusum Sundari had mentioned that Chandrakant was on his way to Suvarnapur to enlist Buddhidhan's help in search of Sarasvatichandra, and that he was carrying a note for Buddhidhan from Vidya Chatura. The letter also mentioned that Gunasundari was about to set off on a pilgrimage to Bhadreshwar Mahadev near Lilapur, and that a decision to invite Kumud to join the pilgrimage had been taken; therefore, 'You should obtain everyone's consent and be ready' to accompany a messenger. These gave rise to further conflicting emotions and confusion, and Kumud cried even more helplessly.

Chandrakant's letter to Navinchandra was somewhat strange. It was written in English.

> Unhappy life: date, day and night are all the same.
> Dear Chandra,
> You can live without Chandrakant, but Chandrakant cannot live without you. Even when Chandra forsakes Chandrakant and

hides in the antipodes, his actions, however discreet, reveal him. I did you no wrong. It was cruel of you to forsake me. In doing so, you also compromised your honesty. What did you tell me at night, and what were your actions the next morning? God's will. But now be kind. I have fought many a battle with fate, and you were the one who took me to victory. But now, you are the cause of my defeat.

The day that is spent without you, may it perish
This human frailty like a mirage
Takes me further away from where you are

My state is like that of the cuckoo. You have been heartless with all. You felt no pity for your father, your friend, not even for that delicate soul! Such heartlessness! So be it. You may pretend to be heartless, Chandra, but your soul is not, and can never be heartless. Let me give you an example. I believe that you have in truth gone to look for the one you abandoned, and to repent. Compassion and heartlessness, wisdom and foolishness, delicacy and adamantine hardness, pleasure and renunciation; you harbour many such contradictions within you. Do not be perturbed. Be kind to me, and stay where you are for a few days. Thereafter you will be free. If it is my destiny to roam endlessly after you, so be it.

Eager to be with you—one whom you are not incapable of recognising.

Kumud Sundari's heart ached. Just then she was called in for lunch. She wiped her tears, composed herself, kept the letters carefully in her cupboard between layers of clothes and went down. On the staircase she sang to herself,

I saw the world
In all its futility today

Emotions like the colours of the rainbow are short-lived. Alak Kishori had insisted that on this joyous and auspicious occasion, all the women also eat together. Her word was accepted even by those who had already eaten. Amidst all these celebrations, Kumud's sombre mood also turned celebratory. Saubhagya Devi was to eat in Buddhidhan's plate, similarly Alak Kishori would eat in Vidurprasad's plate, Kumud Sundari in Pramaddhan's plate and Jamnakaki in Dayashankar's plate. No plates had to be set for these fortunate ones. For all others, plates were being arranged. Meanwhile, Vanleela composed a song on a sheet of paper and showed it to Saubhagya Devi. Alak Kishori demanded that it be sung. She also said the song would be considered good only if it passed Kumud Sundari's test. As Kumud came down, all the women made way for her. She sat down, Alak Kishori and Vanleela sat on either side of her; Kumud held Vanleela's composition in her hand. Other friends sat around them. Saubhagya Devi and Jamnakaki, who had taken the seats previously occupied by their husbands, now turned their attention to Kumud. The cook ready to serve their meals also paused and looked up. The three women sang in their soft and melodious voices.

What would mortals know of Godly play?
The oil He pours shapes the burning flame
The days of sorrow are now past
Joyous times are upon us, behold
He who troubled the meek and good
The evil Shath stumbled and fell at last
In this chess, we have beaten you, ungodly ones
The Rana of Suvarnapur was alert and just
May his glory all ages outlast
May we prove worthy of our victory
Prays Vanleela with folded hands
May this glorious dream forever last

All the assembled women attentively heard the song. They awaited Kumud Sundari's verdict. 'It is well composed,' Kumud said with a smile, and the women got up to begin their meal. One said,'The words flow in a rhythm'; the other remarked, 'Yes, the meaning is also very clear'. One of them went up to Vanleela and asked, 'What does beaten in chess mean?'. Vanleela was enthusiastically pulled in all directions.

Alak Kishori caught Vanleela by the arm and sat her down beside her. All the women sat down to eat. They joked and laughed during the meal. Thus the past, the present and the future were forgotten in the unfolding of the present.

16 Buddhidhan and Saubhagya Devi

Before Kumud Sundari came down for lunch with the rest of the women, all the men assembled at the Counsellor's residence went up to Pramaddhan's drawing room. Buddhidhan moved around, talking to the officials. Those whom he spoke to, or even acknowledged by merely looking in their direction, felt especially privileged. Vidurprasad passed around paan. Pramaddhan reclined in an armchair, grandly issued orders, chatted with his friends, and laughed loudly and incessantly. Navinchandra sat quietly in a corner, torn between his decision to leave Suvarnapur and his desire to observe the unfolding developments. Finally, at around two in the afternoon, all the officials and other guests began to leave in groups. Buddhidhan was exhausted and wanted to rest after the heavy meal. He retired to his room. Pramaddhan also went into his room. Navinchandra fell asleep on a couch in the drawing room.

The court was to assemble again that evening at five. But the general assembly was postponed to the next morning. Only trusted aides were to meet and confer that evening. It was decided to send Pramaddhan and Tark Prasad to Lilapur to brief Russell Sahib of that day's events and obtain his consent for future plans. They were asked to return before the assembly convened the next morning. Russell Sahib's Shirastidar Rambhau had, through Tark Prasad, made certain inappropriate demands on Buddhidhan. He had also threatened to ferment trouble with the Sahib if his demands were not met. This new problem had caused the postponement of the assembly.

Buddhidhan went to his room and found Saubhagya Devi waiting for him. Just looking at her face, all his troubles vanished for a while. He took her hand in his and asked her how she had passed the day. Devi did not reply. Buddhidhan said, 'Today is a festive day. God willing, tomorrow, too, shall be a day of celebration. Devi, do you recall my delirious words during my long sickness? I will touch Dayashankar Kaka's feet as soon as I receive the robes of my new office tomorrow. He has been like a father to me.' This pleased Devi. 'In our days of poverty in Lilapur, once when we were standing at the window, we saw an English madam pass by in her closed carriage. Devi, do you recall what you had said that day? I did not tell you this, but I have got a carriage made for you. From tomorrow, you must travel in it every morning to pray at the Rajeshwar Mahadev. We have seen this auspicious day only because of His blessings.' Devi's joy climbed a notch higher. She said, 'Alak told me that Kumud has made the temple garden look even more beautiful. We should spend some more money on the temple. Kumud has a sense for these things. We should let her and Alak decide.'

'Yes, of course. Our wealth is for our children.'

Husband and wife took delight in each other. Buddhidhan looked at her fondly and with desire. Devi's body seemed different to him. He sensed there was going to be an addition to his family. Her shyness confirmed his belief. Their children were married and old enough to be parents themselves. Devi's joy at being a mother again was shadowed by doubt and perplexity as to what her children would think when the news became known. Saubhagya Devi, like a good Arya woman, expressed a noble desire. And Buddhidhan, like a good Arya husband, accepted. 'We should adopt Vanaprastha even while remaining householders. The responsibilities of being a householder should now be passed on to the children,' she said. Her wish fulfilled, Saubhagya Devi's joy knew no limit.[1]

1 Author's note: In the West, Malthus' advice has not been followed.

Arth, the pursuit of worldly desires, is the preserve of men; but the pursuit of amorous desire and moksha are enjoined upon both women and men. Saubhagya Devi's pursuit of sexual desire had reached its end. She had matured from being a girl to a woman. Today, she freed herself from the bond of desire that had given her youthful pleasures, and chose a bond of piety and abstinence. It was not for her to contemplate moksha—her moksha was her husband, in this life as in the next, in this world as in the world to come; its location was insignificant for her. She would travel as her husband's shadow in all his pursuits of artha, dharma, karma and moksha, and partake in the fruits of all his efforts. The husband accepted his wife's wish to be freed of sexual desire, and also the new basis of their relationship. What more could she want? Her moksha was her husband, as voiced in the song:

Vraj is dear, Vaikunth I would not go,
For how would I find my Nand Kunwar there?

Oh, you pious women of India! Your instincts are noble indeed. Saubhagya Devi had cultivated a sense of religious duty by listening to the instructive tales of the *Shastras* and *Puranas*, thousands of years old, which have brought noble aspirations to the illiterate masses of India, surrounded them with examples of good morals and right conduct, and guided them to lead lives devoid of wealth, prestige and ego, and yet made their minds aglow with an inner light. These instructions are now mocked by stupid, arrogant reformers, and neglected by the passage of time. Saubhagya Devi's husband had become the Karbhari of Suvarnapur, and her desire to lead a religious life was fulfilled the moment she expressed it. She was no longer a conjugal partner to her husband, but a spiritual companion. Devi felt blissful, and thought, If I were to die this very moment, with my eyes on my husband and my heart filled with pure joy, I would be truly blessed. She continued to hold his hands but her eyes lowered reverentially to Buddhidhan's feet. Her gaze turned inward. Just as the quiet flow of the river captures the reflection of the moon, her heart reflected the image of her husband.

With the new boon she had been granted, she felt only an emotional attachment towards him. She felt as if she were standing on the shore, watching, while he churned the sea of Suvarnapur's administration. She pictured him, Krishna-like, riding on the serpent Kalia that was Shathrai, while she was the gopi who witnessed his triumph from the banks. She continued to hold his hands, but her bejewelled toe moved to some inner rhythm. Her youthful passions were leaving her just as a new phase of her life was about to begin. She wept joyous tears as she bid farewell to a dear friend and welcomed new joys. Unaware of her tears, Devi was aware only of her husband's radiant face etched deep in her heart. She was in a trance. Her eyes were focused on his feet. A song escaped from her lips, as if on its own.

Gone is my churner, gone is my churner
How do I churn the milk?
The water dances, the wind dances
This whole world dances
Upon the now tamed Shesha,
The very universe plays
As if swaying to tinkling anklets
The milk brims over
So do my sobs
O' thief of Govardhana, O' son of Nand
Seeing my reflection in the water, I weep
As the dawn eclipses the moon
Says Kabir, Listen O' you sadhus
The world sings of the joy in
The house of Nand
But gone is my churner, my churner is gone

The beauty of her song enveloped Buddhidhan. He was filled with a joy pure and intense and, for a brief while, he was freed from the bondage of life.

17 Pramaddhan and Kumud Sundari

The men had dispersed, but the women were to spend the day with Alak Kishori. Kumud Sundari was in that group of women. And, Pramaddhan? What was he doing?

Buddhidhan's son could not sleep that afternoon. His head was full of excitement, of dreams of a new life. His authority was absolute, that is, as long as Kumud Sundari was not present. He respected his educated wife but lacked the courage to respond to her. Kumud tried her best to further his education and mould him in her own image. This he did not like. He wanted passion and desire from his wife, not learning. He also grew tired of her superior aesthetic sensibility. Love for him was animal passion. He felt constrained in Kumud's presence as one often feels in the presence of elders or superiors. He sought enjoyment with equals among his friends and flatterers, and with Padma. As the days passed, he grew even less fond of Kumud. Moreover, his position in the palace had now altered, he was flattered by all. He did not like feeling insignificant and inferior before his own wife. He felt it was degrading for an important official like him to have to suppress his desires in the presence of his wife.

That afternoon, since Kumud Sundari was not there in the room, Pramaddhan felt a great sense of freedom and abundant joy. He talked to himself, paced restlessly about the room, lay down upon the bed for a while, then got up again and went and stood at the window overlooking the street. He played with the gold buttons of his starched kurta, impressed passers-by with his imposing mien. He went into the room, picked up a mirror, twirled his moustache and admired himself. Meeting his own proud eyes in the mirror, he said: Now you watch me, Pramaddhan! Now I am an officer with a salary of two hundred rupees. Navinchandra, despite his lofty education will only get a paltry hundred rupees, while I will get two hundred! I will occupy the post hitherto occupied by Narbheram. And what shall I do with the money? Pitaji has said that I must maintain dignity. That means I must be proud. I will promote my friends. Won't Pitaji agree even to this much? But how am I to spend these two hundred rupees? I don't have to worry about household expenses. I don't have to worry about savings, Pitaji saves enough. All right then, I should allocate my expenditure. I must give fifty rupees a month to Padma. I have to spend at least twenty five rupees on perfumes and suchlike if I am to visit her. I will need to spend another fifty rupees on clothes and other sundry expenses. So how much is it then? Fifty, and twenty five, and fifty more—that makes it hundred and fifty. So I still have fifty rupees to spare. That Kumud never says or asks for anything. But do I have a choice of giving her nothing? The rest will go to her. It is because she says nothing that I am free to spend without accounting for it. So that makes it two hundred.

Thus the budget was allocated, the money accounted for. British officers who are paid thousands make mistakes of crores of rupees while making budgets for India. So why should it bother anyone if illiterate Pramaddhan should forget to account for twenty five rupees in his excitement and exhilaration!

He put aside the mirror and sat on a chair near the table. Kumud Sundari's things were on the table. On one side were books of English poets, next to it was Sanskrit poetry; on the other side there were books on physics and the *Manusmriti* in Gujarati, and facing him were pages of the *Ramayana* with a book mark placed in it. Pramaddhan stretched his legs under the table and picked up the *Ramayana*. He looked at the image on the first page, made an attempt to read a page, but gave up. He kept it carefully back in its place. He had bought all these books for Kumud. She spent the difficult hours of the day reading them. He stared at the books for a while, and felt as if he were looking down a deep well. He made a face and got up from the chair.

Next, he picked up Kumud's sarangi and idly plucked a few strings. He liked Kumud's playing but found her singing dry, for unlike Padma she did not sing songs of Krishna and love. How can there be a song without Krishna! He put away the sarangi and stood with a finger on his lip, solemnly admiring his own portrait on the wall. Then he turned around and, facing the bed, saw a philosophical book in English lying on a pillow. What's this? God knows why, but she needs to read and read and read! Otherwise she is listless. A book can be kept upon the table. But on the bed! Pramaddhan promptly picked it up and put it on the table. He felt like reading something, but didn't know what. He opened a cupboard and looked, but found nothing to match his taste. Eventually, he picked up an English novel, a romance that he had bought, and lying down upon the bed, he began to read it out aloud. Just then, he heard some noise in Navinchandra's room. He got up, opened the door and found Krishna Kalika there, alone. What was she doing there? This young woman of loose morals had become infatuated with Navinchandra.

Reader, as you already know, Krishna Kalika had tried to make Alak Kishori the instrument of her lust, and failed. For sometime after that incident, Alak Kishori remained cautious and tried to distance herself from Krishna Kalika. But true to her nature, before long she had forgotten all about it and regained her former affection for Krishna Kalika. Saubhagya Devi had doubted her daughter's virtue and was worried. But by the time the episode of Kumud Sundari fainting, and coming to, was over, Saubhagya Devi had become aware of Alak Kishori's repentance. Pious herself, she believed that her daughter could not but be chaste and pious, too, and she admonished herself for thinking otherwise even briefly. We also know that Kumud's doubt and distress in the matter was resolved by Vanleela. Moreover, unable to keep it a secret from her beloved bhabhi, Alak Kishori had herself told Kumud all about it; she had abused Krishna Kalika, and gratefully praised Navinchandra. Taking advantage of the moment, Kumud counselled Alak, advising her to forsake such a degrading friendship with Krishna Kalika. One day in her naiveté, Alak went and told Krishna Kalika that Kumud had advised her to keep away from her. Thereafter, Krishna Kalika did her best to reduce the impact of Kumud's counsel on Alak. Alak Kishori repented having told Kalika about Kumud's advice. For some days she kept it to herself, but eventually she again told Kumud. Kumud became cautious, and her attempts to wean Alak away from Kalika's influence became more subtle. She stopped giving her advice and instead became even more affectionate towards Alak. Gradually, Kumud turned Alak toward Vanleela. Vanleela was friendly, intelligent, and more playful than Alak Kishori, but she was also more mature. Kumud praised Vanleela before Alak, spoke of her virtues and thereby fostered warmth and affection for Vanleela. As Alak's eyes opened to Vanleela's virtues, Krishna Kalika appeared lowly in comparison. Thus Kumud Sundari managed to create a distance between Alak and Kalika without criticising her or even mentioning her vile name. Krishna Kalika was related to Shathrai. Alak Kishori suspected her of carrying stories of her household to Shathrai. She had made a conscious effort to distance herself but could not bring the old relationship to an abrupt end.

Today, Alak Kishori publicly displayed affection for Vanleela and made her sit beside her at lunch. This was too much for Krishna Kalika; her pride was hurt and she glared at Vanleela. She resolved to find a way out of her situation. After lunch, as everyone sat talking, she got up unnoticed and sneaked up to Navinchandra's room in the hope of finding him alone. Navinchandra was not in his room. She immediately thought of another plan. Let that rand Alak be, she told herself. I don't need her. If I can take Pramad in my hands, I can get something for my husband. He will get him a good job, and I shall take my revenge on that bitch Kumud. She is after me with a vengeance, the rand!

Just then Pramaddhan opened the door.

Kumud Sundari had seen Krishna Kalika get up. Her eyes followed her as she climbed up and disappeared into Navinchandra's room. Kumud made an excuse and got up. But she did not feel like shadowing Krishna Kalika. Let her be, she thought. Why should I watch over her debauched ways? But though she seemed engaged in the conversation around her, Kumud's mind was on Krishna Kalika. There was no sign of her for a while. Finally Kumud grew anxious and impatient, and climbed up the stairs. She peeped into Navinchandra's room. There was no one in it. The door to her room was shut. She tried to push it open. It was latched from within. 'Who is it?' Pramaddhan enquired. She again pushed at the door. He shouted, 'Wait, I am opening it!' After a few moments, Pramaddhan opened the door. He was alone in the room. Kumud did not enter. Pramaddhan asked her in. She replied, 'I am coming,' but she stood near the door. Her eyes were on the terrace. Soon enough, Krishna Kalika quietly sneaked out from Navinchandra's room and crept down the stairs. But Kumud ran after her and caught her by the wrist. Pramaddhan turned pale and hid inside the room. Kumud seethed with anger, her cheeks flushing a deep red, and tears of indignation welled up in her eyes. Her eyes blazed, but she was speechless with hurt and rage. At first Krishna Kalika was frozen numb with shame and would not dare look up to meet Kumud's eyes. But when she did not see a way out, she turned brazen and said in a cold flat voice, 'Let me go'.

'Aren't you ashamed!'

'Why should I be ashamed? You should be.'

'Wretch, you are not even worthy of conversation. I will let you go today. But if I ever see you again in this house, you would not know where to run. This is not Shathrai's house. Don't you ever cast your eye on us again.'

Krishna Kalika was about to retort, when she remembered that things had changed now, the scales had tilted between Shathrai and Buddhidhan, and that Alak Kishori was no longer on her side. She knew Pramaddhan was powerless; she also knew the influence Kumud Sundari wielded on the household. Krishna Kalika was bathed in cold sweat. She hissed softly, 'Will you let me go?'

'Only on the promise that you will never enter this house again as long as you live.'

'What if someone calls me?'

'Not even then.'

'I cannot give any such promise.'

'Then I won't let you go.'

'Do you want to imprison me? If yes, tell me so, woman.'

Kumud Sundari realised it was pointless to battle with this shameless woman. She could no longer bear to defile herself by her touch. 'Go! Leave at once! But if you hold your life dear, do not enter this house ever again.' And Kumud let go of Krishna Kalika's hand and watched her run down the stairs. Kumud entered her room. Pramaddhan was sitting with his head on the table. He did not have the nerve to lift his head. Kumud Sundari went up to the window facing the street and looked out. She heard loud wailing and saw a dead body being carried, followed by a handful of ten or fifteen mourners. They were the closest relatives of Shathrai. The body was his son Dushtarai's. Some women followed at a distance. Khalaknanda was among them, she was wailing the loudest. Kumud Sundari could not see Rupali, Dushtarai's wife. Even Shathrai and Karvatrai were not among the mourners.

Pramaddhan raised his head and asked, 'Who has died?'

'Dushtarai' replied Kumud. As Pramaddhan got up to come to the window, she turned away from it. Kumud stood in the middle of the room, pondering the destinies of Dushtarai and Pramaddhan. Are the sons of Karbharis all fated to be debauched? What Rupali did to Dushtarai, Krishna Kalika or Padma or some other woman may do to Pramaddhan. What would be her condition, then? As she stood thinking, she spotted something on her bed. She went closer and saw a flower from Krishna Kalika's hair and buttons in a chain of her blouse. She picked them up and stood by the bed. Then she noticed that the latch on the door that led to Navinchandra's room was open.

Pramaddhan stood at the window and watched the women mourn and wail. Krishna Kalika had joined the mourners and stood facing him. As she beat her chest, she realised that the chained buttons of her blouse were missing, and was frightened. She was brazen enough to come back to Pramad's room to retrieve them, but seeing Kumud's livid face flash before her, she abandoned the thought. She wept both for her buttons and the dead relative. Her tears did not allow her to look up at Pramaddhan. Pale and nervous, Pramaddhan turned around to face Kumud. He tried to pretend that nothing had happened before her sudden arrival.

Kumud stood leaning against the bed, toying with the flower and the chain, silently talking to herself. Dear God! Is it no longer within my power to reform him? Have all limits been crossed? I am in the room, and he stares at that woman from the window! He does not wish to even look at me. He is no longer restrained by my presence. Are all windows for change firmly shut? And then she thought, What is it to me? Why should I care? I was forsaken by a learned man before marriage, and then by an uneducated man after marriage. This thought pained her and she was overcome with emotion. She abruptly went to the window and flung the chain and the flower with some force at Krishna Kalika. Then she collapsed on the floor, put her head between her knees and wept her heart out. Pramaddhan looked at her, but neither moved nor said a word to comfort her. She felt even more violated and sobbed aloud. Fortunately, no one heard her crying. Pramaddhan was taught by his friends that a woman's tears are only a ruse and should be ignored, a man should not give into such womanly traps. He remained at the window, unmoved.

Kumud Sundari beat her head upon the floor in anguish. The beast felt some pity then and melted. Pramaddhan came and sat down beside her, and gently said, 'Come, now. What is all this?' He took her hand in his lap. The mere touch of her provoked in him a pure thought. He realised he had committed a crime and had hurt her. He again asked, 'What happened?' Kumud felt that she still occupied some space in her husband's heart. She felt hopeful of changing him. This gave her solace. She wiped her tears, responded evasively, saying, 'Nothing'. She freed her hand from his clasp, got up and sat on a chair.

Pramaddhan had been raised by servants. As he had grown up, selfish and debauched friends had led him down the path of vice. He had enjoyed much freedom, without the incumbent responsibility, from an early age. Even so, he was not untouched by the pious atmosphere of the house. He was Buddhidhan and Saubhagya Devi's son, after all. The goodness latent in him was awakened. He pleaded with his hurt and angry wife. She remained silent, but he continued his attempts to engage her in conversation. He asked her questions, he tried to tell her of the day's tumultuous events at the palace. But he did not once mention Krishna Kalika. Neither did Kumud. Pramaddhan gave her the news that he had been assigned the responsibility of going to Lilapur and that he had been appointed a salaried official. He told her about the postponement of the evening assembly due to some machinations of Rambhau. He talked about Navinchandra. He told her about Dayashankar Kaka's advice that Buddhidhan should buy back his ancestral house at whatever cost and fulfil his father's desire to build a Mahadev temple in memory of his mother. Pramaddhan talked on and on. Kumud Sundari sat there, gazing intently at the hands folded listlessly in her lap and paid no attention to his words. She only lifted her eyelids once ever so slightly at the mention of Navinchandra. Pramaddhan eventually did succeed in calming her passions somewhat. At last she looked up, happy that her husband had at least made an attempt to assuage her hurt.

As she got up, Kumud felt a sudden rush of affection for her husband. No, she told herself firmly, It was a trap laid by that vile woman. My husband is simple-minded. She thought of his inherent goodness, his desire to make amends, and the guilt on his face. She surprised both of them by putting her delicate arms around his neck and embracing him and felt as if all her virtues had transmigrated into him. Oh Arya woman! Your heart has far greater capacity for happiness than what can be obtained from a divorce court! Let the joys of the divorce court remain the preserve of the foreigner alone! Kumud felt that her husband's heart had become pure and transparent like glass. She tried to erase all traces of Krishna Kalika from it. Without disturbing the pleasure of innocent and affectionate conversation of these rare and joyous moments, Kumud also told Pramaddhan a few things. It was Krishna Kalika who informed Shathrai about the secret meeting between the Rana and Pitaji at the Rajeshwar Mahadev. She spied for Shathrai, and she also knew about Jamal Khan's evil designs, she told him. Kumud, intelligent as she was, felt that with this startling information, this woman, an enemy of the family, should have been erased from her husband's mind for good.

Under the gentle ministrations of his left hand, her hair came undone. She looked up at him and sought his consent to visit her mother at Bhadreshwar. He gave his consent by a light caress of her face. She liked the sudden sensual warmth of this touch that had come after a long estrangement. But why and how did this happen? How did the bitter fight turn into affection and love? Did they both long for each other? Did she forget his sin? Did she whisper love to him? Do couples not communicate emotion without words? Are words necessary to respond to such messages? When did such love rise unspoken, unasked in Kumud? When did Pramaddhan become aware of it? How did they respond to each other's touch? Where did uncultured Pramaddhan acquire this subtle art? Why did the learned and sensitive woman forget her insult and hurt and adopt the love of the unlettered? The answers to these questions are not to be found in the *Puranas*, this philosophy has not been discussed in the *Vedas* nor in the *Vedanta*, English learning is not about to discern its secrets, and it cannot be understood in everyday life. But the two hearts for whom it was meant understood it and responded intuitively. Such is the miracle of God's creation. The Arya mind has the capacity to forget the past, be content in the present, and make the future beautiful even by force. May God preserve this capacity for ever.

18 The Karbhari and his Administration

The king who gives up the two vices of lust and rage,
and allocates wealth where it is due,
One who listens well and acts fast,
such a king is seen as exemplary by all.
One who can make men believe in him, and who punishes those
whose crime is established beyond doubt,
One who knows his limits and knows pardon,
Lakshmi embraces such a king.
One who remains unperturbed in crisis and with a clear mind
pursues any enterprise he takes,
One who, when the time comes, bears suffering and endures,
for such a great soul, sagacious as he is, for a king like him,
enemies are already won.
And existing enmities he does not fan, nor does he quell them;
he does not swell with pride, nor shrivel in dejection,
One who does not do what should not be done, those who are
noble call such a person as possessed of nobility.[1]

It was evening. As the momentous day wound to a close, the excitement, too, had begun to ebb in Suvarnapur. Shathrai had become old news. Pramaddhan and Tark Prasad had left for Lilapur. At such a time, Buddhidhan walked about all by himself in the vast

[1] These verses in Sanskrit in the Gujarati original have been translated by Arindam Chakrabarti for this volume.

magnificent assembly hall of Suvarnapur palace, reciting to himself these verses. The soft lights from the chandeliers soothed his tired eyes.

Until today, Buddhidhan had never felt completely at ease in the palace. The Rana's trust in him was a matter of public knowledge now. With Shathrai out of the way, Buddhidhan no longer needed to play hide and seek, something he had always found distasteful. The Rana and his Karbhari for the first time experienced the joys of mutual trust and openness. A long journey had come to an end. The man who took pride in his Karbhari ancestors was now himself one—the Karbhari, the Chief Administrator of Suvarnapur. And the man who was the king was now a ruler in the true sense of the word.

But the fate of Shathrai and his cohorts still remained to be decided. In the native states, factional power changes with a change in the administrator, and the new karbhari abhors all those who have served under the previous administration. Buddhidhan knew that when power is distributed in all factions, it gives the impression of a just administration, which is liked by the reform-minded individuals of Bombay, and those trained in the new education system. But he found that to maintain even the appearance of a balance of power was extraordinarily difficult. If power were vested in two, neither would be able to exercise it unhindered. It may prevent the abuse of power, but it may also not allow for the exercise of power for good ends. How could he trust the other faction? Pity or generosity may be taken as a sign of weakness; people of the state and opposing factions may both interpret such gestures as inability and ineptitude. Moreover, it would also allow them to continue their machinations and to pose a threat. Just as an uncouth woman does not respect a meek husband, subordinates do not respect superiors who seem timid of opponents, and given a chance, such subordinates would join the contending faction. What would be the implications of this? How should he administer the state? When two factions are mired in mutual mistrust and bias, it renders both ineffective and allows for a third view to prevail. This makes for uncertain politics. Who should be made responsible for the state? Who can be held accountable? Both factions would want praise and acknowledgement, but neither would accept criticism. The people would obviously blame the Karbhari, as they will only see a partial picture. They would be in the dark about who holds actual power, who wields authority, and whom to petition for redress. Power divided among various factions can only lead to the oppression of the people.

Why do the English educated insist that there be no factions? Why do they say that all factions must have equal rights? Buddhidhan asked these and countless other questions of himself. In the absence of any worthwhile answers, he grew increasingly bewildered. What do they see in the British system? Isn't the English Parliament also similar? One party rules. If people believe in one party, that party is right and the other is wrong. I think that these people just talk, they have no experience whatsoever. They can only talk. Among the reformist sections of Bombay, there are fads, and if they adopt one fad, they will not leave it until they get a new one. They just need someone to give them a fad. The Sahibs that I have worked with are not like them. From where did this lot pick these things up? They are neither Hindus nor English! But this Navinchandra seems learned. He says that in England there are parties and opinions, and the opinion that wins the trust of the people rules. But among our people, relations are more important than opinions. But Buskin Sahib told me that in England, individuals must follow the party discipline even if they hold a different opinion. He must be right. Navinchandra is wrong; he is inexperienced, he must have read it in some book. But Buskin Sahib has had personal experience of such things, so he would know. But what choice do I have anyway? Power should be vested in one person. Can two men share a wife? Can a woman have two husbands? We are better off than the English! If I hold one opinion and 'vote' for another—it is called a vote, isn't it! Is that not tantamount to lying? Among us there is only one vote—that of the superior officer. All others have to follow instructions. Even then, can there be a state without factions? Even the Gods have factions—devs and rakshasas. Isn't the religion of the English also like that? For their God, his angels are always right and Satan is always wrong. Satan is regarded as cunning, false, evil, and destined for perpetual hell. Our Gods are not so partial, even a rakshasa can be reformed—if not in this life then in the next one. Buddhidhan laughed at this thought as he lay down to rest.

Ultimately, Buddhidhan came to the conclusion that the age-old ways were good and right. There could be no danger in following them. Now the problem is, he said to himself, who is in my faction and who is not? Then he laughed at his own stupidity. Those who are mine are with me, of course, and all the rest are in the other faction. How foolish of me to ask such a question! But then he remembered something, and his face fell. When he was ill, Dushtarai had insulted his mother. It was pointless to now seek redress against a dead son from his own father. What would happen, for instance, if his own people were to do wrong? The people of Suvarnapur will have nowhere to turn, they would be crushed. Intoxicated by power, even Pramaddhan could do wrong. Who will have the courage to bring his complaints to you, Buddhidhan? Now he was really perplexed. There will be so many impoverished like I was once; they would be crushed and insulted by my own people. Who will protect those orphans and widows? Oh God! Does the Karbhar involve so many problems? I do not want such a Karbhar. Why should I bear such burdens? My Goddess is my mother. I have fulfilled the pledge that I had taken. I have taught a lesson to Shathrai and Dushtarai. I have fulfilled the aspirations of my father. I have attained the highest office. They certainly did not say that I should hold the office forever! I did not take a pledge to be the Karbhari. Devi aspires to lead a life of renunciation—that aspiration remains to be fulfilled. God has given me enough to last a lifetime. The Rana can make anyone he wants the Karbhari. If he agrees, we could even invite Vidya Chatura. Then I won't have to worry about Pramaddhan. I will hand over all responsibility to him; and Devi and I will take Vanaprastha and retire to the forest. Yes. That is final. For how long should I struggle and strive! What for!

Buddhidhan suddenly felt at peace with himself. He had no more desires. No new aspirations. He was ready to experience the joys of renunciation. He got up. The Rana had still not had his dinner. The assembly hall was warm, and he was perspiring. He told a servant, 'Call me when the Rana is ready for me,' and he went out to sit near a fountain in the garden. He looked up as the stars appeared one by one in the darkening sky and remembered some passages that he had learnt as a young boy.

> I wandered over the country rugged with numerous impassable tracts but did not gain anything; giving up the proper pride for race and lineage I served (but) to no purpose; banishing all sense of self-respect, I dined in strange houses, fearing like a crow (of being driven away at any moment); but thus waxed still, oh Greed—delighting in wicked deeds—and art not satisfied.[2]

Buddhidhan remembered the days of his childhood when he had to take meals at Shathrai's house. Tears welled up in his eyes. He came to a fountain. Some wrought iron benches purchased from Bombay had been placed around the fountain. He sat down on one of them.

> Intent upon propitiating them, I endured with great difficulty the taunting words of wicked men; checking in my tears I even laughed with vacant mind; I steadied my heart, and even bowed to the wicked. Disappointed Greed, in what other way wilt thou make me dance?[3]

Shathrai kept coming back to his mind. The days gone by flashed before him like a dream. He lay down on the bench. The wind cooled by the fountain soothed him. Once he was impoverished; today he shared the wealth and luxuries of the ruler of Suvarnapur. But the future that lay before him was bereft of luxuries! Much of the glory and triumph of the morning assembly had lost its sheen and headiness.

[2] M. R. Kale, ed. and trans. *The Niti and Vairagya Satakas of Bhartrhari*, Verse 4, 2nd ed. (Delhi: Motilal Banarsidass, 1902, 2013), 137.

[3] Ibid., Verse 5, 138.

> That delightful city, that great king, and the circle of feudatory kings, and that assembly of eminent scholars at his side, the ladies (of the court) with their faces like the disc of the moon, and that group of haughty princes, those bards, and those stories—a bow to Death through whose (destructive) power all these things have become things of past.[4]

The grand assembly of the morning was already a thing of the past. It had become memory. Did anything of it survive now?

> Is there not a delightful mansion for habitation; is not music [and company] pleasing to the ear; is not the happiness of the company of one as dear as life itself to (a man's) great gratification? But wise men have resorted to a forest considering all this as unstable as the shadow of a small lamp flickering in the wind (caused by the wings) of a moth madly falling upon it.[5]

Deep in thought, he shut his eyes. The cool breeze and the fragrance of flowers calmed him and lifted his worries away. Buddhidhan slipped into the world of dreams. He saw Saubhagya Devi looking at the reflection of the full moon in the pond at Rajeshwar Mahadev. He was seated next to her. They had both renounced the responsibilities of householders. He said to her, 'Beloved Devi, do you not find our love as pure as this reflection? There are ripples in the water but not in the reflection. The reflection remains whole and sways with it. Our life is also like that. In the true sense, this reflection is false, it will disappear. The real moon is the one in the sky. Similarly, this worldly life is illusory; it will disappear. The true life is Brahma—it is moksha. You and I must finally attain that moksha. Devi, you are ignorant; but your conscience is clear and your mind is pure, just as you are beautiful and your complexion is unsullied. Chaste woman, knowledge for you consists of only one thing—chastity—and a soul as beautiful and pure as you must find moksha. You shall be one with Brahma. Devi, I too

[4] Ibid., Verse 42, 145.

[5] Ibid., Verse 81, 152.

have contemplated none but you. I am with you. When you unite with Brahma, you will find me as a companion. Devi, everywhere you go, I shall be with you.'

As he dreamt, a soft smile played upon his lips. Vishnu, as he sleeps blissfully on the Shesh Nag, contains the whole universe within him. In his dream, Buddhidhan had touched the true meaning and higher goal of life. All his efforts from childhood had borne fruit. He slept a blissful sleep on the iron bench moist with dew.

Rana Bhupsinh finished his dinner and instead of asking for Buddhidhan, he walked down to meet him at the fountain. A barber accompanying him raised the lantern he carried. The Rana saw his old friend fast asleep. Meanwhile, Narbheram, Navinchandra, Vidurprasad and Jaymal had also gathered there. Narbheram was about to wake up Buddhidhan, when the Rana stopped him. 'Narbheram, Buddhidhan has stayed awake for long years. After many years he has slept so fitfully. Let him sleep undisturbed.' Bhupsinh, too, had regained his peace and composure after long years. Shathrai's removal had given him the sudden calmness of a man who becomes aware that what had passed before was only a nightmare. The Rana felt content that Buddhidhan who used to visit his small and bare house in Lilapur today walked about freely in his palace. The memories of days gone by and struggles shared quietened him. The affection he felt for his old friend worked as a balm on Buddhidhan as well. It soothed his mind much as the fountain soothed his body. 'Jaymal, keep a pillow softly under his head so as not to wake him up, and also arrange for our seating here,' the Rana ordered.

His orders were immediately carried out. A silken pillow was slipped under Buddhidhan's head. A couch with silk cushions was brought for the Rana. A carpet was brought for the others. Silver, golden and gilded lights were placed around them. The fountain shone and sparkled in the light of a myriad lamps. The Rana puffed on his hookah from a golden pipe. People sat around him. Servants stood at a distance, whispering amongst themselves. At the Rana's command, a young singer presented himself, settled on the carpet, and began to strum his sitar softly. A servant brought baskets laden with flowers, their sweet heady fragrance filled the air.

The wind, saturated with the fragrance of flowers from the baskets and the garden, merged with the droplets of cool water in the fountain and the crystal clear sounds of the sitar, sprayed the fragrance and music upon all those present there, much as an elephant sprays itself while bathing. The wind brushed against the trees in the dark and shook their branches, scattered the clouds high across the skies. The wind brought with it the rustle and deep green silences of distant forests. Turning soft and fragrant like a woman's hands, it played upon the body, entering the elaborate folds of garments to caress and cool the skin. It touched all those present, touched their bodies and minds, showering them with joy and pleasure. Its only fault was that it did not make a distinction between the powerful and the lowly; it treated the Rana and his servant alike, just as it treated the sleeping and the awake. The wind, the lights, the fragrance, the music, the coolness of the fountain—all lifeless and yet moving—entered Buddhidhan's subconscious, and they aided and nurtured his pleasant dreams.

Buddhidhan moved from one dream into another. Then, as he gradually came awake through layers of sleep, all the thoughts he had just before he slept off came back to him. His eyes remained closed, and his hands lay unmoving upon his chest. Like birds who sing from their nests at the first rays of a new sun, thoughts crowded his mind afresh, though to the others he still appeared fast asleep. Sleep had erased the confusion that had clouded his mind. His thoughts were crystal clear now: I know what Karbhar is. I will be honest and will not hesitate to use my—the Rana's—authority even over my own people. If the populace is convinced that though I grant my officers certain powers, I am open to any complaints about their misdeeds and eager to reprimand them if necessary, people will come to trust me, and the officers will also remain in their limits. They will expect neither encouragement nor forgiveness for their misdeeds. People will bring their complaints to me, and I shall give them justice. Granting authority and dispensing justice are two different things. One involves trust and a bond of closeness, while the other requires dispassionate neutrality. Do the English, who are so intent on doing the right thing, remain just while granting authority? I would commit a crime before God if I do not give authority to those who are trusted by my people.

All those who appeared to be in Shathrai's faction are not necessarily his men. The correct step would be to remove only the top men and retain all other officers, with a warning that henceforth competence will be the sole criteria of judging them, and that their past actions will be forgiven. It is not likely that all those who supported Shathrai when he wielded power would remain faithful to him even now. Those who sided with him out of necessity will now take my side for the same reason. I have no need for them, and I need not fear them either. They should only remain faithful to the Rana, not to Shathrai or me. If I ensure that all the top officials remain supremely efficient and incorruptible, the subordinate officers will also follow their example. The initial appointments will have to be made based on trust, but thereafter, they will all be judged by their virtues and by their work. It would be ungrateful indeed for me to desert the Rana at this stage, especially since he has shown so much trust and affection for so long. Once the administration has been set on course, I will be a free man, won't I?

Buddhidhan opened his eyes with this thought. A novel scene lay before him. He was quite alone when he had fallen asleep. And now, all these people here, this splendour, soft strains of music, all these beautiful lights ... Was he still dreaming then? He rubbed his eyes and looked around him. He recognised signs of the Rana's affection and generosity. Rana Bhupsinh removed the pipe of the hookah from his mouth and said with an amused smile, 'Buddhidhan, did you sleep well?'

A surprised Buddhidhan sat up hurriedly, 'Ranaji, you? Here?'

'You were fast asleep and I did not wish to disturb you. So we all decided to wait for you to wake up.' Like the old days, the Rana invited him to sit beside him on the couch. Buddhidhan opted to sit below. He signalled to the servants to withdraw. Once alone, they conversed at ease.

'Buddhidhan, at long last, I am at peace today. If something still worries you, do tell me.' Buddhidhan smiled. 'Ranaji, do worries ever cease? Life itself is one big worry—one problem gets resolved and the other follows on its heels.'

Navinchandra was surprised to hear the worldly but uneducated Counsellor speak like a philosopher, and listened with interest. The Rana laughed and said, 'Tell me, Buddhidhan, what troubles you? I know that all my troubles are gone. If there are any, they are now for you to resolve!'

'Ranaji, what shall we do with Shathrai?'

'What is to be done; a criminal deserves punishment.'

'Buddhidhan bhai, Dushtarai's death has diverted attention from the real thing. Shathrai's brother-in-law had gone to Lilapur. Garbaddas has disappeared; most likely he has gone to seek support from the outlaws of Dhirpur.' It was Narbheram who gave this news.

'Ranaji, did you hear that?'

'Yes. But it is not for me to worry about these things. I can give you a short and swift resolution if you like. We Rajputs do not know of any longwinded methods. Those are for the likes of you,' said the Rana with a nonchalant puff on his hookah.

Narbheram butted in, 'I think they will try and take Rambhau on their side. They will give protection to the outlaws, which will bring a bad name to the new Karbhari. They will then carry tales to the new Sahib at Lilapur and try to prejudice him against us. Their plan would hinge upon what we do with Shathrai and Karvatrai.'

'Buddhidhan, let us for a moment accept that Rambhau succeeds in prejudicing the new Sahib against us. Should that worry us? Should we imagine that he will be unjust and not even give us a chance to present our views? Should we always be worried about what the Sahib or Rambhau or his soldiers do or think? The welfare of our people is no longer Shathrai's responsibility. Should we not be concerned about our people rather than concern ourselves with such matters all our life?' the Rana asked.

Buddhidhan replied, 'Ranaji, what you say is absolutely right. But recall our old days. The engine of our train could not have moved without the Sahib's help. Today, they are the masters—they have the power and they exercise it. That means that hitherto Shathrai ruled; and now the Sahib will rule. We are mere puppets. The Government should intervene and restrain us only when we oppress our people. That is their responsibility. But should they interfere in everything? Are we to accept even a lowly soldier as our master?'

Narbheram spoke, 'Maharana, the newly appointed Sahib is from the army. He is a nephew of Dobak Sahib. He has a bad temper and harbours animosity. He can be easily swayed. He is not very enthused about his work and cannot tolerate any disregard of his orders. He is susceptible to flattery, though. All of Rambhau's fingers will be in gravy now.'

The Rana's brows knotted in irritation. 'Buddhidhan, this means that they are the masters and we are their slaves. I do not wish to hear any further on this. We can be good to them. But if you want to be completely pliable, don't mention it to me. You deal with them. Let us deal with what we have to. Tell me, what have you decided?'

Buddhidhan replied, 'I do not think it would be a good idea to punish Shathrai.'

'What!' The Rana stared at him. 'So shall we honour and felicitate him tomorrow?'

'No, Ranaji, not that. It is not as if Shathrai has not been punished already. Dushtarai is dead. Rupali has brought dishonour to the family. His Karbhar is gone. The punishment now should just be sufficient to ensure that our administration can work unhindered.'

'Sure! And his brother-in-law will show you the way to run a smooth administration!' retorted Bhupsinh.

'Ranaji, anger will not benefit us. We must also realise that had we removed him in haste when all court officials were still faithful to him, how difficult it would have been for us. I have another plan that I think would be more suitable. The Mughal emperors of Delhi had devised a policy. Whenever some nobleman became overambitious, they sent him away from Delhi as a governor of some small region. He would wield absolute authority over that region, feel that he had some power, and so remain content. Once content, he would not be as ambitious as before and so would cease to be a threat. But, if we reduce the enemy to a mendicant, he has nothing more to lose, nor to fear. There is no one more dangerous than such an enemy. He may or may not be able to improve his lot, but he can harm others. Hence, I feel that we should allow Shathrai to retain his village, but we must draw up a new deed for it. The new deed should be made out to him personally, in which we must state that if he satisfies you, the village can become a hereditary holding. Moreover, we must make a condition that he and Karvatrai must reside in the village itself, work for its uplift, and that they should not leave the village without your consent. We must also stipulate that he should not meddle in the affairs of the state. His livelihood will be tied down to it and his self-interest will be to protect it. He will not risk cutting down his own livelihood. He will remain afraid and always remain under our control. Shathrai does not believe in God, but if he does so now, he will thank God. People will praise your mercy. Neither Rambhau nor the Sahib, and nor for that matter will anyone else be able to raise a finger of criticism against you. Those who oppose you will be silenced and will expect mercy for themselves as well. Most importantly, Ranaji, God shall be pleased with you. We will fulfil our objective, the animosity and bitterness will diminish, and you, the people and God, all will be pleased—What more can one hope to obtain with one action?'

The Rana listened to him quietly. His displeasure was clear in the beginning, but now he appeared to be deep in thought. He finally submitted, 'All right, Buddhidhan. What you say makes sense. Do it your way.'

Navinchandra was pleasantly surprised. He thought to himself, A minister who combines mercy and wisdom must be applauded. A king who submits to the counsel of a wise and trusted minister must also be praised. A king so fiercely independent and stormy in temperament submitted so easily, like a child, to superior wisdom! Are all kings like him? If they were, what more could one desire? One has read that kings are incapable of recognising the wisdom of others, or worse, they prefer to sleep in ignorance rather than use their own or someone else's intelligence. There must be numerous such examples in the world. God has created both men and monkeys.

Narbheram spoke up, 'Bhai Sahib, you have shown us the path of the good and the just—but I am certain that they will see this as a sign of weakness. They will say we are afraid of punishing them and that we are unable to clearly establish their crime.'

Buddhidhan laughed. 'Narbheram, do you think I have not considered that? Pramad and Tark Prasad have gone to meet Russell Sahib. They will tell him everything. The opposition will have no basis to make any claims thereafter. Russell Sahib trusts us, and he will give the new Sahib a thorough briefing on Suvarnapur. After that, they can try all the games they want. We will deal with Rambhau and bring him around. But we should do nothing to Shathrai just now. Let all his attempts fail at Lilapur and elsewhere. He will recognise defeat when he sees it; and then, if he so wants, he will fall at the Rana's feet and seek pardon. And Ranaji will pardon him. The mercy of the ruler of Suvarnapur cannot be obtained as easily as one finds things on the road. The world will also know that the Rana knows how to punish as well as how to pardon. The Maharana knows no fear from such people.'

Bhupsinh sat up erect, twirling his moustache with a smile—his pride and his Kshatriya ego were satisfied—and he looked upon his Counsellor with affection and respect. Ego boosting words have a magical effect on most people. Navinchandra witnessed such scenes for the first time. The Rana was not in full agreement with his Counsellor, but he restrained himself nevertheless. Narbheram had said things that should have made his displeasure even more pronounced. But Buddhidhan's words swept away all his objections and doubts like the wind that sweeps the road clean of all dust. Not just that, the Rana felt that the Counsellor should do what he deemed best. Navinchandra was impressed by Buddhidhan's ability to make his ruler do what he wanted him to do, while appearing to accommodate his desires. But he also pitied those who had to serve such a master, who had to spin a web of deceitful words to either please or not displease the master and hide their true feelings. Navinchandra felt that such a servile attitude corrupted one's conscience, ultimately corroded one's self-respect, and was hence destructive. This corruption and destruction appeared to him mutually supportive. He slipped into a world of his own, and then he heard these verses surface in his mind, he knew not from where.

The man of virtuous soul commands not, nor obeys.
Power like a desolating pestilence, pollutes whate'er it touches;
and obedience,
Bane of all genius, virtue, freedom, truth,
Makes slaves of men, and of the human frame
A mechanized automation.[6]

Navinchandra leaned against a tree and recited the last lines of the poem. He felt as if he was back in his own house in Bombay. The passions of the English poet inebriated his mind as he conversed with himself. This was a ploy of the Counsellor to make the Rana pliable. Such is the desolation of corruption! Power made this charade an imperative. O Rana, this is the evil outcome of your power! One man commands another man, one man submits to another man—both these are undesirable. But as the power of these thoughts waned, his Indian upbringing came to the fore: God, such is Your will. Thy will be done! I think the fault lies in my own perspective. Such a good king and so wise a minister; when such great things transpire between them, it can be nothing but the will of God. If all were to think like me, how would the world ever function! Does it not happen that a subordinate suggests something as an equal and autonomous person, and that suggestion is accepted? What do friends and couples do? Does Saubhagya Devi conceal her true nature from Buddhidhan? Is she not

[6] Author's note: From *Queen Mab* written in 1813, Percy Bysshe Shelly.

independent? And despite that, does she not follow her husband? Is she compelled to conceal and hide in the face of Buddhidhan's desires? And in doing so, does Devi deny herself? No—because the desires of both come together harmoniously. She does not desire anything contrary to what her husband desires; even when that happens, she openly expresses herself and finally their desires harmonise. Is such a thing not possible between a master and a servant? Was this charade by the Counsellor truly necessary? Was there no other way of meeting the same objective? But fear gives birth to untruth. Fear of the master makes his subordinates speak untruth. The master who is displeased with the truth and the subordinate who fears the master are both to be shunned. With this conclusion, Navinchandra snapped out of his reverie and turned his attention back to the immediate context. As he listened attentively to the Karbhari, his busily churning mind now occupied the zone between present reality and abstract thought.

But once again, his recessive thoughts gave one last warning. His forehead creased as he said to himself: Masters in your speech, in your movements, in all your thoughts and actions, at every single moment—please remember that even the lowliest of your servants is a human being just like you. He deserves as much autonomy as you do. God placed you on a higher station not so that you can crush those below. 'A dog wags its tail, falls at the feet of his master, and falling on the ground exhibits his mouth and maw; but the lordly elephant looks grave and eats after hundreds of flattering words.'[7] Masters, treat your servants not like dogs but like elephants. And servants, there are duties higher than those of filling your belly; the responsibility of securing a livelihood does not destroy your eternal obligations. With this thought, his mind at last quietened. The churning subsided.

Meanwhile, the Rana and his trusted Counsellor had considered and debated many issues, and resolved a few. They had decided what they wanted to do with Shathrai. Narbheram spoke guardedly about Rupali and Khalaknanda. Buddhidhan did not engage in this

[7] Kale, *The Niti and Vairagya Satakas of Bhartrhari*, Verse 31, 118.

conversation. He felt there was nothing to be gained by bringing Jamal Khan to trial and awarding him a punishment. Buddhidhan did not want to give Jamal the opportunity to even utter his daughter's name during the trial or after his imprisonment term was over. And he was right. Moreover, the Maharana's queens were involved, and however vile they may be, it was undesirable to discuss their affairs in public. This was why they decided to avoid a public trial and punishment for Raghi, Mahva and other accomplices of theirs. Ranjit was a confidant of the Counsellor. He did not deserve to be punished. Like Shathrai, Ranjit was privy to the secrets of the old tunnel and knew that it opened into the queen's quarters in the palace. It was Ranjit who had informed Buddhidhan about machinations involving the queen. He had suggested a way of bringing this conspiracy out into the open. Jamal and others were thus sent into the tunnel. Ranjit was sent to lead the group to allay any suspicions that Shathrai might have. Once inside the tunnel, Ranjit threatened them with dire consequences if they refused to act according to his plan. As per the plan, the tunnel caved in and the entire group was captured by Vijay Sen. The assembly was dumbfounded. Nothing was said, leaving everyone to make their own conjectures and arrive at their own conclusions. The capture of Shathrai's trusted men from the tunnel and the public knowledge that Shathrai resented the Rana's growing power and his trust and affection for Buddhidhan, coupled with rumours about Shathrai's involvement in Parvatsinh's death—all these pointed to Shathrai's guilt. This was an inevitable conclusion for most people. In case some dull minds still failed to grasp it, Merulo's accusations sealed the case.

The man who had seamlessly orchestrated all these events now tried to soothe his troubled conscience and absolve himself of any guilt. What am I to do if that is what the people choose to believe? I committed no crime. Nor did I force anyone to commit a crime. I did not ask anyone to lie. I only helped those who had dug their own grave to fall into it. I also did that to protect my own life, my family, and in order to fulfil my pledge. I followed the commands of my ruler. I did it for his sake. How was it wrong if I placed Shathrai's men in the dark tunnel that was symbolic of his sins? The goal was accomplished. I am not going to have those involved punished wrongly. God, You are my witness—I have not sinned against You. If I have committed any wrong, I will ensure that innocent pawns are not punished. That is my repentance. Tomorrow, I could be in Shathrai's place. If I show mercy now, I might be shown similar mercy in future. How long can any ruler be trusted? And thus, Buddhidhan tried to row his boat through the sullied and troubled waters of Karbhar. But the dark waters drenched him and filled his boat as well. Many seen and unseen markers guided his morality. No one else had any inkling of his troubled mind. God did not make our mind and conscience transparent to others. It must be for our own good. Pure soul and impure body—their union is somewhat apparent but largely concealed from human eyes. It is for the better. Purity and impurity are human artefacts. They have no place in the world of Gods. We must accept the time and space of the world we inhabit; east and west, north and south are irrelevant once we leave the earth. While dealing with this world, one must cultivate a penetrating, clear and unsullied this-worldliness. But while contemplating the highest truth, one must develop a holistic vision. O' reader, be aware of this state and nurture a detached view to closely examine Man who combines aspects of purity and impurity and revolves like constellations around the antipodes. Reflect with equanimity on this human condition and learn from it. Because you, too, are human.

There was a state guesthouse in the forest a few miles away from Suvarnapur. It was meant for the Sahibs. It was decided to send Jamal there as a caretaker on a reduced salary. He would be assured of a pay rise provided his conduct was good. Raghi was similarly sent away. Mahva was made a postman. He had to carry official letters to distant villages. Ranjit was made the police chief of the area under whose jurisdiction Shathrai's village fell. This was a motivated move. Shathrai would feel happy that his man had been appointed. Ranjit was Buddhidhan's trusted man and he was to keep a watch on Shathrai and his men. Ranjit was properly briefed on his responsibilities and was promised a gradual but substantial pay rise. Maharana was furious with his queen for her role in Shathrai's plot, and determined never to look at her face again. But Buddhidhan advised against it. Instead he suggested that Bhupsinh should marry again and get a new queen. The old queen should be told that her prestige and position would be reconsidered based on her conduct.

Indian mothers tend to cry after punishing their children. Indian people have a similar mentality. During the Mutiny, people had complained to the Sahibs about the cruelty of Malharrao; but when he was punished, the same people pleaded that he be shown mercy. Unaware of this mentality, the foreign rulers were perplexed by the people's attitude. Buddhidhan was well acquainted with this mindset. He knew that there was an outcry against Shathrai, but that if Shathrai were to be imprisoned or otherwise punished, people would suddenly turn sympathetic and criticise the Rana and him. Brahmins and baniyas would not want even a man-eating tiger to be killed. Buddhidhan's strategy was therefore to wisely ensure that the tide of public sympathy does not turn in favour of Shathrai. He and Bhupsinh decided on a plan that combined punishment with compassion and administered this concoction to the guilty. The Counsellor confidentially predicted that it would meet with the people's approval as it would satisfy their desire for revenge as well as their expectation of compassion. He predicted that people would praise Bhupsinh for his actions. His confidence in his predictions inspired faith in others.

Navinchandra recognised that Buddhidhan was an expert politician and possessed all the capabilities to be the chief administrator of the state despite his lack of English education. As he reflected on this, the topic of conversation changed. Decisions regarding the opponents had been taken. Now it was time to reward the supporters. Everyone was more interested in this pleasant duty. Buddhidhan began forming his 'cabinet'. Everyone became attentive. There was no difficulty in giving Karvatrai's position to Tark Prasad. In his time, Shathrai had also acted as the superior of all mahal officers. Buddhidhan separated this task from the office of the Karbhari, and appointed Narbheram as the superior of all mahal officers. Narbheram was pleased with such a high position. Buddhidhan wanted to ensure that Narbheram, although a trusted man, should not have the temptation to turn traitor. This objective was achieved. There was no possibility of a dispute about Narbheram's suitability for the new position. Pramaddhan was given the position hitherto occupied by Narbheram. Jaymalshankar was to replace Dushtarai; Vijay Sen was made his assistant. Vidurprasad was made the representative at Lilapur; he was not too pleased with the posting and felt jealous of Jaymal, but he chose not to object. It was decided that Buddhidhan would be the new Karbhari. The old position of the Counsellor was abolished. The arrangement satisfied everyone.

These appointments were to be made public. Buddhidhan had a soft corner for Navinchandra. But he did not think it fit to give an unknown, inexperienced outsider an independent position so soon. It was his plan to send Navinchandra to Lilapur along with Vidurprasad. He intended to call back Vidurprasad to Suvarnapur in a few months once Navinchandra became acquainted with the work and was known among the people. Buddhidhan had brought him to the assembly to read English newspaper reports concerning Rambhau to the Rana. Navinchandra was thus introduced as a man to be trusted.

Buddhidhan wanted to keep Garbaddas in his old position. But Garbaddas had incited Rambhau, telling him: 'You ask for your reward in the form of a position in the state. If they decline, threaten them that you would use your position in Lilapur to harm them. If they give you the desired position, accept it. I am not capable of being the Karbhari, but I can make efforts to obtain that position for someone as experienced and prestigious as you. Buddhidhan fulfilled his aspirations with my assistance, but now he refuses to show gratitude. With your support, I will take my revenge. You look after the arrangements at the Agency. The Rana and I trust each other fully.' Rambhau liked this advice. He sent a message to Buddhidhan through Tark Prasad. If he wanted money, Buddhidhan would have readily met his demand. But his demand was dangerous. Buddhidhan clearly saw that Rambhau and Garbaddas were flexing their muscles and were in collusion with each other. He found a way of countering the duo. He realised that Garbad had acted from fear and he decided to allay his fears. He sent him a message that indicated his trust: 'Tomorrow in the morning assembly, you will be asked to report on the treasury, and Shathrai's mismanagement of it. Your assistance would be required in the future as well. Our efforts of many years have borne fruit. For all these years you have pretended, on my suggestion, to be on the other side. But now is the time for you to come out in the open. You must remove all traces of mistrust. Ranaji had taken a pledge to reward all those who have supported him and punish those who opposed him. You must not waste any more time.' Buddhidhan decided that Garbaddas should be given the task of conveying the message to Rambhau. Garbaddas had cast his net. Now he was in a fix as to how to extricate himself. He had incited both Rambhau and the outlaws. Buddhidhan feared that it was beyond Garbad's capacity to rein them in. Meanwhile, Navinchandra translated for the Rana a few letters that had arrived from the Sahib. But Rana did not want any more papers read to him; they held no interest for him. He impatiently asked, 'Buddhidhan, almost everything is now settled. There are some minor matters, but you deal with those. I am only concerned with three things. One, how do you intend to accomplish your plan regarding Shathrai?—You have decided to wait for Tark Prasad to return. Second, you will be honoured with a presentation of robes tomorrow—that should be the first item in tomorrow morning's assembly. Third, you mentioned that we should commence some work that would bring us glory all over the country. Now it is for you to decide what that should be. It should bring glory to our name and immortalise us. You must work towards it. The Sahibs submit to fame.'

They talked late into the night. The world was already asleep. Sleep drew the Rana to itself and sent him into the embrace of a queen he despised. Buddhidhan, Narbheram, Jaymal and Navinchandra got into their horse-drawn carriages and submitted themselves to the skills of the coach drivers. The sound of hooves and rumble of the carriages pierced the quiet of the night. All other senses were numbed by the enveloping darkness. Navinchandra's mind cried out, Darkness! Darkness! Wretched citizens of Suvarnapur! They could not spare even fifteen minutes for you in the last four hours! Unless, I am making a mistake. But wasn't everything they did for the people? Wasn't the removal of a corrupt and cruel Karbhari for the good of the people? But somehow his mind did not accept this.

A lantern faintly lit the passenger compartment of the carriage, almost hiding itself from the dark. Buddhidhan's eyes shone in that light. They had left the palace grounds and were speeding through the night in silence. Buddhidhan spoke, his words seeming to emerge from the darkness itself, piercing it. Everyone listened carefully. 'Narbheram, make sure everything goes smoothly tomorrow. Tark Prasad will return tomorrow morning. God willing, the Sahib would have given his consent to various things. We have not said a clear no to Rambhau. We have told him that his demand has been placed before Ranaji. Once all the major decisions receive the Sahib's consent, the other functionaries for assisting the Karbhari will be appointed. Most likely you will be considered at this stage. It is another matter that we are not going to consider Rambhau—of course, we will not tell him that. We will give him hope and buy a month's time. Eventually, we will get him out of Lilapur as well, just as we got rid of Sadashiv Pant. Rambhau is a snake who should not be nurtured; at the same time we also don't want to make an enemy of him so soon. We will keep one important position vacant; so he will think it has been reserved for him. I have already told you of the arrangements regarding Garbaddas. You must go see him as soon as you reach home. You must have already alerted Vijay Sen regarding the outlaws.'

'Yes, sir,' Narbheram replied.

'Some of Shathrai's friends are also part of that plot. In just six hours, they have created enough trouble. This news must have reached Lilapur.'

Jaymal said, 'I have heard that Shathrai's brother-in-law has rushed to meet Dobak Sahib.'

'Is that so?' asked Buddhidhan. No one spoke for a while.

Jaymal broke the silence. 'Ranaji said that once the matter about Shathrai is settled, he intends to gift you the village of Ujaliyu.' Buddhidhan had himself prompted Jaymal to make this proposal to the Rana, which was accepted. But pretending to be unaware, he said, 'Ranaji is very kind, but he should not act upon it right now. It would be justified once I have done something good for the state.'

Narbheram said, 'Buddhidhan, it is not good to keep Goddess Laxmi waiting at the doorstep. One should never refuse wealth. Ranaji might change his mind tomorrow. One should not stop those who wish to be generous. I had thought about it, but as the saying goes, one has to ask even one's mother for food. If this has occurred to Ranaji without anyone's prompting, what could be better?'

'Narbheram, I feel that it may not be proper.'

'Let propriety be. Take my advice. If you don't take it, you will have to live without it. An opportunity once gone does not return. Bhai Sahib, I am not a mendicant like you. Let me tell you, get something for me, too, at the right time. I speak straight from the heart. Don't you trust me?'

Navinchandra was stunned by this cold, calculated plunder. But then he thought to himself, How can one blame these illiterates? What else do the educated English do? What do civil servants do except plunder? They annex native states for no reason. Every year crores of hard-earned rupees of poor Indians cross the seas like Hanuman! Even if it drowns in the sea, it is lost to us. But it causes so much harm. This plunder will at least be distributed among the people of Suvarnapur. It will be taken from the people, but it will stay with the people. But Navinchandra's patriotic heart bled at the thought of this plunder. Tears rolled from his eyes in the dark. He thought, Buddhidhan, I do not blame you. But I desire that you be pure and unsullied. You cannot be a thief and a liar just because the world is made up of thieves and liars. Let those without learning turn demonic. But are you any less diabolic? Navinchandra felt overwhelmed by a profound despair, and a vast distance between himself and the administrators of Suvarnapur. 'My poor countrymen! What can I do for you? I see no way forward!' These words escaped him as if of their own volition. But those preoccupied with other concerns, driven by self-interest and immersed in machinations did not hear them. The rumbling and rattling of the carriage did not prevent Buddhidhan and Narbheram from holding their conversation effortlessly. They made plans and predictions, took decisions, plotted, granted favours, worried about things and also took pleasure at the turn of events. Their plans were such that they would fatigue the memory, exhaust the imagination and numb ordinary intellect. Hope and hopelessness, fear and fearlessness, joy and dejection, all these troubled them. Their shallow reason took giant steps. They considered favours to be dispensed and punishments to be awarded. They suspected many a fool and the cunning of many became apparent to them. Many good men were castigated for the company they kept. Someone who had said or done something out of place a long time ago was now denied a position for that wrong. Many such inadvertent actions were similarly punished or rewarded. Some deeds escaped their attention. Power and authority gave them the capacity to do good as well as harm. Darkness nurtured this authority.

Narbheram got down at his house. Jaymal got down in front of his house, and found his old father Dayashankar patiently awaiting his return. Buddhidhan exchanged a few words with Dayashankar. He felt good that he was able to reward old Dayashankar's son for all the support he had given in times of hardship. He ordered the coach driver to move on.

The horses trotted off. Buddhidhan now addressed Navinchandra and said, 'I have thought of a position for you.' He told him of his plan. Navinchandra heard him patiently and turned pensive. He felt grateful for the trust and affection. But he did not want this position. And he did not know how to respond without sounding ungrateful. It was against his nature to show false gratitude, and it was against the norms of conduct in the native states not to appear overtly grateful. He finally said, 'Bhai Sahib, your affection for me is deep, and so is your trust. I am grateful. But I am a wandering foreigner, as you well know.

A friend of mine is likely to visit us in a short time. I will await his arrival. I also wish to witness the honours ceremony for you tomorrow. After which, with your permission, I would like to resume my travels.'

Hitherto, no one had ever declined to accept a favour done to them by Buddhidhan. He felt deeply hurt and insulted. Navinchandra was a rank outsider after all. Buddhidhan felt that his trust and affection had been misplaced, and that he had erred in offering the job to him. It was a mistake unbecoming of a Karbhari, and Buddhidhan resolved never to repeat a similar mistake. But he felt relieved that Navinchandra, by his own stupidity, had prevented any potential damage. When one blows on a piece of hot iron, the breath produces a slight vapour. The blot of ill-feeling on Buddhidhan's emotions corroded even his positive sentiments. He felt indifferent and cold towards a man who had hitherto been a recipient of much warmth, affection and trust. He felt he had nothing more to do with Navinchandra. Concealing his true feelings, Buddhidhan calmly asked him, 'Navinchandra, who is it you expect? And where do you intend to go hereafter?' And they talked of this and that, until they reached home. The carriage came to a halt and the passengers alighted from it and entered the house.

Before Buddhidhan had left for the palace in the evening, Alak Kishori had met him on the way and said: 'Father, I have something to ask of you. Do find a suitable position for Vanleela's husband. She doesn't ask for anything, but I think it should be done. That day you refused to help Krishna Kalika's husband. But you can't refuse me today. That bitch Kalika! I don't like her anymore.' Buddhidhan had replied: 'If you don't like her, how long will your affection for this one last?' And Alak had said: 'Father, the two are very different. That Kalika is an evil wretch. But even bhabhi likes Vanleela. You have to do this for me.' Buddhidhan had replied: 'All right. I will try and do something since you have brought your bhabhi into the picture.' As he climbed the stairs, Buddhidhan suddenly remembered this conversation. He had been unable to decide as to who should replace Navinchandra. That decision was now made. The mere presence of Saubhagya Devi in the house freed his mind of all rancour. He said, 'Navinchandra, no one in the family would like your decision to leave us. Alak would be the first one to pick up a fight with me about it.'

'Bhai Sahib, I too will never forget this affection. I have been received and looked after as if this were my own house. But what is to be done? Those who come must go.'

Samar Sen was guarding the door. Buddhidhan called him and said, 'Samar Sen, Vidya Chatura has sent a letter to say that a gentleman called Chandrakant from Bombay is to visit us tomorrow. Most likely he will be here in the morning. I will be at the palace. Look after him well when he comes home.' Navinchandra heard this. He thought for a while and said, 'Bhai Sahib, I am somewhat acquainted with him. The way from Ratnanagari passes by Rajeshwar Mahadev, doesn't it?'

'Yes, but the time of his arrival is uncertain, or else I would have kept someone to wait for him there.'

'I will go. I should be back before lunch.'

'There is no need. How long will you wait there?'

They went their separate ways. Navinchandra, absorbed by new thoughts, went to his room and closed the door behind him. It was midnight, but sleep eluded him. He opened a window, removed his formal clothes and sat down in a chair, contemplating the lonely sky and the dark night. Outside his room, the night held sway. He felt like a man drowning.

19 Night Life: The Rising Curtain and the Ordeal by Fire

The Crescent-moon, the Star of Love,
Glories of evening, as ye there are seen
With but a span of sky between—
Speak one of you, my doubts remove,
Which is the attendant Page and which the Queen?

—*Evening Voluntaries*, William Wordsworth.

The chaste, virtuous woman did not harbour any ill will towards her husband. She attended to all his needs till he left for Lilapur. She then went down and joined the group of women gathered around her sister-in-law. Everyone teased her for the time she had spent with her husband in broad daylight. The banter gave her and others joy. They spent the day around Alak Kishori as if they had nothing else to do. Saubhagya Devi had made a practice of listening to a katha, a narration of Puranic tales, every afternoon. Today the *Savitri Akhyan* was being recited. There were more women in attendance than usual. Alak Kishori had no interest in such narrations. She and her group did not disperse even after the katha had commenced. Their chatter disturbed the listeners. Saubhagya Devi sent a message to Alak Kishori to go and sit somewhere else. They wanted to move to Kumud Sundari's room. But she went and sat down to listen to the katha; so they moved out of the house and sat on an otalo meant for women, where Alak Kishori held court like a queen bee.

After the katha, Kumud tried to tiptoe back to her room. The pious tale of virtuous Savitri worked like a balm on her. But the nightmarish encounter with Krishna Kalika still haunted her. Her tears refused to dry up. People thought her tears were due to the tragic story of Savitri. Saubhagya Devi had observed Kumud through the day and she suspected something was wrong. She called Kumud and asked her to join the other women. Kumud feared she would break down and she made an excuse and declined the suggestion. She went up to her room, closed the door and latched it from inside. She sat down at the table and picked up her books. But she could not read, her mind would not focus. She looked all around her, at the bed, the window, the door connecting her room to Navinchandra's room, the spot where she had sat crying, and at the door where she had stood, forlorn. Her heart was in turmoil; memories flashed before her, jealousy fired her imagination and she saw in her mind what she had not witnessed. Her eyes had the look of a woman crazed. Her breath came hard, her heart beat faster, her lips felt parched, and finally she slumped into the chair. She didn't know how long she spent sitting there, motionless. Her reverie was broken when she heard knocks on the door and got up. It was Alak Kishori and Vanleela. It was five in the evening. All the other women had left; Vanleela had stayed back with Alak Kishori. Vanleela had noticed Kumud's altered mental state. She had also heard some talk about some trinkets being flung at Krishna Kalika and suspected that she had a role to play in Kumud's apparent distress. Concerned, she had come to visit her friend, but chose not to mention anything in Alak Kishori's presence. Kumud's face looked drawn. She somehow regained her composure and joined in their conversation. But she could not bring herself to smile; her heart was empty of any trace of joy. They climbed up to the terrace and cooled themselves in the evening breeze after a hot summer day.

Vanleela said, 'Bhabhi, you have spent the whole day in your room. You could do without our company, but we could not.'

Kumud could not think of a response. They took out a chess board, but she could not concentrate on the game. Kumud and Alak played. Alak, who was defeated by Kumud every day, easily won the game as Kumud made a series of rash moves. Vanleela had gone down to Kumud's room while the game was in progress. She returned with a recent issue of *Buddhiprakash* from Kumud's table and handed it to her saying, 'Bhabhi, they have published a poem called "Chanda". It is beautiful. But I cannot understand it fully. Please explain it to me.' The crescent moon had risen in the sky. Melancholic clouds began to lift under its soft incandescent light. Kumud said to Alak Kishori, 'Alak behn, the moon addresses the evening as her friend. The moon described in the poem is similar to one in the skies. Listen.'

Enticing the dusk, my dear friend,
I bedeck myself and sail to meet you
The evening breeze lovingly sweeps
The courtyard, scattering
Petals of a myriad hues
Gazing upon his calm visage
My river of joy runs over
How beautiful she looks
All draped in orange,
A bright star dazzling upon her forehead
Overcome with joy, I touch the star
And so it is that I play with my friend
But when she comes to embrace me
I am startled and frightened
For there stands a dark sorcerer
Woe betide the night, she has
Separated two loving friends
My dear friend has flown away
Fluttering her tiny wings
While the sorcerer has me in a grapple hold
Making sport of me in the palm
Of her hand
Then she swallowed me whole
She does not know that I am
Immortal in my own temple

As she softly sang the poem addressed to the moon, Kumud's face seemed to glow with a hidden joy; but it also betrayed anxiety. An image of Krishna Kalika flashed before her eyes at the words 'dark sorcerer'. She abruptly got up, agitated, and looked down at the road from the terrace. Then collecting herself, she returned to her seat. It was late in the evening when Alak Kishori and Vanleela left her. Kumud Sundari stayed on the terrace alone. She gazed at the darkening sky and recited the poem to herself over and over again. The words affected her deeply. 'Krishna Kalika, what wrong have I done you!' Kumud said out aloud in anguish. Her sorrow rose up like smoke from a burning volcano and turned the eyes of the Gods red. She lay down and fell into a disturbed sleep. The wise have said: Keep the women happy. Where women suffer, wealth and prosperity disappear. As if to prove them right, at that very moment, as he lay on the iron bench beside the fountain in the royal palace gardens, Buddhidhan was seriously debating refusing the Karbhari's position.

Kumud lay there on the terrace for about an hour. Her maid prepared her bed and came up looking for her, and she escorted Kumud to her bedroom. Just as the thought of renouncing the Karbhari's position vanished from Buddhidhan's mind, Kumud too forgot about Krishna Kalika. Back in her room, she picked up *Buddhiprakash*. She lit a lamp, put a protective glass over it and read the magazine. She re-read the poem 'Chanda', reading aloud the verses that described how the rain played with the moon.

The mischievous rain clouds come
To harass me
Devising ways to wreck
My happiness
But I will never rage against
The rain clouds

She sang the lines over and over again. She reminded herself that she was no longer hurt or angry with Pramaddhan. Her heart filled with affection for him and a poem rose unasked to her lips.

Pramaddhan is my true husband
All else is false
Pramaddhan, he alone is mine
All others are distant
Pramaddhan is my true beloved
All others are unloved

She recited these lines repeatedly to herself, changed their sequence, even tried to set them to tune on her sarangi. Kumud felt a quiet joy as she recited these lines bereft of any poetic merit. She repeated with emphasis every syllable of Pramaddhan's name. She felt shy repeating his name as if she were in the presence of others, as if she had uttered his name for the first time ever. She felt the romance of his first touch. The slow utterance of his name syllable by syllable filled her with a novel sensation of pleasure—she trembled and closed her eyes. She got up, and balancing one leg on the bed and the other on the window ledge, she brought down a framed photograph of Pramaddhan from the wall. She sat down on the chair and showered his photograph with kisses, pressing it close to her heart as if it held her very life. A shiver of excitement akin to the moment of union ran like a current through her body. Kumud Sundari, intelligent, sensitive, refined by education and her love of books and poetry, forgot all about her husband's shortcomings, forgot her pain and misgivings, and focused her mind on his virtues. She became one with him. She romanced the photograph. She held it to her chest and sang: 'Pramaddhan is my true beloved/All others are unloved', moving her hand as she sang as if to brush aside 'All others'.

The Indian mind seeks happiness in that which is destined. The Indian land, despite the desultory influence of Western culture and learning, trembles at the thought of forsaking age-old ideas and norms of conduct imbibed through the affectionate nurture of parents. They continue to live in the joint family.[1] Those who play with 'geography and

[1] Author's note: The English family comprises only a husband, a wife and their children. For us, the family implies old parents, their adult children with spouses, grandchildren, and the families of brothers and sisters as well.

astronomy'[2] are infatuated by illiterate women whose beauty radiates like the fire on which they cook. Such a couple in fact feels love for each other. Such a celebration of destiny is unknown to those whose intellect is lower than the Indian mind. Among the many resources that arrest the slide of this land of Aryas into a sea of sorrows is the Indian mind. This sensibility now flowered in Kumud Sundari's heart like a lotus. She sang to herself a song so noble and pure that it is beyond the comprehension of non-Indians.[3]

Gradually, her excited mind came to rest. She sensed the arrival of sleep slowly enfolding her in its arms. She decided to change her clothes and retire for the night. As she raised her arms to remove her blouse, the crumpled chit of paper with words written in a golden hand slipped out, brushing against her soft breasts, and got caught in the folds of her sari before falling onto her toes. She picked up the chit and read the familiar verse inscribed on it.

Enchanting Night!
Do not allow separation from the waning moon to blind you
By day, holding the hands of the one you desire,
Become a joyous bride.

[2] *Man plays with geography and astronomy,*
While the woman's mind is contained by the cooking fire.
Natives! What sort of a mismatch is this?
—*Bal Lagnabatrisi*, Navalram

[3] Author's note: People of the West are capable of affection for material objects and animals such as dogs. They are no stranger to love, but they have no sense of being bound by destiny. This brings them to grief. Wordsworth's poem 'The Idiot Boy' captures the tragic love of those moved by a strong sense of possession. It describes the love, the grief and joy of a typical English mother for her 'Idiot Boy'. This poem would remind many Indians of similar emotions.

She kisses o'er and o'er again
Him whom she loves, her Idiot Boy;
She's happy here, is happy there,
She is unhappy everywhere;
Her limbs are all alive with joy.

Sleep evaporated as her mind awakened to her own moon. Sarasvatichandra! Sarasvatichandra! She moved to a different state; her resolve melted. Human life is like a twisted rope. Each thread has its own existence and there are times when they are not in harmony with each other. Superior intellect, deep learning and a refined sensibility make these threads and their enjoining more subtle and complex. Though engrossed in thoughts of Pramaddhan, Sarasvatichandra did not wane from her thoughts. Though chaste and faithful to her husband, she could not erase the man who was to be her husband. King Dashrath sacrificed Ram for the sake of truth; Ram abandoned Sita for the sake of his people. And yet Dashrath repeated Ram's name until his last breath, and Ram could never forget Sita. Pious Kumud Sundari sincerely and with firm resolve strove to make her foolish and debauched husband the master of her heart, she joined her image with his and shut out all else. But just as light penetrates closed eyes, receding sounds echo in the ears, and dreams inhabit sleep, the image of Sarasvatichandra remained where it was, deep in the recesses of her mind.

Kumud went to her cupboard and took out a bundle of letters from a golden box. She left the cupboard open and sat down on her chair. She carefully opened the bundle of letters bound in silk cloth. As, one by one, she read the letters she had received from him as a young bride-to-be, she forgot her present and slipped into her adolescent past. Sarasvatichandra's learned discourses revived her thirst for knowledge and made her feel as if she was being educated once again, despite being in a family that did not value learning. She read his letters over and over again. And then his photograph came into her hand. She kept it on her table and gazed at it for long moments, her eyes caressing every feature on his face, looking into his eyes, drinking in his beauty. Memories flooded her mind. She looked at him reverentially one minute, and chided him the next as if she were his rightfully wedded wife, she smiled at him playfully, she talked to him aloud, she laughed; and then as her thoughts returned to his present state, she wept. She pressed her palm upon her breasts to calm her racing heart. Years after abandoning her in the forest, when Ram met Sita again, he must have experienced similar emotions. Oh Kumud Sundari!

> Indifferent through despair, ruffled by harsh treatment, paralysed as it were on account of this long separation, pleased by its inherent goodness, and deeply affected by the touching words of your husband, your heart appears to melt with love, as it were, at this moment.[4]

The bright flickering light of the tiny lamp was the only witness, the only friend that Kumud had on that dark and tumultuous night. The lamp became her refuge, her Tamasa river. Her beautiful liquid eyes reflected its flame. She closed her eyes and felt Sarasvatichandra's presence. Her eyelids grew heavy with sleep and she slept off on the chair for a while, but she soon woke up feeling uncomfortable. She got up and lay down upon the bed, leaving the letters and the photograph on the table. Pramaddhan was not there to share her bed tonight. She slept alone. In sleep, her waking desires became her dreams. Time and orientation changed, and dream became reality for her. She experienced new joys and her heart rose beyond considerations of sin and virtue. In this dream world, Kumud Sundari became one with Sarasvatichandra in every respect.

Buddhidhan had not yet come home. The soldiers sat talking on the otalo. One of them began to sing.

> *When will my lover come home?*
> *Come home to me*
> *O' when will my lover come home?*
> *O' when?*

He sang aloud as the others shouted encouragement. Kumud Sundari's dreams were disturbed by the noise. In the state between sleep and wakefulness, she sat up in bed and looked around for

[4] Kale, *The Uttararamacharita of Bhavabhuti*, 29–30.

Sarasvatichandra. She was jolted by the lines, 'When will my lover come home?' and felt hot tears roll down her cheeks. She did not want them to stop. She was fully awake now. She got up, sat down at the table, and poured her heart out on a paper. A sheet of paper is like the earth for many, it absorbs misery just like the earth absorbs rain. Sarasvatichandra's 'Enchanting Night' came back to her, and her tears turned into words.

The moon has gone, promising
To rise again
But the dark night persists
Creating a deluge in my mind
Woe be upon the life that
Bears witness to this

She paused, resting her chin on her hand. She thought of Sarasvatichandra's present condition, her own desire for him, and the knowledge that this violated her virtue. She sighed deeply and continued.

Leaving her husbandless and bereft, he journeys to a foreign land
She holds his name close to her heart to keep despair at bay
Refusing to submit to dejection
She sets her heart asail
Two lives lived as one:
This playfulness now costs you dearly

Tears filled her eyes. Oh! Sarasvatichandra! What was my crime? Even Nala left Damayanti in a better state. Oh God, Oh mother, Oh Goddess Amba! Kumud put her head down on the paper, her tears smudging her written words. She knew that as a chaste, married woman, this pining was wrong, but she could not control her emotions. She recited verses from the *Uttararamacharita* describing Ram's condition.

> Verily you did not approve of the queen's staying in my house and, therefore, I abandoned her in a forest like a straw; nor did

> I mourn her loss. But the various objects of long familiarity move me; and so being helpless, I weep to-day; please forgive me.[5]

O Ramchandraji, you are the embodiment of right conduct, you are the epitome of piety. If you too were subject to this state, pardon my transgression. I am an ignorant worm. I can no longer bear to be alive—it is beyond my endurance!

Just then, she heard Buddhidhan and Navinchandra talking as they climbed the stairs. Navinchandra's voice had a strange effect on Kumud. She was convinced that he was no one but Sarasvatichandra. Her past was indelibly etched upon her mind. She had shunned amorous desire, but she could not erase her love for him; she still feared her passions. Sarasvatichandra—Navinchandra—Sarasvatichandra—why are we fated to be bound thus? Oh my cruel heart, why can't you accept the new reality and be at peace? Dear God, why are you angry with me? Her heart in turmoil, Kumud's hand moved feverishly on the sheet of paper.

The heart reincarnates bonds of love
From a life past
The vision falters upon a glimpse
Of an idol once beloved
The beloved, though proximate,
Says nothing
Where then do I lay bare my heart
Torn asunder?
A body held by morality can
Remain still
But the mind refuses to listen
The mind will not submit to morality
Two lives lived as one meet
Like rivers
And the helpless one caught
In their midst
Must seek her own salvation

[5] Ibid. Act 3, Verse 32, 25.

Kumud was stunned by what she had written. She flung her pen away and stared at the darkness of her room and beyond. She read and re-read the lines. 'The beloved, though proximate, says nothing.' Sarasvatichandra, you belong to me, as I to you. And yet we cannot even speak to each other. How long can I endure this? She closed her eyes in torment, but found him standing before her—as she had seen him for the very first time. She recalled the verses in his very first letter to her.

O Vaidarbhi! You are blessed with so many virtues
That even Naishadha is drawn to you
Why should one praise the moon just because
It makes the ocean turbulent with tide

Frightened yet thrilled by the immediacy of his image, she watched as he took her shy, hesitant hand in his, and was filled with pleasure at the touch. She recited these lines to herself:

As the moon rises full, my heart smiles
The ocean inheres in it
It murmurs softly, filling me with joy
Its waves dance within me.[6]

She was delighted by the allegory of the ocean for Sarasvatichandra. Pleasant images came to her mind, and she smiled, her smile soothing as a moonbeam. Her agony vanished as she felt her joy overflow in all directions. This comparison is perfect: he is as vast as the ocean, while I am a wretch without virtue, she thought. The ocean softly murmurs, filling me with joy, its waves dance within me. It is true—what merit have I earned that I would possess a great soul like you? Even that momentary association was no less fortunate. Her heart sank. Her deep sigh extended itself to envelop the world in its melancholy, and the night became dark as before.

[6] Author's note: This poem, 'Chanda', is composed by Narsinhrao, son of our popular poet, the late Bholanathbhai, and was published in an issue of *Buddhiprakash* of 1883.

Navinchandra entered his room, closed his door and latched it. The noise startled Kumud. The human mind has the ability to find opportunities to fulfil its desires. In rare and fortuitous moments, such opportunities present themselves to match desires. Kumud's eyes now turned towards the door that connected her room to his. The door was unlocked. Kumud Sundari, did the conviction that Navinchandra was in fact Sarasvatichandra turn your head? Did the incident between Pramaddhan and Krishna Kalika prompt you to forsake your chastity? Was it a fortuitous moment where solitude, opportunity and desire came together? Sometimes, inflamed passions are reined in by the question: Does he too desire me? Oh woman crazed by love, did that question occur to you? Did the thought come to you that, if he did not love you, why would he follow you here, forsaking his wealth and family? Did this question lessen your anxieties? Do not passions become unbridled when one believes that the other reciprocates the intensity of our desires? When you compared your husband with a man who was to be your husband, did not the one you desired to marry appear irresistibly attractive? Was not your heart flooded by the memories of previous encounters with him? Reader, ask your conscience, search your experience, and give an honest response to all these questions. Oh debauched ones, reveal your experiences and provide us the means to evaluate this situation. Oh pure ones, search your memory for a similar moment and reveal to us the weakness and the dangers of such a situation. Be kind and compassionate towards this young woman entrapped by circumstances and pray to God that good sense prevail. If a brahmin, recite the Gayatri mantra. A brahmin prays only for righteous conduct. His brahminhood is contained in this prayer. A brahmin desires nothing but rectitude. Oh pure Gayatri, give light to this daughter of a brahmin. Will you do this? That only the One who is omniscient knows. The world knows that not all desires of humans are fulfilled. Can purity remain eternal? Wealth is so very fickle. Is purity likewise? That is the will of God. Foolish and cunning man! Forsake your pride and pretence. Be humble and virtuous. Those who counsel others, examine your own conscience.

Poor Kumud! She got up and approached the unlatched door. She turned back. She went to the door twice, only to turn back. She considered her virtues. She imagined the dangers of her transgression. She sat down on her chair. She remembered the poems, 'I despise this knowledge'[7] and 'A shepherd without virtue gains no knowledge'.[8] She got up again, touched the door and came back to her chair. She put her head down on the table, unable to think. The lines comparing Sarasvatichandra to the ocean came back to her. She desired to be in his arms, to hide herself in his broad chest. The desire aroused her, tempted her and trapped her. All reason deserted her. She stood up, put one leg on the chair and the other on the floor, and tried to think what to do.

Vanleela's house was close to Buddhidhan's. Vanleela did not have parents-in-law. She lived with her husband. At this moment, they were together on their terrace, his head was in her lap and she sang to him. In the silence of the night, her faint voice carried. The song drenched Kumud Sundari and sent a shiver through her body.

If you stay awhile, I will tell you, Biharilal
I have withered away for you, Biharilal
My body is eager, Biharilal
Day and night, I find no respite, Biharilal
Tend to our love forever, Biharilal
So we may be as the fish and the sea, Biharilal[9]

How can one describe the effect of Vanleela's song? As she heard the song, Kumud Sundari understood her own unbearable pining. 'Tend to our love forever', these words echoed in her mind. She was gripped by a fierce yearning, and she surrendered her mind, heart and body to it. All her doubts disappeared. Her hesitation ended. She made up her mind and walked resolutely towards the unlocked door. With each deliberate step, her mind and body altered, new urges overwhelmed

[7] Author's note: *Sudama Akhyan*, Premanand.
[8] Author's note: *Bhramar Pachishi*, Premanand.
[9] These verses are from a contemporary song sung by women.

her, unseen dreams maddened her. She felt inebriated, she could see colours and fantastic apparitions dance before her eyes. Her desires overpowered her discerning mind just as Bhima had vanquished Duryodhana. Her passions were as fierce as the demon Hiranyaksha who subjugated the entire earth. Her yearning was fiery like the burning sun that scorches the earth. Virtuous and wise Kumud Sundari had lost all her autonomy. Strains of Vanleela's song softly broke the silence of the night, impatient and urging.

The night is alight
O Kanha, your eyes are enchanting

The song intermingled with sounds of laughter, and then the insistent voice became distant and receded altogether. Kumud Sundari, felt pangs of jealousy, and remembering the bewitching gaze of her own Kanha, she lost all control over herself. Torrential rains cause spates in a river calm and quiet, its uncontrollable force drags with it all impurities; a powerful gust of wind shakes a delicate creeper bedecked with flowers. Kumud Sundari felt an electrifying excitement course through her. The distance between them became unbearable. Her gaze became unsteady with passion as she saw his image before her. She felt possessed and powerless to resist. She murmured, My body is eager, Biharilal. Her eyes travelled beyond her body and beheld the beloved as if there were no doors and walls between them. She was drawn to him as the sea is drawn to the moon. She was propelled towards him like a fish riding on the crest of a tidal wave. She was like that fish of pure water hurtling towards capture as she thrashed in the nets of her own desire. She did not offer any resistance to the inexorable pull of her desires and allowed herself to be swept away by the waves. Her eyes closed themselves to everything except his image. They did not want any light, any knowledge or even a single rational thought to penetrate her conscience. They reflected only the bewitching eyes of the beloved. O Kanha, your eyes are enchanting, she murmured, biting into her lower lip, her body moving to the rhythm of her song. She sang it repeatedly, emphasising a different word each time.

Kumud stood near the door. The song had ceased to reverberate in her ears. She no longer murmured or even breathed. She was ready to lie down on the fiery bed of passion. She was now intent only upon her beloved. Like a soldier awaiting the clarion call to sacrifice his life on the battlefield. Her hands trembled like those of someone about to jump into a deep well. Her breasts, the seat of countless dreams and desires, throbbed with anticipation, the arousal of rushing blood made them painfully tender. Gripped by delirium, her delicate young body trembled. She knew fear, as if she had suddenly come face to face with death. The whites of her large eyes became prominent, her beauty deserted her and her soft features took on a harsh ghostly pallor. But Kumud Sundari could not see these changes; for bereft of self-awareness, though conscious, she was like a dead body.

Then as if guided by some unseen power, she put her palms flat on the door and pushed. But, unused to such tasks, her hands lost their nerve and hung limp as if abruptly severed from the wrist.

Krishna Kalika had left the other side of the door unlatched. This friendly act now seemed like a boon to Kumud. The door was waiting to be opened. Kumud Sundari, why don't you push the door open? Why do you stand there petrified? How long will you wait? Are you not overcome by sleep and fatigue? What are you frightened of? Who? It is midnight. There is not a soul around to see you or judge you. Kumud stood still. But in the flickering light of the lamp her shadow moved, looming large over her. The shadow of the extended hand moved over hers as if to say: No! Kumud Sundari, are you without anchor, have you lost the ballast? Has your chastity run its course already? One night without Pramaddhan—and is your virtue shaken? Were you chaste until now only because an opportunity like tonight never arose before? Doesn't even God help the virtuous? Will He remain a mute witness to your fall? Will He not extend a hand to stop you from falling into hell?

Blinded by desire, she did not see the shadow. Disregarding all norms of this world and the next, brushing aside all limits and restraints, mocking her own fear and muting her conscience, her hand moved serpent-like to open the door. But the moment her hand touched the door, she was startled as if it had singed her. The shadow hand seemed to be stopping her from opening the door. She stood there transfixed, staring at the flickering shadow. It was as if Gunasundari's loving soul had traversed space and time to rescue her daughter—to Kumud, the shadow seemed to embody her dear mother's soul. She clasped her hands tightly together. The tide turned. Her conscience was reborn. Just as Lord Krishna had come to Draupadi's rescue in Duryodhan's assembly, Gunasundari had rescued Kumud's chastity. Grateful tears flowed from her eyes, her sense of relief more profound than Draupadi's in the unseen presence of her divine saviour. Words tumbled out of her, she knew not what she said or to whom. Oh Chastity, you have been saved from certain death! Oh mother, you have saved me from being sullied! Oh mother, I remain pure! Goddess Sarasvati bestowed her grace upon Kumud in form of a song, which rose to her tremulous lips.

Saviour of the helpless, He rushes to their aid
Startled, Sri Krishna suddenly awakens
Lord of the fourteen worlds, He rises at once
Rukmini asks: My Lord, who calls you?
It is Panchali! Don't you know her?
Today, my devotee is in grievous anguish
I must go to her at once!
Govinda says: Bring Garuda, ask why later
Garuda is on his way, lest the dark night set
Lord Narasimha has set out
With her eyes closed, Draupadi sees Him
Saviour of the helpless, He rushes to their aid

My Lord, You came to my rescue! Who else could have saved me? Kumud Sundari folded her hands in prayer. Her voice regained its sweet melodiousness, her eyes shone with a new light, and tears of joy and gratitude flowed down her cheeks as she sang. Lifted of its burden, her heart beat fervently and pure. She was suffused with new hope. She looked at the shadow and smiled through her tears. Her tears fell to the floor as if washing her mother's feet. She felt perfectly calm. Her mind was clear. She rested against the doorframe and felt as if she were in her mother's embrace. How can mere mortals like us know or fathom in what form God will come to our aid?

With relief came repentance. Cleansed by tears, her heart regained its autonomy. Moving away from the door, she accidentally brushed against her sarangi which stood against the wall. As she looked at it, she felt as if the strings were playing of their own accord. Their sound reverberated through her. She then remembered the song she had sung to protect Navinchandra from committing a sin.

She who resides in the heavens white
Fell down onto the Lord's head
Having fallen once, she fell again
... A fallen mind is destined for dissolution

Stunned by the truth of the last line, Kumud realised with horror the full import of what she had been intent upon doing, and stepped back, suddenly afraid of the sarangi as if it had admonished her. Dear God! What was I thinking? Oh pure Sarasvatichandra, I could never have been a true companion to you. It was just as well that you abandoned an unchaste woman like me!

In life after life give me wisdom, O' Lord
Let my mind and body be pure and not stray
Keep the desires of a hundred lifetimes at bay
This is all I ask of you, O' Lord

Where passion and desire had possessed her, noble thoughts now swept her mind and heart. Kumud Sundari sat down on the chair and picked up the letters that had produced in her such potent yearning. She read them again with a tranquil, unsullied mind. They were memories of a life past, nothing more. She pressed them to her heart once, carefully folded them into the silken cloth, and put them back into the cupboard. The clock struck one past midnight. Returning to the table, she sat down and reflected upon her previous state of mind, the reasons that had led to her intense uncontrollable desire, and how God's grace had saved her from a terrible disaster. She brought before her mind images of virtuous women: Gunasundari, Saubhagya Devi, Vanleela, Alak Kishori. Her pride melted with the sombre realisation that she had proved inferior to Alak Kishori. Kumud discovered a newfound affection for her impassioned, impulsive, arrogant, even somewhat stupid but unsullied sister-in-law. She felt fortunate that she had a friend in Vanleela, who, with all her playfulness and curiosity, was utterly devoted to her husband. Kumud had an intimation of the joys that Vanleela must have shared with her husband earlier that night, and she blessed her from her heart: Oh Vanleela, may your bliss be eternal! Kumud felt as if Saubhagya Devi, whose only desire was to follow her husband, had come to bless her and said: 'Follow my example, Kumud'. Kumud even looked up to receive Devi's blessings. Then she clearly heard her mother Gunasundari's voice: 'My own Kumud, hitherto, I have always been your guide. Now be on your guard and look after yourself. Ensure that you do not become a blot upon your father's illustrious and virtuous family, and that you do not bring my nurturance to disrepute. Honour is important. You are wise; do not let your honour go to dust. You have been educated with great care; do not let it go waste. Do not bring disrepute to our age-old Sanskrit learning and wisdom. You were imparted English knowledge in the face of social opprobrium; do not allow it to be blamed for your conduct. Do not be counted among the impure and fallible, in this world or in the next. Do not surrender to your passions like ordinary people. Kumud, you are beautiful; do not become demonic. Do not lose your inner light. Never allow your pure and transparent conscience to be so sullied that even you would not wish to gaze into it. Daughter, my wise daughter, each of your actions must be deliberate and conscious. Today, we are. Tomorrow, we will not be. When we gave you away as a gift in marriage, we lost all claim upon you. But remember your mother's love for you always, don't ever forget your mother. No matter whether you are alone, among your husband's family, in a distant land, or in the shelter of God, do not forget your mother's counsel. Your conduct is known only to you and to your Maker. Who are we to do or say anything? God does everything; we are only His instruments. We gave you to that family. You do not belong to us anymore. We cannot advise you. But mine is a mother's heart. It speaks of its own volition. Whether you heed my advice or not is for you to decide. But counsel you I must. Now you are an adult. Do what pleases you, but in this one matter, you must follow your mother. Joy and sorrow come and go; but what is once done can never be undone. Are you listening to me, Kumud?' Kumud began to sob and felt as if her mother had put a loving hand upon her shoulder. She looked back and heard another voice. 'Kumud, my daughter, God is your witness. I am a father only in name. He alone is the true Father to both you and me. Whatever you do, seek His advice. He shall never give you wrong advice. He shall always guide you. He is omnipresent, you shall find Him everywhere. You may forget me, but never Him. His wrath and grace are unique. They cannot be undone. I might have forgiven your transgressions, but you will recognise God's wrath only when it visits you. You will not even be able to plead forgiveness.' She saw her father's affectionate yet stern face. She got up and looked around, and was startled. All around her, Kumud saw faces—her father, her mother, Vanleela, Alak Kishori; Buddhidhan seemed to be near the window facing the road, Saubhagya Devi appeared to be sitting at the window facing the terrace. She also saw Sarasvatichandra standing near Navinchandra's room, looking at her quizzically as if questioning her chastity. She saw her younger sister Kusum Sundari seated next to her, a mocking smile on her face. She was frightened by all these apparitions. Are they all here to judge me today? Was it a dream or reality? Kumud ran around the room looking at the walls, at the ceiling, at the floor, on the table, on her bed. She heard Kusum Sundari sing a song teasingly.

O' sister mine, driven to madness by love
Your deeds will come back to haunt you
O' sister mine, driven to madness by love

Kumud could bear it no longer and flopped down on the chair, crying, God, I will never entertain such thoughts ever again! She put her head down on the table and sobbed her heart out, her tears smudging the papers. Her divine punishment over and cleansed by repentance, Kumud felt calmer. She looked up. The apparitions had vanished. She was alone in the room once more. She knew that she had received God's forgiveness. Her heart felt light. But her need for repentance still remained. She could not stop her tears.

Eyes red with tears, yet how you weep
Two streams course down your face
Like the blood in your veins
Vaidarbhi pines in the forest

She was filled with self-loathing for having strayed even momentarily. She recalled her parents' counsel. The wise truth of their words heard in a trance-like state now made her feel terrible. She felt alienated from everyone: husband, beloved, mother, father, chastity and God. She asked herself, Will I ever be worthy of my loved ones? How will I, a sinner, ever face them again? She pleaded with the earth, O' Mother, forgive my transgressions and take me in your embrace. She searched for Goddess Amba in her mother's image and tearfully sang.

O' Ma Amba, glance below your feet
Take pity on me, judge not my deed
You gave me this human body, Mother
Do not forsake me, for without you I'm distraught
I see you in all ten directions, Mother
Without you, who can show me the way?
O' Ma Amba, without you, all is desolate

Her tears cleansed her. She felt pure. Kumud felt in control of herself and stopped crying.

Human essence, instinct and ability determine our modes of engaging with the world. Like everything else, they can be put to good use as well as bad. We are unable to fathom the will of the Creator. Human autonomy is subject to God's will. Actions good and bad are decided by the orientation of this autonomous action. Abilities either aid or obstruct this process. Human ability tends to be either inert and passive or conscious and active. The inert tendency is governed by instincts, while conscious action is determined by intellect and tends to either support or hamper instincts. Vulgar people believe that autonomy is the unrestrained exercise of instincts. Others claim that autonomy is the unfettered play of intellect. Inert abilities are natural to animals and persons governed by animal passions; they are therefore easy to cultivate. The cultivation of a discerning intellect requires effort. The use of intellect for righteous ends is the ultimate grace of God. It is a state of bliss. The intellect emerges superior only through great conflict. Rare human beings remain pure without experiencing conflict; they are truly fortunate. In rare instances, the pure emerge triumphant despite undergoing many trials. Even before the final triumph, one has to face many blows and obstacles, but this is not seen as a blot. Most are unfamiliar with such trials. Oh ignoramus, see not the momentarily retreating steps or the wounds received while confronting the enemy. Do not consider the warrior to be a weakling. Consider instead the great courage of the warrior, respect him, worship him. Human frailty is limitless. Bear in mind that your resolve is yet untested and your weakness is not for all to see. Praise those who show some resolve and pray to God that He may grant you similar strength. Compassion for the weak and praise for the display of strength in the right manner is not possible without deeply felt experience and a generous and cultivated piety.

Kumud Sundari proved to be momentarily weak, but her virtue finally triumphed. Oh those who aspire to test her noble and steadfast virtue, sharpen your intellect and put it to good use. Examine and judge yourself so that you may acquire the fitness to judge others. Those who shine by their own efforts and learn from their own imagination have a powerful conscience and possess virtue that triumphs over the most powerful of attractions. Sing their praise with abandon. Cleansed by tears, repentant and wiser, the ever growing light of Kumud Sundari's heart illuminated her mind. A smile soft and grave returned to her now radiant face. Her eyes closed in contentment. A pure light enveloped her from head to toe, shattering the darkness that had engulfed her before. She rose and wondered what to do next. She felt exhausted and decided to sleep. As she lay down on the bed, her mind conversed with itself anew.

Without doubt, I can claim no relationship with Sarasvatichandra. God, let not my impure heart sully that pure man by craving for him. Allow me to be imbued with the presence of my husband. Make me worthy of the husband I have.

But I can still be of service to Sarasvatichandra. Can I not reason with him to return home to Bombay and perform his duties towards the country? Would it be right for me to approach him with this request? No. But will it also be right for me to allow this precious gem hiding from his father and friend to descend into the darkness of anonymity? No.

Will it compromise my purity if I approach him? Yes. I can neither trust myself, nor him.

Then I must not go to him.

But what if he disappears before Chandrakant arrives? He may leave at daybreak. What must be done must be done tonight. It is my responsibility.

But will he disappear? How can one be certain about a man as adventurous as him?

Virtue need fear nothing. Men are weak when faced with women. If I am true to myself, there is no danger of passion overwhelming either his or my mind. No desire can overpower me now. God is my witness.

It would be dangerous. But it is an imperative.

No, I need not harbour any doubts regarding my chastity or my intentions. Mother, your counsel, your purity is my shield, and this shield is inviolable. I am your daughter. And my husband? No, I need not look at his deeds. I must be true to myself. Who am I? Who are my parents? What could be more vital than my chastity, my honour in this perishable, ephemeral world? Pious Devi, your blessings will not forsake me. All impure thoughts are now consigned to hell.

Kumud got up and stood near the bed, lost in thought. Then suddenly she began to sing as if possessed, her tone pleading and worshipful.

Come, Ma Amba, come soon
Keep your hand on my head, O' Mother of this world
Purge me of these demonic passions
And fill my heart with your pure light
Shine it serenely upon my face
Such that my Chandra is neither enchanted nor swayed
I cannot bear to see him thus eclipsed
My heart breaks to see the darkness engulf him
It is midnight, and I have submitted neither to fear nor custom
I have found the courage to accomplish this pious task
We were enticed by love and the arrows of memory sharp
Blunt though they may now be
They should not pierce our hearts
Cause this miracle to happen
Hold me to your breast, Mother, help me keep my pledge
Rest my head in your lap, keep my honour intact
I seek release for my once beloved
I seek that my virtue remains unsullied
Whether I call you Father or Mother of the world
You remain a mother to me
As I enter this ordeal by fire
Ma Amba, help me emerge unscathed

She looked up at the sky framed by the window and said aloud: Ma Amba! Your power is miraculous. Men are mere playthings in your hands. You can rescue him from sorrow. You can bring him laughter or make him weep. The sun may or may not rise, but you as the dawn are the dispeller of darkness and the saviour of the world. Ma Amba! Ma Sarasvati! Laxmi! Vidhatri! The Goddess of Fate and Kalika are all your forms! Amba! I am your daughter. I feel your power rise within me. Sarasvatichandra, if demonic passions were to rise within you, my power will turn them to ashes. Sarasvatichandra, I pray that you accept my counsel. Allow me to offer you a service worthy of our former love. Oh pure intellect, come reside within me.

Kumud sat down at her table. She inadvertently picked up the sheet on which she had previously scribbled her musings and wrote on the back of the same page.

> You who are no longer mine! I have no right to speak with you, but the mind conveys what it must through this note. If you have any pity left for this mind, if you feel anything at all for the heart that pines for you, heed this prayer. If you will, do what I pray you to do. A bat cannot see the light, such are the fruits of its deeds. But you can, so do open your eyes. As,
>
> *The vapours that rise from the earth*
> *Return from the heavens as rain*
> *This world is such that our actions*
> *Are fated to remain small*
> *You soar above this earth on the*
> *Many-hued wings of Garuda*
> *Any wonder then that our time together was fleeting?*
> *Winged celestial who descended upon this earth*
> *Fly back. For this is no land for birds.*
> *Spread your golden wings and imbibe beauty*
> *Measure the skies and bathe in the pool of sunrays*
> *When you soar above the mountains, forests and skies*
> *Your light will be as one with the sun*
> *And we who are earth-bound*
> *Will worship your glory with all our hearts*
> *I may not be able to fly, but allow me*
> *To rejoice in beholding the flight of my beloved*
> *Or else, to weep in despair*
>
> Love has the power to search out the beloved from the bottom of the earth. Eyes can be cheated, but the recognition of the heart is something else. Damayanti recognised Bahuk as Nala. I have

> said what I had to. When the boon-giver turns a stranger, who can measure his cruelty? The one who must suffer shall suffer. It is for you to decide what that suffering shall be.
> How does it matter to you who wrote this?

She picked up the letter and told herself, I will put this into his pocket. If he is awake, I will drop it on him and return. I will not speak to him. I will not look at him. Ma Amba, be with me. So saying, Kumud got up. She held the letter that contained all her musings of that night, voluntary and involuntary. There was no hesitation in her step. She had moved heaven and earth to muster courage to open the door. Now she pushed it open easily with her foot and stood inside the other room.

Was there anyone in the room? Who? What was he doing? What went on in his mind and what did he do when he found Kumud Sundari standing beside him?

Navinchandra had returned late with Buddhidhan. He was in his room. The dramatic events of the day, first glimpses of Buddhidhan's administration, thoughts of the day to come, memories of home, thoughts of Kumud, and plans of his impending departure all crowded his mind and kept sleep and peace at bay. He lay down exhausted, but was restless. He could hear Kumud Sundari's faint soliloquy, her singing, and her intermittent sobs, which beat down on his ears torturously. Sleep eluded him. He got up from the bed and took out a piece of paper from his bundle of composed poems. He added a few more to the existing ones. He lay down again and read his new compositions by the light of the lamp placed on a chair at the head of the bed. Sleep crept in stealthily under his tired eyelids, and the pages fell onto his chest as he entered the world of dreams.

Just then, Kumud Sundari opened the door. Sleep vanished that very instant.

Who was that? Kumud Sundari? The question filled his mind. He was stunned. He did not know if what he saw was a dream. His imagination took over; he attributed various desires to Kumud Sundari, and found his own awakening. He felt his virtue was no longer steadfast. He struggled. The mind decided that the eyes shall not open, but the eyes decided that they wanted to observe her stealthily. The anxiety of anticipation gripped him, his heart pined as the body became petrified.

Kumud Sundari entered the room and looked at him. He looked asleep. She carefully put her letter inside Navinchandra's pocket, and turned back to leave. But then she saw the paper lying on his chest. Her curiosity surfaced. She tried to pull the paper free from his grip without waking him. Either because he let go of it or because of her dexterity, she managed to slip it out of his hand, untorn. She immediately recognised the writing. He was Sarasvatichandra! She looked at him intently, wanting to ascertain that he was asleep. It was the same body that she had joyously looked upon at her father's house. He looked withered and pale. But that was to be expected. His ribs were clearly visible. His face had lost its ruddy glow. Kumud Sundari realised that this millionaire's son had taken to wandering like a vagabond only for her sake. Her desire for him had turned to ashes. But her anguish at his suffering became unbearable. Tears coursed down her cheeks. She stifled her sobs in her throat, but they racked her body. She stood still for five minutes or ten; but the man remained steadfast to his decision and did not open his eyes. Finally she began to read the writing on the paper. The ink was still fresh.

I left my father and mother, left my pure beloved
Caring not for despair, I renounced them all
For my father, I abandoned my love
I heeded not your entreaties, o' brother dearest friend
I discounted your sighs and renounced the world
I hardened my heart, futile were the signs of love
Now all that is left for me to do is
To watch her delicate heart break
I have not the right to wipe her tears
I cannot bear witness to this.
O' generous beloved do not waste away
Forget that which cannot be forgotten
Bear with that which is destined

O' generous beloved, virtuous, pure and wise
Bear with what cannot be forsaken
Play the hand dealt to you
O' generous beloved, deeming it a dream
Forget that which cannot be forgotten and
Bear with reality.
O' generous beloved, destiny cannot be averted
So drink deep from the well of destiny
O' generous beloved, o' friend and true brother
Close your affectionate eyes and
Let the one who must leave go
Consider our bond false and broken, forget this ingrate
Let the one who must leave go.
I had prosperity. I had a father.
I had a beloved. I had a brother.
None of them might I now take with me.
O' dear brother, erase me from memory
Let me work for our wretched people
O' brother, this land is richer for your presence
Why impoverish it by searching for me?
Abandon this quest, cease thought of me
I do not wish to live in this world
I shall not return
What I have renounced I shall not reclaim
Even what remains I shall surrender
What do I need of this world?
O' life mine, why did you poison my beloved?
Discarding she who was dearest
You cheated this naïve dear
O' life mine, why did you poison my beloved?
What will become of her?
You have killed her
Now break cruel heart.
Let my wretched eyes weep day and night
Why should they have respite?
O' life mine, why did you poison my beloved?

You do not deserve to live in this world
You deserve neither life's pleasures nor
The quietude of renunciation
Body smeared with ash, heart in turmoil
Such will be my renunciation.
Abandoned, the river lies inert
She will never break free of the mountain.
Affixed to the earth, head in the skies
The mountain may only watch the river weep.
Unbound, I may don any garb I choose
My path is as unbridled as kites that fly
Like them, I too shall soar
To be like the ocean waves
Neither above nor below
Is there succour to be found
Destitute and formless am I
I shall be like the forest breeze, invisible but
Carrying aloft the fragrance called Kumud
My forehead is inscribed with the wealth of the world
And its renunciation
I am the people, and I the king
But in my heart, only you reside.

The poem was smeared with the author's tears. Some smudges appeared fresh. Kumud's heart was torn asunder. Her anguish like an abyss knew no depth. Her tears flowed incessantly. Her pain became unbearable. She blabbered deliriously.

Friend, unrecognised, he roams in the wilderness,
He, burning like a volcano, shall not return,
His wounds are countless, his memory cannot be erased,
I occupy his heart and he is lonely, friendless, unknown,
These bonds cannot be broken.

Kumud forgot where she was. She felt dizzy and fell to the ground unconscious like a creeper struck by lightning. The paper fell from her hand. Blood drained from her face. Although he had decided not to open his eyes, hearing her fall Sarasvatichandra jumped up. At moments of crisis, the strongest of resolves melt. Lord Krishna picked up the Sudarshanchakra in the midst of battle for the sake of his devotee. Love respects its limits, but when faced with a crisis, its force dissolves all pledges. Such is the unfathomable play of God.

She had come to plead with him to return to Bombay. She had her answer. Each stanza of his poem had scorched her heart. Sarasvatichandra's undying and unsullied love, his sacrifice in spite of that love, his refusal to go away despite his renunciation, his pure and loving counsel expressed in the poem, his Bhishma-like resolve to remain steadfast to his decision, and the realisation that his resolve was because of his love for her. She was so overwhelmed by sadness that she fainted. Her unconscious body lay at Sarasvatichandra's feet. He looked at her just as Lord Shiva had looked at the unconscious Uma at the sacrifice performed by Daksha. Many thoughts clouded his mind.

Hitherto he had remained incognito. He had also concealed his feelings. Now he was no longer in hiding. His face betrayed his true emotions. He looked as if he were in his own house looking at the unconscious body of his own wife. His intellect had hitherto been clouded by romantic notions. He had concealed his sorrows by pretending to be an outsider. As his mask shattered, his intellect and emotions also ruptured. What if someone were to open the door right now and come in? He was after all a guest in another man's house. This was not the time to ponder the appropriateness of his action. Kumud had snapped under the weight of pain like the levers of an overwrought clock. She had suffered enough through the day and the night, and now she lay unconscious at his feet. Sarasvatichandra was stunned. He could not think what he should do. He felt numbed by the harm he had caused. He sat next to Kumud who lay broken like a garland of flowers. He cast aside customary morality and took her head into his lap. He knew he was violating norms, but felt that everyday morality did not apply to the extraordinary situation he was faced with. And yet, he was able to restrain himself. His hand moved to caress her face, but stopped, continuing to hold her head. His mind provided no answers as to how he could give succour to the unconscious woman. How could he call anyone else for help? He felt completely helpless.

Finally, he spoke softly into her ears, 'Kumud! Kumud Sundari! Please wake up! Why do you do this? Both of us will be needlessly put to shame. False allegations will be levelled against us. No one will believe us!' Confused and unable to think clearly, Sarasvatichandra kept repeating these words, but to no avail. Kumud remained unconscious. As time went by, the possibility of someone in the family rising early also increased. He became fearful. His mind could no longer be judicious. He impatiently caressed her face and shook her gently by the shoulders.

But Kumud Sundari remained unconscious and incapable of knowing what was happening to her. She lay there lifeless like a sparrow on a cold night. Her clothes had come undone like the small, delicate and dishevelled feathers of the sparrow. She had worn a soft, sheer malmal sari to sleep in for the night. It clung to her body, enticing his eyes. Her fair skin shone like a silvery cloud upon the horizon that concealed the young moon, mesmerising and frightening him. Her body was soft and silken under his tremulous hands, which tried desperately to massage her back to life. But her eyes remained closed like a stubborn flower bud. They dispelled any signs of desire. At last, the tragedy of the moment triumphed and guided the righteous effort.

Ultimately, either by some great effort of will, or by the magical touch, Kumud Sundari regained consciousness and opened her eyes. She realised that her head was resting in Sarasvatichandra's lap. She sat up and moved some distance away from him. For some reason, he held her hand as she tried to move away, but let it go just as suddenly. Kumud stared at him. This silent exchange continued for long moments. Finally, Sarasvatichandra got up and sat on the bed. Kumud Sundari also got up then and went and stood near the window, his poem still clutched in her fist. Both felt quite calm.

Unnatural resolves dictated by fear melted as those fears subsided. Kumud gathered the courage to speak. Just then, in the distance, some women labourers could be heard singing to the rhythm of their work.

Stay eternal, unbroken, enchanting
Intoxicating night
For how will I pass the day
Without my beloved?

A shiver ran through Kumud when she heard their song. The words 'intoxicating night' echoed in her heart. A woman sang lustily in a voice rich and sonorous:

Play with colours, my beloved
Sun, we will worship you with pearls, delay your rising
My beloved plays the hunter
Riding on a steed of love
Some offer diamonds and pearls
I offer you my life

Despite herself, something within Kumud responded to the simple allure of the song, and she felt angry at her own body for growing tense in anticipation. Her own weakness saddened her. She blamed her love for Sarasvatichandra for it. She knew it was her moral duty to purge herself of this love and sadness that had once again threatened her purity. She became resolute. She decided to speak her mind. The momentary weakness and frailty disappeared like lines drawn on sand, washed away by the waves of her determination.

Sarasvatichandra was deep in thought, his eyes riveted upon the floor, pondering his action. I was sullied by wealth and prestige, he thought, and I allowed the moment that should have been pure to become blemished. I gave Kumud Sundari a reason to change the good opinion she might have had of me. He was quite annoyed with himself. Snatches of songs that people returning from a theatrical performance were singing also disturbed him. It would have been better had I not come to Suvarnapur at all. If I could fly, I would have flown away this very instant. He looked up and was filled with compassion for Kumud Sundari. He realised he had wronged her. He recalled the words that a repentant Dushyant had spoken to Shakuntala: 'O fair-bodied one, let the unpleasant feeling caused by my repudiation pass from your heart.'[10]

Just then, like the rustle of winds or a divine revelation, words began to flow out of Kumud Sundari. Sarasvatichandra could only see her piercing gaze. As her words fell upon his ears and impaled his heart, they became real. She spoke like a temple idol; her voice had the ring of silver bells, combining delicacy, beauty, purity and gravity. Kumud Sundari shone with a light never seen before.

'You have snatched away from me the right to speak to you. But today for some reason not known to me, I speak. These are my final words to you.

'You have lost by your own choice the right to know my past, or be concerned about my present and future. You wanted it so. It was your wish. It is not right for me to speak of myself. But I plead with you: do not put another unfortunate woman in a condition such as mine.

'I have kept a letter in your pocket. In that I have written all I have to say to you. I do not believe you will do me even that favour of considering my plea. It was foolish of me to write that note. I wrote as I could not contain myself.

'Sarasvatichandra, have mercy and return to Bombay. Are all learned men like you? Is cruelty integral to learning and intellect? Return to Bombay and meet your father, do not be so cruel. Be like a kite without strings, or like waves in the sea, or the forest breeze! No one can prevent you from being so heartless! I am alive but thrown amidst blazing flames. Is there any escape for me? I will burn, wither, weep or die—but I will bear my heartbreak. I will bear with all that befalls me. What is it to you? Your freedom will remain undiminished. That is all you care for.

[10] M. R. Kale, trans. *Abhijnanasakuntalam of Kalidasa*, Act 7, Verse 24, new ed. (Delhi: Motilal Banarsidass, 1898, 2010), 281.

'I do not want you to respond. It is enough for me that you consider what I have said. May God show you the right path.'

Kumud choked on her tears which flowed despite herself. Her tormented eyes seemed to admonish him and say: 'You have made it impossible for yourself to embrace me and comfort me even in moments of such intense suffering.' She ran towards her room and locked the door without once looking back at him. She flung herself on the bed and cried her heart out. After a while, somewhat calmer, she got up, picked up Sarasvatichandra's poems. She read them again. They were imprinted indelibly on her mind. It seemed futile to preserve the paper on which they were written. She tore up the paper. She then brought out all his letters. Her heart broke at the thought of destroying them. She pressed them to her heart, kissed them, bathed them in tears and stacked them as if she were laying her beloved's body on the funeral pure. She set fire to them, and wept at this act of cremation. She carefully collected the ashes in a beautiful glass bottle, put a label on the bottle and wrote 'Soul Ash'. She pressed the bottle to her heart, kissed it and kept it on the table where she could see it daily. She dried her tears and gazed at the bottle. At last she lay down. She lay awake until three o'clock. Kumud Sundari felt certain that she had finally erased Sarasvatichandra from her life for ever. She thought of her profound sacrifice and felt purged and purified once again. Her heart felt lighter. She had emerged unsullied by God's grace and by a tremendous effort of her own will. Her ordeal by fire over, the strong-willed and virtuous Kumud Sundari at last surrendered herself to sleep.

20 Leave Taking

After Kumud left his room, Sarasvatichandra felt as if some powerful force had gone, leaving a serene calm in its wake. He saw her retreating back, and the closing door. He slumped back into bed with a sigh. Was all of that a dream? Was that Kumud Sundari herself? How did she faint? Did he really hold her in his arms? Did he truly caress her face? What was it she said? Has she gone? Forever? Shouldn't she be the one in a pitiable condition? Was his own frailty not proven? Many such thoughts crowded his mind. He was overwhelmed by a complex of emotions including love, sadness, helplessness, self-loathing, and compassion. It was all too much for his exhausted mind to bear. He fell asleep, and woke up at seven the next morning.

Pramaddhan had returned from Lilapur, triumphant. The Rana, after this successful mission, had decided to present robes of honour to Buddhidhan the same day. Narbheram and Jaymal were given the responsibility of making the arrangements. Buddhidhan's household was bustling with these activities when Sarasvatichandra woke up. He went down to the drawing room after brushing his teeth. Pramaddhan was boasting of his success in Lilapur to a group that had gathered around him. At the door, bards were reciting their compositions in praise of Buddhidhan. Charan women, tall and buxom, sang songs in beautiful melody, evoking feelings of pure devotion towards the Rana and his administration. As the day progressed, a large crowd gathered outside Buddhidhan's house. The entire street was full of people. The house also had many visitors; administrators, friends, well-wishers, and anyone with a fleeting acquaintance with the family called to pay their respects. The drawing room was filled to capacity. Sarasvatichandra's room was opened for visitors.

The women occupied the courtyard and the surrounding rooms. They were decked up in beautiful brightly coloured sarees and adorned with gold and silver ornaments studded with diamonds and pearls. They looked like a garden in full bloom. Saubhagya Devi shone like the moon among the stars. Alak Kishori flashed through the gathering like lightning that eclipses the brightness of stars and the moon. Kumud Sundari was like the sombre and alluring Venus. Dayashankar Kaka and the old family priest were busy instructing the women in the preparation of things required for worship. Flaring red kumkum, fragrant and colourful flowers, incense sticks, silver and golden plates and other objects for worship added to the glory of Buddhidhan's house.

Meanwhile, the Rana sent a ceremonial procession to invite his appointed Karbhari to the palace. Drummers and trumpeters came first, followed by an elephant, followed by a horse carriage in which sat a bhayat, Narbheram and Jaymal; a troupe of riders on horseback and soldiers on foot followed the carriage. The procession stood outside Buddhidhan's door, waiting to receive him.

Sarasvatichandra moved around vacantly amid all this bustle. Kumud Sundari's letter was still in his pocket. He wanted to read it, but found no spot where he could do so undisturbed. Last night he had fallen asleep without reading it. He knew that Chandrakant was on his way to Suvarnapur. Pensive, and fighting to contain a melancholy which threatened to overwhelm him, he remained untouched by the joyous and festive mood around him. On the street outside, the number of horse carriages had multiplied, the excitement in the air was feverish and palpable. Only Sarasvatichandra stood alone and aloof from it all. He realised it was desirable for both Kumud Sundari and him that he not be anywhere near her. But it was hard for him to let go of her. I had abandoned you, Kumud. But unbeknownst to you, you drew me to Suvarnapur. It is not easy for me to break free of you. How should I leave? When should I leave? Should I wait for Chandrakant? What should I do with him? Will I be able to shun him coldly when I see him? I do not desire to return to Bombay with him. His search for me has brought him here. Oh God! How many people have I made unhappy! Kumud Sundari, what fate awaits you now? If you can, do forgive me, my dearest Kumud. But I must leave—I cannot bear to see you lifeless again.

Sarasvatichandra was not the only one who experienced a profound sadness in these festive moments. Vanleela had mentioned Pramaddhan's transgression to Alak Kishori, who in turn had told Saubhagya Devi, and she had informed Buddhidhan last night. Buddhidhan was saddened by the degradation of his son. My daughter-in-law, defiled by my own son under my own roof! And I am powerless to do anything? How will I then bring other culprits to justice? No, this cannot be made public, and hence he cannot be punished. Buddhidhan saw Krishna Kalika's husband outside on the street, and thought, This young man is now my responsibility. Will he dare bring this complaint to me? No, of course not. What punishment can be given which does not make the matter public? How can an aggrieved party be satisfied that justice has been done unless that justice is publicly awarded? If I do not have the capacity to satisfy a complainant, I should give up my Karbhar. Has anyone been able to give up the Karbhar? No one has shunned wealth, except under duress. No, I have decided—I will somehow punish Pramaddhan. The world shall see my justice. I do not want to go to hell. Mother, I have not forgotten the insults you had to bear. I will not allow such a thing to pass. Pramad, how shall I punish you? What should be your punishment? What if I punish myself?

Just then Sarasvatichandra entered Buddhidhan's room. Concealing his grief, he said, 'Come, Navinchandra. How are you?'

'Bhai Sahib, servants from Ratnanagari have arrived to accompany Kumud Sundari back to her parents. They inform me that Chandrakant will spend a few days in Bhadreshwar. I need to see him urgently. I have come to seek your leave.'

'Go tomorrow if you must, but you should attend the court today. There is also a celebration at home. Have lunch with us and leave at night; take a vehicle along. And isn't Chandrakant supposed to come here?'

'Yes, but for some reasons I must leave immediately. I will have my lunch there. You have shown extraordinary kindness towards me, Bhai Sahib; you would naturally like me to extend my stay here. But please accept my request.'

Buddhidhan was worried about Pramaddhan. He was also preoccupied with palace matters. Since last night, he had felt differently towards Navinchandra. He did not want to insist when the other was so intent upon leaving, and so he said, 'As you wish, Navinchandra.'

'Bhai Sahib, please do forgive me if I have ever hurt you by my words or deeds. You have been most generous to me.'

'Do not mention it.'

Sarasvatichandra took his leave. The Karbhari, engrossed in his own affairs, forgot to show the courtesy of arranging a vehicle for his departing guest. Sarasvatichandra sent his belongings to Rajeshwar Mahadev with Murkhdutt, who was a daily visitor to the house. He then went to Saubhagya Devi and Alak Kishori and sought their permission to leave. Quite naturally, they insisted that he stay back, at least for that day. He told them he had already obtained Buddhidhan's permission. Hearing this, Saubhagya Devi gave up her attempts to persuade him and expressed her regret at his sudden decision. Alak Kishori said, 'I will talk to Pitaji—you must stay for this one day. What could be so urgent?' But finally, she too gave up.

Sarasvatichandra looked once at Kumud Sundari, and turned to leave. Hot tears welled up in his eyes which he did not want seen, his legs refused to move, but he somehow dragged them on with slow deliberate steps, nearly stumbled at the threshold, and at last, stepped out of the house of Buddhidhan.

Kumud Sundari was sad that her counsel had been futile. She had no opportunity of exchanging any last words with him. Watching his receding figure, her heart sank into an abyss. She was filled with dread about the future. Kumud moaned aloud as if in pain and fell backwards, but was caught by a woman standing behind her. The celebrations were abruptly halted. She was helped to her feet, given water, and surrounded by concerned eyes and questions. She said it was nothing but a painful knot in her stomach. She composed and becalmed herself by an effort of will, and joined in with the celebrations, which were then resumed. But her heart went with the wanderer.

Sarasvatichandra walked past all the hustle and bustle and revelry. He walked invisible and silent through the jubilant crowds. He left his heart behind in the Karbhari's home.

21 Walking Away

Sarasvatichandra was eager to read Kumud Sundari's letter. He hurried out of the house. If anyone had seen the letter, the consequences would have been disastrous for Kumud Sundari. Murkhdutt met him at Rajeshwar Mahadev. Sarasvatichandra had his lunch with him. During lunch, the two of them conversed.

'Bhai Navinchandar, where will you go from here?'

'I intend going towards Bhadreshwar.'

'Have you arranged for a carriage?'

'I will take a ride in a passing cart.'

'Did not Bhai Sahib arrange a carriage for you?'

'I did not ask for it. I want to go alone.'

'Don't tell anyone on the way that you have been his guest.'

'Why?'

'Shathrai's outlaws are at large. They harass anyone who they take to be from Bhai Sahib's faction. Kumud Sundari is also going to Bhadreshwar. I told Behn Alak Kishori that her departure should be delayed, or else there should be adequate protection arranged for her.'

'Let them be. What should I be afraid of? I will spend some time in the garden. Please stop any cart passing this way, and call me.' Murkhdutt went out.

Sarasvatichandra went into the garden. He sat on Murkhdutt's bed and read the letter. He knew their separation was final. As he tried to clear his mind and think of a way ahead, the tears now coursed freely down his face. Kumud Sundari, what can I do for you? All you want is that I should return to Bombay. You are truly a pure woman. Some women are courageous and do not submit to men they dislike. Are they virtuous? But you kept your resolve despite such deep and abiding love for me. Is your virtue not superior? Sita felt no love for Ravana, naturally she turned away from him. But you did much more, Kumud Sundari. You counselled me. Until now, I was never aware of my own frailty. This was the second instance in which you have saved me. How fortunate and blessed I would have been had I not abandoned you! Now, it is my fate to leave you. Should I follow your advice?

If you can, do pardon me, but I cannot do what you ask of me. I will not return to Bombay. I must atone for what I have done to you. I will roam the land, I will face what hardships come my way, and I will remember you. I do not desire prestige or worldly glory. For whom? I had agreed to be a householder for the sake of my father. You enticed me to worldly desires. But my father's conduct gave me the liberty to break free from worldly bondage. I abandoned you and renounced the world. Why must I dream those dreams again?

Dear Chandrakant, why did you have to go to Bhadreshwar? Am I to meet Kumud there again? Events of last night have forced me to leave Suvarnapur in haste. I cannot wait for you here. I cannot meet you here. And I do not want to be in Bhadreshwar. Then where shall I meet you? Can I not go away without meeting you? Do I have these attachments, still? Yes, let me go away somewhere else. I will send him a note.

Isn't that a cruel choice, Sarasvatichandra? How heartless of me. Have I not inflicted enough cruelty already? I wonder how father is. Did my leaving pain him? If I felt pained, why would he not feel likewise? God, be kind and let Chandrakant tell me that father has forgotten me. Chandrakant, I have hurt Ganga bhabhi as well. How many have suffered because of me? How many more will suffer?

His reverie was disturbed by Pramaddhan's confidant Ramsen.

'Navinchandrabhai, you have to come back to Suvarnapur immediately.'

'Why?'

'Bhai Sahib has gone to the palace. But he has done something unexpected. He knows about Padma and Krishna Kalika.' And Ramsen related the news in detail. Buddhidhan had been told about both these women, and was deeply pained by the debauchery of his degenerate son. Krishna Kalika's husband was enraged. Buddhidhan had called him and promised to punish Pramaddhan. He had not yet awarded the punishment, but the rumours had already reached Pramaddhan. Frightened, he decided to seek his father's forgiveness through Narbheram, but did not have the courage to open up before an elderly person. Pramaddhan thought of Navinchandra, and sent Ramsen to call him back.

Sarasvatichandra heard him in silence, then said, 'Bhai Ramsen, it is you who encouraged Bhai's bad habits. You are responsible for things to have come to such a pass. If Pramadbhai fails to reform himself, he will get what he deserves. But you are certain to lose your livelihood. Go back and help Bhai to reform. I will not meddle in such affairs. Bhai Sahib will take action only after due deliberation. If I intervene, the first thing I would say is that you should be sacked. Hence, go back. My intervention will not benefit anyone. Tell Pramaddhan to change for the better, and be like his father. Whatever punishment Buddhidhan gives will be appropriate. Go back. I will not return.'

Ramsen went away without another word, his head hanging in shame.

Murkhdutt had heard their conversation. He came forward and said, worried, 'Something untoward will certainly happen. Bhai Sahib does not tolerate such things. Pramaddhan may take poison. Who is to say what should be done? Anyway, Navinchandrabhai, a cart is waiting outside. But it may not go to Bhadreshwar.'

Sarasvatichandra retorted, 'Bhadreshwar can go to sleep! I just want to leave this place! I will go *anywhere* the cart takes me. I just want to leave!

They both came out of the temple. Sarasvatichandra stood at the temple gate; the cart was waiting there. Murkhdutt followed with his belongings. It was a large cart pulled by two bullocks. It was long and covered. The rear part was so low that it almost touched the ground. The driver's side was raised. There were three other passengers, an old woman, an unhappy looking man of about forty, and a woman of about twenty. They seemed to be banias; the old woman was a brahmin. None of them were good looking or fair complexioned. Murkhdutt had found out that the cart was headed towards Ratnanagari.

'Chandarbhai, you want to go to Bhadreshwar, but they are going to Ratnanagari. There is a village called Manoharia some ten miles away. The road forks there—one goes to Bhadreshwar and the other towards Ratnanagari.'

'All right, I will go with them.' He took his belongings from Murkhdutt, and gave him five rupees.

This was the first time that Sarasvatichandra was going to travel by such a cart. The cart was lined with hay which was covered by a thick cloth. Sarasvatichandra sat right at the back. It was ten in the morning and the sun was fierce. The millionaire's son set out like Dhruva. But the sun showed him no mercy. For the unhappy man, the heat was the least of his worries. The slow-moving cart passed through dusty roads, taking a jewel among men as its load. Murkhdutt walked behind the cart for some distance, advised Sarasvatichandra to be cautious, requested the cart driver to take good care of him and took his leave. He turned back and soon disappeared from view.

Sarasvatichandra lay down and covered himself with a dhoti. He was still unaccustomed to hardships. What with the discomfort of the noisy cart, the dust rising from the dirt road, the prickly hay, and the harsh blazing sun, he found strange thoughts and images filling his despondent mind. The road seemed like a tunnel and the clouds of dust took on strange forms. One moment they looked like the surrounding trees, one moment like the clouds, and a while later like the warp and weft of the dhoti with which he had covered himself. The clucking noises and harsh guttural sounds the cart driver produced from time to time, the sharp piercing calls of eagles circling high, the raucous cacophony of crows, the echoing calls of *kabar*, the excited chatter of sparrows, the high-pitched squeaks of squirrels on the trees, the grating sounds of reeds breaking under the cartwheels, and the rhythmic lurching and squeaking of the moving cart filled his ears. The sun's rays pierced the thin dhoti and his closed eyes. He was bathed in perspiration. His body swayed as the cart laboriously made its way up a hill. Tired as he was, he could not sleep.

His mind, too, had no respite. Kumud Sundari's poem resonated through it. Will I be forced to meet her at Bhadreshwar? What if I do not go there at all? Should I not meet the man who has travelled so far to meet me? I will stay at Manohariya and meet him there; he is certain to pass that way. He will give me news of my father. Does my father remember me at all? What state would he be in? Should I return to Bombay? Should I not? What should I tell Chandrakant?

I have seen for myself how the Karbhar is obtained, how the Karbharis operate. But I still need to see how the native states are administered, under what conditions people live. I have left behind Suvarnapur. Shall I go to Ratnanagari? In any case, the cart is headed towards it.

It is good that Pramaddhan is to be punished. But why do I need to know about it? Oh, Kumud Sundari!

One should be careful of the outlaws. It is good that Murkhdutt has warned the cart driver.

As the cart lurched along, the cart driver sang lustily to himself.

O' beloved mine, your teeth are pearly white
Come visit me, we will tie a secret knot
O' beloved mine, my home lies across that field
Come visit me there, I will leave the door ajar
O' beloved mine, your hair is serpentine black
Come visit me, we will spend an enchanting night

Sarasvatichandra found the song absorbing. Kumud Sundari seemed to be knocking at his heart. The cart driver remembered he had women passengers and abruptly stopped singing. They moved on in silence in the oppressive heat and dust for a while. Then the old woman began to sing.

The desire to live is high as the mountains
But we die at the foothills
When you die, you die alone
No relations accompany you

Sarasvatichandra was moved by the song and tears filled his eyes. His heart was wrenched between thoughts of death and Kumud Sundari. Eventually, he fell into a disturbed sleep. The cart moved on, unmindful of the beating heart, the many-layered dream world and the consciousness flowing through both the heart and the dreams. In his dream, Sarasvatichandra entered an unknown world. He knew where he wanted to go but did not know what he wanted to do there, he had no idea of what lay in store for him, what new experiences. How could a man about to be reborn possibly know?

Three horse-riders followed the cart at some distance. They kept an eye on the cart even as they talked among themselves. The sounds of the trotting horses reached Sarasvatichandra's ears. Far on the horizon, a cloud of dust rose. Sounds of beating drums and trumpets could be heard. The experienced cart driver grew increasingly nervous; the sounds could be a sign of the presence of outlaws from Dhirpur. He wondered if he should warn his passengers. Then he saw an ascetic walking beside the cart. The cart driver decided that silence was a sign of wisdom.

The old woman sang songs of popular poets, snatches of which penetrated Sarasvatichandra's subconscious.

Countenance neither sorrow nor joy
For each is formed by destiny
No one can will either away
For they are wrought by the Lord
Forsaking bodily desires, a jogi inhabits the forest
Disenchanted with the world, he is melancholic

He who once slept on soft beds, whose house was rich and vast
Now has not even hay to lie on and shelters in the shade of trees
Once rich embroidery and fine clothing adorned him
Now he carries a coarse blanket to keep the chill away
Once thousands rose at his call and armies marched
That man now walks barefoot, that man now walks alone

In his dream, Sarasvatichandra saw Kumud running after the cart, suspended in air. She seemed to be singing. The old woman sang another song.

Attachment to the body is false
It cannot remain yours
Think it over, oh mad one
Why has thought deserted you?

He opened his eyes, and Kumud disappeared behind the clouds. The old woman continued her song.

Deceiving the simpleton, the ash-smeared mendicant walks away
Says Bhoja Bhagat: The sea of life drowns us all

Sarasvatichandra felt as if Kumud's grandmother had chided him. Saddened, he closed his eyes and slipped back into his dream world. The cart moved on at its slow lurching pace. It was noon. The sun beat down mercilessly on everything below it. He felt as if he was about to enter a dark cave bereft of sunlight. He felt he was sinking to the bottom of the sea. Surrounded by darkness and silence, he searched for light—for Kumud Sundari. The dense impenetrable darkness enveloped him like a snake's coils. He was falling, falling, falling endlessly to the bottom of the sea. As he fell, an old English poem he had read in a life past came to his rescue. He could hear in it echoes of his own thoughts.

While the sound whirls around,
Down, down!
As the fawn draws the hound,
As the lightning the vapour,

As a weak moth the taper;
Death, despair; love, sorrow;
Time both; to-day, to-morrow;
As steel obeys the spirit of the stone,
Down, down!

Through the gray, void abysm,
Down, down!
Where the air is no prism,
And the moon and stars are not,
And the cavern-crags wear not
The radiance of Heaven,
Nor the gloom to Earth given,
Where there is One pervading, One alone,
Down, down!

In the depth of the deep,
Down, down!
Like veiled lightning asleep,
Like the spark nursed in embers,
The last look Love remembers,
Like a diamond which shines
On the dark wealth of mines,
A spell is treasured but for thee alone.
Down, down![1]

The cart moved on weighed down by the immeasurable sorrows of this man. It moved towards a fiery future, like oblations offered in a sacrifice. It moved on, like Sarasvatichandra's fate, towards an uncertain, inexorable future.

[1] Author's note: *Prometheus Unbound*, Percy Bysshe Shelly.